Organizational Strategy and Policy

SECOND EDITION

FRANK T. PAINE

Professor of Management,
College of Business and Management,
University of Maryland
College Park, Maryland

WILLIAM NAUMES

Associate Professor of Management,
Clark University,
Worster, Massachusetts

1978
W. B. SAUNDERS COMPANY
PHILADELPHIA • LONDON • TORONTO

W. B. Saunders Company: West Washington Square
Philadelphia, PA 19105

1 St. Anne's Road
Eastbourne, East Sussex BN21 3UN, England

1 Goldthorne Avenue
Toronto, Ontario M8Z 5T9, Canada

Library of Congress Cataloging in Publication Data

Paine, Frank T

Organizational strategy and policy.

Includes indexes.

1. Decision-making. 2. Management. I. Naumes, William, joint author. II. Title.

HD30.23.P3 1978   658.4'03   77-77106

ISBN 0-7216-7948-2

Organizational Strategy and Policy   ISBN 0-7216-7048-2

© 1978 by W. B. Saunders Company. Copyright 1974 by W. B. Saunders Company. Copyright under the International Copyright Union. All rights reserved. This book is protected by copyright. No part of it may be reproduced, stored in a retrieval system, or transmitted in any form or by any means, electronic, mechanical, photocopying, recording, or otherwise, without written permission from the publisher. Made in the United States of America. Press of W. B. Saunders Company. Library of Congress catalog card number 77-77106.

Last digit is the print number: 9   8   7   6   5   4   3   2   1

PREFACE

This revised text is presented along with a new paperback volume, *Cases in Organizational Strategy and Policy*. The purpose of this revision is to provide a conceptual framework for information gathering in the field of strategic management (or general management) and for organizing and analyzing such information. Precise analytical and behavioral assessment guides are given, using a contingency framework. The text deals with the general management tasks of identifying threats and opportunities in the environment, forming strategies to deal with these conditions and developing capabilities and resources consistent with the environment-strategy requirements. Its focus is not limited to those who are or want to be top executives, because general management is not the exclusive province of the chief official. General management skills are needed at many intermediate levels by those in operating or advisory positions. The strategic management viewpoint is also important to stakeholders dealing with the profit or not-for-profit organization from the outside, such as investment bankers, management consultants, consumer pressure group leaders and public policy specialists.

The very favorable reaction to the first edition of *Organizational Strategy and Policy* is appreciated. It was an attempt to meet the need for a practical unifying text which (1) was based on empirical research, (2) blended into an integrated theory of management, (3) described the complex processes of management, and (4) integrated the behavioral and management sciences into policy. This goal seems to be accomplished to the extent that the concepts and ideas have been used in many different situations, ranging from students without any significant organizational experience, to groups of experienced managers and staff personnel from profit and not-for-profit bodies.

In this second edition, while maintaining special attention to integrating behavioral science into policy, movement is made to practical analytical approaches of studying the organization and its environment based on recent research, thinking and practice. Ideas taken from practicing consultants are used. The ideas are quite useful to small organizations as well as larger ones.

The text has been thoroughly rewritten and simplified. Superfluous material has been eliminated throughout. Some of the new features include:

1. A small business case, Bike Lock Co.; a new company with potential is presented and used for examples of case analysis in Chapter 1 and in many sections of the book.

2. The discussion of the descriptive model has been expanded to include various strategies for "negotiation" with the environment such as "muddling through with purpose," "the art of imprecision" and "coalition formation" (Chapter 2).

3. The treatment of the important diagnostic process has been expanded, adding material on recognizing and responding to "weak signals" (Chapter 3).

4. Environmental segments, which have distinct growth prospects, threats, trends or opportunities, are thoroughly discussed (Chapter 3).

5. Understanding of the cost structure of business is emphasized, including major cost elements and how they behave, identifying present competitive positions, gaining a competitive cost advantage and focusing efforts in your business (Chapter 3).

6. The importance of power relationships and political tactics in and around organizations is fully recognized and explored (Chapters 2, 3 and 8).

7. Expanded coverage is presented on the characteristics of general management work (Chapter 3).

8. Precise instruction is given on the analysis of vulnerability and the impact of threats and opportunities in an increasingly turbulent environment (Chapter 4).

9. The discussion of the Strategic Mix and the Portfolios for the whole organization is strengthened. Analysis for the whole organization is discussed, including reallocation among businesses and the use of flexibility, resource and stakeholder strategies (Chapter 5).

10. Strategy analysis for the individual business is emphasized, including defining customer/client groups where there is a sustainable economic advantage and gaining a defensible position through the use of various business strategies (Chapter 5).

11. Added to the financial analysis program from the previous edition is a marketing concepts review section, which is useful for small as well as larger organizations, profit and not-for-profit units (Appendix to Chapter 5).

12. Evaluation of small and medium-sized businesses is highlighted. Essential factors for consideration in 14 areas of management concerning these businesses are discussed. Peter Drucker's rules for such organizations are presented (Appendices 2 and 3 to Chapter 5).

13. Added to the Assessment and Organization Development program are specific ideas for developing and using a strategic issue information network. Scenarios and various

evaluation and change strategies are discussed (Chapters 6 to 8).

14. A situational approach to designing the planning system is presented, with a focus on appropriate balancing *adaptations* to the environment and *integration* of on-going activities (Chapter 8).

15. An intervention program is discussed for the analysis of strategic activities of individual managers or groups of managers (ASAM) (Appendix to Chapter 8).

16. Finally, the overall contingency question of balancing the environment-strategy-capability is discussed, using new research. An integrated contingency model of strategic management is developed (Chapter 9). The general problems of forecasting environmental uncertainty or turbulence, determining gaps in strategy and gaps in capability, and effecting strategic change ahead of the turbulence is an underlying issue throughout the book.

For whom is the book intended? The book was written primarily for use as a framework for information gathering and for organizing and analyzing such information by three main types of policy analysts:

The top level or middle manager, who is involved in policy formation and implementation on a regular basis.

The consultant or researcher interested in understanding and in developing the policy formation process.

Most importantly, the student of policy, organizational behavior or organization theory, who, by the use of case analysis, field or library projects, computer games and/or role plays, may be enabled to develop conceptual and administrative skills.

Thus, it is written for those who are interested not only in an intellectual appreciation of policy but also in the practice of applied information processing on complex policy issues.

Though some practice materials (e.g., cases, role plays, case problems, discussion questions) are included, the book, if used in a policy or management course or in a training program, may be supplemented by the companion case book, a computer game, and a field and/or library project for additional information processing. In addition, the book may be used emphasizing Chapters 1 to 5 and 9, with Chapters 6 to 8 optional.

It has been our experience that use of the text with the practice materials would be expected to aid the reader, be he student or practitioner, in the following ways:

1. Conceptualizing the policy formation process as a social process in which an intellectual process is embedded.

2. Developing comprehension, skill and knowledge for diagnosing and dealing with the specific and unique policy and strategy situation.

3. Gaining understanding of the complex realities, challenging questions and conflicting responsibilities in policy making.

4. Analyzing the organization's environment and its policy-generating structure.

5. Designing and proposing approaches that will help to prevent organizational stagnation.

6. Developing administrative and communication skills in presenting and developing solutions to policy problems.

7. Integrating and tying together concepts, principles and skills learned separately in other more specialized courses.

8. Being cautious in accepting the many prescriptions that exist in the literature of policy (e.g., long range planning is good per se).

To meet these objectives in a policy course, it seems useful for the student or practitioner to play the role of advisor to top management in the organization under consideration. The reader steps back, asks a series of questions and analyzes all aspects of the organization and its policy making process, including the personalities and self-interests of the organization's top personnel.

We would like to express gratitude for special support and assistance to the Manchester Business School, Grigor Machelland, Director; and the University of Maryland College of Business and Management, Rudolph Lamone, Dean. Their actions were helpful to Frank T. Paine in his development of the new material for this revision. Both this revision and the earlier version were the primary responsibility of Dr. Paine.

A note is included here on the use of "he" and "his." The convention of the masculine pronoun is used because, as many authors have discovered, there is no effective English-language singular that includes both sexes.

It is impossible to credit all of the people who have helped to create this revision and shape its contents one way or another. Many users, reviewers, and/or colleagues have played a constructive role. The following are some of them: Charles Summer, Max Richards, Henry Mintzberg, H. Igor Ansoff, Chuck Hofer, Dan Schendel, George Steiner, Carl Anderson, Gordon Mandry, Derek Channon, Jim Leontiades, Tom Lupton, John Barnes, Peter Patel, H. Thanheiser, Rocco Carzo, Jr., Bernard Taylor, Bruce Coleman, Mike McGinnis, John Sims, S. Kyle Reed, Richard Cyert, James March, Raymond Bauer, William Guth, John Miner, William Newman, Bud Pederson, Robert Katz, Henry Eyring, Lonnie Zienkiewicz, Lindsay Lucke, Lisette Cohen, John Neifert and Thomas O'Connor. We will, of course, take the blame for any errors of commission or omission.

Credit should also be given to our wives, Johanne and Peggy, for all their patience and support in this project and other projects.

FRANK T. PAINE
WILLIAM NAUMES

CONTENTS

1 POLICY FORMATION AND THE CHOICE PROCESS 1

    QUESTIONS TO ASK 2
    WHAT IS POLICY FORMATION? 4
    WHAT ARE MISSIONS, OBJECTIVES, POLICIES, STRATEGIES, PROGRAMS AND ROLES? HOW ARE THEY RELATED TO EACH OTHER? 5
    THE CHOICE PROCESS—SOME IDEA ON WHAT SHOULD HAPPEN 11
    THE CHOICE PROCESS—SOME IDEAS ON WHAT *ACTUALLY* HAPPENS 13
    THEORIES RELEVANT TO THE CHOICE PROCESS 16
    OVERVIEW OF DECISION THEORIES—NORMATIVE AND DESCRIPTIVE 17
    A CASE STUDY PLUS FOLLOW-UP 19
    SUMMARY 20
    DISCUSSION QUESTIONS 21
    APPENDIX TO CHAPTER 1 23
        The Bike Lock Company (A) and (B)

2 CONCEPTUALIZING THE POLICY-FORMATION PROCESS 30

    POLICY FORMATION AND CLASSICAL DECISION MAKING 30
    A DESCRIPTIVE MODEL OF THE POLICY-FORMATION PROCESS 33
    "NEGOTIATING" WITH THE ENVIRONMENT 42
    SUMMARY 53
    INTERGROUP POLICY EXERCISE 54
    DISCUSSION QUESTIONS 55

3 ASSESSMENT GUIDES: THE CURRENT SITUATION 57

OBJECTIVES OF ASSESSMENT OF POLICY FORMATION 58
USE OF THE GUIDES 58
FRAMEWORK FOR ASSESSING POLICY FORMATION 59
SUMMARY 83
APPENDIX TO CHAPTER 3 84
    A Program for Analyzing Some Aspects of the Present Financial Condition of the Organization

4 THE CHANGING SITUATION: ENVIRONMENTAL TURBULENCE 93

ANALYSIS OF IMPACT OF THREATS AND OPPORTUNITIES 94
SUMMARY 108
DISCUSSION QUESTIONS FOR CHAPTERS 3 AND 4 108

5 STRATEGY DEVELOPMENT 110

OUTLINE OF STRATEGY DEVELOPMENT 112
STRATEGIC MIX AND THE PORTFOLIOS 113
SEGMENTATION PROCESS AND BUSINESS STRATEGIES 120
DETAILING PROVISIONS FOR PROCURING AND ALLOCATING RESOURCES: LINKING STRATEGY WITH OPERATIONS 134
A COMPUTER PROGRAM FOR REFORMULATING ORGANIZATIONAL STRATEGY 135
SUMMARY 137
DISCUSSION QUESTIONS 138
APPENDIX 1 TO CHAPTER 5 140
    A Review of Marketing Concepts and Ideas
APPENDIX 2 TO CHAPTER 5 145
    Assessment Guides for Small Businesses
APPENDIX 3 TO CHAPTER 5 153
    Helping Small Businesses Cope

6 ASSESSMENT AND ORGANIZATION DEVELOPMENT: AN ACTION-RESEARCH PROGRAM ... 156

WHY ASSESSMENT AND DEVELOPMENT? ... 157
EVALUATION STRATEGIES ... 158
WHAT IS AN ORGANIZATION DEVELOPMENT APPROACH TO STRATEGY FORMATION? ... 161
ACTION-RESEARCH PROGRAM ... 163
USE AND LIMITATIONS OF ACTION RESEARCH ... 164
INFORMATION GATHERING AND PROCESSING ... 165
SUMMARY ... 192
DISCUSSION QUESTIONS ... 193

7 MANAGEMENT SCIENCE AND COMPUTER PROGRAMS ... 195

USE OF MANAGEMENT SCIENCE APPROACHES IN STRATEGY FORMATION ... 196
REASONS FOR SUCCESS AND FAILURE OF MANAGEMENT SCIENCE PROGRAMS ... 210
COMPUTER-AIDED STRATEGY ANALYSIS ... 212
SUMMARY ... 216
DISCUSSION QUESTIONS ... 217
APPENDIX 1 TO CHAPTER 7 ... 219
   Solution to Problem I
APPENDIX 2 TO CHAPTER 7 ... 220
   Solution to Problem II

8 THE ACTION THRUST IN STRATEGY FORMATION: DEVELOPING INDIVIDUAL AND GROUP INVOLVEMENT ... 221

STRATEGIES FOR EFFECTIVE CHANGE AND IMPLEMENTATION ... 222
INDIVIDUAL AND GROUP PROBLEM SOLVING ... 226
OVERALL STRUCTURING OF THE ACTIVITY: THE PLANNING SYSTEM ... 227
TIMING OF THE ACTIVITY ... 231
SELECTING PROBLEM-SOLVING SITUATIONS ... 232
TYPES OF STRUCTURED ACTIVITIES— INDIVIDUAL AND GROUP ... 235

EFFECTIVE GROUP SESSIONS 239
FEED-IN OF ACTION RESEARCH AND
MANAGEMENT SCIENCE DATA 240
QUESTIONS AND ANSWERS REGARDING THE
ACTION COMPONENTS 246
SUMMARY 249
DISCUSSION QUESTIONS 249
APPENDIX 1 TO CHAPTER 8 251
    Managerial Activities and Capabilities

9 ENVIRONMENT—STRATEGY—CAPABILITY 256

TRENDS IN STRATEGY AND STRUCTURE 256
BALANCING THE ENVIRONMENT—STRATEGY
CAPABILITY 259
INTEGRATED CONTINGENCY MODELS 262
STRATEGIC MOVES IN EACH QUADRANT 266
RELATED INFLUENCES ON CAPABILITY 269
OVERALL SUMMARY 272
DISCUSSION QUESTIONS 275
APPENDIX 1 TO CHAPTER 9 277
    Some Action Steps in Case Analysis
    Example of Policy Material Used at Ohio
    State University

AUTHOR INDEX 285

SUBJECT INDEX 289

1

QUESTIONS TO ASK

WHAT IS POLICY FORMATION?

WHAT ARE MISSIONS, OBJECTIVES, POLICIES, STRATEGIES, PROGRAMS AND ROLES? HOW ARE THEY RELATED TO EACH OTHER?
- Basic Missions and Strategic Business Units
- Organizational Objectives and Objectives for Each Unit
- Policies and Strategies
- Programs, Roles and Structure
- Need for Coherent Means-End Chain

THE CHOICE PROCESS—SOME IDEAS ON WHAT *SHOULD* HAPPEN

THE CHOICE PROCESS—SOME IDEAS ON WHAT *ACTUALLY* HAPPENS

THEORIES RELEVANT TO THE CHOICE PROCESS

OVERVIEW OF DECISION THEORIES—NORMATIVE AND DESCRIPTIVE
- Group Theory and Elite Theory

A CASE STUDY PLUS FOLLOW-UP

SUMMARY

DISCUSSION QUESTIONS

APPENDIX 1. THE BIKE LOCK COMPANY (A) AND (B)

POLICY FORMATION AND THE CHOICE PROCESS

An organization exists in a changing environment. Changes are occurring in economic conditions, consumer behavior, social values, technology, politics and even pollution standards. In fact, there are a large number of environmental threats and opportunities that may be of importance to an organization. Their significance for the organization must be determined, and time and effort must be spent in studying their impact on the organization's activities now and in the future. In addition to the difficult job of proper identification of the challenges and opportunities, the organization is faced with (1) setting missions and broad objectives; (2) designing actions to fulfill these objectives; (3) developing and allocating the financial, human and physical resources to carry out the plans; (4) monitoring the results and the organization to see that the desired ends are being accomplished and, when necessary, altering the actions or organization to more nearly accomplish the objectives; and (5) structuring the interpersonal and intergroup relationships within the organization to facilitate accomplishment of the desired future performance levels. These several elements constitute the field of policy.

As you can see, managers at the policy level are dealing with weighty and complex matters. The manager will have some of these matters within his grasp, but some are part of the broad framework of society and include various interest groups and various uncertainties.

This book is concerned with what the policy analyst or general manager can do in a business or nonprofit institution to study and to improve the process of dealing with these complex policy issues. Recognition is given to the similarities in top management functions and responsibilities in all types of performance-oriented organizations. The book deals with ideas useful to organizations of various sizes and organizations with various technologies. Its focus is on managers with significant policy-making responsibility. It has application, as well, to managers and staff with broad responsibilities in a significant segment of an organization (e.g., a strategic business unit, a profit center or an operations bureau). It covers the more general policy-making issues and problems that affect the long-term development of the performance-oriented organization. The emphasis tends to be on private business firms, and the book deals to only a limited extent with important but specialized topics such as labor relations policy, executive staffing and mergers.

This book is primarily concerned with organizational strategies and policies. While these decision forms may come from public institutions, they are still related to a specific organizational unit.

We are not looking directly at national or public policy, a form of decision process which requires a much broader scope than the focus of this book. It essentially defines the values and concerns for society as a whole. As such, however, public policy provides an important input for the decision process for organizational policy. This input is discussed at greater length later in the text.

The manager, even at the top level, is influenced by policies and activities other than his own. Sometimes, if he is at or near the top, he has opportunities to influence his organization's major policies and to take part in activities that contribute to the vitality of the total organization. His actions, however, must be responsive to requirements and changes outside his control. Nevertheless, he shapes his own policy formation process to meet internal requirements and to respond to specific situations. He must help individual policy analysts and policy formation groups to achieve a proper understanding of their role in the total organization (perhaps vis-à-vis other individuals or groups) and to improve their effectiveness in identifying and making choices.

QUESTIONS TO ASK

Assume you are being hired to help to design and to implement an approach for improving the policy formation process in a private or public organization. You should be sufficiently informed and self-critical to be aware of the flimsy base on which prescriptions for strategic management have been posed.[*] Some advances are

---

[*] P. H. Grinyer: Some dangerous axioms of corporate planning. *Journal of Business Policy*, 3 (No. 1):3–9, 1973.

now being made in behavioral and management science concepts and in assessment and development techniques to replace relatively unsystematic observations and anecdotal evidence. Still, a cautious, 'I don't know for sure" approach seems to be appropriate. This book will use such a cautious approach, but hopefully will provide some guidance in establishing a model and a frame of reference for your thinking and your search.

There will be many questions to ask in your search for an approach to improving policy formation. One set of questions that you might be asking has to do with the nature of the choice process and policy formation.

1. What is "policy formation"?
2. What are missions, objectives, policies, strategies, programs, roles? How are they related to one another?
3. What is a strategic business unit?
4. By what methods and processes *should* significant decisions or choices be made?
5. How are choices *actually* made in policy formation?
6. Of what relevance is normative and descriptive decision theory?

Study of this chapter should provide the reader with some answers to these questions.

Another set of questions has to do with conceptualizing the policy formation process and is taken up in the second chapter. The second chapter questions are aimed at uncovering and describing what the policy formation process actually involves:

1. How does policy formation relate to the rational or classical decision-making models?
2. What are environmental demands and environmental support?
3. What are some significant aspects of the policy generating structure?
4. What is the role of the general manager or policy maker in coordinating conflicting sets of interest? What is the role of power relationships or coalitions?
5. How do the structure and the environment interact to form organizational objectives, organizational strategies and so forth?

You would surely want to deal with a set of questions on the ways of assessing and improving the policy product or, from a different perspective, with questions dealing with approaches to study of the process of policy formation. In other words, the questions aim at guides and methods for studying and developing the policy process and policy product.

1. What are some guides for assessing the current situation of the organization and its environment? (Chapter 3)
2. What are some guides for analyzing the impact of opportunities and threats? (Chapter 4)

3. What are some guides for developing strategies? (Chapter 5)

4. What are some methods for assessment and development of the organization, its strategies and its policy formation process? (Chapter 6)

5. What is the role of management science and the computer at the policy level? (Chapter 7)

6. By what processes is there an "action thrust" in strategy making that involves others in planning actions, coordinating actions, executing actions and evaluating actions? (Chapter 8)

7. Is the environment-strategy-capability in balance? What are some action steps in case analysis? (Chapter 9)

This chapter will introduce you to the choice process and policy formation. It provides background material helpful to understanding the nature of this important but complex subject. The material following this chapter suggests answers to some of the additional questions you may have about conceptualizing, assessing and developing the policy formation process.

WHAT IS POLICY FORMATION?

Definition

Important broad definition.

Policy formation involves the decision making and the activities in an organization which tend to (1) have wide ramifications, (2) have a long-time perspective and (3) use critical resources toward perceived opportunities or threats in a changing environment. Policy formation is a dynamic social process within which an intellectual process is embedded.

It involves wide ramifications. Policy formation activites are related to the total system (or a significant segment of it), such as a change in organization goals, or managerial strategies that have implications throughout the organization or business unit (e.g., a major change in the direction or scope of the business or activity the organization is in).

It involves a long-time perspective. The directional decisions in policy formation can be expected to have effects on the organization for an extended period of time.

It uses critical resources toward perceived opportunities in a changing environment. The most important human, financial and other resources are brought to bear in certain situations seen as providing the organization with an oportunity to manage the elusive environment. To understand how effective the policy formation process has been, it is necessary to have some criteria for what an effective policy formation process would look like. This question will be dealt with in a later chapter.

It is an intellectual process. In policy formation, key individuals perceive, analyze and choose between alternatives, *interrelat-*

ing such policy elements as basic missions, broad organizational goals, policies and strategies.

It is a continuing dynamic social process. Policy formation is not just a chore to be undertaken a few times each year when top management meets to decide critical issues. Policy formation is a continuing dynamic social process of implementing and revising policies in the human organization as changes occur in resources and in the environment. "Negotiating" and trade-offs frequently occur.

All these characteristics of policy formation will be examined with the view toward understanding and improving the choice process, which significantly affects the welfare of the organization and the individual. Before looking at what *should* happen in the choice process, however, it is important to make a few comments on how the various components of the policy formation process may be described or defined.

WHAT ARE MISSIONS, OBJECTIVES, POLICIES, STRATEGIES, PROGRAMS AND ROLES? HOW ARE THEY RELATED TO EACH OTHER?

In the conduct of business or agency operations a hierarchy of rules for conduct may exist either explicitly or implicitly. The hierarchy in descending order is referred to here as missions or scope, objectives, policies, strategies, programs and roles. In the following discussion we shall present a few highlights of the nature of these elements so that the policy analyst can differentiate between them. Later these topics will be discussed in more detail. You will notice that the phrases "policy formation" and "strategy formation" are being used interchangeably to refer to a number of kinds of significant activities and elements in an organization. There is no classification of elements or of activities that has a common acceptance. However, many writers and practitioners will agree that, while it is not essential for all to distinguish between elements in the same way, it is essential that one see the means-end relationships among such components as missions, objectives and policies. One of the ways of distinguishing between some of the elements and examining the means-end relationship is what follows next. Alternative ways will be discussed throughout the book.

What is the hierarchy of rules of conduct?

Terms ušed interchangeably!

Basic Missions and Strategic Business Units

As mentioned, policy formation includes the making and interrelating of decisions on the use of limited resources with potential opportunities, risks and threats in a changing, uncertain environment. On the basis of information about such environmental factors and taking into consideration personal values or self-in-

Scope of operation— product and market or service and client.

terests of top managers and/or "influentials" in the organization or associated with it in some way, decisions are made on the basic mission or direction of the organization. The mission or domain may be described as the scope of operations in terms of product and market or of service and client. An organization may define its mission as the railroad business. However, it will be one thing if its mission is commuter or passenger business near a large metropolitan area and quite another if it is freight hauling in the midwest. Deciding upon the basic mission is a *fundamental* component in policy formation. For example, the Southern Pacific Railroad Company decided it was in the transportation business (not just the railroad business) and expanded its activities into trucking and pipelines. Too broad a mission may be dangerous, since problems tend to increase in relation to opportunities.

For many organizations, however, it may be useful to consider a break out of the scope of operations into more than one overall mission. That is, the environmental conditions (e.g., regulations, technology, types of customers, competitors) for a pipeline business may be different than those faced by a trucking business. For purposes of analysis they may be viewed as strategically independent. Various strategic business units (SBU) (divisions, bureaus, profit centers, product lines, departments) may be identified if they sell a distinct set of products or services to an identifiable group of customers or clients in competition with a well-defined set of customers. *Each unit and its environmental segment* can be analyzed then for its own unique pattern on such factors as future growth potential, user benefits, competitive position, cost and margin behavior, competitor strategy and net cash flow.

Organizational Objectives and Objectives for Each Unit

Hoped for results, goals or targets.

Objectives may be described as "hoped for results, goals or targets." They can be quite general (e.g., quality service) or very specific (e.g., reduction in force—[RIF], 5 per cent by June 30th). The more specific the goal, the easier it is to appraise how well it has been fulfilled.

Objectives or goals can be derived from different considerations. They may be based on extensive analysis of the external environment, or they may be dictated, without any research analysis, by the top manager or other influential people associated with the organization unit. They may also have been derived from complex power plays within the organization.

Whatever this derivation, a check needs to be made on the relationships between the objectives for each unit, the organizational objectives and the various missions. We shall return to this point shortly.

Policies and Strategies

Policies may be described as broad guides for managers, supervisors and other employees for the achievement of objectives. It is important to recognize that the policies stem from fulfilling objectives. For example, an objective of quality service may have a policy of extensive monitoring of service activities. Obviously, each objective may require more than one policy in the attempt to reach the objective; thus, another policy stemming from the objective of quality service may be the decision to recruit only the very top-rated management personnel. It may be a decision to allow divisions to acquire only quality oriented companies, after approval of the central office.

Broad guides.

Now one may see the hierarchy or means-end chain in basic missions, objectives and policies. In the above example the extensive monitoring was a *policy* designed to fulfill a basic objective of quality service. If we use our previous example of a basic mission being the transportation of goods and passengers, the hierarchy looks as follows:

Transportion of Goods and Passengers
Quality Service
Extensive Monitoring

The means-end chain is a reflection of the fact that every step in the hierarchy is a means to an end. The chain occurs because all the missions, objectives, policies (and strategies) are linked to one another.

While policies are seen as broad guides to action, strategies may be viewed as specific *major* actions or patterns of action for attainment of objectives. They may be planned ahead of time or emerge over time based on ad hoc decisions.* A strategic action for a company might be to deploy resources into new operations in Germany; another might be to compete head to head with another company for the instant photography business, such as Eastman Kodak's decision to develop a technically superior in-camera development process. Such strategic actions may result in the need for strategies for marketing, technology, finance, geographic area definition, changes and so forth; in other words, a cluster of strategies may be required overall (organizational strategies) and for

Specific major actions or pattern of actions.

Are they consistent with gaining a defensible segment in the environment?

---

*As we shall see later in this chapter, an organizational strategy (or corporate strategy) may be defined not only as a plan which encompasses the mission, policies, objectives and more specific goals of the organization, but also as a plan of action for achieving those objectives and goals. Subsequent decisions are based on the plan. On the other hand, organizational strategies may be described as a stream of significant decisions which emerge over a period of time into a pattern. In this case the decisions, made on an ad hoc basis while trying to adapt to various uncertainties, determine the strategy. Corporate strategy is similar to organizational strategy, but the phrase is sometimes reserved for use in referring to business corporations. The term *business strategy* is sometimes reserved for use in referring to the strategy of an SBU.

8 / POLICY FORMATION AND THE CHOICE PROCESS

each unit (a business strategy). Some strategic actions may alter the missions and/or the objective.

Organizational strategy may be viewed as an integrative concept.

A cluster of strategic actions over time might involve, for example, (1) picking particular product-market segments or niches that are propitious in view of the needs of society and the organization's capabilities, (2) selection of the underlying technologies and ways for attracting financial and other inputs, (3) deployment of resources into particular geographic or major research area and (4) disposing of a particular line of products which do not fit acceptable levels on significant criteria. An overall strategy, then, is the sum total or pattern of these past and present actions or decisions.*

An example of a strategic action stemming from our previous means-end chain would be the decision for greater integration of the organization by adding assessment and development activities formerly purchased from other organizations. The activities might be seen as a systematic attempt toward planned changed in the organization to fulfill the policy of extensive monitoring. The actions might include market research and auditing of the rapidly changing external environment, as well as additional auditing of the internal environment of the organization.

Programs, Roles and Structures

Programs—generalized procedures in response to particular actions.

Programs can be described as generalized procedures that are used in response to a particular type of stimulus. You have heard of programs being "built" into the computer, which takes inputs, executes a set of steps and produces outputs. Humans, as well as machines, learn and use programs as an economical (they are not new each time but reflect the learning of past actions) way of responding. For example, the financial analyst in response to a request carries out a capital budgeting program, or a manager in response to a difficulty carries out a problem-solving program.

As with strategies, there are sets of programs linked to each other. One set might describe the various assessment and development activities used to measure progress in terms of time, resources, quality and quantity. Another related set might describe such methods as periodic status reports, data analysis, interviews, questionnaires and problem-solving conferences. Thus, to the above means-end chain could be added:

Assessment and Development Activities
Problem-solving Conferences, and so forth

---

*It should be noted that to the extent actions or patterns of actions serve as guides or constraints on future action, they (strategies) become similar or equivalent to policies.

POLICY FORMATION AND THE CHOICE PROCESS / 9

The means-end chain could be extended to the level of the individual manager, supervisor or employee in the organization. If it were extended, the individual's role prescription as well as his actual role performance would be added. The role prescription includes the pattern of behavior expected and the functions, duties, authorities and responsibilities assigned to the holder of the position. For example, part of the role prescription for a manager might be as follows:

Determine whether significant factors have been included in goal or target setting of subordinates.

The role performance is a description of the actual pattern of behavior that is followed by the individual and the actual functions and duties he performs. It may be quite specific. For example:

Roles — behavior patterns of the individual.

In carrying out his leadership role, he frequently chats informally with his subordinates. Through this contact he keeps current on important milestones and he uses his recognized competence to influence the pattern of activities among his subordinates.

The structure of an organization deals with the coupling of the roles (and programs) of various members of the organization and the resulting flow of information and authority. It is important to note that in carrying out roles, managers and other influentials use programs to make determinations on the other aspects of the hierarchy, such as missions, objectives, policies, and strategies. We shall return later to the policy making structure of the organization and discuss roles and programs more fully.

Structure defined.

This means-end chain that has been constructed to this point appears as follows:

>Transportation of Goods and Passengers
>Quality Service
>Extensive Monitoring
>Assessment and Development Activities
>Problem-solving Conferences
>Determinations on Whether Significant Factors
>Are Included in Target Setting
>Frequent Informal Chats with Subordinates

This means-end chain, of course, is a simplifcation in that even in the smallest agency, department or business concern there are a number of interrelated elements—environment, strategies, capabilities, resources. It seems important to recognize the fact that, contrary to an assumption sometimes made in economics, there is no such thing as a single objective for a company or organization. Each organization has a network of goals and a network of means to attain those prescribed goals.

But there is more— Environment- strategies- capabilities- resources.

While evaluating an overall organization and each business unit, the classification of basic missions, objectives, policies, strategies, programs, capabilities and resources is difficult and inexact. Evaluation, however, cannot proceed effectively without knowledge of these elements and how they are interrelated.

Classification difficult and inexact but must have knowledge of elements.

TABLE 1-1 SOME ORGANIZATIONAL FEATURES THAT ARE LIKELY TO VARY WITH A CHANGE IN STRATEGY

Centralization versus decentralization of authority
Degree of division of labor
Size of self-sufficient operating units
Mechanism for coordination
Nature and location of staff
Management information system
Characteristics of key personnel

Need for Coherent Means-End Chain

Environment-strategies-capabilities. Are they consistent or balanced?

We have indicated that for each organizational situation the means-end chain needs to be examined for interrelationships and for mutual supportiveness. That is, basically are the managerial capabilities (roles, style, processes, power, knowledge, etc.) consistent with the strategies? Are the strategies consistent with gaining a defensible segment in the environment? Do the review procedures generate useful data for strategy formation? Are the clusters of strategies designed in such a way as to facilitate policy fulfillment? Is, say, centralized decision making congruent with expected participative leadership practices? Are pay and promotion procedures supporting desired role performance? Does the use of standard operating programs in the process of choice tend to inhibit large changes in strategy? Do the complex power plays in the choice of objectives lead to only those strategy alternatives which are politically feasible?

The determination of mutual consistency is, needless to say, a difficult task. Strategies, for example, are subject to continuing formation, implementation, interpretation, change and obsolescence over time. With each shift in strategy the appropriateness of the means-end chain needs to be examined anew. One of the comparisons for the business policy analyst is: Do we have the right organizational structure for our new strategies? To complicate the matter there are several structural features (among other types) that are likely to vary with a change in strategy, as William Newman has discussed.* At this point we shall just show you a sample of features (Table 1-1).

This discussion of the means-end chain has given you a preliminary indication of the information processing that the policy analyst must do in dealing with complex policy issues. The

---

*William H. Newman: Strategy and Management Structure. Presented at the Annual Meeting of the Academy of Management, Atlanta, Georgia, 1971. See also A. D. Chandler: *Strategy and Structure*. Cambridge, MIT Press, 1962.

nature and importance of these issues necessitate attention on a continuing basis to the choices that are being made.

The choice process is the next subject to be examined. After a brief introduction to the choice process, some ideas on what *should* happen will be discussed, following which some ideas on what actually happens will be indicated.

THE CHOICE PROCESS—SOME IDEA ON WHAT *SHOULD* HAPPEN

Assume that you have agreed to accept the challenge of trying to develop an approach for improving policies and the policy formation process. Assume further that you are asking some of the questions that were outlined previously in this chapter in order to get a general orientation as to the nature of the present policy situation. The development of an approach for improvement in policy formation demands some early analysis of the choice procedure; that is, given the fact that resources and capabilities are limited, choices must be made between competing alternative strategies or policies. We ask then by what methods and processes should significant decisions or choices be made?

What methods and processes should be used?

Some ideas on what should happen can be derived by examining organizations such as Digital Equipment Corporation (D.E.C.), American Motors and HMH Publishing Co. (Playboy). They have aimed their products at *particular niches in a larger market*. D.E.C., for example, decided against attempting to compete directly with I.B.M. Instead, it built expertise in a much smaller market, that of mini-computers. While I.B.M. was building large machines, D.E.C. took the opposite approach and built smaller, more compact machines for lower prices. It felt that the mini-computer market would expand once the computer had become fully accepted. The mini-computer was felt to be the answer for those large and small corporations that have problems that could best be solved by use of computers—problems, however, that could not be programmed economically on the large full scale machines.

Find a niche.

The success of D.E.C. over the last several years points to the effectiveness of its corporate strategy. This strategy, as we can see, was designed to take advantage of competitive factors in the environment. D.E.C. hoped it could *match its own internal strengths* in computer design, as well as company size, *with a perceived need in the environment*. In this manner D.E.C. tried to turn a potential weakness, its size and the competitive situation, into an opportunity *by formulating a set of objectives and an action plan that skirted its weaknesses and these threats* and capitalized on its strong points in the total environment.

Match internal strengths and perceived need in environment.

Skirt weaknesses and threats.

Additional examples of directing product appeal to particular market segments as mentioned are American Motors Corporation and Playboy Enterprises. A.M.C. found that it did not have the resources to compete head-on with the Big Three in the auto industry. It saw its sales and market share decline as it spread its efforts and image over a broad range of models. It made a decision to return to its formerly successful strategy of producing small quality cars. A.M.C. felt that this niche strategy, combined with the knowledge that imported subcompacts were selling well, would help it to regain its lost share of market and profits. This strategy has proved relatively successful for the company.

What is A.M.C.'s current corporate strategy?

What is Playboy's current corporate strategy?

Playboy Enterprises, on the other hand, has attempted to tie its diversification efforts into a consistent image of the company. Its products and services are all tied in to its philosophy of the kind of life style the successful urban male should follow. The various enterprises of the firm are designed to enhance that life style.

These examples, however, only give us some insight into parts of what we should consider as a total strategy for an organization. They do not really give us a picture of the framework that the general manager should use during the strategy formation process.

The approaches taken by most policy texts are really concerned with what should be done during the policy formation process.* Although their definitions differ, they are meant to provide a framework to be followed by the general manager to provide an effective organizational strategy.

The general manager is theoretically "the" strategic decision maker; "the" comprehensive rational planner. He should stand in the middle of the environment, exploring the situation around him in order to plan—hopefully—for an "optimal" fit between resources and objectives. Another point that he should consider is the consistency of the objectives with the environment, both internal and external. After finding a competitive niche in the automobile

---

*See, for example, H. I. Ansoff: *Corporate Strategy.* New York, McGraw-Hill Book Co., 1965; W. H. Newman and J. P. Logan: *Strategy Policy and Central Management.* Cincinnati, Southwestern Publishing Co., 1975; F. Gilmore; *Formulation and Advocacy of Business Policy.* Ithaca, Cornell University Press, 1970; R. Katz: *Management of the Total Enterprise.* Englewood Cliffs, N. J., Prentice-Hall, Inc., 1970; C. E. Sumner, Jr., and J. O'Connell: *The Managerial Mind.* Homewood, Ill., Richard D. Irwin, Inc., 1976; J. T. Cannon: *Business Strategy and Policy.* New York, Harcourt, Brace & World, Inc., 1968; R. H. Buskirk: *Business and Administratative Policy.* New York, John Wiley & Sons, Inc., 1970; W. Glueck: *Business Policy: Strategy Formation and Management Action.* New York, McGraw-Hill Book Co., 1976; F. J. Bridges, K. W. Olm and J. A. Barnhill: *Management Decisions and Organizational Policy.* Boston, Allyn & Bacon, Inc., 1971; H. N. Broom: *Business Policy and Strategic Action.* Englewood Cliffs, N.J., Prentice-Hall, Inc., 1970; E. P. Learned, C. R. Christensen, K. R. Andrews and W. D. Guth: *Business Policy, Text and Cases.* Homewood, Ill., Richard D. Irwin, Inc., 1976; T. J. McNichols: *Policy Making and Executive Action.* New York, McGraw-Hill Book Co., 1976.

market, A.M.C. decided to take on the Big Three across the board. It felt that to be an effective competitor, it should also produce a full line of cars. What the general manager(s) failed to consider was the relevant environment facing it. A.M.C. failed to consider its own weakness with respect to its competition. The other firms were better able to compete, financially and in other ways, in the general auto market. A.M.C. had allowed itself to take its previous success in one particular submarket as a sign of strength in the total market.

We now see that one phase of strategy formation involves a more general determination of objectives. Another phase looks for specific areas of strength and weakness in the environmental segment. A third phase involves formulation of an action plan consistent with the previous analysis. Included in the total process must be a method of evaluating the total strategy to ensure the success of that strategy.

THE CHOICE PROCESS—SOME IDEAS ON WHAT *ACTUALLY* HAPPENS

We have briefly introduced a normative, theoretical framework for policy or strategy formation. If we were living and managing in a theoretical world, this framework would produce ideal strategies for organizations.

As we well know, however, we operate in a world with a wide variety of uncertainties and difficulties. These factors can lead to considerable variance from the process as we have outlined it. This should not lead us to scrap the entire process, however. It should lead us to try to understand why the variances occur and how we can adapt the basic process to account for these variances. A brief anecdote concerning policy formation in practice might help to highlight some of these problems and solutions.

Recently a large electronics firm decided to diversify into related areas. A financial planner was included in a new ventures division. His primary responsibility was to cooperate with the engineering department for planning for large scale, capital improvements.

He and an engineer proceeded to gather information concerning the future direction and objectives of the total organization forecasts regarding sales and expense constraints, although with some degree of difficulty. The difficulty appeared to be primarily politically motivated within the organization. They were, however, finally able to obtain all the technical data they felt were necessary from a planning standpoint.

Based on this data, which they were able to get all relevant managers within the organization to agree on, they proceeded to formulate a consistent and feasible plan of action. After several weeks of consultations and revisions, they presented their plan to the plant and division managers.

The plan took into consideration the various constraints the firm had to face. The final figures of the plan were presented in terms of total square feet of building area and equipment required to achieve division objectives from a capital improvements point of view. This information was designed to fit into an overall strategy for diversification and expansion.

To the surprise of the analysts, the upper level managers were unimpressed with the presentation. The analysts left the presentation session determined to find out why this "well formulated" plan had not been accepted. Further discussions with other top managers in the corporation led the analysts to what they felt was a solution. They discovered that the symbols of status and success within the organization revolved around the numbers and growth of the personnel beneath a given manager on the organization chart. They felt that this could well have influenced the managers' reactions to the formulated plan.

With this knowledge, the analysts reconstructed their presentation to point up the numbers of people involved in the proposal. Fortunately this was relatively simple to chart since this information was a necessary basic consideration in arriving at the original plan. Effectively, all they did was to make the same presentation but to use different terms in defining their purposes. The result was that the superiors accepted the presentation and included it in the total strategy.

What this demonstrates is that all decisions are not made in a vacuum. Eventually human managers must make a commitment of resources for a particular strategy. These commitments are not always based on a rational analysis of a completely known environment.

In this factual example the decision of the managers was influenced by status factors that would not necessarily affect the overall success or failure of the strategy. Moreoever, the analysts did not have this information available to them at crucial stages of the policy formation process.

In this instance, this part of the strategy could be reformulated with relatively little waste of time and energy. Many times, however, much time and energy seem to be wasted because of lack of proper understanding of all the factors affecting how significant decisions are actually made in an organization.

Prescriptions are meaningful only when grounded on valid description.

Theories and concepts may provide a solid foundation for understanding the basic strategy formation process. They are very practical or useful if they give us an appropriate framework for thinking and for making policy choices. However, prescribing what we should do is meaningful only when it is grounded in valid description.

Organizational processes theory.

Thus, as we have asked: What actually happens in the choice process? The organizational processes theory* provides us with some additional clues.

---

*R. M. Cyert and J. G. March: *A Behavioral Theory of the Firm.* Englewood Cliffs, N.J., Prentice-Hall, Inc., 1963. For empirical support see E. E. Carter: The behavioral theory of the firm and top-level corporate decisions. *Administrative Science Quarterly, 16* (No. 4):413–428, Dec., 1971. See also T. Petit: A behavioral theory of management. *Academy of Management Journal,* Dec., 1967., pp. 341–350.

One point of departure is to view the organization as a coalition. It includes a variety of individuals and subcoalitions, e.g., bureau chiefs, product managers, engineering managers, members of the Board of Commissioners, heads of research, union officials, vice presidents, stock holders and others. They are all participating in the organization because they share some goals; there is presumed to be some net benefit for their participation. However, there may be conflict over unshared goals and over the distribution of benefits. Different organizational units (say two service bureaus) have different functions or activities but are rivals. This conflict can become a motivation for constructive thought and analysis based on in-depth research and detailed information (experiments have shown interpersonal conflict to be associated with this rivalry).

Organization is a coalition.

Conflict over unshared goals.

However, the managers or executives involved, caught up in the organization rivalry, learn to maintain their viability in organizational life. First, they learn that it is better not to have a proposal turned down. "No's" may get to be a habit; the "no's" may damage their image, their effectiveness and their future. Second, they learn that for many issues or proposals the uncertainty is so great that a slight change in the calculations or emphasis may mean that the organizational standards or cut-off points may be met or missed. For example, breakeven analysis is frequently used in financial planning. A slight change in the predicted expenses and capital outlays might produce a breakeven point at a level below the predicted volume of sales. Third, the executive may learn that in his organization analytical time is a scarce commodity. That, together with a common — as opposed to rational — thinking about sunk cost, may mean that once a study is authorized, written up and reviewed, it becomes, as time goes on, increasingly difficult to reject. Thus, the initial authorization to make such studies is a key leverage element. Finally, and most generally, the executive, say one who is heading up an SBU, is viewed as changing his aspirations, postponing goals, making trade offs, developing allies and attempting to change the aspirations of others. He is responding to the costs and benefits in the social context.

Learning to maintain viability.

Thus, if our description is accurate we have a situation in which the sum of the proposed projects is not necessarily combined into a set which is meaningfully consistent with the organization's mission or objectives. To the contrary, given that subgoals exist and are important, the executives are negotiating, trying to maintain a winning coalition. A coalition is sought that provides support for the proposal and for the right of the exective to go ahead and proceed with the proposal. Much time may be spent writing up the proposal so that it meets the agency or corporate standards, but this may be a time-consuming and relatively unimportant part of the game.

Negotiating to maintain a winning coalition.

Need to understand more about the choice process.

The manager or policy maker needs to understand the process. The formal descriptive postulates presented are exceedingly limited. More normative as well as descriptive content is needed for prescriptions. It seems, though, that the general manager rarely has the formal power to be "the" strategic decision maker. It is true that entrepreneurs may dominate an organization, but even here the formal power is enhanced or diminished by the skills or lack thereof in communication, negotiation and persuasion. The general manager may be viewed as a participant in the complex process of arriving at organizational committments. Thus, we see that general manager is not "the" strategic decision maker.*

THEORIES RELEVANT TO THE CHOICE PROCESS

In summary to this point in our analysis of the choice process, we see policy initiators making an analysis and choice but doing so within a dynamic social process. Policy makers (or initiators) are seen as allocating and mediating among conflicting sets of interests. They form judgments specific to the situation, balancing each issue off against a wide range of other issues, present and future. And in doing so, they attempt to maintain a coalition of support.

You may want to investigate the theories further.

Furthermore, in our discussion to this point we have developed some considerations from theories relevant to the choice process. These approaches have been reviewed elsewhere (for excellent reviews see Bauer and Gergen, 1968; Khandwalla, 1976; Mintzberg, 1977),† so we shall not review them extensively here. Moreover, later in this book use will be made of some of the more important variables (e.g., programs, roles, self-interests) from previous studies, with explanations provided where appropriate.

The next section will provide a brief summary of types of theories relevant to the choice process. It may be appropriate for the student of policy formation to conduct further investigation of many of these theories. This overview is included to indicate the range of possibilities.

---

*See J. L. Bower: *Managing the Resource Allocation Process*. Cambridge, Graduate School of Business Administration, Harvard University, 1970; W. D. Guth: Toward a social system theory of corporate strategy. *Journal of Business,* July, 1976, pp. 374–388; F. T. Paine and C. A. Anderson: Strategic management: An intervention approach. *Proceedings of the National Academy of Management,* August, 1977, pp. 122–126.

†R. A. Bauer and K. J. Gergen (eds.): *The Study of Policy Formation.* New York, The Free Press, 1968. See also F. Kast and J. Rosenzweig (eds.): *Contingency Views of Organization and Management.* Palo Alto, Science Research Associates Inc., 1973; P. Khandwalla: The techno-economic ecology of corporate strategy. *Journal of Management Studies,* Feburary, 1976, pp. 62–75; H. Mintzberg: Policy as a field of management theory. *Academy of Management Review,* January, 1977, pp. 88–103.

OVERVIEW OF DECISION THEORIES—NORMATIVE AND DESCRIPTIVE

Decision theory may be separated into two categories, normative and descriptive. Normative theory is concerned with the particular decisions an organization ought to make, and descriptive theory is concerned with the way organizations actually go about making decisions. Further, normative theory has as its purpose the provision of rules that will hopefully improve choices and consequences, while descriptive theory sets out to describe the patterns of behavior that characterize action.

The way they "ought to" versus the way they actually do.

Normative theory is, in essence, the theory of rational choice in complex situations. It characteristically involves an individual decision maker and decision values expressed in dollars. Using normative theory, management scientists propose ways of guiding the decision maker in business or public bodies in what he ought to do; that is, given an explicit statement of the decision maker's preference, exposition of the alternative actions open to him and an indication of how the alternatives are related to the preferences, management scientists develop programs or generalized procedures which will indicate an optimal choice. As a practitioner or student of management and policy formation you probably are familiar with some of these programs or generalized procedures, such as statistical decision making, simulation and mathematical modeling.*

It is disturbing that these programs as publicized in some quarters might appear to give clear solutions to major policy problems. Such is not the case; exact solutions actually are not provided and should not be expected. The major weakness in providing a policy formation model is that normative theory may rely too heavily upon the concept of a single best solution. Management science programs can be helpful—as a point of departure. The strengths as well as the inadequacies of some of the procedures will be discussed in the next and subsequent chapters.

Major weakness of normative approach is that exact solutions are not provided.

Descriptive theory is more behavior oriented and may have a more pragmatic value to policy initiators in that it attempts to improve understanding of what actually is occurring. Furthermore, it tends to describe the complexities of a set of interrelated problems requiring solutions or in need of decisions. Thus, it has a better quality to fit to the complex policy formation situation.

Descriptive theory has better quality of fit.

Descriptive theory itself is further broken down into two categories that are particularly adaptive to the business and government world, theories of individual choice and theories of collective choice. Theories of individual choice obviously involve single decision makers and are exemplified by the classic theory of eco-

---

*These procedures and others will be amplified as we proceed.

nomic man, the theory of consumer demand and the classic theory of the firm.

Individual choice and collective choice.

Theories of collective choice often refer to decisions made by a coalition of several decision makers, and rivalry and conflict between decision-making units. Such approaches are typified by the Harvard Business School and the Stanford Business School case studies, the institutionalists (e.g., Selznick*), the experimental economists (e.g., Fouraker†), the Carnegie group (the organizational processes theory already mentioned) and Allison's bureaucratic politics theory.‡

Bureaucratic politics theory.

Group Theory and Elite Theory

In addition, descriptive decision theory is frequently viewed as including two particular categories, group theory and elite theory. Group theory places heavy emphasis on interaction within a group and sees the group as the primary source of influence over the attitudes and behaviors of individual policy makers. A major criticism of group theory is that it tends to subordinate the individual.

In contrast, elite theory places considerable emphasis on the individual. Elite theory often includes concern for the recruitment of elites, their socioeconomic characteristics, their perception and communication patterns and their circulation habits and, most importantly, their patterns of decision making. The theory hopes to explain expectations of elites and, therefore, the values they can be expected to pursue.§ Elite theory, while isolating important analytical variables such as perceptions and decision-making patterns, is criticized for not being tied to dynamic process variables. Policy making, so the argument would go, needs to be seen as a process of turning inputs into outputs.

Policy making needs to be seen as a process of turning inputs into outputs.

Our brief review of decision theory is designed only to provide a sample of the approaches that might be useful to the study of policy making and a sample of the criticisms that seem to reduce the appropriateness of these approaches for our purposes. That is, though the approaches have considerable merit, they do not provide rigorous support for prescriptions in policy making.

---

*Phillip Selznick: *Leadership and Administration.* New York, Harper & Row, 1957.

†L. E. Fouraker: Level of aspiration and group decision making. *In* Messick and Brayfield (eds.): *Decision and Choice: Contributions of Sidney Siegel.* New York, McGraw-Hill Book Co., 1958.

‡G. T. Allison: *Essence of Decision.* Boston, Little, Brown and Company, 1971.

§See, for example, W. D. Guth and R. Tagiuri: Personal values and corporate stragegies. *Harvard Business Review,* September-October, 1965, pp. 123–132, and G. W. England: *Personal Value Systems of Managers—So What?* Minneapolis, Industrial Relations Center, University of Minnesota, January, 1973.

Either the approach was based on nonoperational assumptions (e.g., a single decision maker) or it was devoid of acceptable normative content and could not be used alone to support prescription.

In short, the theory relevant to choosing policies and strategies is in its infancy. It would seem that, as already alluded to, advances in descriptive theory would be a major help in the development of a sound base for normative theory. It would seem also that we need field research allowing the comparison of policy formation in many types of organizations. Advances in field research would probably be aided and abetted by advances in normative theory. Better normative and descriptive content is needed for policy prescriptions.

What is needed for policy prescriptions?

A CASE STUDY PLUS FOLLOW-UP

One way of adding to our descriptive content and learning about policy is through the use of case materials. A case study of an actual organization is given in the Appendix to this chapter to illustrate some of the elements in the policy formation process. Reading the Bike Lock Company (A) case provides an introduction to organizational strategy formation specifically for small businesses. It offers the student a simplified small business situation which must be analyzed in terms of its potential for growth and expansion. Key variables to be evaluated include the technological aspects of the product, the environmental segment, the market for the product, the financial requirements of the business and the planning process for expansion.

Carl Reily, a businessman possessing both experience and education, desires to invest in a new business venture. After searching for a suitable opportunity, he locates Joe Last, an entrepreneur with a small but profitable bike lock company which produces high-priced, quality bike locks. Together with Mike Mulligan, Joe's brother-in-law, the two men decide to investigate the possibilities of expanding the small business.

The Bike Lock Company (A) case can stimulate your thinking about the problems and possibilities involved in starting and expanding a small business. As such, it provides a conceptual overview of organizational strategy formation.

Position in the Course

The case is most appropriate as an introduction to business policy formulation. It is simple enough to be used early in the course, even *before* you have read the rest of the text. A useful exercise may be to analyze the case intuitively prior to formal study of the Assessment Guidance (Chapters 2, 3, 4 and 5), balancing the Environment-Strategy-Capability (Chapter 9) and

Action Steps in Case Analysis (Appendix 1 to Chapter 9), then return to its analysis following such study. This practice may serve to illustrate the benefits of systematic analysis as you compare your initial reactions to the case and your later, perhaps more knowledgeable, analysis.

The case can be used in conjunction with its follow-up case, The Bike Lock Company (B), which provides more details about the proposed expansion. Test yourself by generating alternatives and analysis before reading the (B) case.

Analysis

An analysis of the Bike Lock Company cases should include (1) an evaluation of the capabilities (strengths and weaknesses) of the existing company, Last's Custom Lock Company; (2) a discussion of key decisions that must be made prior to expansion; (3) a discussion of the impact of various threats and opportunities in the expanded firm's environmental segment; (4) a discussion of alternative strategies which might be considered for gaining a defensible segment; (5) a discussion of capabilities and resources needed to follow each major strategy; and (6) a discussion of the consistency of the environment-strategy-capabilities. Also, in policy you will use your knowledge and skill learned in more specialized courses. For example, discuss the procedure for making a market survey for Bike Lock (try it first and then look at the Appendix to Chapter 5, Review of Marketing Concepts and Ideas).

SUMMARY

"Policy formation" is a general term referring to a dynamic social process of which an intellectual process is an integral part. Policy formation deals with such crucial questions as, "What can this organization do better than anyone else?" A hierarchy of rules of conduct exists explicitly or implicitly, including basic missions, objectives, policies, strategies, programs and roles. The key directional decisions in this hierarchy (1) have wide ramifications, (2) involve a long-time perspective, (3) affect the use of critical resources toward perceived opportunities and threats in a changing external and internal environment and (4) need to be checked for consistency. These characteristics necessitate continuous attention and emphasis on policy making by top management.

This book is concerned not simply with intellectual appreciation of these complex issues but with developing conceptual and administrative skill in dealing with them. The book deals with ideas useful to organizations of various sizes and various technologies. Its focus is on managers with significant policy-making responsibility. It has application, moreover, to managers and staff with strategy and policy responsibilities in the strategic business units of an organization. For students, the book is designed to provide some guidance for (1) case analysis, (2) field and library projects and (3) role playing. Case analysis is also discussed in the Appendix to Chapter 9.

A person searching for an approach to improve policy formation would ask a number of questions including those on relevant theory and method, on the significant variables and relationships in the social process and the intellectual process of policy formation, and on alternative ways of assessing and developing policies and organizational processes. A mere beginning is made in this chapter at answering some of these questions.

The choice process is analyzed on a preliminary basis, first in terms of normative ideas and approaches and then in terms of describing what actually seems to happen. Management science programs, for example, have provided some useful ways of dealing with uncertainty. The normative approaches at the present time, however, do not give exact solutions to major policy issues. A check into what actually happens in some policy choices in real organizations provides useful insight.

We see policy makers analyzing choices but also allocating and mediating among conflicting sets of interests. Not only are they dealing with conflicting sets of interests, but they must balance each issue against a wide range of other issues, present and future. They frequently are negotiators; they are participants in the strategic management process rather than comprehensive rational planners.

Finally, this chapter gives an overview of some of the types of theories relevant to choice activities, points the way for further background study and provides a case study and some ideas for discussion. Next we shall compare policy formation with a typical cognitive model of decision making and then extend our conceptualization of the policy formation process. The conceptualization will help you to identify some of the significant variables that affect the complex problem solving involved in formulating policy.

DISCUSSION QUESTIONS

1. Discuss the importance of strategy and policy formation. What factors should be analyzed before attempting strategy formation?

2. What are the key elements that define decisions as having strategic importance? What is a strategic business unit?

3. Discuss the difference between strategies, policies, objectives, missions, programs and roles. How do they relate to one another?

4. How should organizations relate strategies to their environment? What relationships should be considered when defining an effective strategy formation process?

5. What are some practical problems that can inhibit effective strategy formation? How can they be overcome?

6. Discuss the applicability of decision theory to the strategy formation process. What are the major problems in utilizing these theories?

7. Discuss the strategy formation process as exemplified by the Bike Lock case. What are the strengths and weaknesses exemplified here? What recommendations would you suggest to improve the process?

8. Discuss how you would make a market survey for Bike Lock. (Use your knowledge of marketing.)

APPENDIX TO CHAPTER 1

THE BIKE LOCK COMPANY (A)*

For over a year Mr. Carl Reily had been looking for a small business opportunity in which to invest both time and some money. His position with a large manufacturing firm was interesting and secure, but the traditional mid-career itch was gnawing at him. Carl had developed an impressive record of corporate success following his graduation from engineering school eighteen years ago. He had worked for two companies and progressed to his current level of responsibility as head of a large department; he had also completed an MBA degree at night at a reputable, progressive university which conducted evening degree programs.

In his search for the right kind of business opportunity, Carl Reily had looked at a number of situations including a sail boat manufacturing company, a new air filtering system invented by a local doctor, and a venture aimed at making solar heaters for outdoor swimming pools. None of these projects suited Carl's interests enough to warrant an investment.

One day in the spring of 1978, he was grumbling to his wife about the fact that their son's fairly new ten-speed bike had been stolen over the weekend while the boy was playing soccer on a local field—even though the bike had been locked to a fence. During the conversation the thought occurred to him that perhaps there was a better way to secure bicycles, at least from thieves that rode them away. "If motorcycles, boats, pay telephones, and factory gates can be relatively burglar-proofed, why not bikes?" he mused.

Over the course of the next few weeks, Carl dug into the matter as time permitted. He was able to assemble a fair amount of information on the bicycle industry.

Mr. Reily learned from the Cycling Trade Institute that roughly 1,000,000 bikes were sold in California alone in 1977. Over 30% were of the lightweight, ten-speed variety. Sales projections for both California and the nation were for continued sales increases. For example, total sales in California had doubled since 1971 when 500,000 were sold. There was another important factor. The percentage of the expensive ten-speeders was increasing by about four percent per year reflecting, in part, the increase in adult riders.

From a survey of local stores and bike shops, Carl determined that virtually everyone carried essentially the same lines of lock chain, cable, padlocks, and combination locks. In one store he was told of a local craftsman who made custom bike locks of some special material; otherwise, there was little new in bike security. A stop at the local police station confirmed the magnitude of the theft problem. At least a dozen bikes were reported stolen each day; 75% were "locked," usually with chain or cable that had been cut through.

Mr. Reily followed up on the rumored local bike lock craftsman and, after some searching, finally tracked down Mr. Joe Last, a young man with a shop in his garage and a set of tools and skills for working with unusual metals and locks.

The meeting between Carl Reily and

---

*This case was prepared by Steven Carl Brandt, Lecturer in Management, as a basis for class discussion. Names and details have been modified to avoid conflict with actual people and companies. Reprinted from *Stanford Business Cases 1975* with the permission of the publishers, Stanford University Graduate School of Business, © 1975 by the Board of Trustees of the Leland Stanford Junior University.

Joe Last came at an opportune time. Joe Last was in his second year of business, and his volume was increasing to the point where expansion was desirable. In the previous month, Joe had contacted his brother-in-law, Mike Mulligan, in search of advice on what to do with the business. Mike was in marketing with a large computer company in Los Angeles and had earned an advanced degree in business administration four years earlier. Mike Mulligan, too, was looking for a smaller situation. Until his brother-in-law phoned, however, he had not considered the bike lock business.

After hearing Carl Reily's expression of interest in the business, Joe Last suggested that Mike be invited to join the discussion. A long meeting between the three took place over the following weekend. It became clear early that Mike and Joe were anxious to build a business out of the garage operation. In their minds, the brothers-in-law were convinced that the market for high-quality bikes and bike locks was already huge. They also felt it would continue to grow because of the expanding interest in health and in energy conservation.

Joe Last had found a domestic source of case-hardened steel wire with a narrow titanium cable core. He had combined the wire with a small electric (battery powered) lock that emitted a howl if it was tampered with. The proper key would open the lock without activating the alarm. Joe had developed on his own a unique way of bonding the inner titanium core to the steel lock mechanism; the steel outer wire was also welded to the lock case. The combination of the virtually uncuttable, light-weight cable and a tough, noisy lock provided a lot of security. Neither cutting torches nor freeze-and-shatter techniques could get through the titanium/steel combination with any ease.

Mr. Last and Mr. Mulligan felt they had the sources and the know-how to produce the locks in volume at a labor and materials cost of under $5.00 per lock. Joe had been pricing his output at $9.95 retail and $8.00 wholesale in recent months. He had been selling roughly 300 locks a month. Joe estimated he had produced and sold over 2,000 custom locks in the history of the business. He also indicated that he felt he knew more about titanium bonding and bike locks than anyone else in the country.

The details of the current operations broke down into several functional categories:

Marketing

Joe Last ran one-inch ads twice a week in six local newspapers: the *Palo Alto Times, Foster City Islander, San Bruno Herald Daly City Record, East Oakland News*, and the *Berkeley Daily Gazette*. In each local area he had one or two retail stores—general sporting goods stores or bike shops—that were selling the custom locks. The ads mentioned the retailer by name. A customer buying a bike usually inquired about a lock of some kind. A knowledgeable sales person could usually sell one of the custom locks if he or she tried. However, few of the stores stocked Joe's locks. His price to the stores was $8.00. A customer wishing to buy the custom lock normally had to order it at the store. The store then phoned or dropped a post card (provided by Joe) to Joe. He would deliver the ordered lock to the store in two to three days. All of Joe's fifteen "dealers" were within a forty-mile radius of his garage. The dealers sold the locks at either $9.95 or $10.95, about twice what the other lock arrangements would cost a customer. Joe made the rounds in his battered VW.

Production

Cable, locks, and other parts were purchased by Mr. Last from various distributors. The special cable took some lead time to acquire, so Joe had quite a bit on hand. The locks were imported from Europe, so their procurement required some planning, too.

The manufacturing process

consisted of stripping the ends of the cables, heat treating, bonding, welding, and adjusting the lock tumblers prior to connecting the noise apparatus which was inserted into the lock in place of a small clock that was removed and discarded.

All of the operations were done with fairly simple tools and equipment. It was clear that a certain degree of skill was required to get a smooth, permanent fit between the components. Joe Last had experimented at length before he finally found the right bonding materials and electrical hook ups necessary for the complete bike lock. Such a lock had to withstand a lot of vibration in use, and Joe shock tested each lock thoroughly before delivery. He considered his materials and processes trade secrets.

Both Joe and Mike felt that a number of the operations could be automated or at least mechanized in order to decrease costs and dependency on skilled labor.

The total cost of all the equipment in Joe's garage was under $2,500 new. He had designed most of it himself, and he had constructed it from used parts. Joe had one trained assistant whom he employed as needed to meet delivery promises.

Accounting

The existing company, Last's Custom Lock Company, owned about $4,000 worth of inventory, mostly cable and locks. Aside from about $600 of cash in a checking account, equipment, and several cases of bonding materials, there were no other assets. The main records kept were lists of past customers. Some customers returned for additional locks or new batteries. The business was currently a proprietorship. Accounts Payable were $500, and Joe Last owed his mother $1,200, which she had advanced him on a loan basis to buy inventory.

The weekend meeting ended on an optimistic note. Mike and Joe agreed to develop a list of equipment, space, inventory, and other requirements they felt would be necessary to produce 1,000, 2,500, and 5,000 locks per month. They also were to develop a profile of the known competitors in the bike lock business. Carl promised to review the marketing and financial aspects of the potential enterprise and implied that he might be willing to advance some money to help start such a business if the numbers looked attractive. A follow-up meeting was set for two weeks later.

During the period between the meetings, Carl Reily assembled various pieces of information. People in the area who were using Last's locks were very satisfied. Most had recommended it to their cycling friends. Existing dealers were nonchalant about the custom locks. They didn't represent any significant income, but theoretically the newspaper ads and extra product and service for customers generated traffic for the stores. About 50% of the custom locks sold in the stores were to people who already owned a bike. Everyone seemed to like Joe; his enthusiasm for noisy bike locks was contagious.

The market for bikes in the over $100 retail price range was booming. One major foriegn brand had sold 10,000 bikes in California in 1975; 25,000 in 1977; and 16,000 during the first four months of 1978. Now, in May of 1978, even greater gains were expected despite the fact that a number of newer manufacturers—domestic and foreign—were coming out with colorfully designed ten speed bikes in the $70-$95 retail price range. The recent currency devaluations had boosted everyone's price somewhat since even the domestic manufacturers had to import some of the accessories such as derailleurs.

Joe Last had good but unwritten relationships with the various distributors from whom he bought parts. However, it was clear that Joe's purchases were a tiny part of their operations and concern. The distributors reported that virtually no one besides Joe Last bought either the special cable or the electric locks. The cable was used originally by aircraft manufacturers. There were rumors of a small mail order electric lock dealer in L.A., and one in New Jersey. Apparently the one in L.A. had done some experimentation with bike locks.

The largest distributor of bikes as well as regular bike lock chain, cable, and locks was the Cycle Company of Pasadena. Cycle Company sold to over 800 stores in fifteen western states. The Cycle Company actually bought the chain and cable in bulk and packaged it under its own private lable. There were two major domestic manufacturers of bikes: Schwinn in Chicago, and Murray in Ohio. Schwinn distributed through independent bike dealers. Other makers generally concentrated on chaper, private-label bikes for retailers like Sears and Ward's.

One of the driving forces behind the bike boom was the increasing price of fuel. Mr. Reily had even heard rumors of a possible mid-eastern oil embargo. Inflation and other domestic economic pressures were also pushing up the theft rate of bicycles as they increased in popularity.

Carl Reily sat down a few days before the second meeting in an effort to digest the information and impressions he had gathered. Was this a project he should pursue further? On what basis? It was clear that the capital requirements to set up a manufacturing facility would not be particularly large. It was also clear if the bike lock business was to be expanded, the coming summer months would be an ideal time to do so.

THE BIKE LOCK COMPANY (B)*

Mr. Joe Last, Mr. Mike Mulligan, and Mr. Carl Reily were evaluating the possibility of forming a business around Mr. Last's custom bicycle lock product. Last and Mulligan were both excited about the growth potential of such an enterprise. Reily was a potential investor and advisor. In early April 1978, the three met for the first time to discuss the project and get acquainted. They agreed to meet again after they had investigated several questions concerning the requirements of the new business. A second lengthy meeting followed at which the results of each person's homework were discussed.

Plant

Mike Mulligan reported that producing the custom locks at a rate of 5,000 per month required a building that had the following characteristics:

- Minimum 3,000 square feet of floor space
- At least 25 electrical outlets around the perimeter including at least two points with 220v power
- Large doors to outside
- Air ducts through the roof for exhaust purposes
- Lighting sufficiently good for hand work.

The initial budget for plant and office equipment was estimated to be $3,000. This figure would cover shelving for inventory, work stations for the employees, and several new devices to expedite the poduction and assembly operations.

In addition, Mike and Joe figured that at least $2,500 more inventory of the special cable, locks, and supplies would be required to be sure that the production process could run smoothly, i.e., without interruptions due to material shortages.

Regarding salaries, Mike and Joe indicated that a budget of $2,000 a month would probably be adequate until such time as the volume climbed to over 1,000

---

*This case was written by Steven Carl Brandt, Lecturer in Management, as a basis for class discussion. Names and details have been modified. Reprinted from *Stanford Business Cases 1975* with permission of the publishers, Stanford University Graduate School of Business, © 1975 by the Board of Trustees of the Leland Stanford Junior University.

locks a month. The $2,000 figure reflected their willingness to work at a minimal $800 per month each in order to get the business going and minimize the dilution of their ownership. Neither had much cash that could be invested in the company. The extra $400 was for clerical or other part-time work that might be required during the early days of the enterprise.

Distribution and Marketing

Attention was next focused on the issue of building the volume of locks sold. There appeared to be a myraid of possibilities.

First, existing bicycle shops could be contacted and sold on becoming "Authorized Custom Bike Lock Dealers." In effect, these shops would constitute a highly selective distribution system. The company would perhaps do cooperative advertising with the dealers. The company might also make deliveries, at least in the local area. Presumably, a premium retail price might do well with such a limited distribution system and the higher caliber of bike salesmen employed by the specialty shops. (This was the way the Head Ski Company operated in its early days.)

Second, existing department stores and general sporting goods stores could be set up as dealers in much the same way as Joe had already done with some stores in the metropolitan area.

Third, direct mail was a possibility. Active cyclists could order directly from the company; the locks could be shipped by United Parcel or by mail, whichever way was more economical. Mailing charges would run around $1.50 per lock, parcel post.

Fourth, the new company could open its own tiny stores or perhaps set up booths in larger stores or shopping center parking lots. This approach would be patterned after the Kodak film drop booths with which all three men were familiar.

Fifth, a concentrated effort could be undertaken to sell either lock, chain, or bicycle distributors (wholesalers) on carrying the line and reselling to retailers. An additional middleman discount would be required, of course. The discount would probably be 10–25% for such an item as the custom, electric lock for bicycles.

Sixth, Sears, Ward, Penney, and other national retailers with large catalog operations could be approached to include the new lock in both their stores and catalogs. Joe mentioned he had heard frightful things about becoming a captive supplier of such mammoth companies, however.

Seventh, the idea of trying to sell the locks through the various scouting organizations was kicked around. "What if we could get thousands of boy and girl scouts going from door-to-door selling our locks the way they sell Christmas cards and flower seeds?" said Mike Mulligan. "We would be rich over night!"

It seemed as though there might also be an eighth possibility associated with working directly in some way with the original bicycle manufacturers.

There was general agreement among the three potential partners that a decision on one or more of the marketing/distribution channels was required before a sales program could be developed. There was also agreement that all the production work had to be concentrated in a single plant in order to insure tight control of the quality of the finished product—a point about which Joe Last felt very strongly. It was clear that Joe's special knowledge and skills would be critical to the success of the product operations for some time to come, i.e., at least until the bugs were worked out of any high volume, automated production line that might eventually be designed.

Carl Reily felt that it was fairly important to hit the market hard right at the start rather than dribble into it and thereby encourage competition. He presented figures for having a research report done on the market; the report would include an analysis of the potential customers, media choices and costs, information on various types of retail stores, and a sensitivity analysis of various retail price levels for different prices. The report would cost $7,000 and could be done in four weeks if the group decided to order it immediately.

Carl also outlined some representative ad costs. Full-page, black and white ads ran, per insertion, $1,100 for the regional (Northern California) edition of *Sports Illustrated;* $300 for *Cycling World;* $750 for *World of Cycling,* and $500 for one-sixth of a page in *Sunset.* Ad agency preparation costs would run about $500 per ad.

Point-of-purchase materials (counter displays, pamphlets, decals, etc.) for dealers would run about $50 per dealer for small quantity orders.

Packaging, letterhead, invoices, and other odds and ends normally associated with presenting the company favorably to the public were estimated to run another $1,000, including the costs of incorporation or partnership formation.

In the discussion of the distribution alternatives that followed, it was clear that Joe Last did not favor working with the large national retail chains on any basis. "They would eat us alive," he claimed. Joe did feel that sporting goods stores were good possibilities; however, he admitted that the most any single store had sold for him in a week, so far, was five locks. The average was more like five locks per month. Of course, the promotion budget had been minimal.

Organization

Late in the evening, Mike Mulligan started compiling a list of subjects that needed resolution. The issue of a company name had arisen from time to time throughout the day. What were the criteria for selecting the "right" name? What type of company should be formed—partnership or corporation? Which form best fit this business and how would the ownership be split up, assuming that Reily was going to put up primarily money and the other two would invest mostly time?

When, if at all, should an attorney be brought in? Mike Mulligan suspected that some sort of agreement between the three of them would be required before any money was committed. The three parties had agreed that the figures in Exhibit 1 reasonably represented the current picture of the business. Mike also knew that Joe was adamant about retaining control of any bike lock business using his ideas. Joe, at age 24, was a man of strong opinions on most subjects, but particularly on his bike lock technology.

Carl Reily pointed out that the closing ad dates for the June editions of all the magazines being considered were between May 10 and May 15. This meant that decisions needed to be made quickly if the new enterprise was to be launched prior to the summer months.

At midnight, the meeting was adjourned until the following Wednesday—five days hence—at which time it was generally agreed that some go/no-go decisions had to be made. Money was required to move ahead; money was really not available in any form until there was some basic agreement between the entrepreneur, the potential manager, and the investor. Any basic agreement would, presumably, reflect the existance of a consensus on the initial direction and plans for the business.

Amidst the closing yawns, Mike Mulligan threw in one other idea that had not previously been discussed. "Perhaps we should package the lock production process or pre-assemble the major lock components and sell or franchise the custom lock idea to locksmiths and key-making shops across the country," he said. "That's a wild one," replied Joe Last.

Exhibit 1
The Bike Lock Company (B)
Balance Sheet—April 15, 1978

Assets		Liabilities & Capital	
Cash	$ 600	A/P	$ 500
A/R	100	Note	6,200
Inventory	4,000		
Equipment	2,500	Net Worth	3,300
Goodwill	2,800		
	$10,000		$10,000

Suggested Additional References for Further Research

Banks, L.: The mission of our business society. *Harvard Business Review* 53(No. 3):57–65, 1975.
Camillus, J. C.: Evaluating the benefits of formal planning systems. *Long-Range Planning* 8(No. 3):33–40, 1975.
Emery, J. C.: *Organizational Planning and Control Systems – Theory and Technology.* New York, The Macmillan Company, 1969.
England, G. W.: Personal value systems of American managers. *Academy of Management Journal,* March, 1967.
Glueck, W. F.: *Business Policy: Strategy Formation and Mangement Action.* New York, McGraw-Hill Book Company, 1976.
Higgins, R. B.: Reunite management and planning. *Long-Range Planning* 9(No. 4):40–45, 1976.
Holden, P., Pederson, C., and Germane, G.: *Top Management.* New York, McGraw-Hill Book Company, 1968.
Kudla, R. J.: Elements of effective corporate planning. *Long-Range Planning* 9(No. 4):92–93, 1976.
Leavitt, H. J., Dill, W. R., and Eyring, H. G.: *The Organizational World.* New York, Harcourt, Brace, Jovanovich, Inc., 1973.
McNichols, T. J.: *Policy Making and Executive Action.* 4th ed. New York, McGraw-Hill Book Company, 1975.
Mintzberg, H.: A new look at the chief executive's job. *Organizational Dynamics 1* (No. 3):21–30, 1973.
Newman, W. H., and Logan, J. P.: *Strategy, Policy, and Central Management.* Cincinnati, Southwestern Publishing Company, 1976.
Strategic planning in large firms – Some guidelines. *Long-Range Planning* 8(No. 1):81–86, 1975.
Taylor, B.: Strategies for planning. *Long-Range Planning* 8(No. 5): October, 1975.
Terry, P. T.: Organizational implications for long range planning. *Long-Range Planning* 8(No. 1):26–30, 1975.
Vancil, R. T., and Lorange, P.; Strategic planning in diversified companies. *Harvard Business Review* 53(No. 1):81–88, 1975.

2

POLICY FORMATION AND CLASSICAL
DECISION MAKING

A DESCRIPTIVE MODEL OF THE
POLICY-FORMATION PROCESS
    Inputs—Stakeholders and
      Other Environmental Forces
    Structure—Roles and Programs
    Self-interests
    Political Resources and
      Power Relationships

"NEGOTIATING" WITH THE
ENVIRONMENT

Circular Effects of Policy
  Formation
Applying the Model to Business
  and Public Bodies
Illustration of Model—A Role
  Play
Social Responsibility and the
  Model—A Debate

SUMMARY

INTERGROUP POLICY EXERCISE

DISCUSSION QUESTIONS

CONCEPTUALIZING THE POLICY-FORMATION PROCESS

POLICY FORMATION AND CLASSICAL DECISION MAKING

We have considered to this point some basic aspects of policy formation and the choice process. We have given some examples of what *should* be done and what *is* done in policy formation. We have provided a case, Bike Lock, for preliminary study and analysis.

Assumptions of the classical decision-making model.

Let us now elaborate a bit to develop further a conceptualization of the policy process. We shall start by comparing some basic assumptions of a rational or classical decision-making model with those of a policy-formation model. The term "decision making" as frequently used by management scholars and psychologists implies a specific model of cognitive activity. This cognitive model may assume (1) a problem statement, (2) a single decision-making unit, (3) a single set of utility preferences, (4) a knowledge of a full range of alternatives and consequences, (5) the intention to select alternatives toward maximizing utility and (6) the opportunity, disposition and capacity to make appropriate calculations.*

A practical consequence that would follow from conceptualizing policy formation in the same way as rational decision making would be a hampering of understanding. This impediment to understanding occurs because, as a matter of fact, each of the

---

*See M. Patchen: Decision theory in the study of rational action: Problems and a proposal. *Journal of Conflict Resolution,* June, 1965; and G. T. Allison: *Essence of Decision.* Boston, Little, Brown & Company, 1971.

TABLE 2-1 POLICY FORMATION AND A CLASSICAL DECISION MODEL

Element	Rational or Classical Model	Policy Formation
Problem or issue	Problem statement	Lack of unity in problem statement; two or more interrelated issues
Organization	Single decision-making unit	Multiple coalitions, power relationships, external and internal
Objectives	1. Single set of utility preferences	1. Two or more sets of interests and values (not translatable into a common set)
	2. Intention to select alternatives that will maximize utility on issue	2. May trade off for benefits on other issues
Alternatives and consequences	Strategic costs and benefits associated with each alternative	Programs generate alternatives similar to previous ones
Dominant inference pattern	Opportunity, disposition and capacity to make appropriate calculations and choice	Actions result of programs and "negotiating"

assumptions of the decision-making model may be violated in policy formation. Thus, the student of policy formation as previously discussed from a different point of view would not have a description of what is actually occurring. Furthermore, another consequence is that the classical decision-making model may confuse the policy maker on how he ought to proceed with the process.

Assumptions violated.

In Table 2-1 we indicate some ways in which the assumptions of the classical model may be violated. The policy formation process is seen as occurring in an organization. An organization is viewed as a coalition of subcoalitions and individuals, including, as mentioned, officials representing different functions or projects along with a board of commissioners or directors, union officials, workers and clients or customers. Drawing a definitive and permanent boundary is impossible when circumstances change frequently. The various interest groups participate, as we have indicated, because the sharing of goals allows some benefits. To illustrate this conflict from a different perspective, consider the current controversy over the extent and type of social responsibility expected of American corporations.*

---

*See for example M. J. Green et al.: *The Closed Enterprise System*. Nader Study Group, June, 1971; G. A. Steiner: *Business and Society*. New York, Random House, 1975; S. Prakash: *Up Against The Corporate Wall: Modern Corporations and Social Issues of the Seventies*. Englewood Cliffs, N.J., Prentice-Hall, Inc., 1977.

32 / CONCEPTUALIZING THE POLICY-FORMATION PROCESS

If a corporation allocates more resources to fulfill its social responsibilities, should wage earners and shareholders receive less or should customers pay more? The top manager in publicly held corporations is responsible to the owners, customers, employees, competitors, local, state and national governments, and so forth. If policies are devised that pursue the interests of any one group exclusively, the interests of others may suffer, at least in the short run, and sometimes over a prolonged period.

Of course, the classical model can be modified, and it has been. One modification in approach might be to have the coalition (e.g., Joe, Mike and Carl at Bike Lock) work toward more agreement on the problem or issue statement. Through definition and redefinition it might be possible to develop a consensus on an operational definition. However, the perceptions of problems change over time.

The basic difficulty.

The basic difficulty is conceiving what would constitute the single set of interests and values against which to judge solutions. Members of a group will not have identical values. Furthermore, individuals with substantially the same values may be located at different points in the organization and receive different benefits. Often benefits are widely distributed and costs are highly concentrated. Consider a proposed reorganization of agencies in the Federal government. Benefits may be widely spread to many citizens across the country, but costs may be highly concentrated among relatively few bureaucrats; a few Congressmen might even lose some political muscle if Congressional Committee responsibilities are altered to match the new agencies.

In policy formation involving allocating and mediating among conflicting sets of values and interests, judgments are formed specific to the situation, balancing each issue off against a wide range of other issues, including present issues and those that might exist in the future.

Is there an optimal policy?

Is there an optimal policy? No! Different perceptions of the critical problems and the diversity of interests and values preclude the determination of a single "best" policy. For example, a high cash dividend policy may be "best" for some stockholders but not "best" for those more concerned with plowing back earnings for growth.

Of course, improvements can be made toward more effective and consistent policies. What would the reader, hired to improve the policy-formation results and the policy-formation process, need besides the conceptualization of the policy formation developed to this point, to develop an effective improvement program? The remainder of the book is designed to present the reader with some information to help him to focus on significant variables and relationships as well as to answer critical questions.

What is the approach suggested?

The approach that is suggested is to see the policy issues as involving a complex social process and then to converge on the cognitive aspects rather than hope that the issues can be understood in terms of solely intellectual components. This approach has been proposed by Bauer.* He suggests two reasons for not working outward to the social context:

1. Much of the record and people's verbalization of what has happened and is happening is highly rationalized.

Why?

2. Much of what occurs will not make sense in the more limited context.

In the first instance the analyst may be deceived about the policy process. In the second, he may label the behavior of the businessman or government official as "irrational" when, in fact, the individual involved is concerned with more issues than the analyst has taken into account.

A DESCRIPTIVE MODEL OF THE POLICY-FORMATION PROCESS

In an attempt to clarify and to describe some of the more significant variables in the policy-formation process, an input-output model is presented in Table 2-2. This model of policy formation is designed primarily from the standpoint of the policy maker(s). The policy makers are seen in the role of "negotiating" to find solutions to policy issues which will (1) capitalize on opportunities and gain or utilize external and internal support, (2) satisfy environmental

Summary of descriptive model.

---

*R. A. Bauer: Social psychology and the study of policy formation. *American Psychologist,* 21 (No. 10):933–942, 1966.

TABLE 2-2 A DESCRIPTIVE MODEL OF POLICY FORMATION

```
                                    ┌─────────────────────────────┐
                                    │ Structure--                 │
                                    │   Roles, Programs           │
                                    │   Self-interests or Values  │
                                    │   Political Resources       │
                                    └─────────────────────────────┘
  ┌──────────────────────────┐      ┌──────────────────┐
  │ Environmental Forces—    │      │ Interaction of   │
  │ External and Internal    │─────▶│ Forces and       │
  │         Threats          │      │ Structure        │
  │ Demands  Requirements    │      └──────────────────┘
  │ Support  Opportunities   │         (Transformation)
  │          Capabilities    │
  └──────────────────────────┘
         (Inputs)

  ┌──────────────────────────┐      ┌──────────────────────────┐
  │ Changes in Environmental │◀─────│ Objectives, Strategies   │
  │        Forces            │      │ Role Performance         │
  │                          │      │ Organization Outcomes    │
  └──────────────────────────┘      └──────────────────────────┘

         (Feedback)                         (Outputs)
```

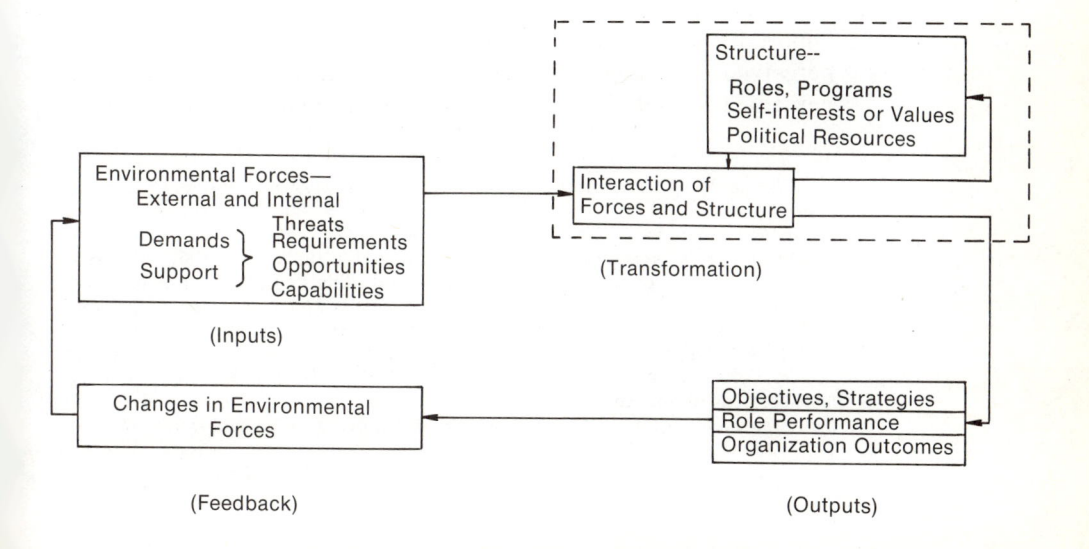

demands or requirements and (3) partially satisfy the policy makers' own interests and desires.

The model assumes that the key inputs affecting policy makers are environmental forces and that these forces interact with a given policy generating structure to *produce outputs* (*organizational objectives and actions*) which are designed to adjust to and adapt to these pressures on the structure. The outputs became part of the environment, and the cycle continues. The structure is a political one in which an authoritative allocation of benefits takes place; that is to say, those in authority allocate benefits to relevant parties (i.e., stakeholders or those with some stake in the organization) in exchange for this support. The allocation, however, may be modified by bargaining or coalition formation. Four concepts related to structure with which the model deals are roles, programs, self-interests and political resources.

Contingency approach.

The model further assumes an open and dynamic situation whereby the environment and the structure continually interact. The interaction is such that certain environmental forces such as technology or uncertainty may be associated with particular types of organizational forms, administrative practices, organizational objectives or strategies. This contingency approach has been suggested by several studies.* For example, Lawrence and Lorsch† argue that organizations facing a stable environment may find a centralized "bureaucratic" organization structure adequate for achieving proper coordination and specialization of activities, while a more uncertain or turbulent environment would preclude effective use of the same form. Other researchers have focused on different dimensions. Hage and Aiken‡ considered the interrelationships between technology and structure and concluded that organizations with routine work are more likely to have greater formalization (i.e., the extent to which rules are used in the organization) of organization roles.

Managerial *perceptions* of the environment are apparently quite important. Khandwalla, in a study of 79 firms, correlated the perceived importance of each of several functional activities with perceived magnitude of different forms of environmental competi-

---

*See J. Woodward: *Industrial Organization: Theory and Practice.* London, Oxford University Press, 1965; T. Burns and G. M. Stalker: *The Management of Innovations.* London, Tavistock Publications, Ltd., 1961; J. D. Thompson: *Organizations in Action.* New York, McGraw-Hill Book Co., 1967; R. Hall: *Organizations: Structure and Process.* Englewood Cliffs, N.J., Prentice-Hall, 1972; F. E. Kast and J. E. Rosenzweig (eds.): *Contingency Views of Organizations and Management.* Palo Alto, California, Science Research Associates, 1973.

†P. R. Lawrence and J. W. Lorsch: *Organization and Environment.* Homewood, Ill., R. D. Irwin, Inc., 1969. See also H. Tosi, R. Aldag and R. Storey: On the measurement of the environment: An assessment of the Lawrence and Lorsch Environmental Uncertainty Subscale. *Administrative Science Quarterly, 18* (No. 1):27–36, March, 1973.

‡J. Hage and M. Aiken: Routine technology, social structure and organization tools. *Administrative Science Quarterly, 14* (No. 3), September, 1969.

tion (e.g., intensity of price and promotion competition) and technological change experienced by the firm.* He found that corporate strategies of firms where managers perceived dynamic, uncertain environments are likely to be significantly different from and more comprehensive than those of firms where managers perceive more static, predictable environments.

In addition, characteristics of successful strategy making (e.g., risk taking, innovation, extent of long-term planning) may vary with the perceived environment. Paine and Anderson studied 62 longitudinal cases involving a variety of organizations and environments.† They concluded that successful organizations tended to follow a strategic mode appropriate for the perceived conditions. For example, of the firms in a perceived environmental uncertainty‡ condition, those which were relatively successful were more innovative and more proactive in searching for environmental information than the less successful firms.

At the present time, however, we do *not* completely understand all the various relationships and contingencies. Thus, the model is presented in a general and simplified form. As we proceed through the book, we shall refer to and elaborate upon some of the concepts depicted by the model, and we shall discuss some of the possible contingencies and relationships.

Simple model— elaborations throughout the book.

The cognitive process of intellectual analysis of internal capabilities and alternative strategies is not denied by the model. It is, however, not emphasized at this point. Later, of course, it will be more fully explored.

Input—Stakeholders and Other Environmental Forces

The organization has obligations not only to shareholders, employees and customers but also to all individuals and organizations with which it has transactions and relationships: suppliers, distributors, competitors, public servants, members of the community, financial institutions and unions. All of these stakeholders, along with such other impersonal environmental forces as the economy, technology and supply of raw materials, provide input to the structure.

---

*P. Khandwalla: The techno-economic ecology of corporate strategy. *Journal of Management Studies,* February, 1976, pp. 62–76.

†F. T. Paine and C. R. Anderson: Contingencies affecting strategy formulation and effectiveness. *Journal of Management Studies,* May, 1977, pp. 147–158.

‡It is important to note that perceived environmental uncertainty may imply such attributes as market turbulence, lack of knowledge about threats and opportunities, competition, short product life cycles, technological change and diversity and societal pressures. See Khandwalla: *op. cit.*; and H. I. Ansoff: Strategic Posture Analysis. Presented at Conference on Analytical Approaches to Strategy, INSEAD, Fontainbleau, France, December, 1976.

The concept of interchange or data input to the structure has been taken from Easton* with some modification. Easton assumes two inputs to a political structure:

1. Demands for scarce resources.
2. Support, i.e., support of the right to decide and support for specific decisions.

What are external and internal forces?

This model treats demands both as *external* environmental pressures, opportunities or threats (e.g., public policy, public opinion, unions) and *internal* environmental pressures (e.g., subordinates, peers, division heads). Support for the decisions and actions may come from customers buying products or services as well as from subordinates or peer groups with appropriate competence and motivation. Support for the right to decide may come from stockholders, for example. Changes in environmental forces and managerial perceptions of those changes are the input data to the structure. Monitoring and predicting the environmental changes are important for policy formation.

Environment filters outcomes.

Two additional concepts are depicted by the model. First, the strategies, outcomes, goals and objectives of the organization are filtered by the environment and must be acceptable to it. Otherwise, the environment will not allow the organization to continue. For example, pollution standards are now being raised and are being enforced to a greater extent. Some plants have had to shut down for failure to comply. Second, the elements that make up the organization's environment are not isolated from and independent of one another. Rather, the opposite is true: they are interdependent,

Environmental forces interdependent.

so that a change in one factor flows to each of the other factors until all are altered in some respect. For example, a governmentally induced legislative change in the area of racial relations in this country has led to changes in the mores of our society and has caused other changes in some aspects of our attitudes toward racial questions. At the same time, aspects of our cultural environment have influenced the government to enact legislation. Also affected by this legislation are the personnel policies and practices that are part of the output which has been forced to alter itself to meet the new legal requirements.

In effect, then, general managers and "internal coalitions" recognize that strategy formation is concerned not only with producing a return for delivering satisfactory services or products but also with achieving social acceptance in the community, influencing government policies, ensuring a continuing supply of energy and raw materials or in general developing a "societal" or environmental strategy. Some actions of major significance may not

---

*D. Easton: An approach to the analysis of political systems. *In* S. S. Ulmer (ed.): *Introductory Readings in Political Behavior.* Chicago, Rand-McNally, Inc., 1961, pp. 136–147.

be, strictly speaking, "formulated" (within the company) so much as "negotiated" implicitly if not explicitly with external parties.* These "external" constituencies or parties—sometimes other organizations, sometimes a coalition of individuals—are kibitzing and seeking direct influence on such concerns as environmental protection, overseas investment policies and employment practices, and even product price and quality.†

Structure—Roles and Programs

Some managers dominate the organization or business unit, seek bold opportunities and quickly decide to enlarge their empire (the entrepreneur). Others more concerned with the planning process follow a highly analytical one-step-at-a-time method of making policy (the planner). Still others react when opportunities and threats come "over the transom" (the adaptor). They adapt to the environment and treat policy formation as an incremental process (i.e., adding on to what presently exists).‡

The entrepreneur, the planner and the adaptor.

These behavioral patterns are examples of role behavior for managers. There are, of course, nonmanagerial roles. They will be discussed later. A primary concern of this model is to explain the behavior of individuals (managerial and nonmanagerial) and, to a lesser extent, coalitions of individuals confronted with policy formation.§ It should be noted, however, that for some organizations the structure may include just one dominant individual who makes the choices. Even the single policy maker must deal with the environmental forces such as influential individuals outside the organization.

What is a primary concern of the model?

Policy formation, as explained, involves choices among conflicting sets of values. A vehicle for managing this conflict in an organization is the structure. Parsons and Shils point out that the most significant unit of social structure is the role. "The role is that organized sector of an actor's orientation which constitutes and defines his participation in an interaction process. It involves a set of complementary expectations concerning his own actions and those

---

*See E. A. Murray: Limitations on strategic choice. *Proceedings of the Academy of Management*, Kansas City, 1976; and F. T. Paine: Analysis of Strategic Activities of Managers (ASAM). Presented at Conference on Analytical Approaches to Strategy, INSEAD, Fontainebleau, France, December, 1976.

†See H. I. Ansoff, R. P. Declerck and R. L. Hayes (eds.): *From Strategic Planning to Strategic Management*. New York, John Wiley and Sons, 1976.

‡See H. Mintzberg: Strategy-making in three modes. *California Management Review*, 16 (No. 2):44–53, 1973.

§For additional insight into the behavior of coalitions of individuals, see J. D. Thompson: *Organizations in Action*. New York, McGraw-Hill Book Company, 1967.

with whom he interacts."* Thus, we can look at the structure as a set of interacting roles. In addition, as mentioned in the first chapter, generalized procedures or *programs* are devised to provide a course of action in response to some stimulus or pressure. Thus, for example, a manager carrying out his role when he hears of a difficulty may use a problem-solving program that includes scanning the environment for information on relevant factors. Self-interests, political resources and tactics, however, affect how the roles and programs are carried out. The discussion of "what actually happens" in the previous chapter illustrated this interplay. The activities were adjusted to account for self-interests and political resources.

Role consensus. Many formulations of the role concept assume that role consensus exists on the expectations applied to incumbents of particular positions; that is to say, there is a high degree of agreement among others on the patterns of behavior that are expected of the incumbent. However, role consensus need not be present and frequently is not. Members of a coalition or a policy-generating structure may have divergent expectations of the role of any one individual. For example, some expect the President to be very conservative; others expect a more liberal orientation. In addition, roles for the individual may vary across policy issues and vary with the political subsystem. For example, some issues are *Role conflict.* utterly crucial for their advocates, and they adjust their role performance accordingly. Their role performance is adjusted for issues of low salience. Thus, role conflict may come about because an individual simultaneously occupies two or more role positions (interrole conflict), or because of contradictory role expectations for the individual as incumbent of a single role position (intrarole conflicts).

To an extent these role conflicts are resolved in the process of policy formation.†

Resolution of role conflict. The major factors that come into play in the resolution of role conflict are legitimacy and sanctions. The first refers to the individual's feelings about the legitimacy or illegitimacy of each of the incompatible expectations that he perceives is held for him in the situation. The second refers to his perception of the sanctions to which he will be exposed for nonconformity to each of the incompatible expectations. For example, he may be told to be innovative and to take risks. At the same time, however, he may note that those who have taken visible actions that fail, find their own future careers in jeopardy. It seems to be a common story in

---

*T. Parsons and E. A. Shils: *Toward a General Theory of Action.* Cambridge, Harvard University Press, 1962, p. 23.
†For discussion see N. C. Gross, W. S. Mason and A. W. McEachern: *Explorations in Role Analysis.* New York, John Wiley & Sons, Inc., 1958.

government bureaucracy, for example, that you make that "one visible mistake" and "your career is dead." If a manager feels that he is judged (legitimately) on the "no mistake image" he creates, there is plenty of reason to believe that this has a profound effect on his behavior and on the policies he supports or adopts.

Self-interests

Our model shows that self-interests or values of top managers are basic and fundamental premises which have affected the policy process. For example, the influential manager may have said, "I want this agency to be best known for its innovations," or he may have said, "I want this company to be much bigger in five years." Or he may have written on a subject such as the socioeconomic purpose of the organization. Edward Cole, as President of General Motors, wrote: "The big challenge to American business—as I see it—is to carefully evaluate the constantly changing expressions of public and national goals. Then we must modify our own objectives and programs to meet—as far as possible within the realm of economic and technological feasibility—the new demands of the society we serve."* Sometimes these kinds of statements are not articulated, but nevertheless "come through" to the organization by the actions of the top executive(s). For instance, it may be known that the top executive wishes to not "rock the boat" or take any serious risk. Each of these interests rooted in top management has provided a frame of reference for others who occupy positions of less importance.

In considering the individual as a policy maker and the choices he will make, March and Simon feel that man behaves rationally only with respect to his own abstractions of the real world dependent on personal values and his own unique modes of perceiving. Therefore, choice is always exercised with respect to a limited, approximate simplified "model" of the real situation.†

Three aspects of a model of self-interest are:

1. Who is the self under consideration?
2. What value is being pursued?
3. Over what time period?‡

Many individuals do not have the information to be clearly aware of their self-interest and to clearly answer these questions. Their "interests" are multiple and complex. In the absence of

---

*Edward N. Cole: Management priorities for the 1970's. *Michigan Business Review*, 22:1, July, 1970.

†J. G. March and H. A. Simon: *Organizations*. New York, John Wiley & Sons, Inc., 1958, Chapter 6.

‡R. Bauer, I. Pool and L. Dexter: *American Business and Public Policy*. New York, Atherton Press, 1963, Chapter 9.

complete information about these dimensions of self-interests, the policy maker is forced to adopt "tactics" that can be altered by new information. New information may change what the policy maker perceives to be his own best self-interest.

Determinants of behavior of policy makers.

As we have indicated, we cannot assume a single and unchanging goal and rational decision making. Individuals have preferences that impose themselves in the policy-making process. Imbalances result in rejecting, clarifying, redefining or changing both individual aspirations and *organizational objectives*. This behavior can be seen as an ongoing series of testing and feedback processes by which the individual both guides his interests and determines his effectiveness. The information sources and perceived self-interests (along with roles and programs) are thus determinants of the behavior of policy makers in the model.

Political Resources and Power Relationships

What are political resources?

A political resource is a means by which one participant (e.g., manager, stakeholder) in the policy formation process can influence the behavior of others. Political resources may be derived directly from his official position in the structure (e.g., legitimate authority) or from other sources (e.g., competence or charisma); other political resources include control of information, social standing, friendship and money.

Political resources of subcoalition.

In addition, the political resources of a subunit or subcoalition may be considered. Hickson et al. have made a comprehensive study of subunit power and policy formation.* They conclude that the power of a subunit in an organization varies directly with the effectiveness of the subunit in dealing with strategic environmental contingencies, the uncertainty of the environment facing the subunit, the degree to which the activities of the subunit are not substitutable, and the degree to which it is central to the functioning of the organization. A description of a powerful industrial relations subunit by Goldner† illustrates coping with uncertainty, centrality and substitutability. The industrial relations subunit studied used the union as an outside threat to exploit uncertainty about the supply and cost of personnel which arose from potential strikes and wage increases. The subunit coped effectively, using its nonroutinized knowledge of union representatives and of contract interpretation; its activities were centrally linked to those of other subunits by the necessity for uniform practice on wages and employment. The staff of the subunit developed non-substitutable bargaining and negotiating skills which enhanced their political resources.

---

*D. J. Hickson, C. R. Hinnings, C. A. Lee, R. E. Schneck, and J. M. Pennings: A strategic contingencies theory of intraorganizational power. *Administrative Science Quarterly, 16* (No. 2):216–229, June 1971.

†F. H. Goldner: The division of labor: Process and power. *In* M. N. Zald (ed.): *Power in Organizations.* Nashville, Vanderbilt University Press, 1970.

Political resources may be used at varying rates according to differences in rewards anticipated for resource use, the degree of optimism associated with the probability of achieving a desired objective, and the opportunity costs associated with the resource use.*

The higher the value of the anticipated reward and the more optimistic the outlook for objective achievement, the more readily resources are employed. The opportunity cost associated with the use of a resource is the sacrifice required of alternative uses.† Furthermore, the opportunity costs associated with political resources can be changed by environmental pressures. For example, the opportunity cost of the goodwill used to support a new product promotion strategy is the cost associated with not having the same goodwill for use in supporting enlargement of the budget for a new market research approach. Environmental pressures may make the new market research strategy more important, and the *opportunity cost* of not supporting it increases. Since the reservoir of goodwill is not unlimited, it must be used judiciously, considering the present and future salience of each issue.

How are they used?

Various political tactics may be used in the policy-formation process. For example, a partial list of "advice" on political tactics might include:

1. Always act like a boss, maintain some social distance; otherwise, you may lose power.
2. Be confident; appear to know what you are doing.
3. Stay flexible; have maneuvering room; keep your options open.
4. Channel, withhold and time information carefully. The policy initiator with pertinent, current, reliable information has power.
5. Form alliances for protection, communication and publicity above, diagonally, and below in the organization and outside with relevant stakeholders. For those above, find out which issues are salient and what you can do for them. At other levels, build the status of your allies with privileges, title, pay, and public endorsement, to name a few.
6. Take counsel only when you desire, from whom you desire; don't say that you "will hear advice from anybody" or you may have pressure and you may have conflicting alignments in your own ranks.
7. When faced with an unfavorable policy proposal:
    a. Don't give in; you will lose power.
    b. Use negative timing, delay.
    c. Don't refuse; you may have a crisis.
    d. Compromise on minor matters.
    e. Move off on tangents.
    f. If it looks like you are going to suffer a reverse, give in. You use political resources built up from giving in as a trade-off later.

Political tactics.

These political tactics are, of course, commonly used by some organization members for their own private gain as well as for maintaining a winning coalition. Some of the tactics are in contrast

---

*R. A. Dahl: *Who Governs?* New Haven, Yale University Press, 1961, p. 274.
†J. C. Harsangi: Measurement of social power opportunity costs and the theory of two person bargaining games. *Behavioral Science, 7* (No. 1):71, January, 1962.

to the proposals of some behavioral scientists and practitioners for open communication, participation and a democratic atmosphere. A rationale needs to be developed for the nonhypocritical use of power or political tactics. However, the tactics are presented here merely to provide a more complete description of the realities in policy making.

In summary, the president and group subunit and department heads of any organization and the members of relevant external constituencies or coalitions all can be seen as players in a power game. The advantages and disadvantages of each player of the game stem basically from his status or position. How well he plays the game, given the initial advantages and disadvantages, depends on his skills at communication, negotiation and persuasion. Each player, from his own environmental location or organizational level, will perceive a policy-issue problem differently than those in other locations or levels. Each player uses the power at his command toward outcomes that will advance his conception of organizations, coalitions and self-interests. These strategic changes result from a pattern or stream of actions that take place as the game continues. The action that occurs over time may be somewhat different from the intention of any one player because there is no one player with all the power. As mentioned previously, even the entrepreneur needs to deal with or "negotiate" with other parties or coalitions. These interactions are discussed below.

"NEGOTIATING" WITH THE ENVIRONMENT

Contingencies affect selection of environmental or conflict strategies.

The general manager has a variety of environmental (or conflict) strategies to choose from in dealing with the uncertainties and conflicts in the environment. The perceived degree of environmental uncertainty in the situation under consideration and the power relationships with the particular stakeholders affect this choice.

He may recognize the futility of trying to push a total package through the organization. Owing to uncertainty he may not be able to determine in advance exactly what the total solution is. He may "muddle through with a purpose," be sensitive to feedback and have a disposition to change tactics. His solutions may be affected by feedback indicating a strike, government wage-price controls, a competitor's technological advance or a crisis of any kind.

Wrapp describes an example of "muddling through with a purpose":*

"Muddling through with a purpose."

A division manager had set as one of his objectives, at the start of a year, an improvement in product quality. At the end of the year, in reviewing his progress toward this objective, he could identify three significant events which had brought about a perceptible improvement.

---

*E. H. Wrapp: Good managers don't make policy decision. *Harvard Business Review,* 45 (No. 5):96, 1967; and C. E. Lindblom: The science of muddling through. *Public Administration Review,* 19:79–88, Spring, 1959.

First, the head of the quality control group, a veteran manager who was doing only an adequate job, asked early in the year for assignment to a new research group. This opportunity permitted the division manager to install a promising young engineer in this key spot.

A few months later, opportunity number two came along. The personnel department proposed a continuous program of checking the effectiveness of training methods for new employees. The proposal was acceptable to the manufacturing group. The division manager's only contribution was to suggest that the program should include a heavy emphasis on employees' attitudes toward quality.

Then a third opportunity arose when one of the division's best customers discovered that the wrong material had been used for a large lot of parts. The heat generated by this complaint made it possible to institute a completely new system of procedures for inspecting and testing raw materials.

As the division manager reviewed the year's progress on product quality, these were the three most important developments. None of them could have been predicted at the start of the year, but he was quick to see the potential in each as it popped up in the day-to-day operating routines.

Art of imprecision. Some effective general managers apparently use the "art of imprecision."* These managers know how to satisfy their subordinates as well as external stakeholders clamoring for statements on objectives by making very general and imprecise public relations statements such as "growth and profits." While managers have improvement projects and objectives in mind, some managers apparently are effective because they do not become committed publicly to a specific set of objectives and an explicit strategy. To do so would constrain the organizational unit when it needs, as it will, to change direction (especially if forced by environmental turbulence or uncertainties). Furthermore, it may be impossible to effectively communicate objectives and strategy to the entire organization. Organizational members will perceive the statements differently according to their various locations in the organization. The pattern of actions and decisions of general managers over time is more meaningful than mere words.

Clarity and acceptance of roles. While the managers may be "imprecise" initially, the patterns they follow can develop into clear and definite expected roles. This predictability and stability over time tends to reduce jurisdictional disputes. There is a risk of loss of flexibility and, of course, conflict situations may still develop. If the role assignments have been accepted as legitimate, however, they are likely to serve as one basis for resolution of differences.

Some evidence exists showing that role conflict and ambiguity have detrimental effects on organization members and organization success.†

---

*E. H. Wrapp: *op. cit.,* p. 91–99.
†For a review of such studies, see J. Rizzo, R. House and S. Lirtzman: Role conflict and ambiguity in complex organization. *Administrative Science Quarterly,* *15*:150–163, 1970; and A. Filley and R. House: *Management Process and Organizational Behavior.* Glenview, Illinois, Scott, Foresman, and Company, 1969.

44 / CONCEPTUALIZING THE POLICY-FORMATION PROCESS

Balance needs for autonomy against getting support.

Hierarchical command. A frequently used strategy is to rely on legitimate authority or the formal right to command. There is, in many instances, the major advantage of decisive and quicker action. Again, however, there is a risk of lack of flexibility and also a risk of lack of acceptance of the decision. Political resources, such as expertise and charisma, may exist in locations other than where the formal authority rests. In this situation, the one with formal authority may move toward more cooperative relationships.

Structural integration. There are a variety of structural arrangements that are used to mediate potential conflicts over values, objectives and allocations. Integrators or link pins may serve as contacts and communicators between organizational units or between organizations. Examples include project managers, sales-production expediters, political lobbyists, interdepartmental committees and joint labor-management teams. One difficulty of link pins may be a tendency for each to represent his own self-interest and thus fail to collaborate in any meaningful sense. Of course, if the reward structure is adjusted so that successful accomplishment of coordination provides a real payoff, this difficulty may be overcome.

Use of "linking pins."

Some evidence on the relationship between structural integration and organization success is provided in a study of six firms in the plastics industry.* An index of integration was closely associated with measures of profit change, sales volume and the number of new products developed over a five-year period.

Superordinate goals, shared values and coalitions. Superordinate goals are compelling goals which cannot be obtained by the resources and energies of the parties separately. For example, departments working jointly on a project involving a new service or product may force a dilemma on such issues as flexibility versus stability of operations, short run versus long run considerations, and objective measurements (e.g., costs) versus subjective measurements (e.g., employee attitudes). The policy initiators may take stands on issues according to their subgoals, and this fact in relation to their "strategic" position (political resources) is one of the determinants in initiating action. When a superordinate goal (e.g., share of market, continuation of the organization, identifying reasons for perceptual distortion, developing a cheap and highly desirable product) can be introduced or mobilized in a given situation, it may serve as a coordination device.† A coalition may be formed. On the other hand, if goals and values are shared and

Coalition: When two or more units join with shared values and common goals.

---

*P. R. Lawrence and J. W. Lorsch: *Organization and Environment: Managing Differentiation and Integration.* Boston, Graduate School of Business, Harvard University, 1967.

†Muzafer Sherif: *In Common Predicament.* Boston, Houghton-Mifflin Company, 1966.

cohesiveness fostered merely within the organization, the result may have negative implications for dealing with stakeholders.

Cooptation. Cooptation is a strategy by which new and possibly hostile parties are absorbed into the leadership of an organization in order to avert threats to its stability or existence. This approach may be helpful when the other parties assume a large share of power. Cooptation increases the probability of future support by the parties coopted. The acceptance on the board of directors of a representative from a bank increases the likelihood of access to financial resources for the duration of the cooptive arrangement. There is a danger, of course, in that the coopted parties are put in a position where they can raise questions and exert influence over many aspects of policy formation.

Cooptation: Absorb other parties into a unit.

Bargaining. Bargaining, by which the organization attempts to engage in an exchange relationship with the environment, is identified with threats, trading off, falsification of position and, in general, gamesmanship. It may occur sequentially between groups or individuals over a period of time—from the time of introduction of a major proposal to the time a decision is made on its acceptance. Thus, one might conclude that initial consensus on objectives by the general managers or the dominant coalition is not a necessary part of policy formation.* The objective in mind may be adjusted and modified as bargaining proceeds.

Bargaining: Engaging in exchange relationships.

Bargaining requires persistence and strength in the struggle between two parties or two coalitions. The negotiator has a problem: If he takes bold action, he is liable to violate the norms of his group and lose status, so his group loyalty may overwhelm organizational logic. On the other hand, if the negotiations stall, he is liable to lose his acceptability to the other group.

A major shortcoming of bargaining, then, is the tendency to move to a distributive relationship in which there are fixed goals for each side. What is one party's gain is the other party's loss. When the bargaining turns out to be of such poor quality, it often results in a "limited war" in which interparty tension is not resolved.† Additional machinery is needed for conflict adjudication, e.g., hierarchical coordination. The emphasis is then on control.

Under certain conditions bargaining is an effective strategy. It can be effective where there are common or complementary interests. Then integrative potential for joint problem solving exists, permitting solutions benefiting both parties, or at least where one party's gain does not represent an equivalent loss for the other party.

---

*E. E. Carter: The behavioral theory of the firm and top-level corporate decisions. *Administrative Science Quarterly,* 16 (No. 4):413–428, December, 1971.

†For a discussion see E. Schein: *Organizational Psychology.* Englewood Cliffs, N.J., Prentice-Hall, Inc., 1972.

Research evidence supports the effectiveness of bargaining, specifically where two individual policy initiators bargain to work out their differences and where group interaction is limited to studying issues rather than planning strategies.* The problem-solving approach discussed next, however, suggests somewhat broader applicability.

Collaborative problem solving. A collaborative problem-solving strategy which has achieved considerable impact in recent years involves meetings of potentially or actually conflicting parties attempting to gain an open and frank discussion of issues and policies. The meetings are designed (frequently by neutral third parties) to open lines of communication and to establish personal and group commitment to improving organizational functioning and organizational policies. This approach has at least part of its origin in organization development.†

A key requirement in the collaboration between parties is to build an atmosphere of trust and to develop a form of leveling in discussion of perceived organizational problems. A low key approach is often used to bring differing objectives, values and perceptions out into the open where they can be dealt with constructively. Also, a basic tactic in problem solving is to find the goals upon which the parties can agree and thereby establish effective interaction. Frequently the group provided with data input is asked to identify priority issues, barriers to actions, plans of actions for themselves and recommendations on plans for others. Evidence exists of the success of this approach in improving coordination and policy formation in both industry and government settings.‡

Circular Effects of Policy Formation

The outputs from the interaction of the structure and the environmental forces include objectives, strategies, role performance and organizational outcomes.

The strategies, as mentioned, are specific major actions or patterns of action (sometimes ad hoc, sometimes planned) to attain objectives. Objectives are targets or hoped for results. Role performance means the actual patterns of behavior of participants

---

*B. M. Bass: Effects on the subsequent performance of negotiators of studying issues or planning strategies alone or in groups. *Psychological Monographs, 80* (No. 6):1–3, 1966.

†G. Dalton, P. Lawrence, and L. Greiner (eds.): *Organization Change and Development.* Homewood, Ill., Richard D. Irwin, 1970.

‡R. T. Golembiewski and A. Blumberg: The laboratory approach to organization change. *Academy of Management Journal,* Vol. II, 1968; F. T. Paine: A conference approach to assessing public management. *Personnel Administration,* June, 1972, pp. 47–52.

relevant to the organization. Role performance would include the interpretation, implementation and acceptance of strategies, and organizational outcomes would include such performance measures as growth, stability, flexibility, return on investment and social responsibility.

Furthermore, the model assumes that once a strategy is formulated it becomes part of the environment. The implementation of the strategy and the reaction to it by the organization member and by individuals and groups outside the organization will comprise new environmental pressures which may necessitate modification of existing strategy and, perhaps, the creation of new strategy. The feedback of output effects and organizational outcomes is necessary since strategy formation is a dynamic process. What was decided yesterday will already exist in a new light today. *Feedback in a dynamic process.*

The feedback is used in such a way as to make the policy process interrelated, cumulative and consistent—in short, incremental.* Existing levels of support for various activities are more or less taken for granted and incremental changes considered. This situation is associated with the widely shared value of mitigation of conflict (or "don't rock the boat"). Such a view of the policy process seems to fail to account for new policy departures. Such events could be treated as random disturbances. A dominant manager may come along and seek bold opportunities. A planning manager may carefully reformulate an organizational strategy. However, old patterns of the interaction process may reassert themselves. *Policy process is incremental.*

The old patterns of interaction may reflect a divided coalition of influencer forces and a complex, rapidly changing environment. This may be the case of the large, established organization with huge sunk costs and many subcoalitions holding each other in check. Some large hospitals, many universities, and a number of corporations would illustrate this pattern of divided power. Also, many governments and government agencies seem to have many controlling groups holding each other in check.

However, a dominant pattern (entrepreneurial) may be exercised (and may be desirable) under conditions in which a powerful individual finds an environment that is yielding and an organization that is willing both to be oriented toward growth and to shift strategy boldly. Young and/or small organizations and organizations in trouble may provide "entrepreneurial-type" conditions. These organizations may have little to lose by acting boldly. The young organizations in particular have made few commitments, and the way is clear to cluster key (and bold) decisions at an early stage. *Strategic mode affected by contingencies.*

Organizations, or segments of an organization, in trouble may

---

*For discussion see A. Wildavsky: *The Politics of the Budgetary Process.* Boston, Little, Brown and Company, 1964.

need an active search for new opportunities and dramatic leaps forward in face of uncertainty.

More emphasis on planning, with its focus on systematic, comprehensive analysis, may be found where there are enough resources to support systematic comprehensive analysis along with a reasonably predictable environment. Planning, after all, is costly and a highly complex dynamic environment may mean that the planning results are discouraging. If planning has been attempted, as it has in many organizations and segments of organizations, it may have taken on a somewhat adaptive character. That is to say it might specify possible end points and alternative routes but allow the manager flexibility to adjust to the feedback along the way.

Core issue — need to prevent stagnation.

The organization might not be able to adjust to opportunities and challenges in a rapidly changing environment. A built-in provision for self-criticism, for challenging present policies and practices, for auditing the environment, and for revising and reformulating strategies is needed. This is a core issue; the organization needs to seek a deliberate way of preventing dry rot or stagnation.

Applying the Model to Business and Public Bodies

The model is seen as applicable to business as well as nonbusiness organizations. Both types of organizations have structures which (1) scan the changing environment for opportunities, threats and risks, and (2) based on premises about the environment and considering self-interests, develop basic missions, objectives and strategies.

The policy analyst should keep in mind, however, that significant differences do exist which affect the nature of his assessment. Bernard Taylor, a well known policy analyst from Great Britain, notes some significant differences between business and public bodies as follows:*

	Business	*Public Bodies*
Environment	Competitive and turbulent	Monopolistic and relatively stable
Main objective	Profit	Public service
Economic objectives	Profit required; bankruptcy possible	No profit required; bankruptcy not possible
Structure	Frequently decentralized into profit centers	Usually a centralized bureaucracy
Accountable to	Shareholders	Congress/Parliament
Control of strategy	Management	Government
Scope of activity	Unlimited; no monopoly	Limited; state monopoly
Major source of funds	Shareholders/banks	Government

*Bernard Taylor: Personal communication, July 17, 1976.

These differences, significant as they are, do not preclude treatment of these business and public bodies with the same model. Adjustments can and should be made, adapting the critical analytical variables to the specific organization.

Illustration of Model — A Role Play

In order to "bring to life" the model of policy formation, you may want to devise and implement a role play or exercise involving one or more groups to illustrate roles, self-interests, conflicts, political resources, trade-offs, coalitions and environmental pressures. Such an exercise might contain the following:

1. A basic description of the organizational policy situation.
2. An analysis of alternative policy opportunities.
3. A description of the policy makers, their self-interests, political resources and environmental pressures.
4. Private information known only to a limited number (one or more) of policy makers.

The description of the Slimey Oil Co. situation which follows illustrates such a role play or exercise. The secret information is not included.

SLIMEY OIL COMPANY (SOCO)

1. SOCO is a large, independent oil refinery located in Baltimore, Maryland, 1978 sales, $100M; profit, $2M.

2. A controlling interest in SOCO was recently acquired by a large conglomerate, Amalgamated Industries. Amalgamated is interested in SOCO because of its asset base ($300M) and has put one of its young executives on SOCO's board to watch over its interests.

3. SOCO is reasonably profitable and internally sound, both financially and managerially.

4. SOCO's key competition comes from the Philadelphia Refining Company (PRC) of Philadelphia, Penna.

5. Because of the switch in 1979 by all the major auto makers to engines that will use unleaded gas, SOCO must rebuild portions of its facilities or lose its customers. This changeover is tying up all of SOCO's cash reserves ($5M) and some of its credit ($3M). The refinery will not have to shut down for this conversion. PRC already makes unleaded gas and is unaffected by the switch.

6. SOCO has learned through its lobbyist that the state of Maryland will pass a law in the next general assembly which will require all companies to cease pollution. This law will take effect in 1980 and would require SOCO to expend a great deal of money on antipollution equipment. This money would have to be borrowed and interest rates are at record highs. Further, a six months' shutdown in production would be required to complete the necessary modifications. Much of the rebuilding necessary to make unleaded gas would also have to be redone. Finally, PRC is under no pressure from Pennsylvania to stop polluting.

After much debate and under pressure from Baltimore area conservation groups and from its stockholders, the Board of Directors decided to meet in executive session and adopt a strategic plan of action.

There are only three alternatives open:

A. Support the law fully and comply. This requires borrowing $20M at 9 per cent and six months' shutdown.
 Effects 1. High interest costs ($1.8M/yr.).
   2. Put in bad competitive position vs. PRC.
   3. Socially acceptable choice.
   4. Don't pay for unleaded change twice.

B. Take law to court and fight for delay. Legal costs would be high, but much, much less than interest costs. The future of interest rate is uncertain and it is unknown if pending Federal antipollution laws will cause the same problems for PRC.
 Effects 1. Maintain competitive position vs. PRC.
   2. Bad public relations; a socially unacceptable choice.
   3. Potential serious financial and legal consequences if court battle is lost; particularly bad if lost early.
   4. Pay for unleaded change twice.

C. Compromise. Fight for delay but also spend some for antipollution. Required spending $5M but very little shutdown—four weeks. Would still have to pay twice for unleaded change.
 Effects 1. Although costs are greater than choice B, still less than choice A.
   2. Better competitively than A.
   3. Still reasonably bad public relations.
   4. Largely avoids legal problems.

MEMBERS OF THE BOARD OF DIRECTORS (7 MEMBERS)

CHAIRMAN _____ Is founder of the company, independently wealthy, *very* civic minded. Has been chairman for 30 years. Strongly supports plan A.

PRESIDENT _____ Has been president for 20 years, during which time the company has enjoyed unprecedented growth and earnings. Supports plan B all the way and has taken public position that if it is not adopted he will retire on the spot.

EXECUTIVE VICE PRESIDENT _____ Son-in-law of president but also MIT honors graduate with M.S. Chem. E. and MBA. Highly competent and well thought of. It is suspected there is strong pressure on him from his wife to support the president. He supports plan B.

CONGLOMERATE REPRESENTATIVE _____ It is known that he supports plan C; Amalgamated doesn't want to rock the boat. He will vote against A or B unless new arguments are presented that give him a better option. Amalgamated will not overthrow the Board.

MRS. _____ A large independent stockholder. Adamantly supports plan A both emotionally and intellectually (believes in conservation). Willing to compromise only as a last resort. She is a civic-minded widow with children in college.

COMPTROLLER _____ Also a stockholder; has been with company since founding. Because of bad financial position that would, in his opinion, result from either plan A or C he strongly supports plan B.

MR. _____ A prominent Baltimore businessman with an independent income. A member of the Sierra Club and a staunch conservationist. Supports plan A all the way. He is a personal friend of the Chairman, the comptroller and Mrs. _____.

Instructions

Your instructor may assign you to play one of the roles as indicated in the exercise. He might also assign some members of the class to be observers of the policy-formation process. Such observers would note their perceptions of the activities in the complex problem-solving situation and report to the class.

In addition, your instructor may wish to provide private information to be known to only a limited number of the policy makers during the meeting. For example, the executive vice president might be given the following information:

If the President wins the vote and you vote against him, he will fire you. He holds a $30,000 note payable on demand on some of your real estate. If he loses and you voted against him, he will call the note.

You are secretly a member of the Sierra Club and strongly support conservation and therefore Plan A, but you must publicly support B initially.

This kind of information would be divulged to all participants only after the observers make their reports. The class discussions will include the question of how the factors (e.g., roles, self-interests, conflicts, differing perceptions of the problem, political resources, trade-offs, coalitions, capabilities and environmental pressures) have affected the complex problem-solving process.

Social Responsibility and the Model—A Debate

There are various points of view on corporate or organizational social responsibility. This section of the chapter assembles some of the more important statements about the role of the corporation in society in order to facilitate comparison and discussion.

In the final analysis, the policy maker is left with questions of judgment, influenced by his role perception and self-interests, and constrained by various stakeholders, all of which he must take in consideration in adapting the organization to social responsibilities.

His judgment may have been affected by one or more of the points of view which we will bring out. You may wish to study and to discuss them. In a classroom situation a debate might be staged with students gathering additional information and examples.* One individual or group might start the argument as follows:

Various points of view on what is social responsibility.

1. The businessman has no way of determining what his social responsibility should be, how much he should spend on it or how he should evaluate the results. If he spends funds in a way other than

Businessman should seek profit for stockholders benefit?

---

*There is a lack of systematic research on impact of social responsibility on formulation of corporate strategy. Read Robert W. Ackerman: Public responsibility and the businessman. *Harvard Business School,* 4 - 371–520, BP 1033, 1971.

the way those to whom he is responsible (the shareholders) would have spent it, he is in effect imposing a tax and deciding on the use of proceeds.

2. Public functions should not be exercised by the managers of private enterprises, lest, if democracy is to be preserved, they become civil servants to be duly elected by the people or appointed by the state.*

Another individual or group might take a different view of corporate responsibility as follows:

Express corporate conscience?

1. Yes, there are economic constraints and the possibility of sacrifices in short-term profitability. However, social responsibility should be included as a factor influencing the formulation of policy and strategy. This explicit inclusion of social responsibility is an expression of corporate conscience.

2. In the long run, those firms that will earn the right profits for their stockholders are discharging their responsibilities to society.†

Convert social problems into economic opportunities?

A third position might be as follows: Business is better qualified than government to find solutions to many urban and other problems provided it is (1) adequately controlled and (2) given economic incentives to do so. Once government has decided on the goals, social problems can be converted into economic opportunities which business can deal with effectively.

Still another position that might be brought up is one relating to how social responsibility can be rendered manageable in the complex organization. Joseph Bower argues as follows: "The central source of motivation, the career system, is so designed that virtually all measures are short run and internally focused. Men are rewarded for performance, but performance is almost always defined as short run economic or technical results. The more objective the system, the more an attempt is made to quantify the results, the harder it is to broaden the rules of the game to take into account the social role of the executive."‡

Reward social role of executive?

Finally, the recommendations of the National Affiliation of Concerned Business Students might be used as a starting point for discussion. The ten "essential first steps" to integrate planning for social action into regular corporate functions are:

(1) *Corporate philosophy*—formulate a philosophy in order to define the role of the corporation in meeting economic and social objectives; (2) *social objectives*—formulate social objectives as part of the yearly and long-range

---

*Milton Friedman: The social responsibility of business is to increase its profits. *The New York Times Magazine*, September 13, 1970.

†K. Andrews: The company and its social responsibilities: Relating corporate strategy to the needs of society. *In The Concept of Corporate Strategy*. Homewood, Ill., Richard D. Irwin, 1971, pp. 118–177; and Henry Ford, II: *The Human Environment and Business*. New York, Weybright and Talley, 1970, p. 63.

‡J. L. Bower: The amoral organization. Mimeographed paper, August, 1970. See also Jules Cohn: Is business meeting the challenge of urban affairs. *Harvard Business Review*, July-August, 1965.

economic growth goals, taking these down to the operating units so every manager knows "where he comes in"; (3) *social accountability* — develop a system to evaluate employees and managers on their progress toward social objectives; (4) *social audits* — develop a system of social auditing to allow a corporation to determine what social needs are most critical, and where the corporation can best use its own resources, and evaluate its progress toward the social objectives it has set up; (5) *social reports* — publish a social progress report as part of the corporate annual report, on the basis that social performance is part of the overall corporate performance; (6) *top executive advocate* — name a high level advocate or watchdog for social considerations within the corporation; (7) *social staff* — set up noneconomic senior executive for social concern to do research and planning to determine social needs and corporate programs; (8) *broaden board of directors* — include groups not now generally represented in order to get needed additional perspectives; (9) *lobbying* — use existing political power to lobby for needed social legislation; (10) *executive brainstorming committee* — appoint a top-level group of executives to study the corporation's role in society, allowing the group time away from daily operations to deal with social considerations in depth.*

Integrate planning for social action into corporate functions.

The discussion of these points of view may center on organizational objectives, including the balancing of economic and noneconomic considerations, personal values or interests and social responsibilities, and the environmental and structural forces affecting the implementation of social responsibility in the complex organization. (See Chapter 4 for an extended discussion of social responsibility.)

SUMMARY

We have elaborated a bit on conceptualizing the policy formation process in organizations. Specifically, we indicate that a classical model of decision making may hamper understanding and may confuse students of the policy-formation process. In contrast to this decision-making model, a policy-formation model to be descriptive must include, at least, the lack of unity on problem statements, two or more issues, two or more sets of interests and no single best solution.

The general approach to be followed in this book is to see the policy issues as involving a complex social process and then to converge on the cognitive aspects. To begin, an input-output model is presented emphasizing the dynamic social process. The model assumes that key inputs affecting policy are environmental forces (support and demands) and that these forces interact with a given policy-generating structure. Policy makers, though they make an intellectual analysis of alternative policies, are affected by their role perceptions, their perceived self-interests, and the use of political

Contingency model is emphasized.

---

*Stanford University Graduate School of Business, *Alumni Bulletin,* Summer, 1972, p. 13.

resources. They monitor and predict changes in the internal and external environment.

The interaction of structure and environment pressures has two parts: The first involves the policy makers' decisions regarding resolution of role conflicts, furtherance of self-interests and conservations of political resources. The second part involves the coordination function in obtaining solutions to priority allocation issues while maintaining a winning coalition of support. Various environmental or conflict strategies for "negotiating" with the environment are discussed, such as "muddling through with a purpose," "the art of imprecision," structural integration, coalitions, cooptation, bargaining and collaborative problem solving.

Balance needs for autonomy against the exchange of commitments to get support.

The feedback of output effects and organizational outcomes is used in such a way as to make the policy process incremental. This may result from a widely shared value of mitigation of conflict. If such be the case, the organization needs some provision to rejuvenate itself and to prevent stagnation. Appropriate review and evaluation of the policy-formation process would determine the need for revisions in the adaptions to the environment. Subsequent chapters will deal with some guides to such reviews and evaluations. They will help you to answer some of your questions on learning about policy in general and on using a framework and methods appropriate to a specific situation.

To add realism and practicality, this chapter has provided (1) an illustration of the model of the policy-formation process, and (2) a potential class assignment that includes various points of view on social responsibility.

INTERGROUP POLICY EXERCISE

Policy formation is seen by some as a negotiation process. Certain people interact in the establishment and implementation of policies. There is a need (1) to negotiate, (2) to gain acceptance, and (3) to have leadership skill in spelling out to potential members of a coalition how the policy will serve their interests.

The instructor will set up three or four groups with four or five students in each. He will assign the groups an important policy choice, e.g., selection of one from three or more types of term projects or a determination of the sequence in presenting individual or group reports. It is necessary that the policy choice have a high potential for provoking both interest and disagreements. Each small group will proceed as follows:

1. Make a decision in favor of one of the alternatives.
2. Choose a reporter who will present his group's preference and views to the whole group.
3. Choose a delegate who will meet with other delegates to make a final decision for the whole group. The final decision is binding.

4. Be prepared to discuss the decision-making process within the small group and within the meeting of delegates.

Time limits will be set for each of the activities, based on the complexity of the policy issue and on the class requirements. Discussion of the exercise may include such aspects as the effects of conflicts on the intergroup decision-making process.

DISCUSSION QUESTIONS

1. Compare and contrast strategy formulation with the typical decision-making model discussed in the text.
2. Why does it seem appropriate to view strategy issues as involving a complex social process and then to converge on the cognitive aspects rather than to hope that strategy issues can be understood in terms of solely intellectual components?
3. What are some of the ways the assumptions of the decision-making model may be violated?
4. How do self-interests and political resources affect strategy making?
5. Discuss the methods of coordination used in resource allocation conflict situations.
6. What is meant by the circular effects of strategy formation?
7. Discuss political tactics that may be used in the strategy-formation process. Do you agree with the appropriateness of their use? Why?
8. Discuss differences in the application of the strategy-formation model to business organizations and to public bodies.
9. Devise a descriptive theory that explains the behavior of the participant in the policy-formation process.

Suggested Additional References for Further Research

Barber, R. J.: *The American Corporation: Its Power, Its Money, Its Politics.* New York, E. P. Dutton and Company, 1970.
Barkdale, G. T.: Making planning relevant to public agency management. *Long-Range Planning 9* (No. 1):59–65, 1976.
Bauer, R. A., and Gergen, K. J.: *The Study of Policy Formation.* New York, Free Press, 1968.
Brearly, A.: The changing role of the chief executive. *Journal of General Management 3* (No. 4):62–71, 1976.
Cannon, J. T.: *Business Strategy and Policy.* New York, Harcourt, Brace & World, 1968.
The corporation and its obligations. An interview with C. Peter McColough. *Harvard Business Review, 53* (No. 3):127–138, 1975.
Davis, K.: Social responsibility is inevitable. *California Management Review 19* (No. 1):14–20, 1976.
Farmer, R., and Hogue, W. D.: *Corporate Social Responsibility.* Palo Alto, California, Science Research Associates, Inc., 1973.

Galbraith, J. K.: *The New Industrial State.* Boston, Houghton Mifflin Company, 1967.

Gluck, F. W., and Foster, R. N.: Managing technological change: Cigars for Brad. *Harvard Business Review 53* (No. 3):139–150, 1975.

Harrison, F. L.: How corporate planning responds to uncertainty. *Long-Range Planning 9* (No. 2):88–93, 1976.

Karger, D. W., and Malik, Z. A.: Long range planning and organizational performance. *Long-Range Planning 8* (No. 6):60–64, 1975.

Kristol, I.: Professor Galbraith's New Industrial State. *Fortune,* July, 1967, pp. 90–91, 194–195.

Lawrence, P. R., and Lorsch, J. W.: *Organization and Environment.* Cambridge, Harvard University Press, 1967.

Lindblom, C. E.: *The Intelligence of Democracy.* New York, Free Press, 1965.

Lindblom, C. E.: *The Policy Making Process.* Englewood Cliffs, N.J., Prentice Hall, Inc., 1968.

Luthans, F., and Hodgetts, R. M.: *Social Issues in Business.* New York, The Macmillan Company, 1972.

Macmillan, I. C.: Business strategies for political action. *Journal of General Management, 2* (No. 1):51–63, 1974.

Marley-Clarke, B. W. G.: Policy planning for environmental management. *Long-Range Planning 9* (No. 5):2–6, 1976.

Nader, R.: *The Consumer and Corporate Responsibility.* New York, Harcourt, Brace, Jovanovich, Inc., 1973.

Punt, T.: Social trends and corporate plans. *Long-Range Planning 9* (No. 5):7–11, 1976.

Riker, W. H.: The theory of political coalitions. New Haven, Yale University Press, 1962.

Rondinelli, D. A.: Public planning and political strategy. *Long-Range Planning 9* (No. 2):75–82, 1976.

Sethi, S. Prakash: Dimensions of corporate social performance: An analytical framework. *California Management Review 17* (No. 3):58–64, 1975.

Simon, H. A.: The new science of management decision. *In The Shape of Automation.* New York, Harper & Row, 1965.

Taylor, B.: Conflict of values—The central strategy problem. *Long-Range Planning 8* (No. 6):20–24, 1975.

3

OBJECTIVES OF ASSESSMENT OF POLICY FORMATION

USE OF THE GUIDES

FRAMEWORK FOR ASSESSING POLICY FORMATION
   Present and Future
   Recognition and Diagnosis
   Asking Questions and Organizing Data
   Part A. The Current Situation
   Segmenting the Organization's Environment
   Missions, Strategies and Basis of Support
   Organizational Objectives and Outcomes
   Policy-generating Structure

SUMMARY

APPENDIX. A PROGRAM FOR ANALYZING SOME ASPECTS OF THE PRESENT FINANCIAL CONDITION OF THE ORGANIZATION

ASSESSMENT GUIDES: THE CURRENT SITUATION

Policy makers have been seen as "negotiating" to find solutions to policy issues that will (1) satisfy environmental demands or requirements, (2) win external support (e.g., customers) and internal support (e.g., peers), and (3) partially satisfy self-interests. "Negotiating" has been described as sometimes like "muddling through," with the impossibility of determining in advance what the solution should be. Thus, policy makers are sensitive to feedback from the environment. They analyze their present situation and forecast what environmental demands and support will be; then, with their self-interests as basic premises, they make choices that may emerge into patterns of decisions or strategies.

General Guides.

This chapter contains general guides for assessment of this policy- (or strategy-) formation process and policy-formation content. Again we are using the phrase "policy formation" as a broad one, including in it decision making and activities related to the long-term development of the organization. Our descriptive model of policy formation allows us to see a complex social process and then converges on the cognitive aspects rather than hoping that policy issues can be understood solely in terms of intellectual components. Our reasons for this approach were elaborated in Chapter 2. Moreover, we have recognized the importance of the cognitive activites of analysis and choice. Our guides to analysis, here, will be seen as putting together the intellectual activities and the social process activities and will be associated with various phases of the model. They are organized into three parts as follows:

Putting together intellectual and social activities.

58 / ASSESSMENT GUIDES: THE CURRENT SITUATION

Part A   The Current Situation
Segmenting the Organization's Environment
Missions, Strategies and Basis of Support
Organizational Objectives and Outcomes
Policy-generating Structure
Part B   The Changing Situation: Environmental Turbulence
Analysis of Impact of Opportunities and Threats
Part C   Strategy Development
The Strategic Mix and the Portfolios
The Segmentation Process and Business Strategies
Linking the Strategies with Operations

Part A is covered in this chapter; Part B is covered in Chapter 4; Part C is covered in Chapter 5.

Since these guides are intended for general use in both business and nonprofit bodies, certain features of the policy formation process for more basic strategic questions are referred to in this book. More detailed agenda for review of special policy areas (e.g., labor relations policy) are discussed in other books, and should be consulted when warranted in specific analyses.

OBJECTIVES OF ASSESSMENT OF POLICY FORMATION

What are the objectives of the assessment?

The primary objective in conducting overall assessments of policy formation is to identify problems, threats and opportunities in the organization's environment and structure and to devise plans that include practical responses to the environmental and structural situation. The second important objective of the overall assessment process is to evaluate the operation of specific strategies and specific managers for corrective action by the organization where necessary. An appraisal of policy goes hand-in-hand with an appraisal of management. Management appraisal may use standards of excellence revealed by the success of policy.

USE OF THE GUIDES

Use by three main types of analysts.

The assessment guides are intended for use as a framework for asking questions and for organizing data by three main types of policy analysts:

Top level and middle level managers who on a regular basis are involved in policy formation and implementation; it is recognized, of course, that they may desire and may need staff assistance in information gathering and analysis.

Assessors or researchers interested in understanding and in developing the policy-formation process.

Students doing case analysis, field projects or role plays to develop conceptual and administrative skills in the policy-formation process; it is recognized that students may find some of the information required to do a complete assessment unavailable from the subject organization or inadequately covered in the case; nevertheless, a partial assessment may be made and will probably be useful.

The guides are broadly problem-oriented in that they are aimed at analysis of policy problems, their implications and root causes. The guides are also opportunity-oriented in that they are aimed at analysis of opportunities, their requirements for success and plans for dealing with them. It should be said that the guides are not all-inclusive but are intended to suggest a number of possible elements that may be considered in the assessment process. The reader should keep in mind the limitations of these guides in the process of isolating critical problems, threats and opportunities. The guides are intended to be supplemented liberally by expertise and judgment as well as to be tailored closely to the unique circumstances in a particular organization. Cost precludes monitoring every variable and using every method. Some elements may be judged *more important* than others for particular analyses. Also some methods or variables may be *eliminated* or de-emphasized for specific assessments. For example, analysis of sales data would be eliminated for most government organizations; analysis of consumer income may be relatively unimportant to an aerospace company. Consideration of the important elements developed in the review and analysis of the relationships between the present position, the achievements, problems, opportunities, capabilities and requirements for success should permit an overall assessment of policies and the policy-formation process and the development of action plans.

General guides are problem- and opportunity-oriented

Some elements are more important; some may be eliminated.

Considerable judgment will be required to arrive at the proper balance and perspective of present position and desired position (where the organization would like to be) in making the overall assessment. Organization and reporting of the organizational strategy will require distillation of the findings resulting from the evaluation into major issues and opportunities and translating recommendations into specific actions on the part of relevant organization participants.

Considerable judgment needed.

FRAMEWORK FOR ASSESSING POLICY FORMATION

Present and Future

Part of an approach for systematic improvement in policy formation demands an examination of the present "state of things" and a forecast of the future environmental turbulence. The examination and the forecasts are not a one-shot effort but need to

Examine present "state of things."

60 / ASSESSMENT GUIDES: THE CURRENT SITUATION

Forecast future environmental turbulence.

be more of a continual monitoring of the organization environment and strategy as well as subsystems, processes and results. The subsystems may include functional groups, top managers, members of the board of directors, middle managers, and members of the work force, or they may be "outsiders" such as union officials, government officials, product or service trend-setters and community leaders. The processes include decision-making activities, strategy development methods, relationships with interfacing groups and communication patterns. The results include such things as competitive position, effective service, share of market, image, budget success, inventory position and patients.

Identify gap between desired position and present position.

In addition to examining the present conditions and forecasting "futures," an approach to improvement would include a more or less continuous indication and modification of the desired position and desired organizational effectiveness. In other words, the approach would include a statement of (1) where the organization would like to be (environmental segment, strategy, capability) and (2) the differential or gap existing between the present position and the desired position. These statements would provide food for thought on where to concentrate efforts toward effecting strategic transfers ahead of the turbulence.

Recognition and Diagnosis

Can you close the strategy gap and the capability gap ahead of the turbulence?

Often, however, an organization or strategic business unit will fail to anticipate and suddenly discover that a fleeting opportunity (e.g., to please a higher level manager) has been missed or that survival of a product line is threatened. The organization unit may have contingency plans or crisis management responses to sudden discontinuities to what is expected. An alternative, more efficient but perhaps more difficult, is before-the-fact efforts to minimize surprises and reduce vulnerability to the environment.

Develop response to weak signals.

Recognition of opportunities and threats may have to begin when the signals are weak.* Early in the life of a threat, for example, the currently available information may be vague and its future course unclear. In other words, a threat is sensed but its source, characteristics, nature, gravity and timing of impact are not completely understood. First, the organizational unit needs to aim its responses at increasing its strategic flexibility or preparedness (e.g., capacity to permit quick repositioning to new products and new markets, diversification of work skills, or even using multipurpose equipment.) This flexibility will assist in reducing surprises. Later, as information becomes more precise, so will the organizational unit's response. It then can define and integrate its diagnostic information and deveop a specific response to the strategic issue.

See H. Igor Ansoff: Managing strategic surprise by response to weak signals. California Management Review, 18 (No. 2):21–33, 1975.

In other words, an identification phase of policy formation begins as the art or act of recognizing the problem, opportunity or threat from even rather weak symptoms, signs, intuitive insights and/or analytical findings and proceeds with diagnosis, i.e., defining and structuring the situation as more precise information becomes available. This is the task facing the manager or policy analyst. The task requires maintaining awareness and flexibility while either searching the diverse bits and pieces of information to pinpoint the problem, opportunity or threat or reviewing a situation that has presented itself. The task may be carried on quickly, given precise information, or over a rather long period of time as signals become stronger.

For example, if a competing unit introduces a new service, familiar prior experience may allow a fairly quick understanding of the nature, impact and possible responses. As another example, however, a sense of opportunity from the development of solid state physics in the 1940's was recognized by the electronics industry. The specific source of the opportunity, the transistor, was still several years off. Once invented, moreover, the full ramifications of the transistor were unclear, as were the aggressive responses that some organizations were eventually to make. Pioneering firms were able to develop knowledge of crystal yields and manufacturing process costs sufficient to make reasonable predictions of the ultimate technology and its profitability. Those firms that for one reason or another held back on this strategic issue were forced to pay a high cost of entry into the new industry.

As you can see, several kinds of diagnostic information may be useful. Facts and opinion could be accumulated about:

1. The potential causes(s) of a threat or opportunity.
2. The usefulness of the unit's own capacity for dealing with a threat or opportunity.
3. The external environment (e.g., understanding the market, potential competition and future product potential).
4. The internal flexibility or degree of specialization of resources and facilities.
5. The external flexibility or degree to which the organizational unit is dependent on the maintenance of the current situation and is therefore threatened by a prospective change.

Important diagnostic information.

Using the framework for assessing policy formation will allow the manager (or the reader) to develop information to answer these important questions and therefore to understand the unit's preparedness and vulnerability.

Remember, however, that the integration or structuring of the information which has been received, through various techniques and sources, is critical. If various aspects of the situation are described, it is usually possible to find out how the aspects are interrelated and why they exist. For example, in pinpointing a problem (opportunities and threats may be handled in the same way)* it is desirable to list all the suspected problems and review the evidence for reliability and adequacy to support their existence as problems. The problems will be seen to exist in a hierarchy; i.e., "lower level" problems are interrelated and can be stated as a "higher level" single problem.† With precise statements of these larger problems it is possible to diagnose the causes of some or all of them. For example, the interrelated "lower level" problems of excessive inventory, rising sales costs and declining cash flow may be combined into a product obsolescence problem. The cause may be an inferior product. On the other hand, the same lower level problems may be combined into a marketing effectiveness problem. The cause in this instance may be some of the characteristics of the marketing program. From a variety of possible causes, the most likely cause or causes must be identified by testing tentative causes and by searching for statements that explain the existence of symptoms and signs.

Pinpointing a problem.

Which "cause" explains the symptoms or signs?

Before gathering information is discussed in more detail we shall indicate some cautions for the policy analyst to observe in the process as follows:

1. There may be incomplete data on the problem, opportunity or threat. It may be possible (perhaps costly, though) to gather the appropriate data or, on the other hand, to make certain assumptions and proceed. As indicated before, however, managers have to make choices with respect to a limited simplified "model" of the real situation. They may have to respond to weak signals.

Cautions to observe.

2. There may be a failure to thoroughly evaluate the symptoms and signs. Premature judgment, acceptance of the opinions of a few as general facts, failure to test tentative causes, and failure to search for exceptions which can be found for the explanations of the problem are elements of this error.

3. There may be a tendency to express the diagnosis in terms consistent with self-interests, such as market researchers indicating a need for more market research or trainers diagnosing the situation as requiring more training. Attempts should be made to have an open-minded and a systematic approach.

4. The knowledge and skill for diagnosis of a complex situation may be missing. The resultant diagnosis may include false "causes," and much time and effort may be wasted in trying to correct them. Advice and assistance from expert or experienced sources may be needed. The case analyst may ask his colleague or his instructor. The manager may call in a staff specialist or a consultant.

---

*Opportunities apparently do not require extensive investigation because response is not mandatory. See H. Mintzberg et al.: *The Structure of "Unstructured" Decision Process.* Working Paper, Montreal, McGill University, 1973.

†See John W. Bonge: Problem recognition and diagnosis: Basic inputs to business policy. *Journal of Business Policy, 2* (No. 3):45–53, Spring, 1972.

Asking Questions and Organizing Data

A framework serves as a general guide for those concerned with policy improvement in asking questions and organizing data. Such a guide is provided in this chapter and the next. While a few illustrative devices or instruments are discussed here, subsequent chapters will cover specific methods for assessment and development. As indicated in Chapter 1, many frameworks or agendas have been proposed for assessing policy. Compared with other frameworks the following framework has more emphasis on role and program variables which are useful in understanding and developing the process of policy formation.* These behavioral and organizational variables have been lacking or deemphasized in other agendas. In addition, environmental segmentation, cost performance, competitive position, strategic resource areas and strategic stakeholders in the environment are stressed.

The following presentation of elements in the assessment process does not indicate a hard and fast sequence of steps to be followed by a policy analyst. For example, some analysts may wish to start with an examination and description of the current policy-generating structure and the social processes involved therein. They may feel that these processes and their effectiveness would affect what markets and service-product the organization intends to develop. Similarly they may feel that examination of the structure prior to an examination of the goals and action plans is appropriate. On the other hand, if General Motors were to decide to go into a new business by acquisition, then it would appear that a new structure would be appropriate to deal with achieving that goal, not that given a structure, goals should be established. Our feeling, therefore, is that in this dynamic continuous process of strategy formation the analyst has some choice in where to begin. Elements of the present situation may be studied concurrently or one at a time. The fact is that a structure already exists in the organization and is generating strategic decisions. Describing the structure will help in understanding the basis of the existing organization goals and action plans and suggest possible changes in them. It is fully recognized, on the other hand, that a given structure may need alteration after strategies are generated by that structure. Thus, the policy analyst is required to keep all the diverse elements of the present situation in mind, and it is a matter of judgment where to begin. Any recommendations that the policy analysts make, moreover, are meaningful only when grounded on valid descriptions of the current situation.

Matter of judgment where to begin.

Keep all diverse elements in mind.

---

*C. Saunders: *What Should We Know About Strategy Formulation?* Professional Papers, Division of Business Policy and Planning, Academy of Management National Meeting, August, 1973.

Part A. The Current Situation

Segmenting the Organization's Environment

The objective of the analyst is to define the organization's environment in terms of analytically meaningful segments. One way of doing this is to subdivide the environment into relatively independent strategic business areas (SBA's). Each SBA has its own distinctive trends, threats and opportunities. These environmental segments have no necessary connections with existing units internal to the organization. A connection would exist if the organization has developed strategic business units (SBU's) that match the SBA's. However, it should be emphasized that an "outside in" rather than an "inside out" approach is used for a clearer view of the outside world.*

Important to use "outside in" view.

To identify segments, consideration may be given to geography, customers or clients, technology and product lines. For organizations operating in a relatively homogeneous geographic area and within one technology, the SBA's will be equated with major product lines. But for geographically diversified organizations a geographic dimension may be necessary. Thus, for example, an organization selling cameras in the United States and Canada and in South America would recognize two district geography-determined SBA's, because of the differences in economic, political and social climates as well as in the maturity of respective markets. If, further, the cameras are sold both to consumers and industrial customers or if significantly different technologies are used, further subdivision is necessary. For public service agency (e.g., a research facility) or an educational institution, if one set of clients are experienced professionals and another set are aspiring trainees, again a subdivision into SBA's is necessary.

For the Bike Lock Company, for example, while it is operating in a relatively homogeneous geographic area and has a given titanium/steel combination (and alarm noise) technology, there would be one environmental segment, SBA_1 (see Figure 3-1; Potential Environmental Segments for Bike Lock). If at some point the bike locks are sold to industrial customers for the purpose of applying them to small industrial vehicles, the analyst would recognize the very different prospects in SBA_2. Furthermore, bikes have been quite commonly used as basic transportation by working adults in many parts of Europe and South America for a long time. If the firm were successful locally, geographic expansion might be a possibility. If so, a geographic dimension may be necessary. Thus Bike Lock would recognize distinctive geography-determined SBA_2's (e.g., SBA_3 United Kingdom bike owners and SBA_4 United

---

*See H. Igor Ansoff and J. C. Leontiades: Strategic portfolio management. *Journal of General Management,* 4(No. 1):13–29, 1976.

| | | Geography | |
Application	Technology	US	UK
Bike owners and purchasers	Titanium/steel combination	SBA$_1$	SBA$_3$
Industrial	Titanium/steel combination	SBA$_2$	SBA$_4$

Figure 3–1 Potential environmental segments for Bike Lock Company.

Kingdom industrial applications) because of the differences in the type of customers and the maturity in the respective markets as well as the economic, political and social climates. If, moreover, an additional kind of technology is relied on, another subdivision is needed. The analyst will thus have a set of distinct but perhaps *dynamic and changing* environmental segments (SBA's).

Each SBA, as we said, presents distinctive growth prospects, threats, trends and opportunities. Each SBA has distinct customer/client groups which currently or potentially provide sustainable economic advantage to an organization which focuses on serving them. Thus, as an analyst proceeds with the following guides, an underlying question is, What has to be done *in each segment* to have a successful and defensible position?

Underlying question: What has to be done in serving each segment?

Missions, Strategies and Basis of Support

A variety of information is involved in an analysis of the current position of the organization. First of all, as our model has assumed, once a strategy (e.g., on resource deployment) is developed and implemented, it becomes part of the environment. In addition, this deployment has received a certain amount of environmental support or the organization would cease to exist. Two questions to help us to consider the present environment of the organization are:

Present deployment of resources is result of strategic moves.

1. What is the present deployment of resources? To each segment?
2. Where in the environment does the support come from? In each segment? These questions may be answered with an analysis of budgetary, sales and other data. At least part of these data are available (1) in some case write-ups for case analysts, or (2) from some existing organizations for field project investigators. Consider the usefulness of the following breakouts of data:

Location of support

   a. Budget and/or sales by service or product category and by SBA (or SBU).
   b. Division of budget among major units, major activities and among SBA's (or SBU's).
   c. Percentage of time spent on major functions, e.g., providing technical services.
   d. Sales by customer category and/or budget by client category.

e. Sales and/or budget by channel of distribution of service or product.
f. Cash flows, return on investment, and/or perceived benefits produced by each major unit of activity.
g. Major sources of financial and budgetary support, e.g., banks, stockholders, congressmen, government officials.
h. Support from employee groups, unions, consumer pressure groups, other stakeholders.
i. Availability of human and physical resources, e.g., raw materials.

The breakouts and the specific categories to use will depend on (1) judgment of what is relevant and important in the situation and, of course, (2) the availability of data. It is recognized that some data will not be available in case write-ups or in empirical investigations. The importance of the information is not diminished by this lack.

What analysis identifies mission?

The result from the analysis of whatever data are available will be at least a partial indication of the actual position of the organization in receiving support and in deploying resources in each SBA. This actual position is important for knowing the way the organization and the environment have defined the organization *mission* at the present time.

Vulnerability problem?

The data may be organized to ascertain whether the organization does have a potential vulnerability problem. In other words, to what extent has the strategic deployment of resources led to concentration of the organization's profits, sales, and cash flow in respective SBA's? An example is shown in Table 3-1. A similar table can be prepared to measure the dependence of the organization on key input resources (e.g., perhaps a governmental agency is highly dependent on an influential chairman of a congressional committee). In the main example used, however, the organization is highly dependent for cash flow, sales and profit on three of its SBA's. While this degree of dependency does not necessarily mean a highly vulnerable situation, further analysis of possible changing circumstances in each SBA is certainly indicated.

Some cases and some organizations will allow a comparison of present records with records from the past several years.

TABLE 3-1 CONCENTRATION OF ORGANIZATION'S PRODUCT MARKET POSITION

	%Sales	%Profits	%Cash Flow	%Invested Capital
Top SBA	30	42	35	25
Top 2 SBA's	52	60	58	45
Top 3 SBA's	72	69	78	50

Thus, for example, one may investigate the rate of growth or decline or the change in product/service mix. Trend information is more helpful in spotting potential difficulties and in judging why results occurred than are one-point-in-time data. For instance, one may notice that the sales trend for Product A is leveling off and the share of market for Product A is declining. These circumstances may be symptoms of a problem, and the causes of the problem need identification so that resources may be applied to finding and implementing solutions.

Both trend information on missions and the present definition of missions have implications in developing future corporate strategies. The missions may need to be changed. For example, National Distillers at one time deployed its resources into and recieved most of its support from manufacturing alcoholic beverages. Shortly after World War II it defined its mission in terms of technological knowledge. This knowledge was said to be fermentation chemistry. The firm deployed its resources in a different manner, received support and became a major chemical and pharmaceutical company. In this instance, a narrower definition of mission might have reduced growth potential.

Western Union recently did a thorough analysis of its future environment, resources deployment and environment support. The decision was reached that support for its present mission would be declining and that it would change from a "telegram" firm to a communications firm. Resources were deployed into such technology as communications satellites.

The Office of the Budget was analyzed by federal administrators for possible ways to strengthen its program toward improving effectiveness and efficiency in government. The decision was made to broaden the mission into nonbudgetary factors in management that are closely related to the budgetary factors and can be overseen concurrently. The Office of the Budget became the Office of Management and Budget, with more authority over agency policies and practices. As mentioned in the first chapter, broadening of the mission may be dangerous, and the threats or risks tend to increase as the organization gets farther away from its present services and/or products and clientele and/or markets. A solid position in a narrower field where the organization has strength may be more appropriate.

Basis of support. The current position of the organization includes, in addition to resource deployment and location of support, the basis of support or reasons for support. The questions are: What are the organization's primary distinctive competences, competitive advantages or special organization knowledges? And, what is the basis of support in each segment? Later we shall ask: To what extent will these factors continue to provide environmental support in the future? The former questions may be answered by a

Basis of support in each segment.

68 / ASSESSMENT GUIDES: THE CURRENT SITUATION

comparison of information on current missions with information on environmental factors.

What information should be gathered and how interpreted? We are looking for factors that stand out as providing a basis for support to the organization. We can save fact-finding time if we restrict ourselves to the key ingredients or requirements for success in the situation.

Restrict information gathering to key requirements for success.

A key requirement for a toy manufacturer might be capability to innovate. It might be, on the other hand, responsiveness to the clients' needs for education, or assistance for a government agency. Control of sources of supply might be the key for a natural gas company; financial flexibility for the conglomerate; location of bases for the military unit. There are a variety of possibilities that may merit consideration. Some of the breakouts of information that may be relevant and important are as follows:

1. Market and product/service situation (e.g., share of market, future growth, elasticity and substitutions, cost position, location, patents, advertising, new products and/or services, scope of line of products and/or services).
2. Market definition in terms of user benefits (e.g., what are the main reasons clients utilize the services of the organization?).
3. Production and supply situation (e.g., cost position, technological position, inventory control, sources of supply, labor relations).
4. Financial situation (e.g., holding and use of assets, working capital, budgeting, solvency and use of financial leverage).*
5. Research and development situation (e.g., payoffs from previous research and development, new possibilities).
6. Legal basis for activities and degree of concurrence with public policy (e.g., accountable to shareholders or Congress/Parliament, EEO position, antipollution activities).
7. Managerial capabilities (e.g., style, power, processes, skills, knowledge).

One breakout of particular importance may be the cost performance relative to competitors. The Boston Consulting Group experience in dealing with hundreds of businesses in the United States and Europe has led to the conclusion that in almost all businesses sustained differences in potential cost position exist among competitors: Identifying the "why," "where" and "how the situation may change" is a critical element in strategy analysis.†

Examine cost elements — importance and variability.

Total costs consist of several elements (e.g., raw materials, production of base products, conversion, distribution, marketing) which are of differing importance and which "behave" differently. The cost structure varies across the product range and across

---

*The Appendix to this chapter, A Program for Analysing Some Aspects of the Present Financial Condition of the Organization, is useful for this section of the assessment.

†J. Barnes: The Boston Consulting Group Approach to Strategy. Presented at Conference on Analytical Approaches to Strategy, INSEAD, Fontainebleau, France, December, 1976.

different customer groups. Analysis of these differences may be helpful in determining where the advantages are—specializing in that product line, that group of customers or that technology. If distribution and marketing costs are a minimal part of value added, as in the case of primary conversion of aluminum, it may be advantageous to focus on producing particular products and selling to anybody interested. Or, consider the case of coated abrasives: there is little variation in price of raw materials to users (the organization and its competitors) and little or no cost advantage on gaining extensive experience producing the base product. A competitive advantage may exist by focusing on the end market, i.e., developing skill at (1) using conversion technology and (2) distributing the specialized products to particular industries. Successful firms have done this.

Where is it possible to get a significant cost advantage?

You may want to buy or ask for and examine the competitive product/service to see what it is like. A mattress manufacturer on the East Coast, for example, buys competitive mattresses and tears them apart to see what materials and what construction methods have been used. He knows the cost of these "things."

Thus a breakout of information on cost position relative to competition may be quite useful. That breakout, if appropriate and possible, along with selected others may lead to a pattern of results

TABLE 3-2 INVENTORY OF ORGANIZATION CAPABILITIES AND RESOURCES

Financial strength	Money available or obtainable for financing research and development, plant construction, inventory, receivables, working capital and operating losses in the early stages of commercial operation.
Raw material reserves	Ownership of, or preferential access to, natural resources such as minerals and ores, brine deposits, natural gas, forests.
Physical plant	Manufacturing plant, research and testing facilities, warehouses, branch offices, trucks, tankers, etc.
Location	Situation of plant or other physical facility with relation to markets, raw materials or utilities.
Patients	Ownership or control of a technical monopoly through patents.
Public acceptance	Brand preference, market contracts, and other public support built up by successful performance in the past.
Specialized experience	Unique or uncommon knowledge of manufacturing, distribution, scientific fields or managerial techniques.
Personnel	Payroll or skilled labor, salesmen, engineers, or other workers with definite specialized abilities.
Management	Professional skill, experience, ambition and will for growth of the company's leadership.

From C. H. Kline: The strategy of product policy, *Harvard Business Review*, 33 (No. 4): 91–100, 1955.

that may be helpful in determinining the organization's strengths or competitive advantage. Such a pattern in simplified form for a business organization might be like that shown in Table 3-2.

Sears Roebuck did an analysis of its basis of support and built its business on a "money-back-and-no-questions-asked" guarantee to its farm customers. To the ingredients of a successful mail-order business, a simple statement of confidence in the customer provided a unique or distinctive touch. This statement of trust helped to build a favorable competitive image, adding support for their products and services.

How does the user benefit?

IBM has an organization that thoroughly analyzes its basis for support and defines the market in terms of user benefits. It is quite effective and efficient in design of product and in production. However, it is not the leader of the office equipment industry because of its physical product. IBM's analysis indicates that it is the leader because it excels in the management of data and information for business and government needs. What it gets paid for is a service rather than a product. It earns its livelihood with its knowledge of business processes.

Another way to come to grips with defining organizational competence or knowledge is to analyze those things that the organization has done well and those it has done poorly. An internal comparative analysis is illustrated by the following example:

> A medium size company working on high-speed planes and missile components had an uneven performance record. There were great successes in electronics but also great failures. Again guidance controls witnessed the same results. A new, technologically ignorant president was brought in. An analysis of manpower and responsibility accounting proved of little insight. Only when each project was investigated did the answer appear. Whenever the company had a tight deadline, the company did well. Its specific ability was to work under pressure. Without this inducement no one, it seemed, cared about the project or contract. Ironically, to achieve a leisurely, nonpressure attitude management worked hard to get government contracts. Apparently its strategy succeeded only too well.*

Analyze comparable organizations.

Some case materials provide the opportunity to analyze two or more comparable organizations in the same business, industry or government area which have had opposite results with similar undertakings. Peter Drucker, for example, contrasts what two quite successful organizations, General Electric and General Motors, can do well and can do poorly.

He cites these two companies as excelling in the field of development of new businesses. GE, for example, during World War II when diamond imports were declining, decided to start from scratch and make their own. In the short time span of five years, they were making synthetic diamonds commercially. In 10 years,

---

*P. F. Drucker: *The Effective Executive.* New York, Harper & Row, 1967 p. 116.

GE became one of the largest suppliers of industrial diamonds in the world.

General Motors, on the other hand, does an excellent job of making existing businesses it has acquired more successful than they were. It has the talent to improve companies that have already achieved a fair size and leadership position in an industry. (For this activity they have been accused of antitrust violations.)

However, the talent of GE and GM has not worked both ways. GE has not excelled at successfully building a business acquired. GM has not been a starter of businesses.* Thus, we have two firms successfully developing new business but using different competitive strategies, that is (1) starting from scratch, and (2) acquiring new organizations. Careful examination of aspects of "policy formation" other than competitive strategy, such as existing financial and personnel policies, the way objectives are set or the way they are organized may unearth reasons for differences in success when using comparable competitive strategies, and for comparable successes when using different competitive strategies.

These examples demonstrate the importance and the complexity of identifying the *present* basis of support in relationship to the other elements we have just discussed—resource deployment and location of support. Before we turn to the question of environmental changes that may affect the organization's mission and the basis of support for that mission, we shall extend our guidelines to examine current objectives and outcomes and the existing policy-generating structure.

Organizational Objectives and Outcomes

Objectives are hoped-for results or goals to be achieved, usually within a specific time period. The attainment of these standards or the lack of attainment is an important aspect of the present position of the organization. In assessing the present situation one must not set up some arbitrary external criteria or standards that may not be applicable; critical judgment of the appropriateness of such criteria and standards is necessary.

Our model has recognized that goals or objectives arise from complicated power plays involving various coalitions in the organization and in the environment; that is, we have said that negotiating to achieve goals takes place among top managers and regulating agencies, and so forth. We are assuming here, however, that top management has the largest say in which objectives are emphasized. Furthermore, if a coalition forming goals has a dominant member, the organization objectives will be close to his

What are management's objectives and targets? For each segment?

Ibid., p. 115.

72 / ASSESSMENT GUIDES: THE CURRENT SITUATION

personal goals.* One question with a high degree of relevance then is: What are management's overall objectives and targets? For each segment or SBA?

Are these fundamental standards consistent with environmental segments?

Of major importance is what management wants to achieve. Many cases give indications of managements' intentions. To the degree these general management objectives are or can be translated into operational targets and articulated to the organization, they provide fundamental standards against which actual performance can be measured. There is, as mentioned, a need to judge the extent to which the objectives are consistent with the current milieu. To make this judgment requires information from other elements in the policy process such as audits of the external environment and determinations on requirements for success. The policy analyst then needs to check back and forth on different elements. Long-term objectives (e.g., five years) need to be considered, but also existing deployments and environmental support for shorter term objectives (e.g., six months) need to be considered and reconsidered.

Setting objectives and targets is something that is done all the time. Many managers do it informally when they resolve to do something about the budget picture, go after new areas to explore, try to increase the rate of growth in sales and in share of the market, improve the service to the public, be more socially responsible, push flexibility in relation to the uncertainties of political, social and technological change, improve stability in resisting declines in the business cycle, and so forth. Pressures from various groups may have affected their decisions. Objectives and targets are interrelated and multifaceted; they may be congruent or in conflict with one another; they may be crystal clear or not definitively delineated.

An evaluation of objectives is intended as a means for assuring that intentions are on an appropriate basis—to improve the predictability that the objectives will eventually be met. Since the clarity, challenge and acceptance of the organization's objectives (as well as perceptions of the reward system) help to determine its direction of effort and its effectiveness,† it is appropriate for the policy analyst (to the extent information is available) to:

Need for clarity, challenge and acceptance.

1. List the main current objectives being concentrated on during a suitable time period. Include major areas that contribute to the success or failure of the organization, (It is necessary to include inputs on the future environment and requirements for success.) For example:
    Growth—What new areas are being explored?
    Profitability—A 10 per cent return on investment.
    Technical and Market Leadership—A certain number of new research projects and new products this year.

---

*See W. Hill: The goal formation process in complex organizations. *Journal of Management Studies,* 6 (No. 2):198–209, 1969.
†See, for example, C. Perrow: *Organization Analysis.* Belmont, Calif., Wadsworth Publishing Co., 1970; and E. Locke et al.: Studies of the Relationship between satisfaction, goal setting, and performance. *Organizational Behavior and Human Performance,* 5:135–138, 1970.

Service—Our clients and supporters (e.g., government officials) remain satisfied.

Management—What specific patterns of behavior (roles) are appropriate to expect in the future? What patterns of behavior are associated with effective management in this situation?

2. Analyze each objective in terms of being clear, measurable, and realistic but challenging. For example:

Clear—What will be the end product? Who is going to take action? When?

Measurable—What is acceptable evidence that there has been accomplishment?

Realistic but Challenging—Is it possible to complete the stated goals? Do they strain each area a bit beyond what key parties believe to be the limits of their capabilities and resources at the moment?

To detect the clarity of objectives may be difficult. Some general managers may be maintaining their flexibility by using the "art of imprecision" previously mentioned.* However, in order to identify these objectives it may be necessary to search for a significant pattern in their outcomes and decisions over time in the organization. For example, has consistent support been given to diversification into new markets? Or has a pattern of low prices and heavy promotion indicated a target of high volume for sales growth?

To detect whether an objective is challenging may require technical expertise in the area and may be a task that depends on technology which is stable and predictable. There are many instances, moreover, in research and development, marketing, engineering and other areas where even the most astute analyst will not be able to determine whether the objectives are challenging. The implementation of this guide is then somewhat restricted, however worthwhile theoretically.

Can you tell if objective is challenging?

3. Analyze each objective in terms of its relevance to the broader objectives of the organization. Does it directly support and contribute sufficiently to the overall mission of the organization? Is it socially responsible? Consider the priorities and whether it will be more effective if emphasis is placed on a limited number (say two or three) within a given time frame. For example:

Benefits—What will be received if objective is accomplished?

Costs—How does the cost compare with benefits expected?

Trade-offs—Is it appropriate to add emphasis on one objective at the expense of less emphasis on another?

It is possible that two or more objectives might be inconsistent. The same could be true for two or more parts of the strategy. It is possible that these apparent inconsistencies are actually meant as

---

*See Chapter 2. See also H. E. Wrapp: Good managers don't make policy decisions. *Harvard Business Review,* 45:91–99, 1967; H. Mintzberg: *Power In and Around Organizations.* In publication; and P. Lorange and R. F. Vancil: How to design a strategic planning system. *Harvard Business Review* 54:139–151, 1976.

counterbalancing forces within the strategy. An example of this might be the inclusion of profit "maximization" and imposition of costly measures over and above what would be necessary to uphold sales of a product. There could be specific reasons for the inclusion of these two inconsistent objectives. If they are to be counterbalancing, they should be rated; one should be given primary importance over the other. If not, the inconsistency should be resolved and one or the other of the inconsistent factors should be dropped.

    4. Review whether the objectives and actions are appropriate for today. Is what is being done now appropriate to the end results that the organization is trying to achieve? Where does the organization go from here? Determine whether significant factors have been included in the objectives setting, e.g., who was involved, what power plays were appropriate, what alternatives were considered, what assumptions have been made.

Caution—goal displacement.

Caution should be observed, for example, in checking objectives that have been made as specific as possible by quantifying them. While such quantification is often possible and desirable, studies have shown that goal displacement and inefficiency may sometimes result.* Managers may tend to overconcentrate their efforts in areas for which objectives have been quantified. Areas in which it is seldom possible to write quantifiable objectives, such as innovation and interpersonal relations, may be de-emphasized, especially if the reward system supports the attainment of the quantified objectives.

An example of excessive emphasis on quantifiable objectives is given by Steve Kerr as follows: "Attempting to measure and reward accuracy in paying surgical claims, one insurance firm requires that managers set objectives about the number of returned checks and letters received from policyholders. However, underpayments are most likely to provoke cries of outrage from the insured, while overpayments are often accepted in courteous silence. Since it is often impossible to tell from the physician's statement which of the two surgical procedures, with different allowable benefits, was performed, and since writing for clarification will interfere with other objectives concerning 'percentage of claims paid within two days of receipt,' the new hire in more than one claims section is soon acquainted with the informal norm: 'When in doubt, pay it out!' The managers of these sections regularly meet or exceed their objectives in the areas of both quality (accuracy) and quantity."†

One approach to evaluating the present situation and to helping the organization to become more effective is to involve participants

---

*See, for example, A. P. Raia: A second look at management goals and controls. *California Management Review,* 1966, pp. 49–58.

†S. Kerr: Management by Objectives and Other Children's Stories. Presented at the Academy of Management Meeting, Minneapolis, Minn., 1972.

in the organization (or an important segment of it) in deliberately and systematically analyzing the objectives, activities and results. This may be a group effort, or it may be a collection of individual analyses of the situation. The group effort provides the opportunity for an interchange of ideas, recognizes the complexity and the interrelatedness of objectives and provides opportunity for recognizing some relevant areas of agreement and disagreement. The top manager may, of course, reserve the right to decide. He may be subject to pressure and need to trade-off on certain issues. In any case if there is involvement of top managers and staff in the examination of present objectives and the development of new ones, it is a far cry from methods in which *the* top manager sets objectives arbitrarily and then concentrates his efforts on getting people to follow through. In contrast, evidence supports the involvement-of-others approach, which recognizes that people are more likely to commit themselves and to contribute more effectively when they have helped to shape the organization's purpose and direction and have set standards for measuring the results.*

Involve others in analysis?

Whether an individual is doing the analysis or there is a group interchange of ideas, there are many additional aspects to organizational objectives and outcomes that may require attention. Consider the relevance of the following questions to the current organizational situation.

Other aspects may require attention.

1. What was the actual performance compared with previously established standards? Also, if the objectives have been analyzed and clarified, was it possible to use these new standards (after a reasonable time period) for comparison with actual accomplishment? Were the objectives accomplished? If not, what led to being off target? What can be learned from an analysis of practices and structural arrangements in the past period?

2. What are the trends in performance indicators? Comparison of present records with records over a period of the last several years may indicate changes in external demands, product mix, financial records, physical facilities, types of grievances, union activity, and so forth. As indicated, trend information is more helpful in spotting potential difficulties and in judging why results occurred than are one-point-in-time data.

3. What are the strategies and financial resources of competitive organizations or comparable units in the organization? Frequently the relative success or failure of an organization is rooted in broad factors that pervade an industry or a geographic territory. Within the industry or territory there may be sizable differences in individual organizations' performances. Careful examination of comparable organizations' practices and policies may unearth reasons for such differences.

Compare with other organizations in same market.

---

*See, for example, H. Tosi and S. Carroll: Management reaction to management by objectives. *Academy of Mangement Journal, 11*:415–426, 1968. They discuss some of the difficulties of using an objectives approach as well (e.g., the interdependence of goals).

If possible, the analyst might rank two or more comparable organizations or organizational units in terms of effectiveness measures. Are there any policies or practices in these units that help to differentiate between them? Are there apparent differences in the way they set objectives and determine policies?

Are there performance differentials? Are there industry performances and organization performances that differ in products, services, application, geography, or distribution channels? Are there differences in types of customers?

What are competitors' strategies and financial resources?

Are there differences in organizational strategies? Are there distinct types of market policies, product policies, financial policies or research policies?

As an illustration of the overall assessment of the objectives and organizational outcomes we shall cite Peter Drucker's discussion of three chemical companies.* The three successful companies have many qualities in common and appear very much alike to the outsider. They are all in the same line of chemistry, have big research centers, plants and sales organizations, are about equal in capital investment, sales and return on investment. Yet each has special and peculiar abilities. One company does well at bringing a product to consumer markets. Another develops many new industrial chemical specialties but fails to "make it" in consumer markets. A third does well in neither market but derives great income from licensing developments from its research to other chemical firms.

These companies have experimented with their basis of support. But they have come to understand what they do best and what their limitations are. They set their objectives and measure their organizational outcomes accordingly in terms of their special ability: the first firm in the consumer market, the second in terms of the industrial chemicals it develops, and the third in terms of fees received from its research and development.

Policy-generating Structure

Questions indicate knowledge and skill needed for negotiating.

As shown in our model, a description of the policy-generating structure would include (1) the roles and commitments of relevant organizational participants and stakeholders and (2) programs or generalized procedures that are used. A description of this structure, if extensive, involves making several determinations. These determinations or questions indicate part of the knowledge and skill needed by those who engage in negotiation over time in strategy formation *and* implementation. The answers provide a description of how the choices are made in the current situation.

---

*P. F. Drucker: *The Effective Executive.* New York, Harper & Row, 1967, pp. 115–116.

There are limits, of course, on what the policy analyst can and should describe. He should consider the questions for (1) the extent of their relevance in the situation being examined, and (2) the extent to which valid descriptive content exists or can readily be obtained.

Several areas that could be explored in examining the current policy-generating structure are as follows:

1. Identify significant participants in the organization. For each segment, if appropriate, identify strategic stakeholder areas (SSA's), e.g., consumer pressure groups, competitors, community leaders, public officials, unions, legislators. For each segment, if appropriate, determine the pattern of distribution of perceptions of problems or issues and changes in these patterns. The organization is an open system subject to a number of competitive, economic, government and other forces that help to shape its character. Participants and stakeholders in the organization will tend to define and redefine the problems and issues from time to time. In addition, they may agree, as the Bike Lock executives did, on what the issues are and what their relative importance is, and what the barriers are to their solution.

Perception of issues by participant and by stakeholders in SSA's.

2. Determine whether the choices are made by one person or by a process of negotiating. Is there a tendency toward entrepreneurial, planner or adaptive behavior? Determine who are the most relevant participants, or those in positions of leverage. There may exist a series of power centers, both formal and informal, in the organization and in the environment. It is important to know not only where they are located but also the nature of their political resources.

How are choices made? Who has leverage?

3. What amount and kind of political resources are located at the various points or positions of leverage? The level of effectiveness will vary and the base upon which the leverage exists may include competence, information and charisma as well as official position.

4. What are the sets of "interests" at various locations? In various SSA's how have these "interests" affected the organizational goals? The "interests" are multiple and complex, so much so that individuals at certain locations may end up on any side of an issue. The fact that prediction is difficult means that a continual monitoring is appropriate if a participant or policy analyst is to have pertinent, current, reliable information. In addition, of course, there may be conflicting sets of interests. A simple example would be a firm in which the sales group was interested in greater variety in the product line (to improve sales) and the production group was interested in less variety (to reduce costs).

Interests of stakeholders.

What are existing reward orientations?

Questions directed at individual as well as group interests may be used. The organizational participants' behavior is influenced by the way they see their own self-interest. A more extended example

78 / ASSESSMENT GUIDES: THE CURRENT SITUATION

may help here. Consider the following list of statements* relating to reward criteria. Determine which ones best describe the extent to which the organization uses such criteria as a basis for rewards.

PARTICIPANTS ARE REWARDED FOR			OPINION		
1. Complying closely with policy	YES	yes	?	no	NO
2. Maintaining tranquility	YES	yes	?	no	NO
3. Allocating efforts and resources to long-term development activities	YES	yes	?	no	NO
4. Responsible management, e.g., staying within budget	YES	yes	?	no	NO
5. Being responsive to top management	YES	yes	?	no	NO
6. Making desired innovations	YES	yes	?	no	NO
7. Relating functional excellence to the marketplace	YES	yes	?	no	NO
8. Developing awareness and capability of subordinates for strategic work	YES	yes	?	no	NO
9. Maintaining high work standards	YES	yes	?	no	NO
10. Isolating strategic work for objective analysis and profiling of strategies	YES	yes	?	no	NO
11. Making progress toward goals and objectives	YES	yes	?	no	NO
12. Maintaining flexibility in strategic plans	YES	yes	?	no	NO
13. Knowing the right people	YES	yes	?	no	NO
14. Keeping subordinates informed on current objectives	YES	yes	?	no	NO
15. Relating functional excellence to the operating goals	YES	yes	?	no	NO

If the participants feel their rewards are based on not rocking the boat or on getting to know the right people, they may feel justified in spending much of their energy in that direction. If the participants feel that they need to achieve impressive short-run results, their efforts in this direction may be at the expense of a willingness to allocate time to long-term projects. Opportunities may be missed. For example, there may be delayed but substantial returns for allocating resources to regional service effort and program refinements, but at the expense of current service.

Thus, the policy analyst may want to know what the reward orientations or sets of interests are at various locations and to check on their appropriateness related to organization goals and actions.

Is conflict handled constructively?

5. Determine the strategies used in "negotiating" with the environment. Various ways of negotiating, such as using hierarchical command, structural devices, cooptations, coalitions and joint problem solving, were indicated in the discussion of the model of policy formation. An understanding of the strategies used in managing conflicting sets of interests in making strategic choices provides an important base for analysis and development of improvements in the policy-formation process.

---

*These statements have been adapted from J. Thomas Cannon: *Policy and Strategic Action.* New York, Harcourt, Brace Jovanovich, 1968. They are used here merely for illustrative purposes.

The following simply stated guidelines* are suggestions for evaluating and understanding the conflict management process:

    a. Within and between groups (e.g., divisions, departments, unions, stockholders) is some conflict considered inevitable and subject to resolution or even as a source of creative thought and action (or is it considered bad and consequently suppressed)?

    b. Do the intragroup and intergroup relationships focus extensively on conflict or are they also aimed at bilateral problem solving and generation of new mission opportunities?

    c. Are there regularized arrangements for continuous surfacing of conflicts, problems and new opportunities? Do these arrangements include concerted auditing of the external and internal environment?

    d. Are there regularized arrangements for continuous resolution of conflicts, for problem solving and for generating and seizing new opportunities?

    e. Are information and administrative systems open, visible and understandable to both unions and management?

As well as the specific patterns of behavior in dealing with conflict, description of the role performance of key participants may be made.

6. Determine how participants in the strategy-formation process are playing their roles and how these roles are linked to each other.

An organization may be described in terms of four basic participants: operators, technocrats, managers and influencers.† They are all playing roles in the organization. Operators carry out the basic, routine work (e.g., clerks, janitors, truck drivers). Technocrats perform technical work toward maintaining and adapting the organization (e.g., management analysts, organization development specialists, budget analysts, long-range planners). Influencers are those in formal or informal positions of leverage (stockholders, public interest groups, regulatory agencies, union officials, managers themselves). Managers are those with formal authority or the right to direct the organization toward effectiveness and efficiency (e.g., Board of Directors, executive director, president, vice-president, division head).

Four basic participants.

Later we shall concern ourselves with the coupling of the roles (and programs) of operators, technocrats and managers in the organization structure. You are probably familiar with some forms of coupling such as the traditional—functional, product, and geographic—forms and the newer, results-oriented and matrix forms. These will be discussed later when we deal with the question of carrying out the organizational strategies generated. Our main

---

*Some of these guides could be applied to evaluating labor relations policy. See C. A. Newland: Collective Bargaining and Public Administration: System for Changing and the Search for Reasonableness. Presented at the National Conference of the American Society for Public Administration, April, 1971.

†For an excellent discussion see H. Mintzberg: *Policy as a Field of Management Theory.* Working Paper, McGill University, June, 1971.

concern at this point is with the pattern of behavior of the managers, especially general managers.

Strategic, coordinative and operating levels of activity.

One way to understand the managerial role is to examine the organization at various levels of activity such as strategic, coordinative and operating.* In a smaller enterprise it is more probable that various aspects of the managerial role will be carried out by one individual. That individual would be involved in determining basic missions, organizational objectives and performance specifications, in planning his activities over the short and long run, and then in executing them to achieve the objectives. In other words, his managerial activity would range from strategic to operating.

In larger, more complex organizations the activities may be assigned to managers at different levels. At the strategic level the managerial role includes relating the organization to its environment and designing comprehensive action plans. At the operating level the managerial focus is on effective and efficient implementation of plans to achieve stated objectives. At the coordinative level the role behavior ranges from strategic to operating in trying to integrate the internal activities that have been differentiated by function and/or level.

Basic general management activities.

Every manager, *regardless of level,* within the discretionary limits of his position, is involved to some degree in the three basic general management activities mentioned before:

1. Defining the scope of this unit's activity (what it will emphasize).
2. Specifying performance criteria for his unit (what standards, limits, policies and procedures will be enforced and reinforced within his unit; what performances will be rewarded or punished and how).
3. Procuring, conserving and then deploying resources among competing demands within his unit.

The purpose of the policy analyst here is to describe in more specific terms the characteristics of general management work (e.g., what activities, how much time in each, with whom do they spend their time) and to analyze variations in managerial jobs and in effectiveness.

The complexity of the general managerial role has been captured in a rapidly growing body of knowledge.** Paine and Anderson† have summarized some of the descriptive findings, especially those that have *not* received much attention in traditional management literature or that differ from normative/rational models.

---

*See T. Petit: A behavioral theory management. *Academy of Management Journal,* December, 1967, pp. 341-350.

**See, for example, R. Stewart: *Contrasts in Management.* London, McGraw-Hill Book Company, 1976; I. Ansoff: Managing strategic surprise by response to weak signals. *California Management Review,* 8(No. 2):21-33, 1975; and H. Mintzberg: The manager's job: Folklore and fact. *Harvard Business Review,* 53(No. 4):49-61, 1975.

†F. T. Paine and C. R. Anderson: Strategic management: An intervention approach. *Proceedings of the Academy of Management,* Orlando, Florida, 1977.

The specific relevance and implications of these characteristics would have to be checked in each organization. The characteristics have been associated with three types of interrelated work activities: (1) relationships, (2) information processing and (3) decision making. The characteristics are:

1. Relationships: Job aspects that involve linking between organizational unit and a wide variety of contacts.
   a. Much time in meetings, unscheduled as well as scheduled.
   b. Some participation in operating decisions (for information gathering).
   c. Dealing with conflicting goals and demands.
   d. Concern with activities which seek cooperation of people over whom he has no authority: political behavior.
   e. Personally selling, trading and bargaining with people external to the organization unit.
2. Information processing: Job aspects that involve receiving, transmitting and storing of information.
   a. Reception of "weak signals" about discontinuities.
   b. Information received which is of doubtful accuracy.
   c. Preference for live action, current and specific information, the verbal media.
   d. Preferred use of informal information systems.
   e. Attention to the discretionary importance of information.
3. Decision making: Job aspects that involve initiating changes, allocating resources and handling crisis situations.
   a. Psychological readiness to face unpleasant and unfamiliar events.
   b. Receptivity to "weak signals" and taking measures to insure internal and external flexibility and readiness.
   c. Use of the "art of imprecision" and "muddling through with a purpose" (seldom spelled-out detailed objectives or policies).
   d. Not fully in control of own decisions.
   e. Some hazard of superficiality is faced; activity is characterized by an unrelenting pace, brevity, variety and fragmentation.
   f. Difficulties involving delegation of authority.
   g. Exposure: the possibility of serious mistakes.

One important conclusion to be drawn from these job characteristics and activities is that the general manager is a participant in the strategic management process rather than a comprehensive rational planner as the normative models would suggest. The realities of the job encourage the general manager to take advantage of opportunities, to maintain a hectic pace and to avoid wasting time. His use of programs is obviously affected.

We have discussed programs as generalized procedures that are used in response to a stimulus.* The manager, for example, carries out a decision-making program in response to information which

---

*For discussion see R. M. Cyert and J. G. March: *A Behavioral Theory of the Firm*. Englewood Cliffs, New Jersey, Prentice-Hall, Inc., 1963. Also see H. Mintzberg, D. Raisinghani and A. Theoret: *The Structure of "Unstructured" Decision Processes*. Professional Papers, Division of Business Policy and Planning, Academy of Management National Meeting, August, 1973.

indicates that he should analyze the environment. The technocrat carries out a sales forecast program in response to a request from management. The computer carries out a program in response to directions from a policy analyst.

General programs and more specific programs.

A program response to stimuli is economical in that it includes execution steps and outputs, both of the kinds which have proved useful in past experience. There are general programs and more specific programs. The steps in case analysis previously discussed illustrate a general program. In fact, the whole set of guides and methods for review and evaluation of strategy formation included in this book represent a general program (or a group of programs). Some other programs that the organization may use are more specific (i.e., more programmed). We have previously mentioned rather specific programs in capital budgeting, simulations, market research, forecasting and mathematical modeling. We could add specific procedures in planning and coordination, using pro forma profit and loss statements, pro forma balance sheets, breakeven charts, cash flow summaries and current operating budgets. Thus, any generalized procedure that is used by the organization in response to a stimulus is a program.

Several questions may be raised about the programs in describing the strategy-generating structure. Consider, for example:

1. How are they actually used?
2. How important or relevant are they to the organization?
3. How are they linked together horizontally and vertically? For example, the informational output from one program may be the input to another; or more general programs may include two or more rather specific programs.
4. How effective are they in aiding the strategy-formation process? How costly are they?
5. Is the organization not availing itself of significant programs which could prove effective and efficient?
6. What triggers managers to respond with strategy behavior?
7. What is the present system for scanning status?
8. How are environments, strategies and capabilities reviewed for balance?

Caution: Use of SOP's may tend to inhibit large changes in strategy.

The use of standard operating procedure (SOP) programs or routines in the process of choice may yield outcomes similar to past outcomes and thus inhibit large changes in strategy. G. T. Allison described the strategy formation process during the Cuban missile crisis.* When U-2 flights over Cuba showed that the missile installations were being laid out in readily identifiable, trapezoidal patterns, the patterns were compared with those observed in Russian missile sites and found to be identical. Presumably, faced with a

---

*G. T. Allison: *Essence of Decision: Explaining the Cuban Missile Crisis.* Boston, Little, Brown & Company, 1973.

novel situation, Russia responded with the application of routine procedures. Similarly, one could presume its Cuban strategy to be an extension of past strategies.

Findings in a study of a large research and development company, for example, suggest that freedom to depart from formal planning procedures improves management's ability to contribute strategy recommendations.* In this company, apparently being "bogged down" in formal procedures of annual budget projections, quarterly revisions with detailed explanations of the revisions, and monthly reviews of technical progress, reduced the time for scanning the environment and developing creative strategy recommendations.

Caution: Sometimes formal planning procedures are dysfunctional.

We have already indicated the need to study the role of general managers and the programs they use to carry out their roles. The top management role is not fully understood at this time. Management programs, as well, are generally complex in nature and ill defined at the present time. Work needs to be done toward understanding the dimensions of effectiveness for top managers.

SUMMARY

The analyst studies the policy-generating structure with its variety of roles and programs and, in general, analyzes missions and strategies, the basis of environmental support and the organizational objectives and outcomes and gains an indication of the current "state of things." The policy analyst, of course, goes beyond this and forecasts what the environmental demands and support will be. The important analysis of the impact of various threats and opportunities is presented in the next chapter (Part B of the Assessment Guides—The Changing Situation: Environmental Turbulence).

---

*As reported in D. Zand: *Policy Formulation and Managerial Behavior.* N.Y.U. Working Paper No. 72–22, 1972, p. 9.

APPENDIX TO CHAPTER 3

A PROGRAM FOR ANALYZING SOME ASPECTS OF THE PRESENT FINANCIAL CONDITION OF THE ORGANIZATION

We have previously discussed financial strength as one aspect of the requirements for success in pursuing alternative opportunities in the environment. For example, the analyst may need to determine the extent to which money is available or obtainable for financing research and development, plant construction, inventory receivables, working capital and operating losses in the early stages of a new venture. Analyzing the present financial state of the organization will provide a sound basis for making such a determination.

The following generalized procedures and examples provide a useful guide to the analyst or manager. The procedures are not exhaustive but do provide the kinds of information most commonly used during strategy formation. Potential outside sources of funds such as banks would require a thorough and professional analysis, including the kind of information generated with the financial analysis program, before deciding to provide financial support to the organization.

The authors acknowledge the cooperation of Merrill Lynch, Pierce, Fenner and Smith, Inc., in supplying these examples. A more detailed analysis can be found in their pamphlet, *How to Read a Financial Report.*

To illustrate the program we shall provide a balance sheet and profit and loss statements for the Typical Manufacturing Company, Inc. Then we shall discuss concepts and procedures such as those involving net working capital, current ratio, inventory turnover, capitalization ratios, leverage, net profit ratio and cash flow.

Exhibit 1

TYPICAL MANUFACTURING COMPANY, INC., AND CONSOLIDATED SUBSIDIARIES

Balance Sheet—December 31, 1979

ASSETS
Current Assets
  Cash, Marketable Securities at Cost,
    and Accounts Receivable $4,500,000
  Inventories 1,500,000
Investment in Unconsolidated Subsidiaries $300,000
Property, Plant, and Equipment
  Land .... $ 150,000
  Buildings 3,800,000
  Machinery 950,000
  Office Equipment 100,000
                                                                            $5,000,000
  Less: Accumulated Depreciation   1,800,000
    Net Property, Plant, and Equipment $3,200,000
Prepayments and Deferred Charges 100,000
Goodwill, Patents, Trademarks 100,000
    Total Assets $9,700,000

LIABILITIES AND STOCKHOLDERS' EQUITY
Current Liabilities
  Accounts Payable $1,000,000
  Notes Payable 850,000
  Accrued Expenses Payable 330,000
  Federal Income Tax Payable 320,000
    Total Current Liabilities $2,500,000
Long-term Liabilities
  First Mortage Bonds, 5% Interest, due 1985 2,700,000
    Total Liabilities $5,200,000
Stockholder Equity 4,500,000
Net Working Capital $9,700,000

There is one very important thing that we can find from the balance sheet (Exhibit 1); that is net working capital, sometimes simply called working capital.

Net Working Capital or Net Current Assets is the difference between the total current asset and the total current liabilities. You will recall that current liabilities are the debts due within one year from the date of the balance sheet. The source from which to pay those debts is the current assets. Therefore the working capital or net current assets represents the amount that would be left free and clear if all current debts were paid off. In Typical Manufacturing, the figures are:

WORKING CAPITAL

Current Assets	$6,000,000
Minus Current Liabilities	2,500,000
Working Capital or Net Current Assets	$3,500,000

Current Ratio

Probably the question in your mind is: "Just what is a comfortable amount of working capital?" Well, there are several methods used by analysts to judge whether a particular

86 / ASSESSMENT GUIDES: THE CURRENT SITUATION—APPENDIX

company has a sound working capital position. To help you to interpret the current position of a company in which you are considering investing, the current ratio is more helpful than the dollar total of working capital. The first rough test for an industrial company is to compare the working capital figure with the total current liabilities. Most analysts say that minimum safety requires that current assets should be at least twice as large as current liabilities. This means that for each $1 of current liabilities, there should be $2 in current assets.

The Current Ratio is current assets divided by current liabilities. In the Typical Manufacturing balance sheet, the figures are:

CURRENT RATIO

$$\frac{\text{Current Assets}}{\text{Current Liabilities}} \quad \frac{\$6,000,000}{\$2,500,000} = \frac{2.4}{1} \text{ or } 2.4 \text{ to } 1.$$

Therefore, for each $1 of current liabilities, there is $2.40 in current assets to back it up.

There are so many different kinds of companies, however, that this test requires a great deal of modification if it is to be really helpful in analyzing companies in different industries. Generally, companies that have a small inventory and easily collectible accounts receivable can operate safely with a lower current ratio than those companies having a greater proportion of their current assets in inventory and selling their products on credit.

Quick Assets

Current Assets	$6,000,000
Minus Inventories	1,500,000
Quick Assets	$4,500,000

Net Quick Assets

Quick Assets	$4,500,000
Minus Current Liabilities	2,500,000
Net Quick Assets	$2,000,000

Quick Assets Ratio

$$\frac{\text{Quick Assets}}{\text{Current Liabilities}} \quad \frac{\$4,500,000}{\$2,500,000} = \frac{1.8}{1} \quad 1.8 \text{ to } 1$$

Thus, for each $1 of current liabilities, there is $1.80 in quick assets available.

Inventory Turnover

How big an inventory should a company have? That depends on a combination of many factors. An inventory is large or small, depending upon the type of business and the time of the year. An automobile dealer, for example, with a large stock of autos at the height of the season is in a strong inventory position; yet that same inventory at the end of the season is a weakness in his financial condition.

There are dangers in a large inventory position. In the first place, a sharp drop in price may cause serious losses. And second, it may indicate that the company has accumulated a big supply of unsalable goods.

How can we measure adequacy and balance of inventory? One way is to compare it with sales for the year to arrive at Inventory Turnover. Typical Manufacturing's sales for the year are $6,500,000, and the inventory at the balance sheet date is $1,500,000. Thus, the turnover is 4⅓ times, meaning that the goods are bought and sold out more than four times per year on the average. (Strict accounting requires computation of Inventory Turnover by comparing annual Cost of Goods Sold with Average Inventory. Such information is not readily available in the published statements; hence an approved substitute is Sales Related to Inventory.)

Inventory as a Percentage of Current Assets. Another comparison may be between inventory and total current assets. In Typical Manufacturing the inventory of $1,500,000 represents 25 per cent of the total current assets, which amount to $6,000,000. But there is considerable variation between different types of companies, and thus the relationship is significant only when such comparison is made among companies in a similar industry.

Proportion of Bonds, Preferred and Common Stock

Capitalization Ratios. Before investing, you will want to know the proportion of each kind of security issued by the company you are considering. These proportions are sometimes referred to as Capitalization Ratios. A high proportion of bonds sometimes reduces the attractiveness of both the preferred and common stock, while too large an amount of preferred can detract from the value of the common. The principal reason is that bond interest must be paid before preferred stock dividends, and the preferred stock dividends before common stock dividends.

The Bond Ratio is found by dividing the face value of the bonds, $2,700,000 for Typical Manufacturing, by the total value of the bonds, preferred stock, common stock, capital surplus, and accumulated retained earnings, amounting to $7,200,000. This shows that bonds amount to 37½ per cent of the total capitalization. Capitalization means the face value of bonds and par value of stocks (both preferred and common) that a company has outstanding. But we must include also the amount of capital surplus and the accumulated retained earnings which have been plowed back into the corporation. The capitalization of Typical Manufacturing therefore consists of:

CAPITALIZATION

Bonds	$2,700,000
Preferred Stock	600,000
Common Stock	1,500,000
and	
Capital Surplus	700,000
Accumulated Retained Earnings	1,700,000
Total Capitalization	$7,200,000

The Preferred Stock Ratio is found in the same way: Divide the preferred stock of $600,000 by the entire capitalization of $7,200,000. The result is 8⅓ per cent.

Naturally, the Common Stock Ratio will be the difference between 100 per cent and the total of the bond and preferred stock ratios—54⅙ per cent in our example. The same result is reached by combining the common stock, capital surplus, and accumulated earnings and dividing by the total capitalization. Both capital surplus and accumulated earnings represent additional backing for the common stock. The capital surplus usually indicates the amount paid by stockholders in excess of the par value of the common stock; the accumulated retained earnings are undistributed profits plowed back to help the corporate growth. For Typical Manufacturing we add to the common stock of $1,500,000 the capital surplus of $700,000 and the accumulated retained earnings of $1,700,000 for a total of $3,900,000. This figure divided by $7,200,000 total capitalization gives 54⅙ per cent as the common stock ratio.

To summarize, the proportion of bonds, preferred, and common stock for Typical Manufacturing is:

CAPITALIZATION RATIOS

	Amount	Ratio (%)
Bonds	$2,700,000	37½
Preferred Stock	600,000	8⅓
Common Stock	3,900,000	54⅙
(Including capital surplus and retained earnings)		
Total	$7,200,000	100

Generally speaking, it is considered desirable for an industrial company to have no more than 25 per cent bond ratio, and for the common stock ratio to be at least as much as the total of the bond and preferred stock ratios. If these proportions are not maintained, a company may find it difficult to raise new capital. Banks are reluctant to lend money to companies with relatively large debts, and investors are reluctant to buy their common stock because of all the bond interest or preferred dividends that must be paid before the common stockholder receives any return.

Railroads and public utility companies are exceptions to most of the rules of thumb that we use in discussing Typical Manufacturing Company. Their situation is different because of the tremendous amounts of money they have invested in their fixed assets, their small inventories, and the ease with which they can collect their receivables. Senior securities of railroads and utility companies frequently amount to more than half their capitalization.

Leverage

A stock is said to have high leverage if the company that issued it has a large proportion of bonds and preferred stock outstanding in relation to the amount of common stock. Speculators are often interested in companies that have a high proportion of debt or preferred stock because of the Leverage Factor. A simple illustration will show why. Let us take, for example, a company with $10,000,000 of 4 per cent bonds outstanding. If the company is earning $440,000 before bond interest, there will be only $40,000 left for the common stock after payment of $400,000 bond interest ($10,000,000 at 4 per cent equals $400,000). However, an increase of only 10 per cent in earnings (to $484,000) will leave $84,000 for common stock dividends, or an increase of more than 100 per cent. If there is only a small common stock issue, the increase in earnings per share will appear very impressive.

You have probably realized that a decline of 10 per cent in earnings would not only wipe out everything available for the the common stock, but result in the company's being unable to cover its full interest on its bonds without dipping into accumulated earnings. This is the great danger of so-called high-leverage stocks and also illustrates the fundamental weakness of companies that have a disproportionate amount of debt or preferred stock. Investors will do well to steer clear of them. Speculators, however, will continue to be fascinated by the market opportunities they offer.

The Income Statement

Some companies refer to this statement as The Earnings Report or The Statement of Profit and Loss. We have called it Income Statement. It appears as Exhibit 2, p. 92.

While the balance sheet shows the fundamental soundness of a company, reflecting its financial position at a given date, the Income Statement may be of greater interest to investors because it shows the record of its operating activities for the whole year. It serves as a valuable guide in anticipating how the company may do in the future.

The income statement matches the amount received from selling the goods and other items of income, on the one hand, against all the costs and outlays incurred in order to operate the company, on the other hand. The result is a Net Profit for the year or a Net Loss for the year.

For example:

Sales for the Year and Other Income	$6,610,000
Costs Incurred	6,255,000
Net Profit	$ 355,000

The costs incurred usually consist of cost of the goods sold; overhead expenses such as wages and salaries, rent, supplies, depreciation; interest on money borrowed; and taxes.

The most important source of revenue always makes up the first item on the income statement. In Typical Manufacturing, it is Net Sales. If it were a railroad or a utility instead of a manufacturer, this item would be called Operating Revenues. In any case, it represents the primary source of money received by the company from its customers for goods sold or services rendered. Net sales is the amount received after taking into consideration returned goods and allowances for reduction of prices.

A secondary source of revenue referred to as Other Income or Miscellaneous Income comes from dividends and interest received by the company from its investments in stocks and bonds, which are carried as assets in the balance sheet.

Cost of Sales and Operating Expenses

In a manufacturing establishment, Cost of Sales represents all the costs incurred in the factory (including depreciation, which we have stated separately for Typical Manufacturing) in order to convert raw material into a finished product. These costs include raw materials, direct labor, and such factor overhead items as supervision, rent, electricity, supplies, maintenance and repairs.

Depreciation is the decline in useful value of an asset due to wear and tear. Each year's decline in value of a machine used in the manufacturing process is a cost or a loss to be borne as an expense chargeable against the production as an additional outlay.

Net Income

After we have taken into consideration all income (plus factors) and deducted all costs and expenses (minus factors), we arrive at Net Income for the year. In condensed fashion, the income statement looks like this:

CONDENSED INCOME STATEMENT

Plus Factors		
Net Sales	$6,500,000	
Other Income	110,000	
Total		$6,610,000
Minus Factors		
Cost of Sales and Operating Expenses	$5,800,000	
Interest on Bonds	135,000	
Provision for Federal Income Tax	320,000	$6,255,000
Net Income		$ 355,000

Net Income is the amount available to pay dividends on the preferred and common stock and to use in the business. To the extent that dividends declared by the board of directors are less than the net income, the excess is plowed back into the corporation and is reflected in the accumulated retained earnings. From the balance sheet, we have learned a good deal about the company's stability and soundness of structure; from net profit from operations, we judge whether the company is earning money on its investment.

The figure given for a single year is not nearly the whole story, however. The historical record for a series of years is more important than the figure for any single year. This is just as true of net income as any other item.

Even though a company shows no profit in a particular year or winds up with a loss for the year, the board of directors may deem it prudent to continue to pay a dividend to the stockholders. Such distribution comes from the accumulation of earnings of former years.

Analyzing the Income Statement

The income statement, like the balance sheet, will tell us a lot more if we make a few detailed comparisons. The size of the totals on an income statement doesn't mean much by itself. A company can have hundreds of millions of dollars in net sales and be a very bad investment. On the other hand, even a very modest profit may make a security attractive if there is only a small number of shares outstanding.

Before you select a company for investment, you will want to know something of its Operating Margin of Profit and how this figure has changed over the years. Typical Manufacturing had sales for the year of $6,500,000 and showed $700,000 as the operating profit.

Net Profit Ratio is still another guide to indicate how satisfactory the year's activities have been. In Typical Manufacturing, the net profit was $355,000. The net sales for the year amounted to $6,500,000. Therefore, Typical Manufacturing's profit was $355,000 on $6,500,000 of sales, or

NET PROFIT RATIO

$$\frac{\text{Net Profit}}{\text{Sales}} = \frac{\$355,000}{\$6,500,000} = 5.5\%$$

This means that for every $1 of goods sold, 5½¢ in profit ultimately went to the company. By comparing the net profit ratio from year to year for the same company and with other companies in the same industry, we can best judge profit progress. For example:

The American Iron and Steel Institute and United States Steel Corporation give the following figures of Profits per Dollar of Sales (that is, net profit ratio):

Year	Steel Industry Percentage	U.S. Steel Percentage
1965	6.0	6.2
1966	5.9	5.6
1967	4.9	4.2
1968	5.3	5.5
1969	4.5 (est.)	4.5

The margin of profit ratio, the operating cost ratio, and the net profit ratio, like all those we examined in connection with the balance sheet, give us general information about the company and help us to judge its prospects for the future. All these comparisons have significance for the long term, since they tell us about the fundamental economic condition of the company.

Interest Coverage

The bonds of Typical Manufacturing represent a very substantial debt, but they are due many years hence. The yearly interest, however, is a fixed charge, and one of the first things we would like to know is how readily the company can pay the interest. More specifically, we would like to know whether the borrowed funds have been put to good use so that the earnings are ample and therefore available to meet the interest cost.

The available income representing the source for payment of the bond interest is $810,000 (total income before interest on bonds and provision for income tax). The annual bond interest amounts to $135,000. Therefore:

TIMES FIXED CHARGES EARNED

$$\frac{\text{Total Income}}{\text{Interest on Bonds}} = \frac{\$810,000}{\$135,000} = 6$$

meaning the annual interest expense is covered six times.

Before an industrial bond can be considered a safe investment, most analysts say that the company should earn its bond interest requirement three to four times over. By these standards, Typical Manufacturing has a fair margin of safety.

Preferred Dividend Coverage

To calculate the Preferred Dividend Coverage (the number of times preferred dividends were earned), we must use net income as our base, since federal income taxes and all interest charges must be paid before anything is available for stockholders. Since we have 6,000 shares of $100 par value of preferred stock that pays a dividend of 5 per cent, the total dividend requirement for the preferred stock is $30,000. Dividing the net income of $355,000 by this figure, we arrive at approximately 11.8, which means that the dividend requirement of the preferred stock has been earned more than eleven times over, a very safe ratio.

EARNINGS PER SHARE OF COMMON

Net Income for the Year	$355,000
Less Dividend Requirements on Preferred Stock	30,000
Earnings Available for the Common Stock	$325,000
Number of Shares of Common Outstanding	300,000 shares

$$\frac{\text{Earnings Available } \$325,000}{\text{Number of Shares } 300,000} = \$1.08\frac{1}{3} \text{ Earnings per Share of Common}$$

Earnings Available for Common Stock	$325,000
Dividends Paid Out on Common	120,000
Current Year's Undistributed Earnings Allowed to Accumulate in the Corporation	$205,000

Cash Flow

You will observe from the net profit shown on the income statement that Typical Manufacturing was $355,000 better off by reason of the year's operating results. One of the elements of cost that were taken into consideration was depreciation in the amount of $900,000. Now, this amount does not represent an actual outlay of cash; it represents rather the annual write-off of an investment in fixed assets, showing the decline in value due to use during the year. Therefore, we can regard the current year as having generated $1,255,000 in cash, thus:

Net Profit for the Year	$ 355,000
Restore Depreciation Write-off, Which Is Not an Outlay of Funds	900,000
Profit for the Year on this Basis—Cash Flows	$1,255,000

Source of Funds and Their Application. A more significant presentation of cash flow for a corporation should show how the funds were used during the year. For example:

Source of Funds			
Net Profit for the Year			$355,000
Add Back Depreciation			900,000
Total Source of Funds			$1,255,000
Application as follows:			
To purchase new plant equipment		$675,000	
To redeem long-term debt		150,000	
To pay dividends		$150,000	975,000
Balance remaining added to working capital			$ 280,000

Exhibit 2

TYPICAL MANUFACTURING COMPANY, INC., AND CONSOLIDATED SUBSIDIARIES
Income Statement—1979

Net Sales		$6,500,000
Cost of Sales and Operating Expenses		
Cost of Goods Sold	$4,400,000	
Depreciation	900,000	
Selling and Administrative Expenses	500,000	5,800,000
Operating Profit		$ 700,000
Other Income		
Dividends and Interest		110,000
Total Income		$ 810,000
Less: Interest on Bonds		135,000
Profit before Provision for Federal Income Tax		$ 675,000
Provision for Federal Income Tax		320,000
Net Profit for the Year		$ 355,000

**ACCUMULATED RETAINED EARNINGS STATEMENT
(EARNED SURPLUS)—1979**

Balance January 1, 1979		$1,495,000
Add: Net Profit for the Year		355,000
Total		$1,850,000
Less: Dividends Paid		
On Preferred Stock	$ 30,000	
On Common Stock	$ 120,000	150,000
Balance December 31, 1979		$1,700,000

4

ANALYSIS OF IMPACT OF THREATS AND OPPORTUNITIES
    Economic Considerations
    Technological Advances
    Social Influences
    Political Input
    Competitive Factors
    Multinational Competition
    Social Responsibility

SUMMARY

DISCUSSION QUESTIONS FOR CHAPTERS 3 AND 4

SUGGESTED ADDITIONAL REFERENCES FOR CHAPTERS 3 AND 4

THE CHANGING SITUATION: ENVIRONMENTAL TURBULENCE

Changes in technology, legislation or social demands may affect entire industries and result in dramatic changes. In-camera development of pictures has significantly affected the photography industry. Recent Equal Employment Opportunity legislation has affected federal government agencies. Pressure from some citizen groups concerned with safety and pollution problems represents a potent factor in corporate and governmental planning. A lack of perceptive managers who can recognize such environmental changes may be disastrous. For example, the Baldwin Locomotive Works stuck with the making of steam locomotives until it lost environmental support and went out of business.

Predicting or recognizing change is difficult, of course, and requires constant vigilance. One problem is that the number of environmental factors (e.g., the domestic and international economy, competition, technological developments, government, legal and political changes and social issues) is so great that it is necessary to determine which are the most significant and to spend time and effort in analyzing them. (A large part of the work of corporate planning staffs is performed in these areas) The opportunities, threats and requirements for National Beer are far different than those for Pittsburgh Plate Glass The forecast of legislation may be very important to a government agency. The forecast of disposable personal income may be very important to an automobile company. The forecast of change in preferences of hair length and hair style is of extreme importance to those owning barber shops. (Short hair seems to be coming back in some locations.) Monitoring activities must focus on those environmental areas or variables that are deemed critical to the particular organization. In other words, those areas that will have a significant impact on the survival of the organization need consideration. Each threat/opportunity will impact on different strategic business areas with varying degrees of strength.

Select and monitor critical environmental factors.

ANALYSIS OF IMPACT OF THREATS AND OPPORTUNITIES

Estimate nature of impact.

Estimates are needed on the nature of potential impact of each environmental factor on each of the strategic business areas (SBA's). Ansoff* indicates several dimensions which may be included: (1) identification of the impact as a threat or opportunity or both, (2) magnitude of the impact (measured by the probable range of loss or gain currently derived from the SBA), (3) probable timing of the critical profit benchmark (using the range from earliest to the latest possible moment), and (4) identification of the present state of knowledge about the environmental factor.

Table 4-1 shows the results of such estimation for an organization with one major threat/opportunity for each of its four SBA's. The percentage of profit that each SBA contributes is indicated. As ignorance decreases. the range of the timing and profit impact estimates becomes narrower. The profit estimates for the self-generated opportunity in SBA's can be calculated within a narrow range—timing one to two years and profit impact two to three times current profit. On the other hand, the environmental factor impacted on SBA_2 is 10 to 15 years off and may be a threat or an

---

*H. I. Ansoff: Managing strategic surprise by response to weak signals. *California Management Review, 18*(No. 2):21-33, 1975.

TABLE 4-1 THREAT/OPPORTUNITY ANALYSIS*

		State of Knowledge				
SBA	Profit Contribution (%)	Sense T/O†	Source of T/O	Concrete T/O	Response Concrete	Outcome Concrete
SBA_1	50		Type of Impact T Timing 3-5 yrs Profit Impact .2-.5			
SBA_2	30	T/O 10-15 yrs .0-.2				
SBA_3	15				Opportunity O generated 1-2 yrs by firm 2.5-3.0	
SBA_4	5	0 4-8 yrs 2.0-5.0				

*Adapted from H. I. Ansoff: Managing strategic surprise by response to weak signals. *California Management Review, 13* (No. 2): 25, 1975.
 †Sense T/O—Conviction that changes or discontinuities are impending.
  Source of T/O—source identified.
  Concrete T/O—characteristics, nature, gravity and timing of impact understood.
  Response Concrete—response identified, timing, action programs; budgets can be identified.
  Outcome Concrete—profit impact and consequences of response are computable.

opportunity. Nevertheless, the impact may be quite serious and early measures toward enchancing the organization's awareness and understanding need to be taken.

Thus the general manager must be attuned to even "weak signals" from the environment. The range of possibilities in the changing situation is broad, as the following discussion of economic considerations, technological advances, social influences, political inputs, competitive factors, multinational competition and social responsibility indicates.

Economic Considerations

A significant factor in any compilation of environmental forces must include economic considerations. All too often we hear of the new enterprise or diversification move taken by an organization only to have it fail because of changes in the economy. Many small electronics firms were founded in the late 1960's with high hopes for participating in the growing aerospace and computer industries. Much to their dismay, these new firms soon found that they had made their move just as the economy tumbled into a recession, taking with it these two relatively volatile industries.

Many of the managers in these new firms assumed that the economy would expand forever. They did not really examine what the effect of a declining economy might be upon their operations. In the case of the small electronics firms, the recession was a prime factor in many of the cuts in capital spending made by their large customers. Aerospace firms found both private and public sector contracts difficult to procure. Large companies everywhere were cutting back on orders for new computers in order to trim their overhead costs. These factors led to a declining market for the struggling young firms, many of which were undercapitalized to start with.

There may have been bright spots in the misfortunes of the recession, however. There were many companies supplying goods for so-called countercyclical SBA's. These SBA's include product industries which do especially well when the economy is down. Examples would include used cars, low priced food and auto parts. However, many of the firms supplying these products were caught short when the recession hit.

Consider effect of economic conditions on each SBA.

Other similar examples could also be listed, including the inability of producers to fully supply the housing industry during its recent, dramatic turnaround. The point to be made is that the manager or analyst who is responsible for formulating strategy within the organization must have a thorough understanding of the effects of the economy on the industry and on his SBA's. The manager who does understand these interactions will have a distinct advantage over his competitors.

The analyst must also be able to distinguish between long- and short-term economic factors. In the previous examples of the small electronic firms. we should see that some of the problems confronting the organizations were short term in nature. The economy was not going to stay down forever. If the analysts had had the foresight to take into account a recession of relatively short duration, many of the firms might still have survived. If the factors had been longer lasting or even relatively permanent, such as a total change in the structure of the economy, it is conceivable that nothing might have been able to save the firms. Such shifts would include changes in savings and spending patterns brought about by psychological, technological and other factors. An example of these latter factors would be the "depression psychosis" that leads to increased personal savings. This, in turn, leads to a decrease in spending by consumers. If the products of the firm are sensitive to this type of change, its environment could be permanently altered.

Long or short term?

The analyst should consider the following points when analyzing economic effects on the firm:

1. How does the course of the economy affect sales of the product of the SBA? Threat? Opportunity? Are short-term or long-term economic effects more important?

Perceived effects.

2. Are economic effects direct or indirect? What is the timing of these effects? Do they lead, coincide with or lag behind economic trends? When are they coming? Impact?

3. Are these economic effects real or perceived? Can perceptions be altered before economic effects take hold?

Technological Advances

Economic inputs are not all that is required for a thorough environmental analysis. Among other key factors to be analyzed one would have to include technological advances. We are living in an age of rapidly advancing technology. How those advances might affect the opportunities available to the individual or the organization is a key input in the policy-formation process.

The story is sometimes told of the Boston patriarch who labored many years to build up a worthwhile estate to pass on to his children. When it came time for him to draw up his will, he chose to set up a rather complex, but unbreakable, trust for the benefit of his family. He left firm instructions as to how his estate should be used to provide for his heirs; he made what he felt was a thorough analysis of then current (turn of the century) conditions and stipulated that his assets should be invested in electric street railway companies. As might be guessed, it was not too long after his death that his required investments started going awry.*

---

*C. Amory: *Proper Bostonians* New York, E.P. Dutton & Co., Inc., 1947.

THE CHANGING SITUATION: ENVIRONMENTAL TURBULENCE / 97

The upshot of the story is that the plans for financial security laid by the head of the family were destroyed because of his lack of understanding of the nature of technological advance in a given area. The strategy adopted by the Bostonian proved inflexible when confronted with new ideas and innovations in the transportation field.

Need a flexible strategy?

The analyst must have a clear understanding, not only of the present state of technology affecting his products, but also of potential future advances. The analyst must also be able to consider the effect that seemingly irrelevant technological changes may have on his organization.

Many organizations have found, to their dismay, that technological events in seemingly unrelated areas have shattered supposedly carefully planned strategies. The previously mentioned example of the steam locomotive firm demonstrates this to some extent. Other examples would include many textile firms which were forced out of business because they could not see the effects that various, newly developed petroleum and chemical-based derivatives would have on their products. Synthetic fibers gained a foothold in clothing and related markets, and many organizations that had not previously been a factor in the market became significant competitors or supply agents. In these roles, they were able to determine the future direction of the SBA, even to the point of having significant inputs in styling owing to constraints or the lack of constraints on the new materials. Early permanent press garments, for example, could not be repressed or altered but had to be worn as manufactured.

Check seemingly unrelated technology.

Some questions to be asked can be grouped in two categories:

1. How are new products methods, new materials, new equipment, new products and/or services likely to affect the SBA (e.g., automatic data processing equipment, plastics, electric automobiles, transistors and information retrieval systems)? When? Response?

2. What use should be made of technological forecasts? The methodology for this type of forecast, which will be discussed later, ranges from mathematical formulas to informed judgment. It may be necessary to use in-depth analysis to develop useful information.

Finding answers to these types of questions will enable the analyst to grasp the potential direction of technological change in the environment. As we may see by analyzing these questions, however, answers may require information on other areas and topics. One of these areas would involve the various social factors in the environment that are shaping the direction of future change.

Social Influences

The composition and thinking society as a whole play a significant part in the policy-formation process. The values or demands of society are used as inputs in the objective-setting phase of developing corporate strategy. The resources or support available in a changing society can seriously affect the strategy of an organization when the strategy is designed to achieve only previously acceptable objectives.

We have seen many organizations forced to alter their corporate strategies, or cease operations altogether, because of changing social factors. The changing size and geographic location of the population have led to a wrenching change in agriculture in this country during this century. Large corporate farms have taken over the role of primary producer formerly held by small family units. This has, in turn, led to an entirely new SBA, often called "agribusiness."

Changes in education level and access to information have also led to differing effects on many organizations and SBA's. No longer can the analyst assume that the consumer has to rely on point-of-purchase information. Markets have expanded rapidly, so that analysts now must consider not only local social influences, but also those of a regional, national or even international origin.

Obviously many of the changes we are discussing here are related to change in other areas. It is quite difficult, however, to distinguish which changes were caused by what factors; the relationship and direction of effects between economic, social, technological and other factors is often quite hazy. This should not make the analyst feel that knowledge of social influence is too difficult to obtain; it should spur him on to seeking better answers to questions affecting his organization originating from social changes.

Examples of the kinds of questions and areas of interest to the analyst would include:

1. How are the size, location and age make-up of the population changing? Threat? Opportunity?

2. How is the educational level changing?

3. How are the values and norms of the population changing (e.g., attitudes toward the desirability for goods and services and the attitudes toward work)?

4. To what extent and when are such changes and other social changes likely to have an impact in the products and/or services of the organization (e.g., demand for mass transit facilities, social welfare services, investment advisory services, second homes, public insurance protection, and marijuana cigarettes)? Response?

5. To what extent and how should survey research forecasting be formulated and used?

Political Input

Social influences usually affect the SBA in several different ways; besides some of the methods already discussed, social changes eventually show up as political influences on all levels of government.

An analyst working in the aerospace industry might have used a great deal of insight in formulating strategies by noticing social trends taking place in the mid-1960's. A growing antiwar mood in the United States could have been a forecast of decreasing defense spending. This change in the views of society eventually led to a slowdown in United States involvement in the Vietnam conflict as a result of political pressures. This slowdown had adverse effects on both aerospace and defense industries.

Political factors are not relegated to appropriations by various legislative units. Large blocs of the economy are regulated to varying degrees by governmental agencies. Present regulations must be analyzed thoroughly to determine legal constraints on the planning process. Future trends in regulations must also be anticipated. The analyst is, after all, interested in future directions and actions of the organization. For this reason, trends in outside political influences should be forecast as much as possible.

There are very few government actions that come as complete surprises to the economy.* Foreknowledge of these actions can often give the analyst the added competitive advantage he needs to create and implement a successful corporate strategy. Questions to be answered to help in forecasting and understanding such actions include:

Forecast government actions.

1. What agencies now hold some type of regulatory power in the area into which we are heading? Is there leeway in the interpretation of these regulations? Are the agencies receptive to innovation in the SBA?

2. Who are the individuals involved in setting regulations or legislation in our future areas of competition? What might be their personal and professional views on our projected moves? Are these individuals likely to be replaced through electoral or other means? What other pressures or groups must they face?

3. Are there indications of wholesale changes in the governmental process (i.e., change of party in power, shift in power from Congress to the President, etc.)? What are the possible predictors of change? How can they be measured?

Competitive Factors

The various environmental inputs discussed to this point cannot be considered as if they were affecting only the organization you are

---

*The obvious exception would be President Nixon's announcement of the imposition of economic controls in August, 1971. There are other less known examples, such as the delayed announcement of policy changes by the Federal Reserve Board's Open Market Committee, which affected interest rates and the money supply.

Reactions to our strategic moves.

considering; all these inputs are felt to one degree or another by any organization in competition with your organization. Their reactions to these inputs must be considered if a corporate strategy is to be feasible and well rounded. Included in any analysis of competitive factors must be a knowledge of the reactions to the strategic moves planned by the organization. Once again the policy formation process is, of necessity, interactive.

"What if" questions may be asked; a simplified example of an attempt to evaluate the strength of a proposed strategy against what a competitor might do is shown in Figure 4-1. The figure shows weaknesses in our strategy if we concentrate on R & D applications and competitor A responds by emphasizing leadership in technology and focusing on specialized high-price goods.

Thus, competitive reactions play an integral part in determining the constraints on strategy formation. American Motors must consider what its giant competitors might do if it decided to attack a new segment of the auto market. Its most profitable years have occurred when it was not competing head on with the full line of products carried by the Big Three. Similar examples can be seen in other industries dominated by a small number of relatively large firms.

For these reasons, an analysis of the strengths and weaknesses of competitors is extremely useful. In the case of American Motors, it would be helpful to realize that its competitors might view its continued existence as a potential defense against antitrust action against the industry. The industry somehow looks more competitive with relatively small firms still operating. This potential weakness of competitors could be turned into a strength on the part of American Motors to fortify their strategic moves in the future.

Polaroid Corporation found itself in a position where it had to weigh heavily the reaction of its huge competitor in the home picture

KEY ELEMENTS OF PROPOSED ORGANIZATIONAL STRATEGY

What if Competitor A's Basic Strategy is	Build Continental Production Capacity	Expand Continental Sales Force	Concentrate R & D on Applications
Component supplier	Effective	Neutral	Neutral
Domestic only	Neutral	Strong	Neutral
Leader in technology	Neutral	Neutral	Weak
Specialized/high price	Weak	Neutral	Weak

Figure 4-1 *Assessing strategy against what each competitor might do. (Adapted from L. V. Gerstner, Jr.: Can strategic planning pay off?* Business Horizons *15 (No. 6):11, December, 1972.)*

business, Kodak, when it made decisions relating to future camera and film developments. It decided to begin producing its own film, knowing that the loss of the market to Kodak could well force Kodak to try to develop its own instant cameras.

As these examples demonstrate, a thorough knowledge of the policies and strategies of competitors is necessary during the policy-formation process. Other questions that should be asked include:

1. What is the competitive environment of the industry? Is competition concentrated among a few firms or is it spread over many firms? How are the competitors geographically dispersed?

2. What policies and strategies are followed by individual firms in the industry? Do they lead the industry in developing new production methods and pricing? What are their strengths in research and development, marketing, promotion, etc.? What are their production strengths? How can we improve our knowledge of competitors?

3. What is the financial condition of the various competitors? Will they be vulnerable to strategic moves because of lack of financial resources?

The basic idea is to determine what peculiar strengths or weaknesses competitors might have that would affect any potential actions by an organization. The human, material and financial resources available to the competition must be analyzed to be able to provide contingency plans in the corporate strategy against any moves initiated by that competition.

The combination of these external environmental inputs is designed to give the manager an understanding of the constraints facing an organization. The strategy-formation process is dependent upon an integration of the analyses of the various internal and external factors in the current and changing situation. Bringing together an understanding of these factors provides the basis for redevelopment objectives for the organization. It also enables the analyst to reformulate alternate strategies for achieving those objectives.

Multinational Competition

The world we live in is becoming increasingly interrelated. Frequently, what happens in one economy or society directly or indirectly affects results in other economies. This is especially true for the major trading partners of the United States, such as the Common Market countries, Japan and, increasingly, OPEC countries.

Competition for sales of many products, such as steel and automobiles, is now international in nature. Similarly, the United States no longer provides the sole market for most goods or services. Granted, the United States economy is the largest, by far, of any in the world. However, the Common Market, if it were one economy, would be as large or larger, depending on the method of measuring the gross national product.

If all societies were similar in composition, the major additional question facing organizations would concern transportation costs. Countries do differ, however, in values, government structure, needs and wants. For example, many firms have found that their trade name is totally inappropriate in some countries, owing to negative connotations associated with the name in foreign languages. Standard Oil Company of New Jersey had to discard many alternatives before settling on Exxon as a global trademark, for this very reason.

Operating in the international sphere also increases organizational problems. The basic management principles are made more difficult by the barriers imposed by distance and by the different customs, laws and economic systems that require different organizational structures. Where the President may hold total responsibility in one system, the Directors or the comptroller may be held responsible for the actions of a different firm.

Tax laws hold opportunities as well as constraints. Transfer pricing between different operating units of a multinational firm has been used as a method of overcoming variances in such laws. The governments involved are beginning to question such tactics, however. Clearly, they view such moves as transfer pricing as even worse than a zero sum game. What one country gains, another country loses, only more so. The multinational firm mananges to end up with an improved bottom line; the nation that loses tax revenues feels cheated. Whether that nation with multinational organizations within its borders attempts some form of retribution depends on the relative strength of the nation. Here, we must remember that several of the largest multinational firms have greater revenues than the gross national product of all but a handful of the biggest nations.

In all these instances the strategy analyst should consider the long-run implications of any actions. It was not long ago that the OPEC nations were weak and ineffective. Considerations of the desires of the Saudi Arabia government may not have been uppermost in the minds of the owners of ARAMCO while energy sources were plentiful. This attitude may have hastened the expropriation of their interests earlier than would have occurred otherwise. Their policy of building schools and hospitals for the Saudis may also have softened the terms of this expropriation, however.

In essence, multinationals must consider the long-range implications of their actions abroad. Positive short-run results may lead to undesirable long-term outcomes for the organization.

Social Responsibility

The combination of the external environmental trends and internal behavioral influences can lead to decisions that often do not directly affect the productive capability of the organization. The concept of social responsibility within the firm involves one of these areas. Nevertheless, this issue must be faced in a society where increasing emphasis is placed on the responsibility of the organization towards its environment.

Problems may arise, however, in attempting to implement these policies regarding the social responsibility of the corporation. The corporation, although legally a separate entity, is nevertheless composed of many individuals. The question arises as to the feelings of these individuals regarding their combined social responsibility. Just as agreeing on an overall strategy for the firm is difficult to arrive at, so is determining the social goals of the organization. First, the question arises as to whether the firm even has as an objective the betterment of the society within which the firm operates.

The claim is made that corporations are limited to performing operations as described in the corporate charter. The philosophical argument put forth is that the corporation is restricted to these areas alone. The rejoinder to these arguments follows the lines of the comments made previously in Chapter 2: The corporation operates within its environment; if that environment prospers, then the firm will probably prosper along with that environment.

However, the question still arises as to whose evaluation of social responsibility the firm should follow. A strictly rational discussion would lead the firm to choose organizational strategies that would lead to its own economic advancement. Examples of this point of view would include the advantages to the lumber industry of reforestation. This industry requires a continuous supply of raw materials for its long-run viability. It would, therefore, be economically sound for it to develop resources for further reforestation projects. The lumber industry assumes that there will be a long-run need for its products. However, it also draws much of its raw material from federal funds. The stipulations attached to these timber sales require reforestation. Also, the government holds title to the land, decreasing the capital investment of the lumber industry. All firms within the industry are faced with similar constraints. This is not true for all industries, however.

Whose evaluation to use?

There are several factors that the individual firm must consider when faced with socially oriented investments, particularly those designed to improve the physical environment. One involves the actions of competing firms, both at home and abroad.

If the environmental actions are not required by law, the question arises as to the competitive position a firm might find itself in if it were the only firm taking environmental action. The policy analyst must question whether the various image, personnel and product gains, if any, will overcome potential cost disadvantages relative to competition. At this stage, the individual firm must truly test its commitment to environmental betterment.

Some policies rationalized on profitability or on legal grounds.

On a larger scale, the country itself must test its commitment when it requires environmental protection through regulations and legislation. If these actions place an entire domestic industry at a disadvantage relative to foreign competition, the country must consider who will be asked to pay for that disadvantageous position.

The analyst working in any of these situations must eventually evaluate the effectiveness and feasibility of his organizational strategy. To do this, he must have some idea of the long-term demand for his product; often, however, social and environmental considerations inhibit his ability to forecast the long-term demand. The petroleum industry, as an example, finds that it needs more refining capacity domestically to meet a growing demand for its various products. It feels constrained in investing in increased capacity, however, because it does not know what types of regulations the federal government may place on its various products, such as gasoline. This problem becomes particularly acute since the cost of an efficient refinery is in excess of $100 million and requires three years to build. This kind of uncertainty present in the environment makes strategic decisions extremely difficult, if not impossible, to make.

Social issues add to uncertainty.

The utility industry finds itself in a similar position. The main differences are that the time involved is longer and the costs are greater. These factors heightened the investment problems and led to a virtual halt in planning for new nuclear power plants in 1971.

The policies just noted have all involved commitments directly related to the product itself, or government regulations involving the product or the production process. As such, these environmental and social policies can be rationalized on profitability or legal grounds.

Less easily rationalized policies involve decisions to support local, regional and national causes not directly related to the product or service supplied by the firm. The question arises not only as to what extent the firm should support various charitable, educational and social causes, but whether they should be supported at all.

Support which causes?

During past centuries support of these causes was often the sole responsibility of the private sector. During this century, however, the government has assumed support in many of these areas. This has led many firms to withhold resources from what are considered nonessential actions. Basically, the decision eventually facing the firm breaks down into several questions shown in Figure 4–2.

These questions have to be considered by the policy analyst if he is to be successful. Likewise, the student of policy formation has to consider these questions if he is to present a total analysis of the environment surrounding *any particular situation.*

Usually long-term investment.

The problem arising with the strategic importance of social responsibility issues is that investments in this area are usually long term in nature. Also, the returns from these investments rarely show up on any financial statements except as expenses. The question arises as to how to take advantage of these investments in the eyes of the investing public.

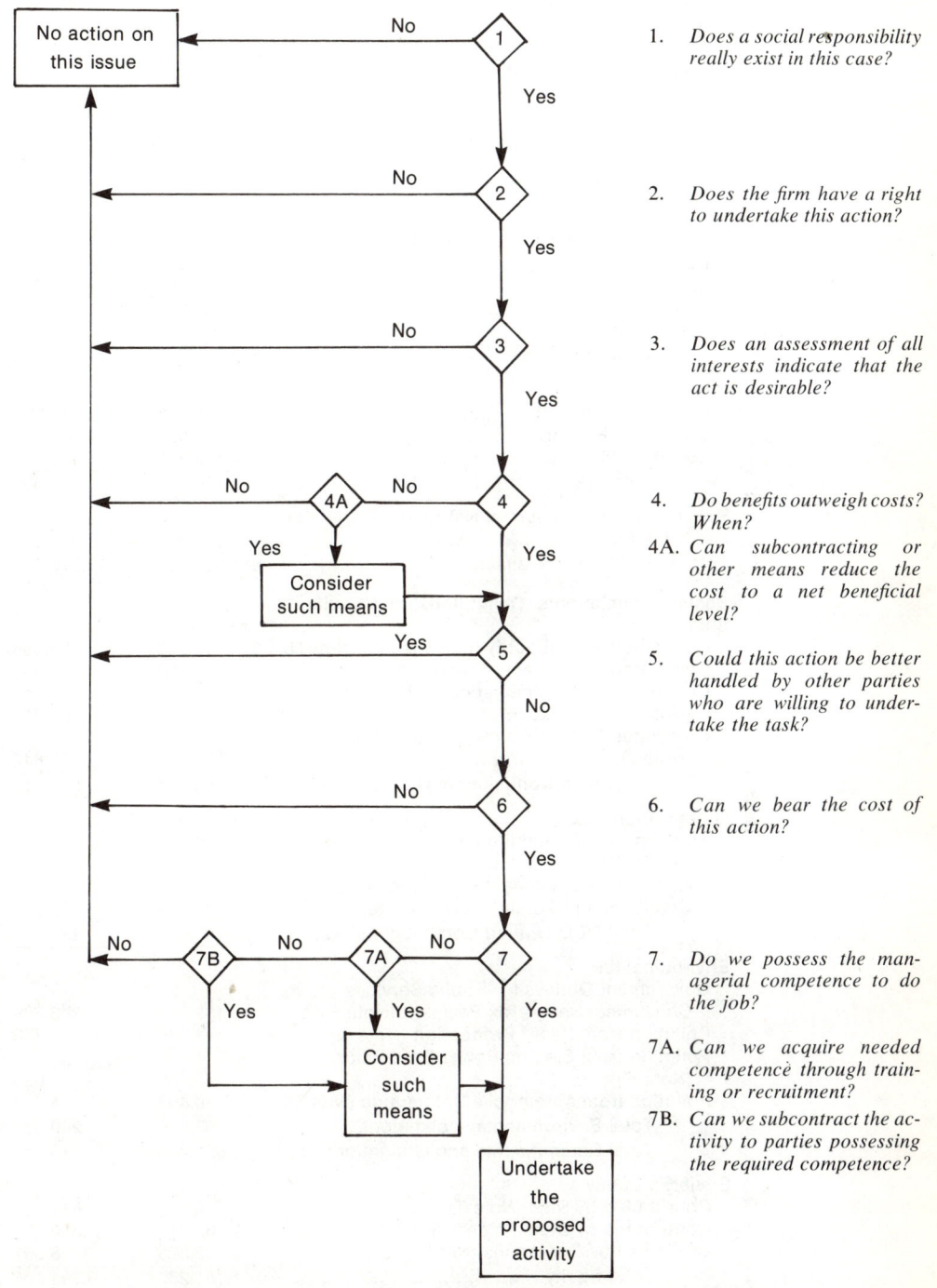

THE CHANGING SITUATION: ENVIRONMENTAL TURBULENCE / 105

1. *Does a social responsibility really exist in this case?*
2. *Does the firm have a right to undertake this action?*
3. *Does an assessment of all interests indicate that the act is desirable?*
4. *Do benefits outweigh costs? When?*
4A. *Can subcontracting or other means reduce the cost to a net beneficial level?*
5. *Could this action be better handled by other parties who are willing to undertake the task?*
6. *Can we bear the cost of this action?*
7. *Do we possess the managerial competence to do the job?*
7A. *Can we acquire needed competence through training or recruitment?*
7B. *Can we subcontract the activity to parties possessing the required competence?*

Figure 4-2 Decision-Making Flow Chart (Adapted from Aldag, R. J.; Jackson, D. W., Jr., "A Managerial Framework for Social Decision Making," MSU Business Topics, *Spring 1975, p. 34.*

Abt Associates Inc. Social Balance Sheet

Year ended December 31, 1971 with comparative figures for 1970

Social Assets Available	1971	1970
Staff		
Available within one year (Note I)	$ 2,594,390	$ 2,312,000
Available after one year (Note J)	6,368,511	5,821,608
Training investment (Note K)	507,405	305,889
	9,470,306	8,439,497
Less Accumulated Training Obsolescence (Note K)	136,995	60,523
Total Staff Assets	9,333,311	8,378,974
Organization		
Social Capital Investment (Note L)	1,398,230	1,272,201
Retained Earnings	219,136	—
Land	285,376	293,358
Buildings at cost	334,321	350,188
Equipment at cost	43,018	17,102
Total Organization Assets	2,280,081	1,932,849
Research		
Proposals (Note M)	26,878	15,090
Child Care Research	6,629	—
Social Audit	12,979	—
Total Research	46,486	15,090
Public Services Consumed Net of Tax Payments (Note E)	152,847	243,399
Total Social Assets Available	**$11,812,725**	**$10,570,312**
Social Commitments, Obligations, and Equity		
Staff		
Committed to Contracts within one year (Note N)	$ 43,263	$ 81,296
Committed to Contracts after one year (Note O)	114,660	215,459
Committed to Administration within one year (Note N)	62,598	56,915
Committed to Administration after one year (Note O)	165,903	150,842
Total Staff Commitments	386,424	504,512
Organization		
Working Capital Requirements (Note P)	60,000	58,500
Financial Deficit	—	26,814
Facilities and Equipment Committed to Contracts and Administration (Note N)	37,734	36,729
Total Organization Commitments	97,734	122,043
Environmental		
Government Outlays for Public Services Consumed, Net of Tax Payment (Note E)	152,847	243,399
Pollution from Paper Production (Note Q)	1,770	770
Pollution from Electric Power Production (Note R)	2,200	1,080
Pollution from Automobile Commuting (Note S)	10,493	4,333
Total Environmental Obligations	167,310	249,582
Total Commitments and Obligations	651,468	876,137
Society's Equity		
Contributed by Staff (Note T)	8,946,887	7,874,462
Contributed by Stockholders (Note U)	2,182,347	1,810,806
Generated by Operations (Note V)	32,023	8,907
Total Equity	11,161,257	9,694,175
Total Commitments, Obligations and Equity	**$11,812,725**	**$10,570,312**

Figure 4-3 How one company measures its social contributions. (From Business Week, *September 23, 1972.*)

One solution arrived at by some authors, consultants and businessmen is to perform a social audit for the firm.* The purpose of the social audit is to measure "the impact of its [the firm's] social programs in terms of costs, benefits, performance, or even profits."† Although no specific ground rules or regulations have been developed for the social audit, examples have been developed. One such example is reproduced here (Fig. 4-3). It was developed by Abt Associates, Inc., to measure their own resources available for social issues.

This type of policy aid could prove to be quite valuable to top managers in plotting strategic decisions and negotiations. Much study must be done before a realistic social audit can be accepted and implemented for all firms. The lack of an effective measurement device should not deter firms from engaging in socially responsible efforts, however.

The key factor is not to feel unnecessary psychological constraints. The students should include a realistic analysis of the social trends of the environment, as previously indicated, as an input into the strategy-formation process. The fact that this topic is included in the Business Policy course should not be considered as simply a gesture toward salving the social conscience of the instructor, the students or the business community as a whole. Social responsibility should be designed to provide an important constraint, or opportunity, for the strategy-formation process.

Constraint or opportunity.

In the final analysis, only those organizations that survive fulfill their responsibility to society. Socially oriented decisions and negotiations have to be consistent with the basic mission of the organization. If the organization is in the profit sector, social objectives cannot be followed to the point where they endanger overall profitability. Similarly, for nonprofit organizations social objectives should not predominate over the primary service objective. A hospital that services too many patients who cannot pay for those services may find it is no longer able to serve the greater community. This is a case in which society must shoulder its share of social costs to insure services to society as a whole.

Likewise, organizations that do not deserve to survive should be allowed to pass from the scene. These types of decisions should be made on the basis of societal costs and benefits concerning the product, service or process provided by the organization.

Policy analysts should understand that most strategic decisions entail some forms of social cost. The question that society must answer is just who will bear these costs: the stockholders, consumers or society as a whole.

---

*For a more extensive discussion, see R. A. Bauer and D. H. Fenn, Jr.: *The Corporate Social Audit.* New York, Russell Sage Foundation, 1972.

†The first attempts at a corporate "social audit." *Business Week,* September 12, 1972, p. 89.

If social costs are to be considered as part of the strategy-formation process, the organization should structure its evaluation process to reward performance in this area. As we have already noted, social responsibility usually entails long-range factors. Evaluation based on short-term, bottom line results are unlikely to generate socially responsible actions A manager confronted with a potential safety defect in a product may be unwilling to initiate a recall if it will negatively affect costs in the short run. In this example, we can see that performance evaluation may be dysfunctional to the long-term objectives of the firm.

SUMMARY

The general assessment guides introduced in the last two chapters are intended to help the reader to begin the process of understanding and analyzing an organization's present situation and to forecast what the environmental demands and support might be. The guides, intended for general use in both business and public bodies, include many of the more basic strategic variables or questions that may be pursued in an assessment.

Can you close the strategy gap and capability gap ahead of the environmental turbulence?

Considerable judgment is required, however, in tailoring the assessment to the unique circumstances of the organization. Some methods or variables may be eliminated for specific assessments; some may be added; some may be judged as more important than others. Consideration of the selected elements in the review and analysis of the relationships between the current position, desired position, achievements, problems, opportunities, threats, capabilities and requirements for success should permit an overall assessment of environmental segments, organizational strategies and the strategy formation process. We now turn to Part C of our assessment guides, Strategy Development (Chapter 5).

DISCUSSION QUESTIONS FOR CHAPTERS 3 AND 4

1. Discuss the need for assessment guides. Who uses them? In what manner are they used by different groups?

2. In what manner does assessment tie in with the descriptive model of policy formation presented in Chapter 2?

3. What effect does the current position of the organization have on the overall assessment? Where does the statement of missions occur in the assessment?

4. Discuss the purpose of objectives in the assessment of organizational strategies. What factors should be considered when determining the effectiveness of stated objectives?

5. How are conflicts resolved in the objective-setting process?

6. Discuss the relevance of external factors in the strategy-formation process. What key questions should be considered when relating organizational strategy with these external factors?

7. Take a stand on the questions of the type and degree of social responsibility for business corporations. Defend your position. What pressures might you be under as a manager in an attempt to effectively implement your ideas?

8. Set up a threat/opportunity table for the organization you work for or for one with which you are familiar. Analyze the impact of various threats and opportunities. What responses should be made?

Suggested Additional References For Chapters 3 and 4

Ackerman, R. W.: Social Responsiveness in the Large Corporation. Professional Papers of the Academy of Management, Division of Business Policy and Planning, Boston, 1973.
Boehm, George, A. W.: Shaping decisions with systems analysis. *Harvard Business Review*, 54(No. 5):91, 1976.
Bowman, E. H., and Haire, M.: A strategic posture toward corporate social responsibility. *California Management Review*, 18(No. 2):49, 1975.
Butcher, B.: Corporate social audit. *Journal of General Management*, 2(No. 1):80, 1974.
Chapman, P. F.: A method for exploring the future. *Long-Range Planning*, 9(No. 1):2, 1976.
Friedman, M.: The social responsibility of business is to increase its profits. *New York Times Magazine*, September 13, 1970.
Gossett, W. T.: Legal counsel as a social adjuster. *Harvard Business Review*, 53(No. 3):6, 1975.
Hershey, R.: Planning for the unthinkable. *Harvard Business Review*, 53(No. 4):20, 1975.
Hussey, D. E.: Strategic planning and inflation. *Long-Range Planning*, 9(No. 2):24, 1976.
Kabus, I.: You can bank on uncertainty. *Harvard Business Review*, 54(No. 3):951, 1976.
Levitt, T.: The dangers of social responsibility. *Harvard Business Review*, September-October, 1958.
Levitt, T.: Marketing myopia. *Harvard Business Review*, 53(No. 4):26, 1975.
Migliore, H. B.: Planning and management by objectives. *Long-Range Planning*, 9(No. 4):58, 1976.
Miller, J. G., and Sprague, L. G. Behind the growth in materials requirements planning. *Harvard Business Review*, 53(No. 5):83, 1975.
Morris, G. K.: Forecasting the impact of social change. *Long-Range Planning*, 8(3):64, 1975.
Nagashima, Y.: Response of Japanese companies to environmental changes. *Long-Range Planning*, 9(1):20, 1976.
Nutt, A. B., Lenz, R. C., Jr., Lanford, H. W., and Cleary, M. J.: Data sources for trend extrapolation in technological forecasting. *Long-Range Planning*, 9(1):72, 1976.
Sandbrook, R.: Key environmental issues for business. *Journal of General Management*, 2(1):64, 1974.
Taylor, B.: Managing the process of corporate development. *Long-Range Planning*, 9(3):81, 1976.
Zettergren, L.: Financial issues in strategic planning. *Long-Range Planning*, 8(3):23, 1975.

5

OUTLINE OF STRATEGY DEVELOPMENT
STRATEGIC MIX AND THE PORTFOLIOS
    Experience Curves
    Reallocation Strategies
    Flexibility Strategies
    Making Trade-offs on Objectives

SEGMENTATION PROCESS AND BUSINESS STRATEGIES
    Defensible Barriers
    Narrowing the Choice
    Synergistic Possibilities
    Gaining and Maintaining a Defensible (and Profitable) Position

DETAILING PROVISIONS FOR PROCURING AND ALLOCATING RESOURCES: LINKING STRATEGY WITH OPERATIONS

A COMPUTER PROGRAM FOR REFORMULATING ORGANIZATIONAL STRATEGY

SUMMARY

DISCUSSION QUESTIONS

APPENDIX 1: A REVIEW OF MARKETING CONCEPTS AND IDEAS

APPENDIX 2: ASSESSMENT GUIDES FOR SMALL AND MEDIUM-SIZED BUSINESSES

APPENDIX 3: HELPING SMALL BUSINESSES COPE

STRATEGY DEVELOPMENT

No certainty on best approach.

Strategy (or policy) makers have been seen as interrelating important or critical decisions in a continuous process of mediating and allocating among conflicting sets of interests. Organizational strategy that results from the process is viewed here as an integrative concept encompassing not only the objectives but also a selection of combinations of resource deployments for achieving those objectives. The organizational strategy may be determined formally in a strategy planning program or intuitively in the brain of a top manager in the organization. Frankly, there is no complete certainty at this point on the best approach to use.

Judgment, experience and well guided discussion are important to success.

However, the assessment guides presented thus far (i.e., environmental segmentation; strategies and basis of support; objective and outcomes; policy-generating structures; opportunities, threats or problems) provide a sound basis for analysis of strategic choices. Though much staff work may be done by others and though there may be much line involvement, the strategic choices frequently are made by top executives working at the conference table. The primary keys to success seem to be judgment, experience, and well guided discussion rather than staff work and mathematical models.* The joint conference effort is especially successful for

---

*See P. Holden, C. A. Peterson, and G. E. Germane: *Top Management.* New York, McGraw-Hill Book Company, 1968; R. Mann (ed.): *The Arts of Top Management.* New York, McGraw-Hill Book Company, 1971, and W. Klein and D. Murphy (eds.): *Policy: Concepts in Organizational Guidance.* Boston, Little, Brown and Company, 1973.

smaller and medium-size companies.* Larger organizations, of course, may do extensive staff work with mathematical and statistical analysis, but still rely heavily on discussion and judgment.

In some cases the analysis of strategy development is written down as a planning document. This chapter will present an outline of such a document to illustrate the elements in strategy development. Following the outline is a discussion of various aspects of those elements. The objective is to provide general direction focused on Part C of the Assessment Guides—Strategy Development. Subsequent chapters will provide a more specific methodology for information gathering and processing toward enhancing environmental awareness and self-awareness and toward implementing strategy. Appendix 1 to this chapter reviews some basic concepts in marketing. Appendices 2 and 3 highlight especially relevant ideas for small and medium-sized businesses.

Before the outline is presented it is important to distinguish between two distinct areas of strategy development: (1) *business unit strategy development, and (2) portfolio strategy development*. The basic differences? Units are concerned with issues such as the marketing mix, cost position, competitive position and mechanics of changing, and new product market segments. By contrast, the organization is (or should be) concerned with the continuing process of resource reallocation among different business units to improve the organizational portfolios. One portfolio would include the mixture of strategic business areas (or units). Others could include the strategic resource areas (SRA's, indicating the importance, availability and cost of human, physical and monetary inputs) and the strategic stakeholder areas (SSA's previously discussed). The main question for the organization is allocating resources, i.e., cash, management effort, skilled personnel and scarce materials, as well as capital for investment. Priorities must be set and decisions must be made about acquisition and mergers, closure or cut back of weak businesses, development of new ventures, and "negotiating" with stakeholders (Chapter 2). *The organizational portfolios.*

Caution should be used in "making the strategy explicit" Mintzberg points to the danger and naivety in that popular prescription.† Frequently observed is a push-pull model of strategy development. The general manager(s) state(s) an explicit strategy (perhaps growth) a priori and is then pulled into a significant commitment by the rest of the strategy-generating structure or bureaucracy. The very fact of making strategy explicit—even an *Caution!*

---

*See F. F. Gilmore: Formulating strategy in a small organization. *Harvard Business Review*, June, 1971.

†See H. Mintzberg: Strategy Formulation as an Evolutionary Process. Conference on Strategy Formulation, Aix-en Provence, France, May, 1976.

implicit one that is evident to all—provides a clear invitation for *bureaucratic momentum* to "take over for better or worse." A notable example is Lyndon Johnson in 1968 finding that his escalation strategy somehow had been implemented beyond his intentions. It had been *overrealized*.

OUTLINE OF STRATEGY DEVELOPMENT

The outline of strategy development is suggestive. It may (and should) be adapted to the particular and unique situation of the organizations under consideration. The outline follows:

1. Strategic Mix and the Portfolios

Develop a compendium of strategic alternatives.

A compendium of strategies or policies is useful as a tool in considering alternatives for the organization and for each SBA (or unit). The compendium could include allocations to change the portfolio mix as well as movements among product/market segments and the enhancement of the units' situation within a given segment. Each alternative costs money; each can be expected to influence the numbers in a certain way.

Important broad strategic alternatives— reallocation, penetration, stability, diversification, flexibility, expansion, integration, divestiture.

The more promising alternatives would be described by adding more specifics to one or more of the following: broad strategic alternatives: (a) reallocation of resources from one business area to another, and/or (b) penetration or saturation of existing markets with existing products or services, and/or (c) stability by maintaining present course (but doing it better with a change in distinctive competence), and/or (d) diversification into new markets with new products or services through internal development or acquisition, and/or (e) flexibility strategy to enhance the potential for the future, and/or (f) expansion of the geographic scope of operations from local to sectional, regional or national, and/or (g) greater integration of the organization by adding functions formerly purchased from other organizations (e.g., switching from subcontracting to one's own manufacturing or data processing), and/or (h) divestiture by cutting back or selling out.

Detailed strategies for major areas or units

In addition, the compendium may include alternative policies to serve as guides for selecting among strategic actions in major areas or units. Policy areas that are likely to provide highly significant guidance and require continuing attention include: (a) concentration or mix of products/services (product policy), (b) types and characteristics of customers or clients to whom products (or services) are offered (customer policy), (c) manner in which prospective users are informed and encouraged to purchase (promotion policy), (d) method of distribution from supplier to end user (distribution policy), (e) how and what to charge for products/services (pricing policy), (f) where and how to obtain short-term and permanent capital (financial policy), (g) how to select, develop and reward key personnel (personnel policy), and (h) how and when to review and evaluate performance (review and evaluation policy). Other areas, of course, may assume temporary strategic importance to an organization, e.g., labor relations at a time of intense conflict or strategies for involving employees more in decision making.

Choosing strategies (or policies) for the whole organization and for each individual business area from a compendium has the advantage of displaying each strategy within the context of potential alternatives. This may lead to more critical choices during the life cycle of products or services.

In addition, a more complete compendium would include strategy alternatives for each SRA (e.g., ways of substituting for short resources or for raw materials that have been banned, e.g., saccharin) and for each SSA (e.g., cooptation or bargaining; discussed in Chapter 2.)

Strategies for SRA's and SSA's.

2. Segmentation Process and Business Strategies

Segmentation means defining major opportunities or product/service/market/customers/client segments which currently or potentially provide sustainable advantage to a competitor who focuses on serving them. The established organization has its domains or environmental segments. However, a (more or less) continuous process of segmentation is needed which includes identifying major possibilities, recognizing barriers or limitations for itself and for the competitors, forecasting and analyzing to narrow the choice and considering synergistic possibilities. A key question is What does the unit have to do to dominate and have a defensible (and, for profit-seeking organizations, a profitable) position? Use of the previous analysis on basis of support is helpful in understanding the competitive positions. Given this competitive position and such various conditions as stage of maturity, degree of product differentiation and rate of technological change, alternative business strategies may be considered. Congruency or consistency checks can be made between various strategies and objectives.

Use previous analysis on basis of support.

"Ideal" strategy development would include strong causal links between each strategy and specific quantifiable development (e.g., increase in sales, percentage from new products, increase in market shares, decrease in manufacturing costs). In practice, the links are somewhat weaker but are sufficient to raise fruitful questions. For example, an attempt to raise market share in a mature industry from a favorable competitive position might well cause increased finished goods inventories.* Thus, a cluster of strategic actions may be developed using the judgment of the analyst.

3. Detailing Provisions for Procuring and Allocating Resources: Linking Strategy with Operations

Provisions might include: (a) Projected major long-term moves to give general directions for various functional areas, SBU's or divisions, (b) specific moves detailing the capabilities and resources that must be gathered and used in functional areas, SBU's or divisions, (c) a timetable of the moves, including sequencing lead times, and (d) operational programs for detailing functional, SBU or divisional plans and budgets.

STRATEGIC MIX AND THE PORTFOLIOS

A business has little value to its stockholders unless it yields cash today or growth and compounded cash later. Since it takes cash

Cash really counts.

---

*Paraphrased from a talk given by P. Patel: A Frame of Reference for Strategy Development: The A. D. Little Approach. Conference on Analytical Approach to Strategy, INSEAD, Fontainebleau, France, December 1976.

114 / STRATEGY DEVELOPMENT

Check market share–growth conditions

to grow, cash is all-important. It is an input and an output. It controls the system.* The strategies to be considered from the compendium of alternatives and the net cash flow of a business or product/service are affected by the market share–growth condition in which the organization finds itself.

Important examples of how organizational strategies are changed and developed under various conditions can be derived using the matrix illustrated in Figure 5-1, Checking the Strategic Mix. The vertical columns differentiate between companies, products or SBU with high or low market shares in their SBA. The horizontal rows differentiate between SBA's with high and low growth potential.

Market share is a common measure of competitive strength. Competitive strength could include other dimensions such as product quality, capacity utilization and strategic expenditures. Growth potential is the most frequently used measure of business attractiveness. Business attractiveness could include other measures such as barriers to competition, size of market and the nature of competition.

Check positions– Life Cycle.

Many new firms start out in the upper right-hand quadrant (I) (e.g., Bike Lock). They start initially with a new product (or service) in a new or growing SBA (a single-product policy). As such their market share is low, but the growth potential is high. Their main

---

*Discussed by J. Barnes: The Boston Consulting Group Approach to Strategy. Conference on Analytical Approaches to Strategy, INSEAD, Fontainebleau, France, December, 1976. For a not-for-profit organization you may substitute "cash in the budget" for "cash."

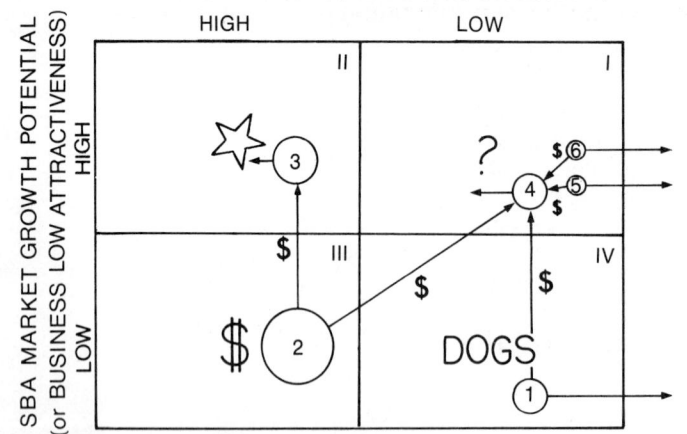

Figure 5-1 Checking the Strategic Mix. The authors are indebted to the Boston Consulting Group, from whose presentation at Stanford University this matrix was derived. The matrix is a diagnostic tool and not a decision making tool. Net cash flow, profitability and invested capital could be added to each circle for additional diagnostic information. Another matrix can be developed to indicate estimated future positions.

objective for change is to move over to the upper left quadrant (II). Here, they have penetrated to become a dominant factor in a high growth SBA. Eventually, if the product follows the typical maturation process, the firm will drop into the lower left quadrant (III).

At this point the firm should consider restructuring its organizational strategy to accommodate a changed environment. Previously the firm may have needed a finance policy of acquiring large amounts of resources from external sources to keep pace with its rapid growth. Now the firm may find that the effect of accumulated experience on costs allows it to produce its own excess resources for expansion.*

Experience Curves

The Boston Consulting Group has noted a tendency that each time an industry (or business) doubles its product experience (sales in units) its costs tend to decrease on *value added* about 20 to 30 per cent. Their evidence from 24 medium to high technology firms seems to hold true for both consumer and industrial products; their evidence refers to all costs—not merely production costs which might be expected to be affected by scale economies and the learning curve. Thus, such costs as advertising, logistics, sales and overall management seem to be reduced with experience.

To illustrate what this means, consider a firm with an annual unit growth rate of 26 per cent. The doubling (and cost reduction if the firm behaves efficiently) would occur in three years. On the other hand, at a slower growth rate of, say, 10 per cent, it would still take only seven years to duplicate its product experience.

Determine cost advantage of accumulating experience.

The firm that has devised a business strategy to gain an increased share in a fast-growing segment thus may have achieved a significant cost-profit advantage over competition: Take a business that has a 5 per cent profit margin, is growing at a 7 per cent annual rate in a market growing at 5 per cent and where prices are constant. When accumulated volume is doubled assume a 30 per cent cost saving (or a 3 per cent reduction per year). The effect on profits is easily calculated. The business's profits would increase from 5 per cent to 8.35 per cent at the end of the first year (5 per cent × 1.07 + 3 per cent = 8.35 per cent). The average business (increasing its volume 5 per cent per year, which means decreasing costs 2 per cent per year at a 30 per cent doubling rate) would increase its profits to 7.25 per cent (5 × 1.05 + 2 per cent). If the faster-growing business could maintain a higher growth rate than average the

---

*For a discussion of the effects of experience on costs, see Boston Consulting Group: *Experience Curves as a Planning Tool.* Boston, Massachusetts, Boston Consulting Group, 1972, pp. 8–9.

Caution

compounding effects on costs and profits would continue to their significant advantage. Even if prices do not remain constant our hypothetical business continues to build up a product experience-cost edge over competition.

However, there is some controversy over the experience curve theory.* Those who contest the experience curve argue that:

1. There is only limited evidence that expanding volume in an industry or in an individual firm can produce these dramatic falls in total costs, and there are certainly areas where costs per unit of volume seem to rise because of large scale working, especially in labor intensive operations where turnover, absenteeism and industrial stoppages may increase.

2. When companies commit themselves to long runs and high volumes of standard products—as Henry Ford did with his Model T—the organization may lose its flexibility and the firm may become vulnerable to a competitor which, like General Motors in the 1920's, chose to compete not on price but on product performance.

3. Even if the experience curve does apply, there is no guarantee that management will be able to reduce costs in line with the curve. We have numerous examples in Britain of companies that have grown in size and whose managements have not been able to reap the profits from higher volumes.

4. The experience curve theory invites companies to commit more and more funds to a few large products in limited market areas. This concentration may increase the risk to the business in the case of change in technology or market. The heavy commitment of the Japanese shipbuilders to large oil tankers and their huge overcapacity after the energy crisis illustrates the danger of overspecialization.

5. The theory assumes a competitive market, whereas in many markets prices are controlled by monopolies, by price controls and by government intervention.

These arguments do not invalidate the theory, but they do emphasize the need for care in applying the concept. For example, does management have the capacity to realize the cost savings while at the same time maintaining a high rate of product innovations?

Reallocation Strategies

For each business fund? maintain? divest?

But let us go back to the strategic mix illustrated in Figure 5–1. What reallocations might take place to improve the portfolio? The organization may be guided by an investment policy of taking its excess resources and applying them to promising new Quadrant I firms or products. The decision pattern in this case may indicate a diversification strategy through acquisition or development. Alternatively, the firm may *fund* propitious Quadrant II firms or products. In this case the firm may be attempting a penetration strategy through extra promotion or lower pricing. The firm may attempt to (1) expand its geographic scope and/or (2) improve its competence, say in distribution. The hope is to find the right combination of resources and products that will follow the path to

---

*See B. Taylor: Managing the process of corporate development. *Long-Range Planning,* June, 1976, p. 90.

excess resources and not tumble into the lower right quadrant (IV).*

The organizational strategy, therefore, has to be restructured as the firm (or SBU) follows a path from I, eventually, to IV. A comment here would be that at the stage at which maturation is about to progress from III to IV, a new organizational strategy would be desirable. Emphasis at this stage could be on preparing the product or division for *divestiture*. At this stage additional expenditures might be limited to only those making the division more appealing to potential purchasers.

Strategic changes contingent on stage of maturation.

Summarizing the strategic changes implied by the matrix, we have followed an organization from the inception of an idea through to the demise of the product or service. Each of the positions in which the organization finds itself requires a different emphasis in its organizational strategy. The early stage requires large inputs of resources and attention to shifting competitive and demand forces. Quadrant II requires a shift to maintaining dominance with only a few competitors (after a shake-out period). At this stage, however, the revenues now starting to accrue still are not enough to offset the continued demands for resources brought on by rapid growth.

Summary of changes.

An organizational strategy for the mature organization (Quadrant III) is to *maintain* its stable position while supplying excess resources to the products or divisions in Quadrants I and II. The cost or risk of increasing market share might cancel any gains. At higher levels of market share there is a growing probability that government, consumers and competition will single out the business for attack. Moreover, it has to constantly re-evaluate its market position so that it can divest itself of areas that threaten to lapse into a Quadrant IV position.

Strong central control may be necessary to effectively carry out the revaluation and divestiture procedure. The person in charge of divisions or products moving into Quadrant IV is not likely to plan himself out of busines. He may be more likely to argue that new growth is just around the corner; he may argue for additional promotion or other expenditures to get this payoff; he may devise calculations that actually meet the financial hurdle established on a traditional capital budgeting basis.

Provide guidelines for resource allocation.

The central policy maker(s) may need to set explicit corporate policies or guidelines to follow in the overall resource allocation process. Use may be made of the simple but powerful approach of

Use portfolio approach

---

*See C. Hofer: *Some Preliminary Research on Patterns of Strategic Behavior.* Professional papers of the Academy of Management, Division of Business Policy and Planning. Boston, 1973. His preliminary research with a small sample (N = 41) of firms indicates that changes in distinctive competence and/or geographic scope were more important aspects of corporate strategy for a significant proportion of the firms than were changes in product/market scope.

sorting products, services or divisions into the four broad *portfolio* categories (or Quadrants): I, sources of growth (future earnings); II, sources of intermediate earnings; III, sources of current earnings; and IV, potential divestitures (immediate cash flow). Using these categories to consider various parts of the enterprise as a group, policy makers are aided in checking that available resources do not flow to a mediocre division or product line at a rate equal to or greater than a high potential division.

Seek dominant winners with cost and pricing advantages

Alternatively, there may be a concentration of the excess resources on a limited number of ventures where there are hopes to capture a large share of a fast-growing market. A limited number of new ventures may be desirable because of the fact that spreading resources among too many alternatives may result in a lack of market dominance for any of them. The solid dominant "winners" in the portfolio are likely to move to a cost and market position (Quadrant III) where they can provide excess resources for keeping a cycle of new ventures coming along.

The organization, if it is at all diversified, needs to consider the balance of its portfolio among Quadrants I, II, III and IV. Particular attention needs to be given to the cash appetites and the cash flows of various divisions and/or product lines in the quadrants. It is true that debt can be used to finance successful growth and thus have a favorable effect on return on equity; it is also true that incurring heavy debt to finance new ventures with high cash appetites may be quite foolhardy, given the environmental uncertainties reducing the possibilities of attaining a dominant "winner." The organization may be wise to avoid acquiring substantial funds from the outside. Rather, it may attempt to move toward a balanced portfolio position which allows some reliance on reallocation of internal resources, as indicated in Figure 5-1.

Balance portfolio?

Flexibility Strategies

Such balance may provide the organization with some degree of preparedness which has been called an *external flexibility strategy*.*
However, in addition to making sure that the organization is not overly dependent on any one SBA, consideration needs to be given to overdependence on any one SRA or SSA. For example, a sudden political event leading to a petroleum crisis might cripple the organization. Further, the cross-vulnerabilities among SBA's, SRA's and SSA's can be so great that a single strategic discontinuity (a sharp break with the familiar past) can cripple the organization by having a simultaneous impact on several strategic areas.

---

*H. Igor Ansoff and J. C. Leontiades: *Strategic Portfolio Management.* European Institute of Advanced Studies in Management Working Paper, 76–16, 1976.

Wide diversification and/or positioning the organization in relatively stable environments may not be the answer. There are trade-offs. Risk and profitability tend to move together. Relatively stable environments are likely to be mature, slow growing and less profitable than "risky" ones. Too wide a diversification can mean the loss of cost advantage from specialization and experience. The choice for general management may be configuring the resources and capabilities of the organization in order to allow quick and efficient transferability. Three important elements are:
1. The flexibility of logistic resources and systems (e.g., diversification of work skills, multiple-use equipment and liquid resources).
2. The flexibility of management structure and process to allow response and innovation.
3. The flexibility of managers, including their readiness and ability to deal with the unfamiliar, and their creativity.

Again, difficult trade-offs are necessary. For example, if relatively independent SBA's are selected for diversification purposes, the potential for enhancing *internal flexibility* is reduced. The equipment and the manpower may be specialized for each SBA. However, the special-purpose equipment and perhaps the labor skills may be made prematurely obsolete when there is unexpected technological change or when the length of production runs is cut short by the shrinking product life cycle. In coming years, as strategic changes accelerate, the trade-offs may move toward more flexibility. If the organization is receptive to environmental signals that indicate potential change, it may push a program for preparedness both internal and external.

Making Trade-offs on Objectives

Repeatedly in the preceding discussion we came up against trade-offs among various criteria which the general manager seeks in choosing a portfolio. This means that as one criterion gains, another one may lose. Recognition of these trade-offs is important in checking the congruency of objectives and targets against the strategies from the compendium of alternatives.

As an example, say an organization has a primary objective of 15 per cent earnings per share. There are different ways to get there but trade-offs along the way. Figure 5-2 illustrates three strategies that might be considered: (1) a high volume strategy, (2) a high asset utilization strategy and (3) an aggressive financing strategy. Each of the alternatives implies a fundamentally different way of operating the company, yet each set of objectives is internally consistent and may allow the organization to achieve an identical overall earning per share target.

Why are trade-offs necessary?

In the high volume approach, emphasis may be placed on adding extensions to the product/service line by acquisition of

120 / STRATEGY DEVELOPMENT

Target	Strategy		
	High Volume (%)	High Asset Utilization	Aggressive Financing
Sales growth	15.0	⟨7.0⟩	⟨10.0⟩
Profit before income tax/sales	4.0	4.0	4.0
Inventory turnover	3.5	⟨4.0⟩	3.5
Dividend payout	60.0	60.0	⟨40.0⟩
Debt/equity	50.0	50.0	⟨60.0⟩

Figure 5-2 Three strategies for achieving 15 per cent earnings per share. (Adapted from L. V. Gerstner, Jr.: Can strategic planning pay off? Business Horizons, 15 *(No. 6):12, December, 1972.)*

development, promoting heavily and lowering prices to build market shares. The high asset utilization strategy may emphasize elimination of low contribution product/varieties, adding products/services that are only sure winners, avoiding promotion expenditures and raising prices even at the expense of volume. In the aggressive financing approach, dividend payout may be held back, the percentage of debt to equity increased and new products added.

The interlocking of sales, earnings and return on investment targets is recognized in each approach. While trading off lower targets here for higher targets there, it may be possible to properly integrate these targets so that alternative ways of attaining a primary objective may be identified. The alternatives most consistent with the organization's or unit's situation may be proposed for action.

In summary, then, the general manager can use the strategic mix and portfolio concepts in strategy development. Each business area (or product/service line) can be categorized by life cycle as fund (Quadrant I and perhaps II) maintain (Quadrant III) or divest (Quadrant IV). Investment criteria and feedbacks can be developed appropriate to each strategy by business and cash flow by business. The organization needs can be identified for a different balance in the portfolio, for more growth, for more cash, for changes in financial arrangements, for more flexibility, and/or for trade-offs on objectives.

SEGMENTATION PROCESS AND BUSINESS STRATEGIES

What product/market or service/client relationships to stress?

Determining organizational needs, of course, is not the only aspect of strategy development. Each individual business is different; each has an environment and strategies which need continuing assessment.

Frequently a determination needs to be made whether there are major opportunities or environmental segments, other than those presently being served, that would fit the organization and utilize its competitive strength. In addition, creative alternatives beyond the "limits" imposed by the organization's ability or inability to operate in the area may be a most important consideration.

The monitoring of the environment gives an indication of problems, opportunities and threats that the organization may face. The importance of the generation of ideas about specific fields of endeavor in which to engage is stressed here. From the preliminary questioning the analyst will have a general, overall view of the organization and its current position in the environment. Then he will work toward creating, through an iterative process, feasible strategic moves by matching strengths with opportunities and suppressing or overcoming weaknesses and threats. As indicated, ideas may come from many sources both outside and inside the organization. For example, customers or clients or potential customers may be helpful if they are asked about their own self-interests; that is, what specific wants or needs can be satisfied effectively and efficiently now or in the future by the supplying organization? What scope or dimensions of the market might be overlooked?

Systematic forecasting of what competitors are likely to do, mentioned before, is something more and more organizations are starting to do. The use of the informal communications network of informed people is an effective method of generating such strategy information. We shall discuss this source of information (and others) in the next chapter.

Given the right support and assuming appropriate competence, research and development staffs within the organization will, of course, provide some ideas. If a policy analyst is going to be successful in improving the search process among the line and staff members he needs conditions to overcome blocks to idea production. One important block is the lack of ease felt by some participants in their dependency relationships to others in the organization. In group problem solving, for example, for some individuals to participate effectively in the work of the group, there needs to be a permissive, informal atmosphere. Otherwise, they may not be sure where they stand and fear immediate evaluation or devaluation of their ideas.* The supportive work environment† and the freedom to make honest mistakes does not mean that quality standards are reduced; the internal environment

Generate ideas.

Match product/ service with specific market segments according to changing perception of values over time.

See Appendix 5–1 on identifying needs, market research, market appraisal and market audit.

---

*See C. Argyris: Interpersonal barriers to decision making. *Harvard Business Review*, 44 (No. 2):84–97, March-April, 1966.
†This environment may not be easy to attain. Various approaches have been suggested: Laboratory training, feedback, group therapy, systemic change. For a discussion of these and other methods see D. Katz and R. L. Kahn: *The Social Psychology of Organizations.* New York, John Wiley & Sons, Inc., 1966; and J. P. Campbell and M. Dunnette: Effectiveness of T-group experiences in managerial training and development. *Psychological Bulletin*, 70:73–104, August, 1968.

should make it seem natural and easy to express ideas in the search for additional or alternative endeavors.

Even brainstorming may be used on occasion to improve the idea production climate. Evaluation and criticism of any presented idea is supposed to be withheld during the brainstorming session. The orientation is on quantity of output of ideas for later synthesis and evaluation. Brainstorming is an example of the staging process that is associated with effective problem solving.* A manager or analyst may find it to his advantage in generating alternatives to state or to separate idea forming from idea testing in his individual or group problem-solving experience. One danger that should be mentioned in group sessions is the occasional occurrence of a common perceptual set or similar way of seeing policies and alternatives.† Frequently various individuals or interest groups will be pushing and politicking for their own alternatives. The various audits of the environment and perceptions of the reward system and self-interests tend to generate alternatives competing for allocations of resources.

Keep an open mind.

Students doing a case analysis or a field investigation will want to put themselves in the position of the manager to the greatest extent possible, gather and interpret relevant, accessible information, and do some creative thinking about alternative fields of endeavor for the organization.

Change mission?

It seems important, then, to keep an open mind in generating promising fields of endeavor that exist or may exist in the future. However, we do need to check whether these product/service/market/customer/geographic area segments fit our current basic missions and utilize or go beyond our current basis of support. Figure 5-3 shows important aspects of the segmentation process.

Defensible Barriers

While we should be careful about ruling out alternatives, it may be helpful to consider whether the organization and its competitors have defensible barriers in terms of environmental demands or requirements for success. To illustrate let us take one example of financial strength and one of raw material strength.

Financial strength. Industries such as steel, public utilities, oil refining and chemicals require large amounts of capital to build efficient facilities; therefore, it is foolish for small organizations to even list this sort of action as a "field of endeavor." An example in reverse is the large chemical company which, because it was

---

*N. R. F. Maier and A. R. Solem: Improving solutions by turning choice situations in problems. *Personal Psychology,* 1962, pp. 151–157.

†M. Dunnette, J. Campbell and K. Jansted: The effect of group participation on brainstorming effectiveness for two industrial samples. *Journal of Applied Psychology,* 47:30–37, 1963.

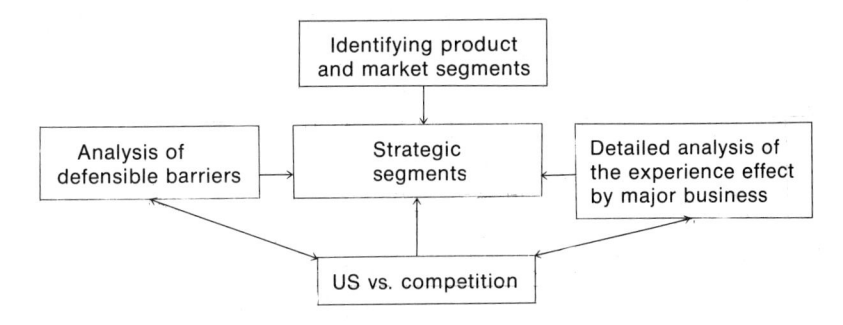

Figure 5-3 The segmentation process. (From J. Barnes: The Boston Consulting Group approach to strategy. Op. cit., 1976.)

producing the basic plastic sheets, attempted to make and sell decorated shower curtains. The firm lost heavily on the experiment because the smaller shower curtain manufacturers and distributors could change their styles and policies more rapidly, meeting retailer demands for many product variations and styles.

Raw material strength. Organizations that own or have assured access to basic raw material resources can realistically consider business that requires these resources. As examples one need only look at the history of the metal and petroleum companies. Chemical and paper manufacturers usually attempt to control timber resources. Large wallboard manufacturers usually control sources of gypsum rock.

Narrowing the Choice

We may wish to narrow the choice of alternative strategic moves by identifying the more promising kinds of activities with, say, market dominance and growth possibilities. A forecast and analysis of the potential of the endeavor(s) in fulfilling objectives in the performance areas of interest may be made. Performances of leading firms in an industry offer indications of industry potential. In addition, developing a profile of the more promising strategic alternatives is an early action to consider.

Profile alternatives

To develop a profile ask questions similar to the following about each segment or alternative that has been identified:

1. What are the required capabilities and resources or barriers to moving from one segment to another? Will they discourage competitors?
2. When and in what amount is each capability and each resource required? How readily available are these capabilities and resources?
3. What does a detailed analysis of the experience curve effect by major business show for the unit? For competition? Do we have a relative cost position advantage?
4. Is the investment appropriate given the overall portfolio position? Given the flexibility strategy?
5. What are the probable results? When? Size? Cash flow?
6. Do requirements leave a margin of error with respect to needs— to meet unexpected business downturns, to cover requirements

if expected results are more successful than anticipated or less successful than anticipated?
7. Is there an acceptable degree of risk? What proportion of organization or unit's resources is committed to alternative?
8. What amount of resources have no assurance of value or continued existence, e.g., specialized facilities or skills? How long will it take to recover capital commitment? How saleable is the usefulness elsewhere in the organization if the alternative is abandoned? How uncertain is the environment?
9. What does preliminary breakeven analysis show?
10. What do the simulated first few operating years look like, e.g., return on investment, profit and loss, balance sheet, cash flow?

In many cases it makes sense to start this profile planning earlier than one is seemingly "ready" to do it. The figures generated may bear little precise relationship to those on subsequent documents, but the earlier this requirement is made, the sooner the proposed kinds of activities will be disciplined into financially sound and complete proposals.

Such evaluation of alternatives may be done readily with computer programs such as PIMS at the Strategic Planning Institute.* The results for several alternative strategic moves, given "most likely environmental assumptions," can be quickly generated.

However, let us illustrate what can be done rather simply in the development of a projected income statement. If the analyst targets a profit figure for the alternative it is possible, using business statistics now abundantly available, to calculate the sales volume necessary to produce that particular profit. Furthermore, the analyst can complete a projected income statement for a typical year of operation, and standard statistics will help him do this. The statistics need to be carefully gathered and adjusted for the specific situation and region.

Caution!

With a targeted income established, only three statistics are necessary to enable the analyst to make a projected income statement. These three statistics are:

1. Profits as percentage of sales

$$\frac{\text{Net profits}}{\text{Sales}}$$

2. Average merchandise turnover for this type of business—the number of times the average inventory is sold each year.

3. Average markup—difference between cost of goods sold and sales expressed as a percentage of sales.

Table 5-1 shows an income statement for a hardware segment with a target profit of $15,000. Dun & Bradstreet's *Financial Statistics*† indicates an average profit of 12%, markup of 35% and turnover of 4/year. Assuming no adjustments are necessary,

---

*See for example: Unique Tool for Marketers—PIMS. *Dun's Review,* October, 1976, pp. 95–97; and C. R. Anderson and F. T. Paine: PIMS: A Reexamination, Presented at the National Academy of Management. Orlando, Florida, August, 1977.

†See Chapter 6 for discussion of various publications and reports.

TABLE 5-1 HARDWARE SEGMENT PROJECTED INCOME STATEMENT*
YEAR BEGINNING JANUARY 1980

Sales		$125,000 (2)
Cost of goods sold		
Beginning Inventory 1-1	$20,312.50 (5)	
Purchasing during year	81,250.00 (7)	
Goods available for sale	101,562.50 (6)	
Less ending inventory	20,312.50 (5)	
Cost of goods sold		$81,250 (4)
Gross Margin		43,750 (3)
Operating Expenses		28,750 (8)
Net Profit from operations		$15,000 (1)

*Adapted from D. Steinhoff: *Small Business Management.* New York, McGraw-Hill, 1974, p. 43.

all the statement figures can be computed from only the four estimates previously determined. The numbers in parentheses indicate the order in which the calculations are made. The calculations follow:

$15,000 is 12% of $125,000   (2)
43,750 is 35% of $125,000   (3)
$125,000 − 81,250 = $43,750   (4)
$\frac{81,250}{4} = \$20,312.50$ (5)
$81,250 + $20,312.50 = $101,562.50   (6)
$101,562.50 − $20,312.50 = 81,250   (7)
43,750 − 28,750 = 15,000   (8)

The projected income statement tells the analyst that if the alternative is going to realize the target of $15,000 net profit, a sales volume of $125,000 will be needed, an inventory of 20,312.50 turned over four times a year and an average markup of 35% maintained. The figures, of course, can be adjusted and various assumptions tested.

Synergistic Possibilities

It may be desirable to test possible combinations of the more promising fields of endeavor with each other. A more thorough analysis is arrived at by generating more alternatives combining fields of endeavor. These alternatives again are evaluated with respect to feasibility (e.g., flexibility, service, stability, growth, self-interest). Combined profiles of conditions of entry, break-even analysis, simulations of first year operations, and return on investment may be developed and analyzed for synergistic possibilities. A simple example of *synergy* is building a restaurant with a motel. Synergy arises when the two actions performed jointly produce a

Test synergy

greater result than they would if performed independently. The motel contributes business to the restaurant and the restaurant makes the motel a more convenient place to stay. Synergy may be sought in the transfer of technical know-how; for example, skills and knowledge acquired on a government military contract hopefully will be applicable to civilian business. The learning period, again hopefully, would be much shorter.

Negative synergy?

There may be negative synergy; that is, the combination of two or more fields may have a negative impact.* We shall use an example of a debatable case of negative synergy. Some insurance specialists argue that if you combine variable annuities with established types of life insurance, the association of the two will lead to substantial reduction in life insurance sales. The rationale is that the life insurance image of stability and sureness would suffer from being associated with a gamble or speculation (variable annuities). More experience is needed to come to a firm conclusion as to whether, in this instance, the synergy would be positive or negative. However, the point is to examine carefully combinations of the more promising fields of endeavors for the advantages and disadvantages of the joint activity.

A brief inventory and profile of alternative endeavors, opportunities and synergistic possibilities may be constructed. This, together with an indication of the expected competitive advantage or basis for support, will be useful in deciding the segments to emphasize.

Gaining and Maintaining a Defensible (and Profitable) Position, or Cutting Back

In developing a detailed strategy for positioning (1) a cluster of strategic moves will need to be identified in such areas as marketing mix, finance, production and research and development, and (2) the set of relevant contingencies must be considered (previously identified from Assessment Guides Parts A & B).

Major changes in the cluster of moves are usually required during three stages of the life cycle—fund, maintain and divest.† In the fund stage, the newness of the product/service compared with competitors and the rate of technological change in product design are major determinants of business strategy; in the maintain stage, product differentiation, cost position and the nature of buyer needs are typically important; in the divest stage, major determinants of

---

*W. Newman and J. Logan: *Strategy, Policy and Central Management.* Cincinnati, Ohio, South-Western Publishing Co., 1971.
†C. Hofer: Towards a Contingency Theory of Strategic Behavior. *Journal of Academy of Management,* 18(4): 784–810, 1975.

business strategy may be buyer loyalty, degree of product differentiation and the price elasticity of demand.

Thus, classifying the business by stage in the life cycle (or quadrant) and considering various contingencies will help us determine an appropriate cluster of strategies. Given the life cycle classification of the business, be it fund, maintain or cut back, a *market share approach* may serve as a major factor in deciding where we should focus effort and investment in the business. The "fund" and "maintain" businesses will be discussed first.

"Fund" businesses might be assigned to increase market share by means of new product innovation (e.g., Polaroid), market niche (e.g., Toyota), distribution innovation (e.g., Avon or Timex) and/or promotional innovation (e.g., Marlboro Country or Avis's "We're No. 2, We Try Harder").

"Maintain" businesses could be aimed at maintaining or protecting the existing market share through product or distribution innovation (a good offense is the best defense). Other "maintain" strategies could be market fortification and confrontation. Market fortification is exemplified by a dominant organization such as P & G plugging market holes to prevent competitors from moving in. P & G uses multiple brands, ties up scarce distribution space and thus discourages some of the competition. Less attractive might be the confrontation strategies involving promotion wars, price cutting wars or even harassment—pressuring dealers and suppliers into ignoring upstarts to avoid losing the established organization's goodwill.

Use market share approach?

There are, of course, many ways of expanding and maintaining a business aiming at market share. Expansion, for instance, can be carried on both internally* and externally. Let us use the Bike Lock Company as an example. Currently being funded for internal growth, it could penetrate the market using strengths and resources currently available within the Quadrant I firm. Internally, it has developed a new type of burglar-proof lock. This undoubtedly could help it to increase earnings significantly over the next few years. Bike Lock saw the need for a new product in the market. It applied resources currently existent within the organization to take advantage of the potential opportunity for expansion.

Similarly, at some point in the future, Bike Lock might

---

*See W. Fruhan: Pyrrhic victories in fights for market share. *Harvard Business Review,* Sept.-Oct., 1972. His research indicates that for some organizations (or divisions) it may *not* be economically worthwhile to seek to increase market share through internal expansion. This tended to be the case where (1) extremely heavy financial resources are required; (2) the expansion strategy may have to be cut off abruptly; and (3) regulatory agencies continuously place new restrictions on the types of competitive behavior which firms can follow. Fruhan analyzed the mainframe computer industry, the retail grocery industry and the domestic air transport industry.

128 / STRATEGY DEVELOPMENT

Develop own capabilities or add from outside?

determine that a threat to growth involved less expensive imitations by larger manufacturers. In this instance the firm might realize that it did not possess internally the marketing and other resources necessary to overcome this threat. Therefore, Bike Lock might choose the external route of acquisition or merger. It might decide that purchasing expertise in marketing was faster and cheaper, in the long run, than trying to develop that expertise internally. It might decide that it needed a major boost in resources to (1) move its production operations away from the expensive "custom made" orientation, and (2) be able to stock sufficiently the distributor outlets.

Bike Lock might, at some point, follow a strategy aimed at *horizontal integration*. It could expand into another area of its basic market. This is similar to an auto manufacturer's developing a product complementary to its basic line to extend its share of that market. Another form of integration also exists in the auto industry. The various firms in that industry practice *vertical integration* as well. The purpose of this strategic alternative is to protect the firm's channels of supply and distribution. The firm expands its operations to control these areas of its market. The auto industry frequently produces the supplies and components it uses to construct automobiles. It also occasionally owns distribution outlets outright. The rest of the outlets are tightly controlled. Once again, the purpose of pursuing a strategy of vertical integration is often to protect existing markets. It also can provide a method of extending market share.

Consider how to protect channels of supply/ distribution.

Thus, expansion can be looked at two ways. On the one hand it protects the business by maintaining its present position within the SBA. The business finds that it has to keep up with any advancements in the SBA to avoid being phased out as a feasible competitor.

Also, expansion can be used to strengthen the business within its basic market. By developing advanced products before competition, the business may be able to increase its share of the market.

Consider newness of product/service.

If the firm is well ahead of competitors in developing new products, it might opt for a *"skimming"* pricing policy. This type of policy allows the firm to take advantage of lack of competition by setting high prices for the short term. This skimming price policy encourages the development of competitive products, however. The originating firm may not have gathered enough brand loyalty to maintain its dominance of the market. What frequently follows is severe price competition and a shake-out of marginal firms (sometimes including the originating firm). This eventually leads to stabilization within the industry, with a much smaller number of competitors.

Consider cost position.

An alternative pricing policy would be to charge a price for the product that is based on favorable costs of production. The originating firm should be able to maintain its *dominance-oriented pricing* in the industry provided it can continue to improve its efficiency as it gathers experience. There is a risk that the firm will not be able to determine the proper price to set. Too high a price will encourage competition; too low a price will unduly restrict profits.

The relative price, of course, is not always the determinant of profits or market share, especially in the case of consumer goods. The brands within a product class may be perceived as (or actually) different in some way, thus permitting some leeway in price policy. Perceived quality and product availability may be critical nonprice variables for both consumer and industrial goods. For example, some people may tend to favor the more well-known company, which is perceived as more likely to "make good" should there be any problem. Product availability may be critical for industrial products of similar quality; in fact in some situations it may allow savings from smaller inventories (in a sense reducing the price). Building distinctive competence in distribution (e.g., speedy order processing, local inventories) in this case may be highly desirable.

Consider degree of product differentiation, nature of buyer needs and purchase frequency.

Many consumer products have a relatively short maturation cycle compared with more industrial products. The cycle seems to be getting shorter.* In the food and dry grocery business categories, for example, 12 to 18 months now does not seem to be an uncommon period of time for the introductory and growth stages. The development and reaction time, thus, would need speeding up. Promotion expenditures on advertising and merchandising are likely to be quite high during the early stages (Quadrants I and II) in an attempt to position the product, gain experience quickly and realize cost savings. It is important to note that there are scale economies in promotion activity and benefits from accumulating experience in these activities. The skills necessary for advertising and merchandising can be purchased, of course, by both large and small producers. If there is little perceived uniqueness to the product, promotion activities become important and the small producer has a chance to gain share with the purchase of unique quality advertising or merchandising.

Consider effects of the length of maturation cycle.

Research suggests that the appropriate cluster of moves for the business area seems to depend on the whole *combination* of contingencies that the organization or division is facing. The combination may add some complexity to the strategy development. To illustrate, the following moves have been proposed† for a product line in the mature stage (Quadrant III), when the degree

---

**Business Week,* March 4, 1972, p. 72.
†See C. Hofer: Toward a Contingency Theory of Strategic Behavior, op. cit.

130 / STRATEGY DEVELOPMENT

Check combination of relevant contingencies.

of product differentiation is low, the nature of buyer needs primarily economic, the rate of technological change in process design high, the ratio of distribution costs to manufacturing value added high, the purchase frequency high, the buyer concentration high and the degree of capacity utilization low, the organization should consider:

1. Allocating more of their R & D funds to improvements in process design rather than new product development.
2. Allocating most of their plant and equipment expenditures to new equipment purchases.

Devise a cluster of strategic changes and policies.

3. Seeking to integrate closer to the end use market or to original sources.
4. Attempting to improve their production scheduling and inventory control procedures in order to increase capacity utilization.
5. Concentrating on market segments, e.g., private label customers.
6. Attempting to reduce their raw material unit costs by standardizing their product design and using interchangeable components throughout their product line in order to qualify for volume discounts.

The efficacy of these moves was demonstrated by the success of Barr-Stalfort in the aerosol packing field.*

To illustrate a different combination of contingencies, we take a mature product line when the product differentiation is high, the nature of the buyer's needs primarily non-economic, the degree of market segmentation already moderate to high, the purchase frequency low and there are barriers to entry in the distribution or technology areas. Then the organization should consider:

1. Focusing their R & D funds first on modifying and upgrading their existing product line, second on developing new products and last on process innovations.
2. Allocating substantial funds to the building of distinctive competences, especially those in the marketing area.
3. Developing a strong service capability in their distribution systems.
4. Seeking to expand the geographic scope of their operations, if possible.

The efficacy of these moves was demonstrated by the success of Beech Aircraft in the light aircraft industry.†

---

*See the Aerosol Techniques Inc. Case (ICH 13G155).
†See "A Note on the Light Aircraft Industry" (ICH 9-370-036). "Piper Aircraft Corp. (ICH 9-369-007) and Beech Aircraft Corp. (ICH 9-369-008).

Not all strategic moves are growth or maintenance oriented. There are often situations in which the business should contract operations. The strategic mix discussed earlier demonstrated that a firm might want to cut loose a "dog" in Quadrant IV. A key point to remember, however, is that a situation or property that is detrimental to one organization may be advantageous to another.

An example of how a firm was able to spin off a losing operation is the sale of Jeep by Kaiser Industries to American Motors Corporation. Kaiser wanted to withdraw completely from the automobile market. It felt it had better uses for its resources. The Jeep unit was a drag on other areas it wanted to exploit which ranked higher in priority.

Check future earning power versus liquidation value.

American Motors, on the other hand, needed a wider product line for its dealers. It also wanted to strengthen its small truck division to take advantage of potential government contracts.

Kaiser was able to dispose of what was for them a losing operation. They stressed points that would be advantageous to a potential buyer. They also accepted a purchase package acceptable to the financially strapped American Motors.

There are also situations, however, in which an operation just isn't very appealing to would-be buyers. RCA found that it could only sell off small pieces of its computer operation. It had to take a large loss in discontinuing this division. Here, the strategy analyst should devise actions that will have the least overall effect on the total organization. RCA deliberately wrote off all potential losses from closing computer operations in a single fiscal quarter. In this manner, the financial community realized that this was a nonrecurring loss. Also, the figure was so staggering, reportedly 250 million dollars, that the financial markets could not react proportionately to it. RCA was willing to accept negative reaction to a bad decision. But it also wanted everyone to know that there would be no lingering effects of cutting loose its bad decision. Basically, it would take its medicine, but nothing more.

Some companies, however, decide not to cut loose but to just cut back a position. The analysis of profitability and risk associated with the business may indicate an overextension in the overall market or in certain submarkets. They may be in a "hot seat" from too large a market share; they may have too many marginal customers. Cutting back may actually increase cash flow. It may involve strategic moves such as raising price, cutting back advertising and promotion and reducing service.

Cut back?

Some examples—faced with antitrust difficulties, Procter and Gamble allowed its share of the shampoo market to slip from around 50% to 20% during the early seventies. Some big supermarket chains have closed down inner-city stores (perhaps with unfortunate social results). American Motors has been given little

132 / STRATEGY DEVELOPMENT

competition by the big three over lucrative contracts for government vehicles (e.g., postal and military jeeps, military trucks).

Caution!

While some research exists to give general support to these strategic moves (given the conditions) and to the regular use of a market share (and contingency) approach in developing strategies, we should caution that hard creative thinking is still needed when formulating strategic changes. The relative importance of the various contingencies has to be examined. The existence of factors or contingencies unique to each situation must be considered.

Before examining the important need to link the cluster of strategic moves with operations, it is important to recognize that the suggested approach to developing and profiling such a cluster is not limited to profit-oriented organizations. A hypothetical set of strategic moves for a non-profit organization using the portfolio approach is illustrated* as follows:

Organization: Measures for Air Quality (MAQ) Program, National Bureau of Standards

Product: Measurement calibration standards and measurement techniques

SBA's: Other Government agencies, state and local governments, industry

Strategies and Objectives:

Quadrant I—Penetration strategy (FY77—FY78)
1. Build distinctive competence in measurement technology, *not* control
2. Tap highly qualified scientists
3. First year—distribute seed money, small amounts of $5K-$20K to encourage people to work on air pollution projects
4. Second year—concentrate on high impact projects (about 8)
5. Earn reputation for MAQ Program and NBS in air pollution community
6. Attend professional meetings to determine problems and markets—what needs to be done and who needs it
7. Financial backing and support—NBS Director taxed each Division .5% for a budget of $250K/year for 2 years to set up the MAQ Program
8. Demonstrate that measurement problem exists, that it will be an expensive one for the country and that NBS has the expertise to have an impact

---

*Personal Communication from Linda K. Cummings, February 28, 1974.

Quadrant II — Stabilization strategy (FY79)
1. Congress appropriated $460K increase due to clear plans about where NBS fit into National problem
2. Program Manager has full control of Congressional appropriation and coordinating function for other agency funds and other NBS funds
3. Continue 8 high impact projects, some of which are reaching development stage, one of which has reached prototype stage and been demonstrated to instrument manufacturers
4. Begin new, more varied, seed projects
5. Determine how far it is appropriate for NBS to go in air pollution — role of the Federal Government and distinction between Environmental Protection Agency (EPA) and NBS
6. Concentrate on standard reference materials (SRMs), the main product of NBS, since this is where NBS expertise lies
7. Convince EPA that NBS should do work on measurement methods
8. Open door policy so that scientists with new ideas can discuss them with Program Manager and be funded immediately if appropriate

Quadrant III — Diversification strategy (FY80 – FY81)
1. Concentrate on one big project — urban particulate SRM (2 years); when finished SRMs for all known major pollutants will have been issued; transfer control to SRM office at NBS
2. Budget of $660K for air, about $300K for water
3. Enter water pollution (Quadrant I); major constraint — no new talent
4. Bide time waiting for new pollutant or new idea — new measurement techniques require innovativeness
5. New product area possibilities:
    a. Collaborative testing — to find out how good different measurement methods are
    b. Chemical kinetics and atmospheric dispersion — relates source emissions to ambient air quality
    c. Removal mechanisms — where does, say, carbon monoxide go when it disappears?
6. Definite shift of emphasis to long-range more difficult projects with no distinct pay-offs

Quadrant IV — Divestiture strategy (FY00)
1. Phase out current work
2. Turn over problem to EPA

DETAILING PROVISIONS FOR PROCURING AND ALLOCATING RESOURCES: LINKING STRATEGY WITH OPERATIONS

After a basic course of action or cluster of strategic moves is determined toward a defensible (and profitable) position, a number of activities are usually necessary to link the proposed course of action with operations. These activities are budgeting, transfer or hiring of various types of personnel, engineering work, material purchase orders placed, etc. Capabilities and resources must be projected. Priorities, sequence and timing of major steps must be developed.

Some organizing programs are necessary. The various activities can be analyzed to find out what work has to be performed, what work belongs together and how each activity should be emphasized in the organizational structure.

The scope of relationships, responsibilities and authority of new positions needs definition. In other words, what kinds of decisions are needed, where in the organization structure should they be made and how should each manager be involved in them?

The qualifications for new positions need to be established. What kinds of people can make our strategy go? Our activity groupings and authority provisions, of course, must take into account people's attitudes, skills, knowledge, power, customs and their limitations.

The allocation of resources (including budget, facilities, equipment) must be determined. This depends on information from the previous analysis to make the allocations realistic. Without that information, allocations would have to be adjusted repeatedly or, in fact, might be damaging.

Measurable checkpoints and expected variations need to be developed. This program involves setting standards and objectives against which actual progress will be measured. The previous discussion about objectives applies here. Questions include how precise should the checkpoints be, what will be measured, when will it occur and what are sources of information?

Various flow-charting and critical path programs* may be used to link or integrate the necessary resource procurements and allocations with timing and sequencing of specific moves. For example, devising plans for implementation requires a detailed accounting of the personnel who will be required at each stage. The various financial and nonfinancial resources necessary to implement the organization strategy must be budgeted so that

---

*Examples of these programs would be PERT (Program Evaluation and Review Techniques), first formulated for the U.S. Navy, and CPM (Critical Path Method).

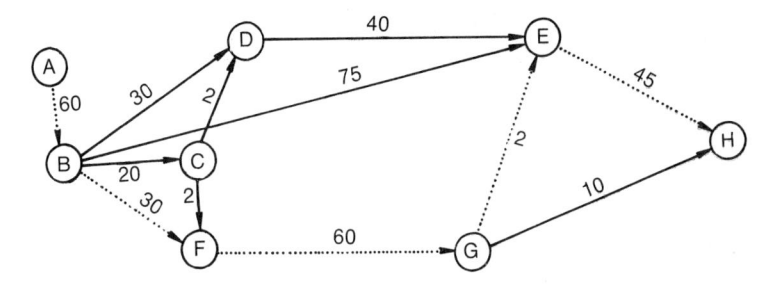

Figure 5-4 Sequence and timing of major steps.

Events

A. Decision to add product
B. Engineering work completed
C. Financing arranged
D. Material purchase orders placed
E. Production started
F. Sales campaign arranged
G. Initial orders received
H. Initial orders shipped

A simplified PERT chart. Events—that is, the start or completion of a step—are indicated by circles. Arrows show the sequence between events. The time (in days) required to move from one event to another appears on each arrow. The critical path—the longest sequence (A→B→F→G →E→H)—is shown by the dotted lines (197 days).

Adapted from W. H. Newman, C. E. Summer and E. K. Warren: *The Process of Management.* 3rd ed. Englewood Cliffs, N.J., Prentice-Hall, 1972, p. 617.

they are available when they are needed. These can all be included in an overall planning chart with cash flows, cash appetites and key manpower requirements and assignments. The PERT chart in Figure 5-4 illustrates simply the tracing of a product development process from the early strategic decision stage through the shipping of the first product run.

A COMPUTER PROGRAM FOR REFORMULATING ORGANIZATIONAL STRATEGY

The previous comments have demonstrated the possible need for a well thought out strategy development process. We have discussed some of the ingredients that make up such a process. How to put these ingredients together is often an insurmountable problem for many analysts, however.

One method for overcoming this problem may be to use a heuristic computer program such as the STRATANAL technique. Basically, this program relies on a sound and thorough analysis of the "total environment" facing the organization.

The program then leads the analyst through a decision process of choosing the right mix of factors for an efficient organizational strategy. The program, through an interactive question and answer technique, requires the analyst to start with a re-examination of the basic objectives and mission of the firm, taking into consideration the effects of environmental trends and organizational capabilities.

Phases in program.

136 / STRATEGY DEVELOPMENT

The analyst then is asked to develop moves and actions covering short- and long-range time periods. Based on these initial alternatives, he is then pressed to include an innovative approach to any changing trends, either internally or externally. These various alternative plans are then supposed to be combined to present the organization with the best overall combination of actions.

At this point the program draws upon the previously stated environmental analysis to allow the analyst to test his combined action plan. This builds an evaluation phase into the process to ensure consistency between the various parts of the organizational strategy.

The final phases of the program are designed to help the analyst to evaluate the feasibility and efficiency of the newly designed organizational strategy. During this phase, the analyst is asked to fill in details required for implementing the strategy. This requires the analyst to determine if resources critical to the successful implementation of the organizational strategy are available. It also tests the acceptability of the total plan to key individuals.

A key factor employed in the program is an analysis of the replies by the analyst to determine if he has understood the planning process or format up to that point. Various prompts and supplemental questions are used if the analytical part of the program determines they are necessary for a better understanding of the strategy formation process.

Figure 5-5 follows the basic path taken by the STRA-

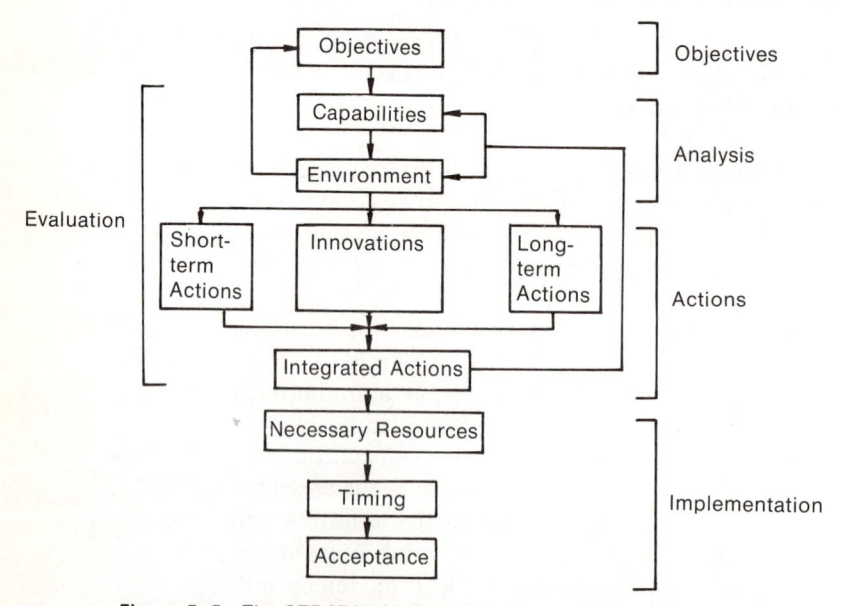

Figure 5-5 The STRATANAL Program. (Source: W. Naumes.)

TANAL program. The various analytical response points have not been included, however.

How effective are such programs? It is too early to make a positive conclusion. They do have merit; they do show promise. There is some evidence, however, to suggest that such programs at the present time are *not* significantly influencing the strategy-formation process within the firm.* In other words, for various reasons that we shall discuss later (in Chapter 7) many top managers are not really finding them useful. Some modifications in content or methodology may be necessary.

Caution!

SUMMARY

Strategy development is a complex process. As we have used the term here it refers to several elements (i.e., strategic mix and the portfolios, the segmentation process and business strategies, and linking the strategies to operations) patterned into a reasonably unified whole. The process by which this unification is brought about is a continuous one involving reallocating the organizational resources to adjust to a complex, ever-changing competitive environment. In earlier chapters it was seen that objective formulation is an interaction process between the structure and its environment and that the manager is a link between that structure and environment. The manager may initiate the development of objectives for change and actions to attain these objectives. Inevitably, as these actions are carried out, they will be affected by influencers, technocrats, other managers, customers and competitors. These "others" will affect what priority of objectives is actually followed, what proposals and calculations are made, what performances are enforced and reinforced or punished, what policies are in fact relevant, and what products or services are supported. Therefore, organizational strategy development is a dynamic process that requires diligent consideration for effective performance of the manager's role.

In this chapter we stressed some initiatives that a manager or analyst may take in developing that strategy. They should be viewed as building upon the situational analysis suggested in the previous chapters. With a general overall view of the organization and its current position in the environment in mind, the analyst will work toward creating, through an iterative process, a feasible organizational strategy and strategies for each area.

Various considerations in initiating organizational strategy are discussed. The portfolio (SBA's, SRA's, or SSA's) approach is

---

*See W. K. Hall: Strategic planning models: Are top managers really finding them useful? *Journal of Business Policy,* 3 (No. 2):33–42, 1973.

highlighted. Each business area may be categorized as fund, maintain or divest. Investment criteria and feedback appropriate to each strategy by business and each cash flow by business may be developed. The organization's needs for a different balance in its portfolios, more growth or more cash may be determined. Trade-offs among objectives and flexibilities may be made in developing various ways of operating the organization or business.

Portfolio approach is highlighted.

Examples of how alternative strategies or policies may be changed and reformulated were given. We followed an organization or product/service through periods of change from the inception of an idea to various stages of growth and decline. The various positions the organization or product/service found itself in should suggest to the manager or analyst broad strategic changes in resource allocation (e.g., penetration, diversification, integration, divestiture, stability, reallocation among areas and flexibility). Detailed strategies that need continuing attention are suggested. We also stressed the need for initiating provisions for procuring and allocating resources, considering overall priorities, sequence and timing of major steps and organizing requirements.

While the development of an organizational strategy is usually done following a rather loosely defined strategy planning program of considering in an iterative fashion the several elements previously discussed, another approach is possible. A computer program such as STRATANAL is designed to lead the analyst through the strategy and policy-formation process. The approach provides a framework for developing organizational strategy.

In summary, this chapter and the previous two give general guidance in analysis for strategy development. A more specific methodology for information gathering and processing aimed at developing and evaluating as well as implementing organizational strategy is given in subsequent chapters. Appendix 1 to this chapter reviews some basic concepts in marketing. Appendices 2 and 3 provide Assessment Guides for Small and Medium-sized Businesses.

DISCUSSION QUESTIONS

1. Discuss the portfolio approach to resource allocation.
2. Discuss alternative strategies suggested by trading-off various objectives.
3. Discuss the contingencies affecting portfolio and business strategies.
4. Discuss the broad and detailed strategies presented in this chapter. Use your previous knowledge of marketing, finance and management.
5. Why are alternative strategies needed within the strategy formation process? What are the key factors necessary in generating these alternatives?

6. How can dynamic computer programs be designed to help the analyst develop organizational strategies? What steps should these programs follow in this process?
7. What timing programs can be used to help in setting and implementing action moves?

Suggested Additional References for Further Research

Bloom, P., and Kotler, P.: Strategies for high market-share companies. *Harvard Business Review*, November-December, 63-72, 1975.
Burns, T., and Stalker, G. M.: *The Management of Innovation*. 2nd ed. London, Tavistock Publications, Ltd., 1966.
Chesser, R. J.: The Development of Behavioral Change Models of MBO Reflecting Moderation Effects of Personality Characteristics. Presented at the Academy of Management, Boston, 1973.
Chevalier, M.: The strategy spectre behind your market share. *European Business*, Summer 1972.
Cooper, A. C., DeMuzzio, E., Hatten, K., Hicks, E. J., and Tock, D.: Strategic Responses to Technological Threats. Professional Papers of the Academy of Management, Division of Business Policy and Planning, Boston, 1973.
Corey, R. E.: Key options in market selection. *Harvard Business Review*, 53 (No. 3):119-128, 1975.
Finn, R. H.: Note: Analyzing a market strategy. *California Management Review*, 17(No. 3):84-86, 1975.
Gilmore, F. F.: Overcoming the perils of advocacy in corporate planning. *California Management Review*, 15 (No. 3):127-137, 1973.
Heenan, D. A., and Addleman, R.: Quantitative techniques for today's decision-makers. *Harvard Business Review*, 24 (No. 3):32,33,36,40,46,51,56,62, 1976.
Hofer, C. W.: Some Preliminary Research on Patterns of Strategic Behavior. Professional Papers of The Academy of Management, Division of Business Policy and Planning, Boston, 1973.
Howell, R.: Plan to integrate your acquisitions. *Harvard Business Review*, November-December, 1970.
Huberman, J.: Management With objectives—or by reaction. *Harvard Business Review*, November-December, 10-12, 1975.
Keeney, R. L.: Setting goals in a professional service firm. *Long-Range Planning*, 9 (No. 3):54-59, 1976.
King, P.: Strategic control of capital investment. *Journal of General Management*, 2 (No. 1):17-28, 1974.
Kitching, J.: Why do mergers miscarry? *Harvard Business Review*, November-December, 1967.
Levitt, T.: Dinosaurs among the bears and bulls. *Harvard Business Review*, 53 (No. 1):41-45, 1975.
Mace, M. L.: The president and corporate planning. *Harvard Business Review*, 43:49-62, 1965.
Macmillan, J. C.: General management policy and creativity. *Journal of General Management*, 3 (No. 1):3-10, 1975.
Naylor, T. H.: Experience with corporate simulation models—a survey. *Long-Range Planning*, 9 (No. 2):94-100, 1976.
Stagner, R.: Corporate decision making: An empirical study. *Journal of Applied Psychology*, 53:1-13, 1969.
Stevenson, H.: Defining Corporate Strengths and Weaknesses: An Exploratory Study. Unpublished doctoral dissertation, Harvard Business School, March, 1969.
Wheelwright, S. C., and Clarke, D. G.: Corporate forecasting: Promise and reality. *Harvard Business Review*, 54 (No. 6):40-42, 47-48, 52,60,64,198, 1976.
Woodward, H. N.: Management strategies for small companies. *Harvard Business Review*, 54 (No. 1):113-121, 1976.
Zarecor, W. D.: High technology product planning. *Harvard Business Review*, 53, (No. 1):108-118, 1975.

APPENDIX 1 TO CHAPTER 5

A REVIEW OF MARKETING CONCEPTS AND IDEAS*

Introduction

It is essential that the strategic unit be in contact with its environmental segment(s) in order to align itself with them. Those activities that enable the unit to respond to the needs of its customers are referred to as marketing. "Customers" is used here in the broadest sense, that is, those in the public who influence the selection and use of the unit's products. To aid the student in his or her review, some of the main concepts and ideas are presented below. These concepts and ideas are useful for profit and not-for-profit units, for small as well as larger units.

Market. Many conceptualize the market as a physical location where buyers seek out sellers, such as a shopping center or a livestock auction. Actually, the market is substantially more complex. The market consists of all interfaces between buyers and sellers that effect the exchange process. The market then is multidimensional and complex. For example, the successful marketing of a new automobile requires that the automobile be appealing to the consumer but that a dealer network capable of reaching the consumer be established, that the car meet federal emission and safety standards, that provisions be made for supplying repair parts and that a plan be developed for promoting the product. These are just a few of the problems.

Marketing. Marketing is the process of facilitating market transactions. Barriers inhibit the automatic occurrence of transactions between buyers and sellers. Marketing activities reduce these barriers through a process of interactions between buyers and sellers that overcome the obstacles to market transactions.

Product. Product is defined as a bundle of attributes capable of need satisfaction. This definition avoids the problem of distinguishing between "goods" and "services." Actually, the product is seldom one or the other. A visit to the dentist usually includes the consumption of some "goods." On the other hand, the purchase of a television usually includes a service (the warranty, which promises that the manufacturer will correct deficiencies in the product).

The word "need" can be summarized as "need as *perceived* by the customer." This eliminates the necessity for protracted debates on when is a "need" really a "need." If the customer perceives that the product will provide utility, then a need exists.

The Product and the Organization's Environment. The definition of the product is an area in which the organization may demonstrate its ability (or inability) to relate to its environment. It is essential that the organization define its product in terms of its customers' perceptions of what the product is rather than in terms of what the organization's management perceives the product to be. The motion picture industry nearly disappeared because it saw its product as motion pictures rather than as entertainment. IBM perceives itself to be in the business of information processing rather than in the business of manufacturing and selling computers.

The Marketing Concept. The marketing concept is a managerial philoso-

---

*Written by M. McGinnis and F. T. Paine.

phy that incorporates an awareness for satisfying customer needs with a recognition of the organization to be profitable (or have budget success). The marketing concept has three components. The first is that the unit should strive to fulfill customer needs. If customer needs are not fulfilled, then the unit will ultimately fail because of low demand for its products. The second component is that the unit should seek *profitable* sales volume. Sales volume in itself is of little help if profits are too meager to enable the organization to achieve its financial objectives. For the non-profit organization the second component may be translated into a defensible position so the organization may survive and flourish.

Implicit in the marketing concept is that a product will be marketed only if (a) there are reasonable expectations that it will fulfill some customer need, and (b) demand is sufficient to insure that an adequate profit (or defensible position) will result.

The third component is that the unit should be organized so that the marketing concept can be implemented. This does not mean that every unit must have a particular organizational format. It does mean that marketing activities should be coordinated so that the objectives of meeting customer needs and generating profitable sales (or a defensible position) are achieved.

Marketing Management

Marketing management is the process of implementing the marketing concept. In reviewing marketing management, the marketing mix, the role of marketing research, identification of needs, market appraisal, market segmentation, product differentiation and the marketing audit will be discussed. Without an understanding of these ideas one cannot hope to participate intelligently in the marketing management process.

Marketing Mix. Management of the organization's marketing activities is generally accomplished by manipulating four controllable variables available to the marketing manager. These variables, known as the four P's, are product, price, promotion and place. Nearly all discussions of marketing strategy consider these variables. Product is usually the most important of these variables. In most cases the marketing strategy is built around the product, which was discussed in the previous section.

Pricing decisions are a crucial consideration in marketing management. Pricing policy must continuously be in touch with the unit's environment. Demand for the product, product costs, customer expectations, the competitive environment, the firm's financial objectives, and the likelihood that high profits will attract competition are a few issues that confront the unit when establishing price. Simply stated, pricing is bounded by two constraints. The maximum price is set by demand. One simply cannot sell a product for more than the customer will pay for it. The other costraint is cost. The unit will not knowingly market a product that does not recover its share of costs. Between these two constraints exists the range within which pricing will fall. The exact price is determined by management after considering the unit's objectives and its environment.

Promotion includes all activities intended to inform, influence or persuade the customer (or potential customer). Promotional activities may exist by themselves, such as advertising or personal selling, or they may be part of the product, pricing, or place strategy. A major consideration in product design is whether it will be perceived as being appropriate for the product. A computer, for example, should look like a computer to the customer if it is going to be successful. For this reason, IBM devotes a considerable amount of effort to the esthetics of its products in addition to their technical performance.

The place part of a decision focuses on selecting the distribution channel. The ultimate objective of the channel decision is to reach the customer. Because customers are often heterogenous, multiple channels may be needed for a product. Ketchup, for example, is marketed through distributors to smaller grocers, direct to large supermarket chains, direct to large institutional accounts, and through a second set of distributors to fast food chains. In addition to channel selection, management of the place decision includes design of the physical distribution system, establishment of customer service levels and management of intrachannel cooperation.

Marketing management requires that management of the four P's be totally integrated. Because each of the decision areas (product, price, promotion, place) are interdependent, it is essential that each be coordinated with the others. This implies that the optimum marketing strategy will be the result of trade-offs between the components of the marketing mix. The unit's internal and external environments will greatly influence the magnitude and scope of these trade-offs.

The Role of Marketing Research. If the organization is to be responsive to its environment, it must stay in constant touch with it. This is certainly true in marketing activities, where undetected changes in the market can spell failure. The managerial role of marketing research is to monitor customer needs to detect changes in the market that may result in opportunities for new products, to identify new uses for existing products, and to evaluate the performance of current products in the market place.

Marketing research activities include market analysis, customer/consumer analysis, motivation studies, analysis of advertising effectiveness, competitive product analysis, and studies of competitive strategies. When done well, the firm should be well aware of its environment. Two words of caution should be mentioned. First, market research activities are the responsibility of many areas of the firm. Second, good marketing management requires that market research information be used. The best marketing research system is of no use if it is not used by management.

IDENTIFICATION OF NEEDS

Organizations starting up, such as Bike Lock, as well as existing organizations can and should try to gather and process information identifying needs that are not being met. Ingenuity and hard thinking rather than complex (and expensive) market research techniques may be all that is necessary. Several approaches may be pursued:

1. Talk with potential customers about (a) what they are buying now and unhappy with; (b) what products they would like to see.

2. Ask yourself what you would like to see as a consumer.

3. Identify future needs that are not recognized, e.g., house sitting or new counseling services.

4. Identify needs now being met but where there is an opportunity for "us" to have a competitive advantage; e.g., if they stress low price maybe we could enter with extra service and somewhat higher prices.

MARKET APPRAISAL

There are a number of questions to ask in the difficult area of appraising the potential of a market. Again, even a small organization needs ingenuity and hard thinking.

1. What specific group do we want to attract?

2. What will be our competitive advantage? Why will people buy?

3. What are the cost implications of our particular competitive advantage?

4. What are the strengths and weaknesses of competition? Yes, recognize even what you don't want to see.

The appraisal itself may proceed in a number of ways:

1. Examine similar organizations with similar conditions. For example, how many students for how many theaters in other campus towns?

2. Survey the current buying habits. Be careful, though, because a yes answer does not necessarily mean a change in actual behavior.

3. Market test the product perhaps in a low-cost, low-risk way. For example, you might take your stitchery to fairs, exhibits or existing stores and try selling it.

4. Will larger organizations share with you their previous research?

5. What does the industry background and figures show? Expected costs? Break-even analysis? Performance statements?

6. What do you need in way of sales to survive? Over what time period?

7. What amounts of cash do you need and when? What can you expect in the way of cash flow?

Market Segmentation. Market segmentation is an important strategy in marketing management. Simply stated, market segmentation is the process of dividing a heterogenous market into two or more submarkets that are homogenous. General Motor's slogan of "a car for every purpose and purse" is an example of a management's ability to determine the importance of market segments. There are many bases for segmenting a firm's market. Some of them are geographical area, age, heavy vs. light users of the product, education and family size. In addition, psychological techniques may be used to identify segments that cut across more traditional demographic categories.

Product Differentiation. Product differentiation is a strategy of creating a perceived difference so that it is unique from other similar products. As part of its strategy, General Motors developed five different brands to reach the various automotive market segments. These brands—Chevrolet, Pontiac, Oldsmobile, Buick, and Cadillac—ensured that for nearly any automotive customer at least one GM model would be a viable contender. This strategy has been so successful that General Motors has been the dominant auto producer in the United States for nearly 50 years.

The Marketing Audit. Like other open systems, the marketing system must remain aligned with a changing environment. Much of this change occurs as a matter of course with routine managerial decisions. While changes in the external environment may be gradual in the short run, they may be substantial over the long run. If the marketing system is to remain aligned with its environment, then it undergoes a thorough explicit periodic reexamination. The *marketing audit* then can be described as a periodic reassessment of the marketing system and its environment.

The marketing audit should be undertaken when major changes occur in the environment. For example, the hand-held calculator industry changed to intensive distribution as prices fell. Firms that were slow to react were left behind. Lacking major changes in the environment, the marketing audit should be undertaken at periodic intervals. While no specific interval is applicable to all organizations, less than one year between marketing audits is probably too frequent and more than five to six years is probably too long.

No area of the marketing system should be immune from the marketing audit. Products, pricing policies, methods of promotion, distribution channels, sales force, marketing research activities, market shares, target markets, and staffing needs are among the items that should be examined. The marketing audit should be as objective and professional as possible. Results should be examined by top management. Recommendations of the marketing audit should be explored and implemented as appropriate within a reasonable length of time. One should remember that the best marketing audit is worthless if no action is taken on its recommendations.

Expansion of Marketing as a Concept

Early thinking emphasized marketing as concerned with economic transactions between buyers and sellers where payment was exchanged for goods or service. In the last decade the scope of marketing has expanded to include the activities of non-profit institutions. Marketing is now considered relevant in situations in which there is an organization, a client group, and a product. Here product is defined broadly to include the benefits provided to the client group. For example, the city library is an organization that offers its products to the general public. While the library may be financed by the city budget, its ability to attract adequate appropriations will be influenced by the level of public satisfaction with its product.

Analysis of the city library might identify several products: entertainment in the form of magazines and novels, self-improvement through books, research assistance for students, a quiet place to relax and browse. Similarly, its markets might be segmented: high school students who use the library for assignments; retired citizens who visit for purposes of keeping informed and entertained; local businesses may use reference services to provide information on markets; the parent seeking information on how to fix the car or a book for a preschooler.

Expanding the marketing concept enables not-for-profit groups to use marketing techniques to better serve their clients. After examining its products and markets the manager of the city library can then evaluate what products to offer, what markets to reach, how to promote the library to its various markets, where to locate branch libraries, where to route the mobile unit and what hours to remain open.

Summary

The marketing system is essential to the organization and its strategic units. It is one of the major interfaces between the organization and its external environment. Marketing research is used to evaluate the reaction of the unit's market to its marketing efforts. The marketing audit is performed at periodic intervals or when substantial changes occur in the environment to totally evaluate the marketing system. Marketing techniques are as applicable to non-profit and public organizations as they are to profit-seeking firms.

APPENDIX 2 TO CHAPTER 5

ASSESSMENT GUIDES FOR SMALL AND MEDIUM-SIZED BUSINESSES*

The following guides may be used in assessing management needs of a small- or medium-sized business. Essential factors that should be considered in 14 areas of management and business concern are given. The information provides an outline of the particulars in which the business person may need counseling or training.

Market Feasibility

Sales in a retail or service business depend on community economic conditions and must be studied carefully. Such study should include population trends (growing, stationary, declining); population makeup (size, age, sex, income); public transportation; shopping habits of residents; number, size and prosperousness of similar businesses.

There are many other questions to ask—depending on the particular business or service, neighborhood, etc. Sometimes a walk-around evaluation or simple survey is enough but at others a more complete study will be necessary.

Market studies can be highly technical, and outside industrial specialists may sometimes have already done the work. In some cities, studies may be in existence and available from the Chamber of Commerce, the State Department of Commerce and other local sources.

Location

Some people going into business choose a location for the wrong reasons—a building is empty, it is near where they live, they are familiar with the neighborhood, there is a business for sale in the neighborhood. Reasons like this often seem to be good enough to business beginners. They do not take time to sit down and make an objective evaluation of the business potential of a particular location. If they did, they might find that the area is in a state of rapid decline, that people are moving out, that urban renewal or freeways are in the offing, or that the location is just not suited to the type of goods or services they plan to sell.

Selecting and making the most of a location is a part of management responsibility, and it has to be guided by management principles. Most people going into business will not know these principles, and without help, they are likely to become a casualty.

In evaluating the proposed location for a business, be sure to include such factors as: nature of surroundings, amount of automobile and pedestrian traffic, sufficiency and kind of space, outlets, storage space and facilities for storing and handling stock or equipment.

In evaluating an existing location, relocation to a more suitable spot should only be recommended as a last resort.

---

*These guides have been developed for the Small Business Administration to assist in the counseling of small business owners by Small Business Institute team consultants.

145

First determine what locational factors are hurting the firm and see if those problems can be aided by less drastic measures.

Money Needs

Before a person going into business can open his store, he must have a financial plan. He must know how much money he will need for (1) capital items such as fixtures and equipment; (2) initial stock; and (3) operating expenses, including his personal living expenses.

Except for personal living expenses his plan will be built on estimates. Operating ratios for various kinds of retail and services businesses provide a tool for making the estimates.

The plan must give in dollar amounts the answers to questions such as:

How much will he have to spend before he can open the door for business?

What operating expenses will he have during his first year?

When can his business reach the breakeven point—the point where sales are equal to expenses?

For an existing firm, the principal questions will involve operating expenses and cash budgeting.

Initial Stock

Initial stock should be a well-balanced selection of merchandise that will appeal to the needs and wants of customers. Factors to consider in determining the opening stock for a small retail store are:

Projected Annual Sales. The annual sales volume a store expects to do and its initial stock go hand in hand. For example, a camera shop with annual sales of about $65,000 should open with about $14,000 worth of stock. In some lines, the possibility of selling on consignment may help to reduce the original investment.

Rate of Stock Turnover. This figure is closely allied to the annual sales volume. It is an indication for determining the dollar amount to invest in initial stock. As a rule of thumb, the faster the goods move off the shelves, the smaller the initial investment in stock. The turnover rate for stock varies with merchandise lines. For example, the rate for a service station is about 25 times a year, while the rate for a small furniture store is about $2^1/_4$ times a year. Stock turnover rates for particular merchandise as given by trade associations and companies, such as Dun & Bradstreet and National Cash Register, are averages. These rates may vary slightly from one area of the country to another.

Stock Assortment. Styles, colors, sizes and price range are some of the factors involved in determining the assortment of the initial stock. For example, the stock assortment for a ladies sportswear shop consists of six types of apparel: blouses, sweaters, skirts, slacks, bathing suits and miscellaneous (jackets, halters and so on). Styles and sizes complicate the determination of the proper mix. Often the choice, on colors for example, is to buy a minimum stock of what seems best and to reorder the best-selling colors early in the season. The stock assortment of a small camera shop might be cameras in a $20 to $50 price range, inexpensive flash equipment, films, flash bulbs and photofinishing services.

Reserve for In-depth Orders. Even in a staple line of merchandise, it is not wise to buy up to the hilt on initial stock. Part of the funds for it should be held in reserve during the first month or two of operations. By that time, sales should show popular items that should be stocked in larger amounts and related items that should be added to the stock assortment.

Source of Supply. Availability is one of the things to consider when looking for wholesalers and others who will supply the initial stock. For example, using a local wholesaler reduces or eliminates transportation cost and usually means a minimum time lag between reordering and receipt of merchandise. Price and credit terms are also important. Fast payment discounts offered by suppliers are particularly important.

Service Business. In a service business, such as a household appliance repair shop, the initial stock consists of the parts and supplies necessary to handle routine repairs. In many service businesses, major parts are bought as needed. Thus, working capital is not tied up in parts that may be used infrequently.

Layout

A major factor in selling merchandise effectively is the interior layout and arrangement of the store. The ways floor and window spaces are used can have a direct effect on sales. Windows should display merchandise to entice customers into the store, and floor arrangements must take into consideration the circulation of customer traffic throughout the store. Aisles should be wide and displays must be attractive, neat and inviting enough to encourage customers to browse.

Some necessities (or those things which most customers come in to buy) can be judiciously placed at the rear of the store, while impulse or luxury items could be placed nearer the front. The purpose is to draw the customers in search of staples past items which usually offer a higher markup. Signs should direct customers to particular items, and merchandise should be clearly identified and priced. An open and uncluttered layout, with small items displayed in plain sight, offers aid to the honest customer while it tends to discourage the shoplifter.

Effective use of natural and artificial light, ventilation, air conditioning and heat will provide comfort, attract customers, and help keep an operation running efficiently. Some basic factors to consider in determining a layout are: type of merchandising, size of store, number of customers expected at peak volume and operating expenses for the whole store and for each section of it.

Service establishments, such as barber shops and beauty shops, should stress customer conveniences and attractiveness. Others which combine service with production, such as laundry or drycleaning establishments, must be sure the work area and public areas are separate to provide display space in the small public section.

A great deal of care must be taken in the purchase of equipment. Before any equipment is purchased or commitments made, there should be a plan for its arrangement. Once installed, changes may be difficult and expensive. One must find out the merits of various makes and how responsible different manufacturers are. A manufacturer should be able to render prompt service and keep machines in operation.

Some retail and service firms may have good reasons for offering pickup and delivery service. The merchandise may be too bulky or heavy to be carried home; the nature of the competition may force such service; or, as in the case of a drycleaner or laundry, the business may demand it. There are a number of factors to be considered by the owner. He must choose the method of delivery, figure the cost for the driver as well as for the vehicle, set up routes to eliminate duplicate service to the same area, and work out a delivery schedule. It may be that the prohibitive cost of delivery by truck, for instance, may make it cheaper to deliver by another method—such as by common carrier. One rule of thumb claims that a truck is not justified unless a business is spending $12,000 a year on delivery service. This should be investigated thoroughly, and Small Marketers Aid 133 has an excellent checklist for reference.

Merchandising

Once initial stock is on the shelves, merchandising is necessary to insure that the store continues to offer an assortment that is balanced to customer demand. As items come on the market, the retailer must consider whether to add them to his line of merchandise. He must price new items, using a markup that will insure income to cover expenses and profit.

Moreover, merchandising is complicated by a dollar limit—the amount invested in the initial stock. The secret is in buying additional stock without investing additional capital.

Stock control is essential to effective buying. If the stock is small, the owner can determine which items are understocked and which are overstocked merely by looking. For size and style goods, a unit control is needed to record sales, stock and purchases in terms of pieces of merchandise.

A never-out list is helpful in keeping up with staple items. For it, the owner has to estimate: (1) weekly sales of each item he lists; (2) the normal delivery period; (3) the normal reorder period; and (4) the amount of stock to keep in reserve for sales exceeding his estimate.

The markup percentage is usually determined by the line of merchandise and by competition. But even so, pricing is an art. The owner should always weigh volume possibilities against customer acceptance, probable markdowns, and expenses.

Vendor relations are important. Usually, the fewer the number of suppliers used, the better. When purchases are spread among many suppliers, opportunities for special prices for volume order are lost. Savings can also be gained by paying the wholesaler's bills on time and taking discounts. Prompt payment also helps initial good relations with wholesalers and other suppliers.

Advertising and Sales Promotion

Advertising and sales promotion go hand in hand. Advertising—such as window displays, word-of-mouth, newspaper, direct mail, radio, and television—is used to attract customers to the store. Planning the items to be promoted, interior display, and personal salesmanship are used to turn customers into buyers.

One of the first steps in advertising and sales promotion is to determine how much money the store can afford to spend. A guide is the advertising ratio—the average percentage of the sales dollar—of similar stores. A new store may have to spend more than the average during the first several months of operation. Advertising should be on a regular basis. The possibilities of cooperative advertising should be investigated.

The type of media to use depends on the locality. The goal is to use those media that reach people who can be expected to visit the store. In a city, direct mail and handbills, for example, offer a way to reach neighborhoods rather than the entire metropolitan area served by the daily newspapers. Also, radio stations serving particular groups are a good bet.

Whether the ad is printed or spoken (radio and television), the layout should be attractive. It should be clear so the reader or listener gets the message.

The message in an advertisement should promote specific items. In this way, advertising, interior display and personal salesmanship can be tied together.

Planning is needed for successful advertising and sales promotion. The time needed in advance of the specific ad depends on the store and the media. In some cases, such as promoting a well-stocked staple item, planning a week ahead may be sufficient. But in others, a month or two may be necessary. Radio, television, major newspapers or newsstand magazine advertising should be budgeted every several months at least, and professional agency services should probably be used.

In a small neighborhood store, window displays are the chief tool for creating traffic. Show windows can be tied in with advertising. Window displays should be planned with the same care used in planning ads, but probably will not require outside agencies.

Interior displays should attract the customer's eye. Effective ones make him stop, examine the merchandise and buy. Price signs should be visible, plain and clean.

Personal salesmanship can be the small store's most effective promotional tool. Each customer can be given individual attention. As the owner and his employees learn customer needs and desires, they can use suggestion selling. In addition to moving items out of the store, suggestion selling makes the customer feel that he is getting special attention.

Advertising is one of the most important selling tools used by service businesses to get new customers. Because of the type of business they are, service shops must show the public that they are up to date and progressive—a leader in their field. Service shops used to do hardly any advertising—just a sign in front of the shop perhaps. Today, chances are, all successful service shops advertise regularly.

The main purposes of service shop advertising are these: (1) To identify the shop as the place where customers can buy the service or merchandise offered. (2) To make the shop stand out from its competitors as the shop that offers *better* service and merchandise. (Be sure that it does.) (3) To get present customers to buy more service or merchandise. (4) To get new customers to try the shop. (5) To hold customer interest between visits to the shop.

The service shop owner should never *think* that everybody knows about his shop. It is not true. Many who do know about the shop know very little about all the services and merchandise offered. And, it is not enough for people to *know* about the shop. They must *think* of it when they need the services and merchandise it offers. Also, new customers are added to the market every day. Word of mouth advertising for service shops is perhaps the most important kind. For this reason, customer relations are even more important here than in retail shops.

Recordkeeping

A recordkeeping system has three main purposes: (1) it should provide a record of all the transactions of a business; (2) it should safeguard the assets of a business by providing for automatic detection of error and fraud; (3) it should serve as a control of operations.

The owner of a small store needs records that will show the score on: (1) sales; (2) cash receipts, (3) credit, (4) purchases, (5) stock on hand, (6) employees, and (7) fixtures and equipment. At tax time, records help him to file an accurate return. But even more important, throughout the year good records help him in doing the things necessary to making a profit.

The type of recordkeeping system may vary according to the merchandise lines the owner offers. For some lines there are packaged systems that require a minimum of paperwork from the owner.

Recordkeeping should be kept as simple as possible. A properly organized checkbook might well be the core of a usable system for many small stores. A set of books should be set up and maintained. The owner need not be familiar with the technical details of bookkeeping; but he should understand the broad areas such as credit. For example, if he gives credit, he should be able to look at his records to see how much credit is outstanding and how many customers are behind with their payments. Such information enables him to take corrective action. For instance, he may need to make a personal call on some of his slow-paying customers.

Insurance, Taxes, Regulations

Insurance, taxes and regulations are facts of life that the owner of a small store has to live with. He should keep abreast of developments and adjust his operations as necessary.

Insurance. The business should be protected by insurance such as fire, lightning and wind storm insurance; use and occupancy insurance; robbery and burglary insurance; and casualty insurance. Public liability insurance provides protection against claims for personal injury, especially to customers. Life insurance on the owner and/or partners protects heirs and partners in case of death. Workmen's compensation and employee's liability insurance (required by most states) protects the store when employees are hurt on the job.

Taxes. Retail stores are subject to local, state and federal taxes. Among the federal taxes a store may be liable for are: social security taxes (shared by employer and employee), excise taxes and income tax (on the firm itself if it is a corporation and on the individuals if it is a partnership or sole proprietorship).

State and local taxes differ greatly from place to place. All 50 states, as well as the District of Columbia and Puerto Rico, have State unemployment compensation taxes.

The other more common types of taxes levied by states are income, property, sales, and occupation or business license taxes. Many municipalities have property taxes and one or more forms of the taxes upon business, usually license taxes. Also, sales and income taxes are levied by many municipalities.

Regulations. The most common types of regulations are those on licensing, trade practices and labor relations.

Licensing controls affect nearly all businesses. The degree of regulation depends on the type of location of the business. Most retail licenses are issued annually. Certain types of businesses, such as restaurants, barber shops and beauty shops, may be subject to regulations (such as health) beyond those of any ordinary license.

Some trade practices are prohibited or restricted by federal and state laws. These laws are designed to encourage competition. Federal laws for encouraging competition include:

The Sherman Antitrust Act—aimed at the elimination of monopolies, it prohibits contracts, combinations, and conspiracies in restraint of trade.

The Clayton Antitrust Act—as amended by the *Robinson Patman Act*—prohibits, with certain exceptions, any direct or indirect discrimination in price between different purchasers of commodities of like grade and quality which injures competition. An agreement with a supplier not to use or deal in his competitor's goods also violates this Act, if the effect is to lessen competition.

The Federal Trade Commission Act, as amended by the *Wheeler-Lea Act*—declares unlawful "unfair methods of competition" and "unfair or deceptive practices" in commerce. Types of acts prohibited include false advertising, disparagement of competitors, misrepresentation, and simulation of competitive products.

Consumer Credit Law—The *Consumer Credit Protection Act,* which was passed by Congress in 1968, requires retailers to inform their credit customers of credit charges both in terms of money and annual percentage rates. Also a store's advertisements that mention figures on credit must provide detailed information on annual interest rates, cash prices, incidental charges, and other conditions. This Act is also known as *"The Truth-in-Lending"* Law; it went into effect July 1, 1969.

Most states have antitrust laws prohibiting agreements in restraint of trade. Several states have laws prohibiting price discrimination between purchasers of like grade and quantity when the effect is to lessen competition. Many states have laws dealing with false and deceptive advertising.

The paramount labor relations law for retail stores is the *Federal Fair Labor Standards Act.* It sets minimum hourly wages and overtime rates for employees.

Many states have laws dealing with health and safety conditions under which employees work, workmen's compensation and unemployment insurance, child labor regulations and special laws affecting women.

In most towns, the Chamber of Commerce will have detailed information on taxes, licenses, regulations, etc., with the municipal, county and state authorities also available for consultation on these subjects. In addition, a reliable broker can be located for information on insurance.

Credit and Collections

The owner should set a credit policy covering the following: (1) credit or no credit; (2) down payment or no down payment; (3) typical down payment and time allowance on installment sales. Credit customers should be selected with care.

Investigate the customer to get the following information: (1) address and length of residence in the locality, (2) occupation and earnings, (3) references, (4) bank references, (5) marital status and number of dependents, (6) property ownership, (7) other credit accounts and (8) extent of debt or payments.

Retail credit bureaus can supply confidential reports.

Limits should be set on credit. Accurate and complete records should be kept on each credit customer. Statements should be sent at regular intervals. Records should be watched for past-due accounts and action taken to collect them.

The collection procedure should be organized in four steps: (1) remind the customer, (2) request response, (3) insist on payment, and (4) take final action. The customer should be reminded shortly after his account has become past due. Customers who do not react to the reminder should be reminded again and asked to respond. Customers who do not respond to the follow-up may not intend to pay their bills. Pressure, such as suspension of credit privileges, may have to be applied in such cases.

Legal action may be needed on customers who fail to pay even after the first three steps of the collection procedure.

Credit can be a useful tool for increasing sales, but it must be used judiciously to insure that increased profits accompany the sales.

Central charge and credit card systems may help relieve a small store of some of the administrative details of credit and collection. But costs are fairly high, and the businessman has no control over the agency's policies (thus he cannot use credit service as a tool to build up goodwill for himself).

Chambers of Commerce, the Better Business Bureau and local central charge or credit bureaus can give information on credit and collection matters.

Personnel

Employees—even one—call for personnel management. In working through others, the owner of a small store or service firm should be a coordinator. This role involves four functions: (1) hiring, (2) training, (3) supervising and (4) recordkeeping.

Hiring should start with the question: What skill is needed? To avoid talking with ill-suited job applicants the owner should spell out what he wants when working with employment agencies, both state and private. A simple application form is helpful in screening and evaluating applicants.

Training may be needed to orient a new employee to the firm's way of doing business. Periodic training may be needed, as in orienting repairmen to new models of appliances. Or training may be continual, as in keeping salesclerks supplied with information about the products they sell.

Supervision involves seeing that employees do their work and do it correctly. In a small firm, supervising and training sometimes go hand in hand, as in correcting an employee's mistakes. Good communication is vital to effective supervision. When employees know what is expected of them they are more apt to cooperate than when the rules vary according to the owner's whims.

Recordkeeping for employees can often be done with the proper payroll records.

The firm's records must show each employee: (1) his earnings, (2) the amount withheld for federal income tax, (3) withholding for social security, (4) withholding for state and/or city income tax (when applicable), (5) number of hours worked and (6) overtime hours worked.

These items are required by various laws. In addition, the records should show deductions for hospital insurance and similar benefits which the firm may provide. When an employee travels or has other expenses connected with his job, his records should show them. A record should also be kept of important changes, such as pay raises.

Note: Equal employment and other anti-discrimination laws pertaining to minority groups and women must be followed and union rules must be considered, where applicable, in the hiring, training and supervision of employees. For firms with several employees, equal employment opportunity reports may have to be filed.

Planning for the Future

Planning for the future is tied in with sales growth. It varies from store to store. In one firm, it may involve only the hiring and training of an assistant to relieve the owner's wife of part-time work in the store. In another store, planning for the future may be more complicated. For example, technicians may need to be hired and trained as sales volume increases in a small service shop. In a third firm, forward planning may involve seeking new lines of merchandise that can be used to increase sales.

The important thing that the owner of a newly established business must recognize is that the future does not take care of itself. Goals have to be set. Plans have to be made and step-by-step actions have to be taken to carry out these plans.

After the first several months of operation, the owner should begin to set some time aside for planning. An hour or so a week may be sufficient. The point is to get in the habit of looking ahead and deciding what has to be done as the business grows.

Technical Skills

Even the person who is proficient in his trade may need help with technical skills when he opens his own service business. For example, a baker who has worked in a production bakery may need refresher training on skills which he has not used for several years. In addition to upgrading latent skills, the owner must keep abreast of the latest developments in his trade. This may be no easy task today, when technology is advancing so rapidly.

Moreover, the owner must recruit and train technical employees as his sales increase. This training may consist of courses in technical schools at night as well as in on-the-job instruction and supervision.

Other (Specify)

This category is designed for the consideration of deficiencies that are not business management deficiencies. For example, a prospective businessman may lack certain basic tools needed in business dealings. Or, he may have the basics but lack training in certain special (non-technical) business skills.

It is up to the person evaluating the prospect to spot such deficiencies and determine how to provide the help the applicant needs in order to overcome them.

APPENDIX 3 TO CHAPTER 5

HELPING SMALL BUSINESSES COPE*

Business growth is a reward for achievement and should be a cause of joy. Instead, for far too many small and medium-sized businesses, growth turns into a nightmare. Just as the company seems poised for rapid and profitable growth, it gets out of control and into severe trouble.

Even if the business survives the crisis—and many do not—it often will have lost its earlier growth potential and remain permanently stunted. And in the most favorable case, the business that then recovers and goes on to success, there will be deep and permanent scars.

I have learned to apply five simple rules to enable a small or medium-sized business to grow without getting out of control and without suffering the severe affliction of the growth crisis.

1. Growth requires investment. It always strains the financial resources of a business. And unless the business is managed for cash flow, growth is likely to create liquidity pressures that might even force the growing business into insolvency. Profits in such a business come second. Indeed, in a rapidly growing business profits are an accounting delusion; they should be considered contingency reserves.

2. The growing business, especially the growing small or medium-sized business, needs to anticipate the financial structure and financial resources it will need—at least two, and better still, three years ahead. It needs to go to work now on obtaining the outside money it will need to sustain its growth.

*From Drucker, P. F.: *Wall Street Journal,* April 21, 1977. Reprinted with permission of *The Wall Street Journal,* © Dow Jones & Company, Inc. 1977. All rights reserved.

Financial Requirements

Financial requirements of a business do not grow proportionately with sales volume. Some areas may need disproportionately more money, others disproportionately less. Receivables, for instance, may have to grow twice as fast as sales—but they may also grow only half as fast or hardly at all while sales double. And this applies in all areas—manufacturing plant and equipment; distributive facilities, such as warehouses or delivery fleets; investment in technical service or in materials inventories.

As a result, capital structure always needs to be changed during rapid growth. Today's structure always becomes inappropriate and a straitjacket. If tomorrow's financial needs and financial structure are tackled today—that is, a few years ahead of the need—a sound business can almost always obtain what it needs in the right amount and in the right form, whether equity, long-term debt, medium-term notes or short-term commercial credit.

If the business waits until it needs the new money, it will have waited too long. Even if it can get what it needs, it is unlikely to be in the right form and almost certain to be very expensive.

Financial planning for the growing business need not be elaborate; indeed it rarely can be elaborate. But it needs to be timely, and that means way ahead of the actual need. The starting point has to be the realization that growth is qualitative, rather than mere quantitative, change in its impact on financial needs and financial structure.

3. To grow without running into the growth crisis, a business also needs to anticipate future information needs.

Growth always requires data beyond those furnished by the accounting system—data on what goes on outside the business and especially data on what goes on in the marketplace.

I remember vividly a small company in the consumer goods business with a very successful innovative product range and a growth rate in sales of 10%—15% compounded each year. The company announced a fairly sharp price increase, but offered to supply present customers with goods at the old prices for the rest of the year. Sales spurted by 50% that year. But after the first of the next year, sales completely dried up. Six months later, they had only recovered to half the earlier level. The company collapsed and was forced to liquidate.

Actually, nothing had happened except a lack of data. The ultimate consumer continued to increase his purchases at a 10%—15% rate. But the distributors had stocked up in anticipation of the announced price increase and were holding back new orders until they had worked off their inventories.

Nobody in the company realized this, however, for everybody (mis)defined "sales" as deliveries to the distributors—the legal and accounting rather than the economic definition (and usually the wrong definition, by the way). The simplest sample of customer purchases—for instance, a sample of the actual sales by 1% of the distributors once a month—would have told the company early what was happening, and would have enabled it to take the appropriate measures.

But lack of such simple data, as anyone familiar with small and growing businesses knows, is all too common. The small and medium-sized business that expects to grow therefore needs to ask: What additional information do we need to have real control and to know what really goes on in our business? What are real results in the business and what are real costs? And it needs to develop this information well before the time at which its absence can cripple it.

4. Small and medium-sized businesses that want to grow need to concentrate on technologies, products and markets. They need to free themselves by sloughing off diversions.

There is, for instance, the manufacturer who sells $12 million a year in his home market, the U.S.—up from $3 million five years ago—and who indulges himself in an "international business," consisting of a joint venture in Japan and two small plants in Europe. After five years of hard work, they sell a total of $1.5 million and lose every year $600,000. Worse, they absorb up to one-third of the time of all the key people in the company, who forever dash off to Osaka or to Hamburg to "straighten things out"—without, however, ever staying long enough to achieve anything.

Or there is "our prestige line," the "flagship of our fleet"—or conversely, the "popular low-priced line," developed in an abortive attempt to get the company's goods to the discount stores and "to make us a factor in the mass market."

Growth makes large demands on energy, especially on managerial energy. It demands concentration on areas where the results are. And it demands willingness to give up areas in which there are only efforts but no real results, no matter how "promising" these areas looked when the company first went into them.

5. The small or medium-sized business usually cannot afford much by way of top management. But if it wants to grow, it better make sure that well ahead of time it develops the top management it will need when it has grown. Small growth businesses start out typically as the brain-child of one or two men. These are usually entrepreneurs with vision, drive, ability and courage. But they are still only human beings, and thus endowed with weaknesses as well as strengths.

There is the company, for instance, started by a man with high product imagination, great capacity for product design and development, and ability in promotion. He builds a fast growing, highly successful small company on his ability. But this kind of man is often a "loner," moody, and ill-at-ease with people, and bereft of financial sense.

Kill the Business

If he is conscientious, he will almost certainly kill the business. He will force himself to work on finance and other tasks for which he lacks ability. By spending so much time on what he cannot do well he will neglect what he can do well. A few years later the growth crisis hits and this kind of company usually goes out of existence, having lost the original advantages its founder gave it.

Equally common is the man who brushes aside as unimportant any concern about people, finance or distribution while he concentrates on product design, development and promotion. Three or five years later his business will also be in crisis. Still, it can often be salvaged; at least it has the right products and they are positioned right in the marketplace. However, it is still likely to remain permanently stunted, while the owner-entrepreneur will probably lose control and be jettisoned in the course of the rescue operation.

What the small and medium-sized business needs in order to grow is to ask: What are the key activities in this business (and people and money are always key activities in every business, although never the only ones)? Then its top people must ask: Which key activities fit the people at the top? Then: Which of our employees have the capacity to take on, in addition to their current duties, the key activities for which the present managers are not suited?

These people are then assigned responsibility for specific key activities, preferably without publicity, without change of title and without paying them a penny more. Five years later, when the business has grown, it should then have the top management team it will need. But it takes five years or so to develop such a team, and if the job is not started beforehand it will not be able to become or remain a larger company. It will buckle under the additional load that growth always imposes.

It is difficult if not impossible to cure the growth crisis of the small or medium-sized business. But it is fairly easy to prevent such a crisis, and vital to do so.

6

WHY ASSESSMENT AND DEVELOPMENT?

EVALUATION STRATEGIES

WHAT IS AN ORGANIZATION DEVELOPMENT APPROACH TO STRATEGY FORMATION?

ACTION-RESEARCH PROGRAM

USE AND LIMITATIONS OF ACTION RESEARCH

INFORMATION GATHERING AND PROCESSING

Finding and Using Some Outside Informants
Developing a Strategic Issue Information Network
Using Face-to-Face Contacts
Using Observation Tours
Using Forecasts
Using Publications and Reports
Using Questionnaires
Breaking Out Returns and Using the Results
Using Market Segmentation Breakouts

SUMMARY

DISCUSSION QUESTIONS

ASSESSMENT AND ORGANIZATION DEVELOPMENT: AN ACTION-RESEARCH PROGRAM

You should be able to discuss models of evaluation, an organizational development approach, and information gathering and processing.

Until now we have discussed conceptualizing and learning about the strategy-formation process and have provided a program (or a set of programs) for improving organizational strategy making. But this general guidance and discussion must be supplemented with a more specific methodology directed toward developing a self-renewing, self-correcting strategy formation system—a system that will continue to expand and improve the choices available to and made by the organization as it copes with changing demands and challenges from the environment. As we have indicated, the organization goes through (perhaps informally) a more or less continuous process of evaluation, choice, coordination, implementation and re-evaluation.

In this chapter we shall discuss, first, some models of evaluation and, second, an organization development approach to strategy formation. The organization development approach suggested includes a diagnostic phase that is data based. The data collection and analysis methods in this book are separated into those methods primarily associated with the behavioral sciences and those primarily associated with management science. In this chapter we shall cover some behavioral science methods; in the next, we shall cover some management science methods. In Chapter 8 the data generated and analyzed are designed to be useful as input to overall assessment and development activities.

The purpose of this and the next two chapters is to provide a readily available methodology for consideration by policy analysts or managers. The various methods subsequently described are not to be interpreted as being the only feasible methods. The collection represents those techniques that have had at least some testing and which seem, with the limited evidence available, at least somewhat effective in assessing and developing (1) strategies and policies, and (2) the policy-formation process. Development of innovative techniques or improvements in the techniques described is encouraged. The field of identifying policy problems and uncovering solutions to those problems is a rapidly changing and developing one.

The purpose of Chapters 6, 7 and 8.

This grouping of methods should *not* imply that all methods presented are to be used periodically in assessments. The policy analyst will be concerned with developing a methodology mix that meets the needs of a particular assessment in conjunction with programs and questions presented in previous chapters. The previous chapters have already alluded to and provided some methods. This chapter and those following will add to and elaborate upon the collection.

WHY ASSESSMENT AND DEVELOPMENT?

If we were to ask ourselves why the use of these assessment and development methods is desirable or necesssary, it would appear that several reasons are related to organizational strategy. First, there is a need for the organization to adapt to the environmental changes and to develop new capabilities and perhaps structural alignments to accommodate these. Second, if the organization were to enter into new services and/or a new market as a result of a strategic decision about where the organization is going, then there might be the necessity to develop additional skills and certainly additional structures to accommodate this new domain of its service area or technological strategy. Third, the organization's status or current stage of development may be less than fully effective in achieving its current goals, let alone any changes in the environment that might have occurred or any changes in the domain of its operations. For example, differences in perceptions about organizational strategy and conflicts in these perceptions may cause ineffective performance. One of the difficulties may lie not in strategy formation but rather in the communication of the organizational strategy to lower levels and in the independence that coalitions at lower levels are able to exhibit in contradistinction to whatever organizational strategy has been established. It might be useful for an organization to discover the discrepancies between intended and actual perceptions of organizational strategy within an organization.

Environmental awareness and self-awareness activities.

158 / ASSESSMENT AND ORGANIZATION DEVELOPMENT

Thus, in summary, an organization may need some sort of systematic assessment and development carried on continuously (1) to adapt to environmental changes, (2) to adapt to a new domain of operations, (3) to maintain its current state, or (4) to improve its "steady state," so to speak.

EVALUATION STRATEGIES

There are a number of ways to choose from in proceeding with assessment of and improvement in organization practices and policy formation in particular. We do not have in the field of policy a neat typology of evaluation strategies, but a few models can be identified. A Continuum of Evaluation Strategies, Table 6-1, illustrates some of the possibilities. These range from an evaluator-centered compliance approach to the client-centered process approach. Some of the difficulties in each approach that may be encountered are indicated and have been discussed elsewhere.* There will be only a brief discussion here.

Compliance.
One of the most prevalent models of evaluation is certainly the evaluator-centered compliance approach. This compliance approach occurs when the evaluator examines the organizational situation, identifies the problem and the solution, and tells the relevant parties in the situation to comply with his solution. This model frequently works quite well when the evaluator is respected and has made an accurate diagnosis. Sometimes, however, the evaluator does not procure an accurate picture; he may have used unreliable sources; he may not have fully thought through the consequences of his recommendations. Sometimes there is resentment and resistance to the evaluator, who may appear to act in a condescending manner.

Doctor-patient.
Another popular model of evaluation is that of doctor-patient. Here the managers initiate the actions of bringing in evaluators (who may be managers themselves) to "look over" some part or all of the organization and to make recommendations. Again, this strategy may work quite well. The evaluators have been invited in, and if

---

*See for example: T. W. Costello: An Organizational Psychologist Looks at Change in Municipal Government. Presented at the American Psychological Association Convention, San Francisco, 1968; W. J. Crockett: Team building—One approach to organization development. *Journal of Applied Behavioral Science* 6 (No. 3):291–306, 1970; W. Dyer, R. Maddocks, J. W. Moffett, and W. Underwood: A laboratory-consultation model for organization change. *Journal of Applied Behavioral Science* 6 (No. 2):213–227, 1970; W. Eddy: Beyond behavioralism organization development in public management. *Public Personnel Review* 21 (No. 3):169–175, 1970; R. T. Golembiewski: Organization development in public agencies; Perspective on theory and practice. *Public Administration Review*, 29 (No. 4):367–377, 1969; A. J. Marrow; Managerial revolution in the state department. *Personnel* 43 (No. 6):2–12, 1966; E. Schein; *Process Consultation: Its Role in Organization Development*. Reading, Mass., Addison-Wesley Publishing Co., 1969.

TABLE 6-1 A CONTINUUM OF EVALUATION STRATEGIES

Evaluator*-Centered			Client†-Centered

Compliance Model
P! S!
	Doctor-Patient Model
	P S
		Purchase Model
		S
			Helper or Process Model
			P? S_1?
			     S_2?
			     S_3?
			     .
			     .
			     S_n?

Evaluator identifies problem and solution; tells client to comply	Managers ask evaluators what is wrong with organizational unit and what should be done	Managers identify problem and request information or service	Evaluator's activities help client to perceive, understand and act upon events in his environment; evaluators provide challenging alternatives; client decides
Possible difficulties: Resentment; resistance; problems tend not to stay solved effectively unless organization solves own problems	Organizational unit reluctant to reveal information; systematic distortion of information; lack of common diagnostic frame of reference; organizational unit unwilling to believe diagnosis; evaluators without exhaustive study unable to learn enough about organizational culture to suggest reliable courses of action	Managers do not correctly identify and/or communicate their own needs; build dependence on evaluator; assumption may be made that organizational change comes through transmittal of information (e.g., a report)	Evaluators may advance solutions prematurely; client may be unwilling or unable to see the problems, to share in diagnosis or to be actively involved in generating solutions; evaluators may not pass on diagnostic skills to client; client may not request services; evaluator may need right to come in

P = problems; S = solution.
*Evaluator may be the manager himself or a policy analyst.
†Client may be manager or a subordinate to the manager.

they do a competent job of evaluation, their recommendations may carry some weight. However, numerous difficulties may be present. For example, the organizational unit that is defined as the patient may attempt to cover up information needed for an effective evaluation. The Watergate case illustrates this difficulty. Thus, the "doctor" may not be able to properly identify the problem and suggest an appropriate solution.

Purchase. A third strategy occurs when the manager identifies the problem and requests information or service to identify a solution. He may define a need—e.g., some activity he wishes carried out—and look for someone with expertise to fill the need. For example, he may wish to know the demands or requirements of a particular segment of consumers, or he may wish an analysis of the efficacy of some complex technology. The success of this approach depends on the appropriateness of the assumptions that (1) the manager has correctly identified and/or communicated his own need, and (2) the manager has accurately assessed the capability of the evaluator and the consequences of his recommendations. Many things have to go right for the purchase model to work.

Finally, an evaluation model we have illustrated in Table 6-1 is the helper or process strategy. Here the evaluator's activities are aimed at helping the complex problem-solving process. In other words, the evaluator (who may be a manager or policy analyst) is trying to help members of the organization to perceive, understand and act upon events in the environment or the organization. The evaluator may assist in setting up a problem-solving process and he may suggest alternative courses of action. A key assumption is that if the organization members being evaluated *see* the problem, share in the diagnosis and are actively involved in generating a remedy, problems will tend to be solved more permanently. In addition, if the evaluator has effectively passed on his diagnostic skills to the evaluatees, they will better able to solve new problems as they arise.

Helper. However, numerous difficulties may be encountered. For example, a trust relationship necessary for the success of this strategy may not be developed. There may be an unwillingness or inability to see the problems, to share in the diagnosis or to be actively involved in generating solutions. Part of the problem may be that the evaluator has real power (e.g., he is the boss) and cannot easily switch to the collaborative helper role. Those being evaluated may distort their responses; they fear that the evaluator-boss may utilize negative information to their detriment.

In an effort to develop ways of diminishing some of the many barriers to effective assessment and to deal with the variegated environmental changes affecting organizations, an organizational development technology has emerged in recent years. Organizational development practitioners have used, built upon and added to such traditional methods as interviews, questionnaires, forecasting and financial and operating data analysis. Such methods, traditional and new, may be fitted into the various models of assessment behavior—Compliance, Doctor–Patient, Purchase, and Helper. Such methods and models or combinations of methods and models may be applied specifically to the strategy formation process.

WHAT IS AN ORGANIZATION DEVELOPMENT APPROACH TO STRATEGY FORMATION?

It would be helpful to have a single, clear definition of exactly what organization development is and what it is not. However, there is no single definition; on the contrary, there are many. For example, the NTL Institute sees organization development as a "short title for a way of looking at the whole human side of organization life."* Others place more stress on its specific application to finance, market, and labor relations variables.† Examination of the literature in the field points up why, in fact, organization development is many things to many people, depending upon how broadly or narrowly they apply the term to their own purposes.

Organization development can be a broad label that includes many activities through which the manager or analyst may make better use of the organization participants. In this book these activities are viewed as both *problem solving* and *developmental* in nature in that they are helpful in solving policy problems while at the same time increasing the capability for solving future problems.

Problem solving and development.

Definition

To further elaborate, an organization development approach to strategy formation is defined as a process (1) planned, (2) organization wide, (3) managed from the top (4) to improve strategy formation through interventions, using relevant analytical and developmental methods. In addition, (5) the approach suggested tends to focus more on coalitions of performers or groups than on individual performers.

1. It is a planned effort.
  There is a systematic diagnosis using multiple methods of analysis, providing an indication of the forces, factors, effects and relationships that impinge on mission accomplishment; a set of action steps is developed for new or improved formation and implementation.
2. It has organization-wide implications.
  Strategy formation is the focal point and, as indicated, involves the

---

*News and Reports, NTL Institute, Vol. 2, June, 1968; see also Bennis, W. G.: *Organization Development: Its Nature, Origin and Prospects.* Reading, Mass., Addison-Wesley Publishing Company, 1969; W. French: Organization development—Objectives, assumptions and strategies. *California Management Review* 12 (No. 2):23–24, 1969.

†See R. Blake and J. Mouton: *Building a Dynamic Corporation.* Reading, Mass., Addison-Wesley Publishing Company, 1969.

widest sort of ramifications in the organization. An organization development program involves the entire organization or coherent system or a significant part thereof.
3. It is managed from the top.
Experience and research indicate that top management involvement, direction and commitment seem to be desirable* attributes of successful development programs; thus, we include this element. Top mangers may be the analysts themselves, or they may endorse the efforts of external advisors or those analysts internal to the organization.
4. It is designed to improve strategy formation through planned interventions and assessments, using relevant analytical and developmental methods.
It is comparable to other organization development efforts. However, it focuses on strategy formation and places more emphasis on market, economic and financial variables than many other organization development efforts. It places somewhat less emphasis on human variables and values. The interventions designed are based on the behavioral sciences. Experience-based learning activities (e.g., sensitivity training and T groups) are not relied on; instead, a shared approach to problem identification and solution is used. Methods are selected and developed for auditing the existing environment and structure and helping the organization to examine its organizational strategy and its strategy formation process.
5. It focuses more on coalitions of performers rather than on individual management development.
Management development aims at ensuring a constant supply of trained individuals to fill anticipated vacancies in the management ranks. The organization development approach here takes the point of view that the way in which participants adapt corporate strategies to the changing environment and deal with conflicting sets of interests has a great deal to do with the effectiveness of the organization. This approach includes concern with the establishment of appropriate systems and problem-solving processes for group and intergroup interaction in developing organizational strategies.

Core issue—prevent stagnation.

As indicated, one purpose of implementing an intervention within the organization is to encourage a renewal process. This renewal process must take place; otherwise, the organization may suffer deterioration. As John Gardner points out, an organization tends to have a predictable life-cycle of decline that may be offset by a struggle for renewal.† A built-in provision for self-criticism, for challenging present corporate strategies and practices, for auditing the environment and for revising and reformulating policies and strategies is needed. This is a core issue mentioned earlier; the organization needs deliberately to seek a way of preventing dry rot or stagnation.

---

*See L. Greiner: Pattern of organization change. *In* Dalton, G., Lawrence, P., Greiner, L. (eds.): *Organization Change and Development*. Homewood, Ill., Richard D. Irwin, 1970.
†J. Gardner: Can organization dry rot be prevented? *Personnel Administration*, 29:3–13, 1966.

The organization development intervention therefore is seen as basically a problem-solving (anti-dry rot) *and* development approach, with its activity focused more on groups or coalitions than on individuals. Outside advisors, assessors or consultants often share the responsibility with managers for the problem-solving and development process, but they also work with managers toward increasing the organization's own capacity to diagnose the external and internal environment and to develop and carry through strategic plans of action.

ACTION-RESEARCH PROGRAM

An element frequently included in organization development activities is the *action-research* program of intervention. As the term is used in this book there are three processes in an action-research program applied to strategy formation, all of which involve extensive collaboration between the analyst and the organization:

Three processes in action research.

1. Information gathering from the internal *and* external environment (e.g., on threats or opportunities, their source, characteristics, gravity and timing).
2. Organization, analysis and feed-in of such information to relevant parties or groups in the organization.
3. Joint action planning based on the analysis and discussion.

Action research is designed to make data available about the organization and its environment and then to help the organization to use that information to make plans for the future.

A variety of sources and methods for an action-research program are covered in this chapter; e.g., personal contacts, publications and reports, observation, interviews, questionnaires and market segmentation. In the next chapter we shall consider models, simulations and statistical decision making. Methods for using data that have been generated for gaining individual and group involvement in *joint action planning* are covered in Chapter 8. The ideas covered in these three chapters seem to be useful in assessing, formulating and implementing organizational strategies based on the framework that has been suggested thus far in the book — *environmental forces, strategy-generating structure, organizational objectives and outcomes, portfolios, segmentation* and *business strategies.*

Multiple sources and methods useful.

The ideas are also seen as being useful in developing the strategy-formation process. For example, group and organization involvement would include a series of sessions including, if appropriate to the unique situation, such focal points as: stating and analyzing objectives, priority setting and action planning, policy group development, intergroup conflict management, and progress review. The plans for the future from action research may include

Use questions from conceptual framework presented previously.

parts that extend for a relatively short period (e.g., six months) and parts that are projected for the long run (e.g., two or five years).

USE AND LIMITATIONS OF ACTION RESEARCH

Lack of rigorous research.

We shall discuss the various methods and provide examples of actual instruments or procedures that have been used in business and government. It is worth reiterating that there is a lack of rigorous research (e.g., systematically controlled experimental studies) that would provide a better understanding of the actual effectiveness of the action-research approach in inducing organizational change and strategy improvement. Much reliance at this point (perhaps too much) is placed on before-and-after studies, self-reports and anecdotal evidence.

The action-research approach, however, has been used in a variety of profit and nonprofit organizations with apparent success. For example, in a study of organization development—action-research activities in the 4000 employee "Sigma" plant, Blake et al. report significant improvement in: (1) productivity and profits, (2) management practices and behavior, and (3) attitudes and values.* Phases of the program included data collection feedback and discussion for group and intergroup development. The before-and-after evaluation, however, did not include a control group. Thus, any changes cannot be uniquely associated with the development activities.

Phillip H. Chase reports success in the utilization of an action-research design at Babcock and Wilcox, a manufacturing firm.† The holding of "Creative Management Workshops" at Babcock and Wilcox is reported to have resulted in an increased desire on the part of the executive participants to play an active role in future problem identification and problem solving.

Some research support.

A team development effort in a large investment and commercial bank is reported as a successful method for coping with overly centralized decision making and changes in the external environment that require concomitant change in the internal environment. Results from interviews and questionnaires and previously existing data on productivity, turnover and absenteeism were fed back and discussed, using teams of managers.‡ In addition, there have been a variety of applications of action-research programs in large and

A variety of applications.

---

*R. Blake, J. Mouton, L. Barnes and L. Greiner: Break-through in organization development. *In* Dalton, G., Lawrence, P., and Greiner, L. (eds.): *Organization Change Development.* Homewood, Ill., Richard D. Irwin, 1977.

†Phillip H. Chase: The creative management workshop. *Personnel Journal,* April, 1972, pp. 264–282.

‡Richard Beckhard and Dale G. Lake: Short and long range effects of a team development effort. *In* Hornstein, H., et al. (eds.): *Social Intervention: A Behavioral Science Approach.* New York, The Free Press, 1971, pp. 421–439.

small organizations in many countries, in government agencies, hospitals, and universities and school systems.*

From the point of view of the student analyst learning about policy there may be lack of opportunity to use some of the techniques (e.g., observation, interview, questionnaire, management science programs, conferences) being presented unless a cooperative organization is available. Nevertheless, the student should have some familiarity with the full variety of sources and methods being used today. Of course, these information sources and the methods for assessment and development of organizations and strategy formation may change somewhat over time. Included in the approaches, however, is a durable characteristic; that is, a systematic way of finding out what any current reality is. The systematic way of learning the "state of things" in the organization and the conditions in the environment has lasting value. Thus, the sources and methods would appear to be useful to the analyst, be he a student or a practitioner.

Systematic way of learning about state of things.

INFORMATION GATHERING AND PROCESSING

A first step in the action-research program is information gathering from the internal and external environments. There are a wide variety of sources: customers, suppliers, subordinates, friends, colleagues, books, reports, forecasts, journals and so forth.

Interviews and questionnaires may be used. The manager or analyst collects, organizes and interprets information to determine the status of those factors that seem to have greatest relevance to the organization.

Scanning status can be quite a job, considering the explosion of information that is occurring in our society and the world. For example, the United States government publishes over 100,000 technical reports each year. The number of journals and the number of published articles are increasing rapidly.

The manager or analyst has several information-gathering and processing problems with which to deal. What information is needed? Where is the information? Has enough information been

Several problems with which to deal.

---

*Numerous illustrations are provided by W. L. French and C. H. Bell: *Organization Development*. Englewood Cliffs, N.J., Prentice-Hall, Inc., 1978; thirteen studies are surveyed by L. Greiner: Patterns of organization change. *In* Dalton, G., Lawrence, P., and Greiner, L. (eds.): *Organization Change and Development*. Homewood, Ill., Richard D. Irwin, Inc., 1977; five case studies are presented in R. Beckhard: *Organization Development: Strategies and Models*. Reading, Mass., Addison Wesley Publishing Company, 1969; see also A. D. McCormick: Management development at British-American Tobacco. *Management Today,* June, 1967, pp. 126–128, B. F. White: A higher dimension for management development. *Report of the Presidential Task Force on Career Advancement,* November, 1966; and G. Foster: The managerial grid at Ward's. *Stores, 48*:42–44, 1966.

gathered? Is the information available to him? For example, he may feel that not enough relevant information is available within the organization itself. Even if the information is available within the organization, he may not know where to obtain it or, if he does, he may feel that for some reason it is unavailable to him.

If this situation seems unrealistic, reference to the anecdote discussed in Chapter 1 might demonstrate some of the problems.

The financial planner (or technocrat) in that anecdote, working for a large electronics firm, found that he needed a certain amount of data concerning market forecasts to plan realistically for capital improvements. His first attempt at gathering this information within the firm led him to the Marketing Department; it seemed natural that market forecasts would be available there. He contacted the marketing manager, who referred him to the market forecasting group. The manager of that forecasting group, after some discussion, agreed to give the financial planner what information he had available. Upon returning to his own financial group, the planner used the information to develop his recommendations. He soon found, to his dismay, that the manufacturing manager disagreed with his action plan, primarily because the manager disagreed with the data on which the plans were based.

The financial planner asked the manufacturing manager what he felt were realistic sales forecasts. The manufacturing manager presented him with his thoughts. The financial planner then went back and asked the market forecasting group why there was some discrepancy between what they thought were sufficient data and what the manufacturing group thought were sufficient data. The market forecasting group stated that the planner had received an early version of the forecast, and that forecasts had changed since then. The planner then asked for the updated forecast, which the group promised to send him. A new set of data was forwarded to the planner relatively quickly. The planner, upon receiving this new information and comparing it to the old information, realized that the two sets of data were totally different. To ensure that he would not waste time, he presented the manufacturing manager with the updated forecast. The manufacturing manager proceeded to tell him that, just as the previous forecast was too low, these data were too high by almost the same amount.

The planner now found himself rather perplexed as to what was happening. Rather than go back to the market forecasting group he decided to try another route. He asked his own superior to attempt to find sufficient data for planning purposes. The superior then contacted the financial Vice-President, who, in turn, called back to the financial planner and asked why he had gone over to the marketing department to obtain this information in the first place. The financial planner stated that he thought that, since it was market forecasts that he needed, the right place was the market forecasting group. At this point, the financial planner learned that although the market forecasting group did indeed have data available to them, they did not originate this data. They were merely information brokers. This was the primary reason they were hesitant about giving this data to the financial planner. It turned out that the person who originated all this data was in actuality in the finance group. Once the source of the data was found, the planner no longer needed the market forecasting group. The upshot of this action was to decrease the importance of the market forecasting group. It became evident to everybody within the organization that if you needed good, up-to-date, effective data, then you should probably go straight to the source rather than to the broker.

The problems that we see here indicate the various reasons information can be very difficult to gather within an organization. The validity of gathered data may be used as an excuse if something goes wrong with the formulated plan. This is evident in our previous anecdote. The financial planner was contemplating relatively large capital outlays based on the data that were supplied to him. The market forecasting group was afraid that if their information was used for these large capital outlays, running into millions of dollars, and something happened to jeopardize the plan, then management would blame their data rather than the plan itself. The planned capital outlay was approved in that organization and something did go wrong with the plans. The organization found that it ran into the credit crunch and encountered a recession that it had not planned on in its forecasts. It did not have enough funds to carry through the investment. The plan had to be scrapped at a considerable cost to the organization in total resources. By this time, however, the planner had already left the organization and was not directly affected. It's to be expected that some of the people within the organization who supplied the information were adversely affected, however. One of the problems we can see from this example is that much of the information that should be used cannot be found within the organization. For instance, information concerning a potential credit problem in the environment was obviously not available within the company. Also, the future of the industry hadn't been thoroughly studied by people within the organization; they hadn't looked to the relevant external sources of information.

We talk frequently in the policy-formation process about changes in the direction of the organization. Quite often this means that we are looking for new and different methods of achieving expanded goals. The search may reveal that pertinent information is just not available from any sources within the organization. Sometimes the source is outside the organization; sometimes, within. The questions arise as to just what are good sources of information and how we utilize them effectively.

A study by Aguilar* indicates that the main source of information about the environment used by managers is the informal information network with subordinates and with friends in the industry. Impersonal sources such as publications and forecasts provided the second most important source. As we have indicated earlier, the manager prefers live action, current and specific information and verbal media. However, studies by Mintzberg and Ansoff† indicate the need for managers (1) to use their sources and

Main source of information.

---

*Francis J. Aguilar: Scanning the business environment. *In* Columbia University Graduate School of Business: *Studies of the Modern Corporation*. New York, The Macmillian Company, 1967.
†H. Mintzberg: The myths of MIS. *California Management Review* 15(No. 1):92–97, Fall, 1972; and H. I. Ansoff: Strategic Posture Analysis. *Conference on Analytical Approaches to Strategy,* INSEAD, Fontainebleau, France, Dec. 1976.

Finding and Using Some Outside Informants

If we need new information that is specifically appropriate to analyze the impact of threats or opportunities (e.g., on market potential, competitors, pricing, customers, technical tidings, government actions, acquisition leads, etc.), where is that information available? Certainly some of the information can be obtained from publications and forecasts. Quite often, however, when considering new approaches or new directions, human resources must be utilized. The problems here are, first, finding relevant and reliable human resources or informants, and then utilizing those resources effectively and efficiently.*

Where is the information available?

The first problem involves two separate phases: Initially we have to be able to spot the informant and, second, we have to be able to approach him. (The first phase could be handled in advance.)

We all have a relatively good idea of the potential areas in which we might need material in the future; therefore, *informal information networks* or potential networks should be built in advance. There are three types of informants which could be potentially useful in achieving this purpose.

Build an information network.

The first type of informant can be called the *deviant*. The deviant is the analyst who has tested out new or untried ground. He has attempted to implement change in a particular area. Examples of this type of person would include inventors, innovators, entrepreneurs. People like Bill Lear of Lear Jet and stereo fame and Howard Head of Head Ski fame exemplify this type of person. An advantage of the deviant is that he makes good copy for the press. This means that it is relatively easy to spot him in the environment. This advantage should be utilized by the analyst by accumulating the names of deviants and situations under which they are operating.

Deviant.

The second type of person can be called the *transitional individual*. This person has gone through a rapid change or is in the process of going through a rapid change in his organization. His particular area of expertise lies in his knowledge of the incremental problems of change. He also is in the public eye, which makes him easily identifiable. On the way up, he is usually the hero for the journals; on the way down, he is usually the goat. An example of this type of person would be Jimmy Ling, formerly of LTV, Inc.

Transitional individual.

The third type of informant is the *marginal* individual. He is marginal not because his information is weak, but because of his

Marginal individual.

---

*See M. Granovetter: The Strength of Weak Ties. *American Journal of Sociology,* 78:1360–1380, 1973.

position. He is the type of person who works on the fringes of an industry or area, not specifically within it. Examples of marginal informants are lawyers, consultants and accountants. They are easy to find, but from a different standpoint; they advertise themselves quite frequently. Also, they are frequently more than willing to discuss the area around which they work. They often give a fresh approach to that particular area; they often see the entire picture rather than just a small portion of it, such as in the forest-for the-trees syndrome.

These various types of individuals provide certain advantages as information sources. The first two categories of informants are usually too busy with what they are doing at any given time to make immediate use of any information you might impart to them. The third individual usually does not want to actively participate in any given area since he makes his living working for people within the area. In this case the consultant, accountant or lawyer could not operate in his traditional capacity if we were also considered a competitor for the market.

Advantages.

One of the key problems in obtaining information from such human sources is discretion. Discretion must be used in the information-gathering process to ensure that the environment won't be changed by merely trying to gather information. The individual who attempts to buy land, for instance, in advance of a large expansion in a particular geographic area will find that if he doesn't use discretion in gathering information about that land, the price may increase simply because of the way he is asking questions.

Use discretion.

Likewise, the analyst gathering information may utilize the strategic alternatives he has previously developed for the information-gathering process. If the individual from whom he is gathering information cannot determine which of the alternatives will actually be utilized, it would be more difficult for the informant to become a potential competitor. Also, if the potential competitor believes that the analyst is creative enough to develop several different alternatives, he may be wary of trying to steal any ideas for fear that the analyst will be able to creatively prevent the informants from using those ideas effectively.

Need for strategic alternatives

The question now arises as to how to find this type of individual. Informants are usually very busy people and therefore don't like to waste their time listening to unrealistic or worthless ideas. They guard themselves from this problem through the use of screening devices. Screens are set up to keep out unwanted individuals and to allow in desired individuals. An example of a process of this type can be shown by looking back to our previous example of the financial planner in the large electronics firm. We saw that he went from individual to individual within the organization until he finally found the person who could actually give him the information he needed. The information-gathering process in this instance, however, took him in several wrong directions and, at one point, gave

How to approach informant?

him incorrect information. Therefore, one of the most important phases of the information-gathering process, where humans are concerned, is not only to find the individual you want to talk to but also to find the screen that will get you through to him.

The student has a ready supply of potential screens available to him in the faculty of his school. Many business or public administration professors have had dealings with individuals of importance of the type we are talking about during their careers. In many instances, professors and college administrators can act as screens. Students with good ideas can quite often utilize their contacts with faculty members as screens. Other people who act as screens are the same people referred to as marginal individuals when describing informants. Accountants, lawyers, consultants and others of that type perform the screening function for other informants. The main factor to be remembered is that discretion throughout this process is of prime importance. Also remember the desirability for developing alternatives before reaching the informant. The informant and his screen may be much more enthusiastic about talking to someone they feel has more to offer. Increased worth to the informant can be demonstrated by the use of several different alternatives.

Developing a Strategic Issue Information Network

Must the manager rely on his own informal information network? Although it gives the manager the current intelligence, which he needs (and may not get from his formal system), such a network is a crude and inconsistent one. It is subject to his time constraints, which are severe for both gathering and disseminating information. The manager frequently can contact only a few informants and can keep only a few close subordinates properly informed.

A staff analyst may be able to help develop a network for monitoring, data storage and dissemination. The network needs to be able to handle quickly and efficiently individual fast-developing threats and opportunities. It needs to be able to present managers with the relevant facts—the ideas, issues, bits of gossip and significant events. It needs to take information from the manager—from sources of information that, because of the manager's status, remain open only to the manager—perhaps through debriefing sessions. It needs to process, store and disseminate the information as an explicit data bank.

The information requirements need careful study. What do managers actually seek; what to they receive; what do they use? The analyst may be able to devise a network that will help go beyond the informal information networks and provide data on technology, market trends and internal operations.

An example of a flexible and responsible information network meeting some of the needs of managers is presented in Figure 6–1.

The functions of four groups of participants are identified: general managers, planning staff, task forces (drawn for capabilities in the type of problem identified) and operating units. The general manager group may be the top manager(s) in a small or medium size organization, or several groups scattered through a large organization. The general manager would maintain informal information networks but the formal network would add input on such strategic issues as vulnerability and internal flexibility, which have previously been discussed. The general manager would use debriefing sessions and use the planning staff as a data bank. In addition, he would assign selected issues to operating units or task forces for planning and execution. Strategic feedback, indicating whether the issue has been well identified, whether it deserves the priority assigned and

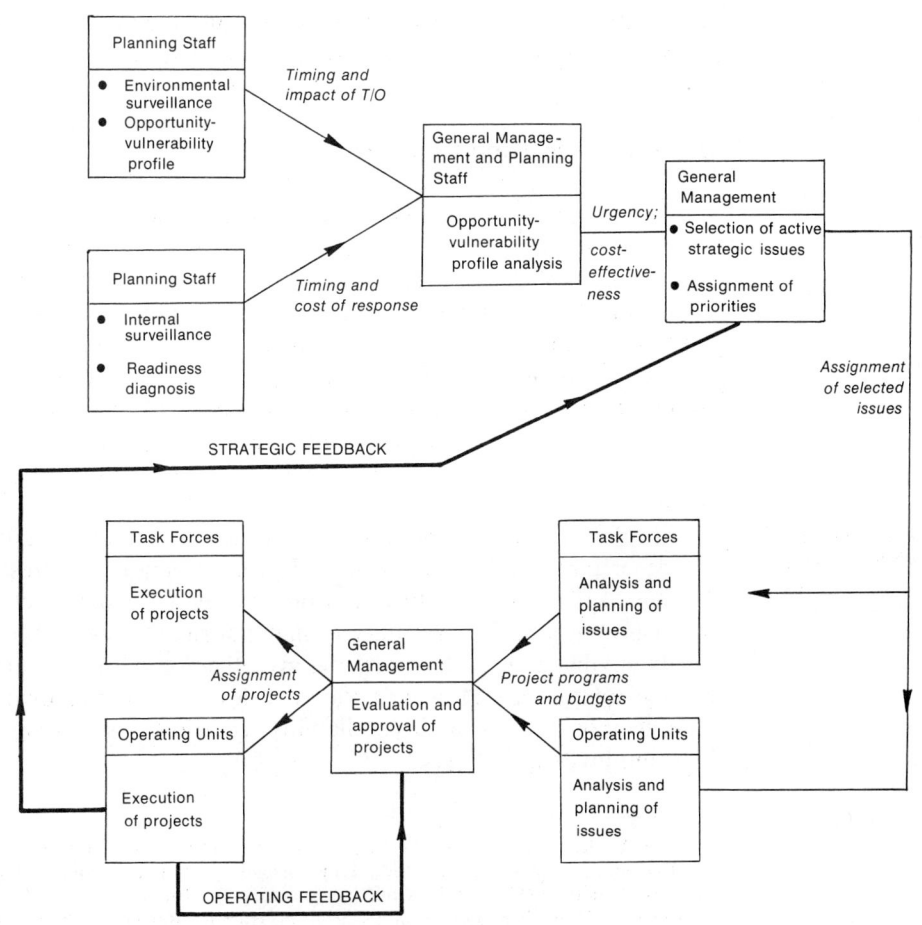

Figure 6-1 Strategic Issue Information Network. (Adapted from H. I. Ansoff: Managing strategic surprise by response to weak signals. California Management Review, 18(No. 2):31, 1975.)

whether the action strategy has been well chosen, would come from these units and task forces. Operating feedback would indicate whether the programs and budgets are being followed.

All in all, the S11 network is a continuous (or real time in character) one, aimed at helping the manager in updating issues and in processing, storing and disseminating vital information. Nevertheless, the manager must be alert to his own role. Can the internal and external relationships be built up for more effective functioning? Can he improve his face to face contacts through improved interviewing? Can he use observational tours more effectively? Questionnaires? What contacts and sources are available only to the manager? Can the planning group or task forces do more of the scanning?

These are difficult questions to answer without a specific situation and specific managers in mind (See Appendix to Chapter 8). In any event, careful study by the manager and staff may allow improvement in their use of face to face contacts (the interview), observation tours, forecasts, publications and reports and even the questionnaire. Discussion of those methods follows.

Using Face-to-Face Contacts

A frequently used method in analyzing policies and strategies is the face-to-face interview. Interviews may be conducted with managers, staff, employees, employee or union representatives, clients or customers, and community organizations and leaders, as well as informants outside the organization being examined. Other sources of obtaining information, such as published reports or observations, provide information about areas of interest that will prompt further investigation, but the interview remains as a significant method for gaining in-depth information on strategy formation.*

Advantages and disadvantages.

The basic interview requires that the analyst actually speak with the other party and question him as to his reactions, impressions, feelings, and so forth before, during or after his experience. The interview has a major advantage of high information yield. It can be highly flexible and can facilitate the investigation of highly complex management issues. However, the interview, as is well known, may involve difficulties in validity, reliability, question bias, retrospective bias and investigator bias.†

---

*See W. Keegan: Scanning the International Business Environment: A Study of the Information Acqusition Process. Unpublished doctoral dissertation, Harvard Business School, 1967; and R. Collings: Scanning the Environment for Strategic Information. Unpublished doctoral dissertation. Harvard Business School, 1968.

†For discussion of difficulties, see R. A. Bauer and K. J. Gergen: *The Study of Policy Formation,* New York, The Free Press, 1968. Also see M. Granovetter: The Strength of Weak Ties. op cit.

Two types of interviewing procedures are of particular use in studying complex strategy issues. The first is the standard structured interview. Attention is paid to standards of reliability by developing standardized questions and asking them of all respondents in the same manner. If the questions have been carefully selected and limited in number with appropriate preliminary analysis, this approach can yield a rich volume of information while saving considerable interview time. A systematic way can be developed to "add" together the descriptions from each respondent. The sum total of their reports compensates for individual bias and distortions skewed by poor or prejudiced reporters. This approach could be considered for *lower and perhaps middle* managers and staff (and for first line supervisors if appropriate). *Structured interview.*

A *less* structured approach that may be appropriate for *outside informants* and for *middle to high level* strategy makers is termed "the focused interview." An interview guide may provide a set of foci for the interviewer, but the interviewer himself determines the exact form and structure of the interview as he sees fit. This approach allows much deeper probing and is sensitive to unanticipated responses. It has a special advantage with persons of prominence. Such persons may resent an overly structured approach and may play such an important policy-making role in an organization that greater flexibility in questioning is desirable. This approach, though perhaps preferable for informants and top management officials, does suffer in terms of bias, validity and reliability. *Focused interview.*

Kahn and Connell* have dealt with the issue of selecting between an open "focused" interview (open-ended) and a standard structured interview (fixed alternative). They list the key factors to be weighed in deciding between the two approaches as: *Factors in choosing approach.*

1. The objectives of the interview (classification of respondents vs. understanding).

2. Respondent's degree of information about the topic.

3. Degree to which the topic has been thought through and opinions crystalized.

4. Respondent's motivations or ability to communicate.

5. Interviewer's prior awareness of the respondent's situation.

The main criterion they present, however, for using one format over another is that relatively complex and ill-defined issues should be evaluated through an open-ended technique.

The interview depends heavily on the interviewer's skill in sensitive probing. Intensive training is necessary for excellence in "focused" interviewing and also, to a lesser extent, for the standard interview.

---

*R. L. Kahn and C. F. Connell: *The Dynamics of Interviewing.* New York, John Wiley & Sons, Inc., 1957. See also R. L. Gordon: *Interviewing: Strategy Techniques and Tactics.* Homewood, Ill., Dorsey Press, 1969.

The many variations in organizational strategies and in emphases of different assessments make it impractical to define precisely the scope and direction of each interview or to establish any single formula for conducting an effective interview. The following listed guides seem to have general application to interviews on strategy issues:

Guides to interviewing.

Because of the sensitivity of some respondents to possible invasion of privacy, not only should an interview be treated in confidence, but the interviewer himself should avoid delving into or giving any impression of delving into areas not related to organization matters or strategy issues. Some situations would dictate that respondents should be advised that their expression of opinion will be treated in complete confidence (keep it "off the record").

Interview findings should be used with regard to the limitations of interviews. The manager or analyst should consider interview findings as one source of information that tends to confirm or to cast doubt upon findings reached through other methods. Interview findings often suggest the need for further study. When it is necessary to base a finding primarily on information gained through an interview, the findings should be appropriately qualified. In the case of group interviews, consideration should also be given to the extent to which one or two dominant personalities within the group may have influenced the responses of the other members of the group.

Interviews should sometimes be conducted at different levels in the organization. Strategy formation and implementation issues may be seen differently at various job levels in the organization.

There are many techniques and methods that can be used to manage conflict between different interest groups and to accomplish objectives. The emphasis and theme of interviews may be on success in attainment of objectives rather than on procedures and techniques.

The phrasing of the questions is important in the interview (as well as a questionnaire). To obtain a more accurate description of strategy formation practices, for example, consider phrasing the question so that the respondent is not describing what he thinks *his* policy or *his* behavior is like. Phrase questions so that he is describing decisions or the way decisions are made when he looks at his peers and when he looks at his boss. The rationale is that, though the objective superior can pinpoint some of the issues in the situation, the subordinate is assumed to see the "real" world a shade more clearly.

Developing and asking good questions for an interview (or questionnaire) is not easy. Many of the pitfalls and suggestions for overcoming this have been discussed elsewhere.* A brief listing of suggestions would include the following:

1. Be honest and utterly objective.
2. Avoid complex or abstract concepts that may obscure the meaning (e.g., some people may not know what a Norwegian correlation is).
3. Avoid too many open-ended questions (some people are hard to shut off).
4. Avoid loading the question (e.g., "Your product needs are not being met, are they?").

---

*For example, see F. N. Kerlinger: *Foundation of Behavioral Research.* New York, Holt, Rinehart & Winston, Inc., 1964; and M. Dunnette and W. Kirschner: *Psychology in Industry.* New York, Holt, Rinehart & Winston, Inc., 1968.

5. Avoid double-barreled questions (e.g., "Are you rewarded on productivity and creativity or on competent leadership and good investment spending?").

Interview Item Content

Ultimately, however, the usefulness of the interview rests with the type of question asked. The type of question could vary with the kind of issue under study (e.g., market tidings, current buying habits, product or service, distribution, investment, competitor's intentions, social responsibility) and the kind of respondent who is being used as a source of information (e.g., customer or client, informant, subordinates, public official, union leader, manager). When measuring how an organization goes about its strategy formation, for example, the objective is to ask about activities that are (1) descriptive of the strategy process, (2) related to the organization's effectiveness, and (3) capable of being changed by the action of the strategy maker.

To illustrate we shall describe and discuss a hypothetical focused interview approach and then a structured interview approach to measuring aspects of strategy formation. A "focused interview" approach might involve two general stages.* The first might be to identify strategy formation issues of interest, individuals involved in the issues, and phases through which the issues pass (e.g., initiation, staffing, data collection, and so forth). The second stage would build on the information so gathered and add to it. Subissues could be specifically delineated and identification and evaluation of useful practices made.

Stages I and II of the hypothetical interviewing project on strategy formation are described in more detail below.

Stage I
A. Identify issues involved in policy or strategy formation. Initial interviews will be with those in formal positions of leadership in relevant organizational units.

Many questions could be constructed from the organizational strategy considerations brought up in the previous chapters.
B. As a second step, information could be gathered concerning other participants in the issue area who have important roles in the strategy process (including people not in positions of formal leadership).
C. Between the inception of an insight into an opportunity and its ultimate implementation many events transpire. These events may be conceptualized as overlapping temporal phases, each of which may affect the effectiveness or outcome. Information could be gathered on the phases through which issues pass (e.g., initiation, staffing, data collection, feedback, analysis, standards, corrective action).

What is crucial to know about the internal and external environment?-

---

*These stages have been adapted from R. A. Bauer and K. J. Gergen: *The Study of Policy Formation.* New York, The Free Press, 1968.

D. Each respondent might be asked to sort a number of individuals on the basis of the subphase in which they are most influential.

E. Respondents could be questioned on the degree to which each strategy issue was salient to him and his own position on the issue.

Combining information from Stage I would provide a map of organizational strategy issues, phases and leverage points in the strategy-formation process in an organization or in a segment of it.

Stage II

Developing map of strategy issues, phases and leverage points.

On the basis of the information collected, the next step would be to sharpen the questioning and analysis on a set of specifically delineated issues and subissues.

Respondents would be asked to what extent, and how, changes in specific practices should be made to improve organization effectiveness and efficiency.

Suggested changes for improvement.

Thus, our "focused interview" example will provide for discussion and analysis of: (1) significant organizational strategy issues and subissues identified in the words of the respondents, (2) an indication of the significant phases that organizational strategy issues go through, (3) a map of leverage points in the organization or part of it and, finally, (4) an indication of suggested changes for improvement.

Example of structured interview.

In contrast, our example of a structured interview will include content relevant to organizational strategy effectiveness such as feedback on planning, the adequacy of staff meetings, the degree of conflict and consistency among objectives and policies, and adequacy of communication. This content is modified from part of a structured interview that was used recently in a federal government agency to assess its management policies and practices. The Instructions to Interviewers are included along with a sample of the questions as follows:

Sample of Structured Interview

Instructions to Interviewers

You are to fill out the interview schedule. The interviewee is not to write at all.

There are several rating questions such as "On a scale of 1 to 5, please rate how clear the quality of work expected is. 1 indicates very poor; 5 very good." *Make sure* that the interviewee gives you only one number.

In general, the format of the interview is to ask closed questions such as in the above example followed by open-ended questions in which the interviewee is allowed to express his opinions in an unstructured manner. Please follow this format. However, do not allow the interviewee to ramble. Throughout the interview schedule, special instructions for the interviewer are placed in parentheses.

The entire interview should take approximately ____ minutes; you should not exceed ____ minutes per interview.

At the end of the session, you may write down any observations you would like to make on a separate sheet. Please complete this structured interview sheet immediately after the completion of an interview.

Structured Interview

LEAD-IN BY INTERVIEWER: This survey is being conducted by _____

_____. The purpose of the survey is to review and evaluate

the effectiveness of organizational strategy in the _____

_____. We are concerned with the whole set of organization and management policies. After we finish the survey, we are going to report

the grouped results to the top management of _____.

No one in _____ will see your individual answers.

First, I'd like to ask you a few background questions.

What is your full name? _____
                            FIRST   MIDDLE   LAST

What is your job title? _____

(Instructions to interviewer: Please note the position of the interviewee, that is, staff, assistant director of the unit, or director of the unit)

_____ staff

_____ assistant director of the unit

_____ director of the unit

How long have you worked for the _____

_____ years and _____ months approximately

The name of the unit is (interviewer: Please fill in; don't ask)

_____

It is located in (Interviewer: Fill in; don't ask)

_____

How long has it been since your boss sat down with you to discuss your overall planning formally? _____ years and _____ months and _____ days

In general, how often does your boss sit down with you to discuss your overall planning? Every _____ years and _____ months and _____ days.

Think of a scale of 1 to 5. One represents very bad impressions, five very good impressions. Now I want you to rate the feedback you receive from your boss regarding your planning. First, how helpful do you feel this feedback is? _____ points. Second, how fair do you feel the feedback is? _____ points. On the 1 to 5 scale, would you say that your boss' evaluation is based on solid facts? _____ points. Do you feel that the boss is too critical? _____ points.

Overall, how would you rate the feedback your boss gives you? _____ points. Why do you feel this way?

Sample of Structured Interview — Continued

In general, how often do you have staff planning meetings? _____ never or about every _____ weeks. Again think of a scale of 1 to 5 where 1 represents very bad impressions and 5 represents very good impressions. How would you rate the amount of participation in these staff meetings? _____ points. How would you rate the contribution of your boss during these meetings? _____ points. Do you feel that the real planning problems are discussed at the staff meetings? _____ points. Finally, on the 1 to 5 scale, do you feel that there are enough planning meetings? (1 represents too few meetings, 5 too many meetings) _____ points. Overall, how would you rate the staff meetings? _____ points. Why do you feel this way?

Again using the 1 to 5 scale where 1 represents strong agreement, and 5 represents strong disagreement, how would you rate the inconsistency or contradiction among policies and guidelines? _____ points. Do you feel that there is conflict between objectives that groups are expected to accomplish? _____ points. To succeed it is necessary to play politics. _____ points. If a project is going badly it would be better to keep it quiet. _____ points. Good ideas get serious consideration from top management. _____ points. Information is dealt with secretively. _____ points. Overall, how do you feel about conflict and communication in the organization?

On the 1 to 5 scale, how would you rate your boss regarding the communication of information and new developments that directly affect organizational strategy? _____ points. On the same scale, how would you rate managers of the _____ who work in the regional offices? _____ points. Why do you feel this way?

USING OBSERVATION TOURS

In addition to conducting interviews or having them conducted, the policy analyst or manager may use an observer approach.* For example, in studying how an organization goes about its policy-formation process, the manager would tour various locations and watch individuals and coalitions going about their daily tasks for a period of time. The manager might then be qualified to answer such questions as:

1. What is the pattern of distribution of perceptions of the organizational strategy?

---

*See E. J. Webb, et al.: *Unobtrusive Measures: Nonreactive Research in the Social Sciences.* Chicago, Ill., Rand McNally & Company, 1966.

2. What are the positions and makeup of relevant coalitions?
3. Which are the dominant coalitions for various issues?
4. How much do the coalitions practice effective teamwork and effective intergroup cooperation?
5. To what extent are goals and targets challenging, clearly understood and accepted?
6. What are the competencies of various relevant strategy initiators?
7. What capabilities are needed to make the strategy go?

Gain firsthand knowledge.

The observer approach would be useful if it is accepted and skillfully applied. The major advantage to this method is that the observer can gain firsthand knowledge and a "feel" for the process at hand. However, normal standards of validity (the degree that a characteristic of an individual or a situation reflects what is felt to be the true characteristic) and reliability (the degree of consistency in a behavior or measure over an extended period of time or recurring number of repetitions) may be prevented by:

Validity and reliability?-

1. Lack of formal criteria of assessment.
2. Lack of independent checks on observation.
3. Lack of recurrence or replication of phenomena.
4. Bias of manager trying to observe phenomena in his own organization unit.

In addition, those truly skilled in the observation approach are in scarce supply and expensive. However, the observations or impressions of managers or policy analysts are relied on frequently in making judgments about the organization's policies and the strategy-formation process. The judgments are, of course, not limited to just those based on in-house observations. Feelings or impressions are used and sometimes are quite useful, for example, in judging competitors' corporate strategies, customer behavior or labor union activities.

Observation of external environment.

Using Forecasts

The manager or analyst, of course, may rely on a variety of forecasts. Some may be available to the public in the library and/or through subscription. Some may be privately conducted at his direction. For example, forecasts in the following areas may be available already, or, on the other hand, may be made by (1) sales (e.g., by industry or by corporate product/service), (2) general economic (e.g., Gross National Product, Personal Disposable Income), (3) technological (e.g., automatic data processing), (4) social values (e.g., attitudes toward materialism or human dignity), (5) social indicators (e.g., measures of "quality of life" phenomena such as noise pollution or personal security), and (6) competition's intentions (e.g., plans to enlarge an agency's scope of operations). Accurate forecasting in such areas is likely to give the organization an obvious advantage in striving for success.

Several forecasts that may be useful.

180 / ASSESSMENT AND ORGANIZATION DEVELOPMENT

Important progress is being made in "futures" forecasting.*
We shall discuss such forecasting in the next chapter.

Using Publications and Reports

Written or published information includes several different subcategories. The sources in one subcategory include various research organizations that are available for both business and nonbusiness sectors. One that comes to mind would be the Stanford Research Institute's long-range planning series. It is available to organizations at a fee. Some libraries carry this series, but many large organizations subscribe to it. The series can be very costly, but is of relatively high quality. There are similar types of series and reports from consulting firms, other research organizations, such as the Brookings Institute, and others that are of equally high quality. The major benefit of these reports is the quality of their research. The research writers usually go to great lengths to determine whether the environment is conducive to various strategic moves in a particular industry or area. The reports are also relatively unbiased in their point of view.

Quality.

The problem with these reports, however, is that they are often quite costly and, also, their material is usually dated. The researcher who writes these reports usually gathered the information from other published sources, so that the combination of publication times built into the various reports and their data lead to, in some instances, considerable lags between the original data sources and the time of reading by the user. It is often impossible to determine just how many sources the material has gone through; whether the reports are second-, third-, fourth-, or even fifthhand information is never really known.

Material dated?

A second source of public information is the entire list of business and specialist publications. Included in this list would be

---

*Several illustrations are included in the following: John C. Chambers, Satender K. Mullick, and Donald D. Smith: How to choose the right forecasting technique. *Harvard Business Review*, 49:45–74, July–August, 1971: Nestor B. Terleckyj: Measuring progress toward social goals: Some possibilities at national and local levels. *Management Science*, 16:755–778, August, 1970; Robert U. Ayres: *Technological Forecasting and Long Range Planning*. New York, McGraw-Hill Book Co., 1969; Kurt Baier and Nicholas Rescher (eds.): *Values and the Future*. New York, The Free Press, 1969. Also see such journals as *The Journal of General Management, Technological Forecasting, Marketing Research, The Futurist, Public Administration Review, Dun's and Modern Industry, The Wall Street Journal*, and *Business Week*. The case analyst, of course, may not have an informal information network or be able to have his own forecasts made, but he, as well as the manager, can rely on published reports and forecasts such as the Department of Commerce: *Survey of Current Business; Standard and Poor's Current Statistics;* Bureau of the Census, *Statistical Abstract of the United States;* National Industrial Conference Board, *Economic Almanac;* Bureau of Labor Statistics, *Monthly Labor Review* and Robert Morris Associates, *Annual Statement Studies.*

publications such as *Business Week, The Wall Street Journal, Fortune,* and various technical and industrial publications. The advantage of these publications is that their data are usually up-to-date. They are also easy to come by and relatively inexpensive. The problem with their information is that they can often be biased in their interpretation of potential opportunity areas, and also their information has varying degrees of quality.

Up-to-date.

Bias?

A third source of information includes the documents published by governments. The federal government, in particular, publishes large amounts of information on just about any conceivable topic or strategic area. This information is readily available for use from large libraries. Vital information, however, is frequently hidden among large amounts of extraneous material in the government periodicals section. Most large libraries do have a government periodical librarian who is adept at researching any given topic in a particular strategic area. If the manager or analyst utilizes these reference librarians effectively he will find that they can be extremely useful to him. The reference librarians in these areas may have little contact with the "real" world. They often welcome contact with people who are trying to research actual problems through government reports. Their knowledge of the various government reports often enables them to spot, on a moment's notice, specific types of information that might be available.

The benefits of this kind of information are that it is readily available and covers millions of different topics. However, it is often unclear just how old this information is. The quality of the information also varies considerably from report to report. Much of the information may be open to bias. The various departments that carry out the research, such as the Departments of State, Interior, Labor, Commerce, and so forth, often have a major interest in the outcome of the report. When evaluating any particular report consideration must always be given to the reason for the research and the research agency that performed it.

Readily available.

A general problem that applies to the entire area of written reports is that, when the analyst does find a particular piece of information from a published report that appears to fit his corporate strategy effectively and properly, he should be wary of that information. If he has seen this information, then others have probably seen it also. Since we are talking about changes in corporate strategy, what we really want is a competitive advantage in the strategy-formation process. If the information relating to the organizational strategy is readily available, then competitive advantage could very well be lost.

Any competitive advantage?

Using Questionnaires

An alternative or supplementary approach to information gathering is the questionnaire. The questionnaire survey for assessment requires a set of questions—open-end and/or closed-end, structured or unstructured—to be answered and returned by the relevant parties under study. Some assessors* have little faith and trust in the questionnaire approach for purposes of developing organizations. This may be for several reasons: too impersonal, the difficulty in giving objective and meaningful interpretation to results, attempted improper use as a scorecard, and unrealistic expectations about the ease of developing leads for assessment for descriptive data.

Many analysts (e.g., Likert)† are more favorably inclined toward the questionnaire. Perhaps the situation here is similar to many other instances in organizations where assessment (or training) techniques seem to follow a pattern of rise in interest and use and then decline or abandonment, and then a rebirth, and so on. The questionnaire approach has probably not been developed to its fullest potential as an important diagnostic device.

Choosing a format.

Two types of questionnaire procedures may be of use in studying complex policy issues. The first is the self-administered, fixed alternative questionnaire. It is praised for requiring the respondent rather than a coder or interviewer to make an attitudinal judgment, for giving greater clarity to the dimensions for answering the question, and for easing data handling via precoding. On the other hand, fixed alternative items may be detrimental in the sense that they provide irrelevant or meaningless frames of reference. That is, the wording may not be appropriate to the respondent.

The other type of questionnaire uses an open-ended format. This type is usually criticized and praised for opposite reasons: e.g., data handling is cumbersome because of the need for coding responses, and response freedom is allowed without researcher-based sets. With advantages and disadvantages for each type, it means that the appropriateness of the response format (open, fixed or a combination) is left to the judgment of the questionnaire developer. Though the open format is cumbersome, this approach has proved useful in assessments; for example, "Write-in responses were extremely valuable in a large government industrial facility. A recurring theme in the write-ins was conflict and polarization, skilled vs. unskilled labor, white vs. black, unions vs. nonunion, etc. This polarization lay at the root of numerous problems, including lack of cooperation, poor morale, and even potential violence at the installation. This issue was isolated as one of the primary barriers to organizational improvement, and later fact finding during the survey was aimed at identifying potential solutions in terms of planned management action."§

---

*See E. Shein: *Process Consultation: Its Role in Organization Development.* Reading, Mass., Addison-Wesley Publishing Company, 1969.

†R. Likert: *The Human Organization.* New York, McGraw Hill Book Co., Inc., 1965.

§See *Evaluating Personnel Management.* FPM Supplement 273-73, U.S. Civil Service Commission, Washington, D.C., 1973.

Questionnaire Item Content

As with the interview, the usefulness of the assessment and development questionnaire rests with the type of questions asked. The type of questions could vary with the kind of policy under study and the kind of respondents who are being used as a source of information. For example, a questionnaire on consumer attitudes toward products or services may be helpful in identifying challenges and opportunities in the external environment. The following is a sample of items that were used in a study of consumer attitudes toward alternative transportation modes in Baltimore (N = 550) and Philadelphia (N = 471).* The respondents were asked to indicate the importance of several factors (time, convenience, reliability, state of vehicle and so forth) for work trips and non-work trips. Each respondent was also asked to check how satisfied he was or would have been if he took (1) *auto* and (2) his most likely form of *public* transportation (bus, subway, train, taxi). For example:

Consumer attitudes.

How satisfied were you with	Very Little	Little Satisfied	Some-what	Gener-ally	Very Well
The time it took to travel					
auto satisfies					
public transportation satisfies					
The cost of the trip					
auto satisfies					
public transportation satisfies					
The feeling of independence					
auto satisfies					
public transportation satisfies					
The time it took to travel					
auto satisfies					
public transportation satisfies					

Some implications for possible strategic moves to change mode use patterns were developed from the study. For example, the researchers concluded that perceptions of travel time, susceptibility to weather, avoidance of changing vehicles, avoidance of waiting, avoiding the unfamiliar and independence were *more* significant than cost, reliability of destination achievement, state of vehicle, congestion and diversions in choosing between auto and public transit.† Also, significantly different preferences were

Implications for Strategy.

---

*F. T. Paine, A. N. Nash, S. J. Hille and G. A. Brunner: Consumer attitudes toward auto versus public transport alternatives. *Journal of Applied Psychology* 53(No. 6):472–480, 1969.

†It is interesting to note that the DIAL-A-RIDE bus system has been developed to take advantage of some of the more important travel considerations.

found between the inner-city segment and the suburban segment of respondents.

However, for our main example of a questionnaire let us use the same concept as we did with the interview; when measuring how an organization goes about its policy-formation process, the objective is to ask questions about activities that are (1) descriptive of the policy process, (2) related to organization effectiveness, and (3) capable of being changed by the action of the policy makers.

The policy-formation questionnaire that follows is one such instrument. It attaches an agreement-disagreement scale that can be used to measure such dimensions as planning adequacy, reward orientation, goal consensus and clarity, conflict and inconsistency in policies and standards, and skill utilization depth. (Additional dimensions could be added.)

Content Related to Organizational Effectiveness

A large body of research has shown these dimensions to be associated with organizational effectiveness.* It is recognized that for any particular organization all of these dimensions may not be appropriate criteria of effectiveness. The choice of criteria will depend on the objectives of the organization and the requirements imposed on it by its environment for continued survival and mission attainment.

Measuring organization climate.

In fact, these are measures of the organization climate. The theoretical construct of organizational climate according to Forehand and Gilmer refers to the environment within which organization participants operate.† The significance of this construct lies in the longstanding proposition that behavior is a function of the interaction of a person and the environment. The combination of items (or scales) proposed are possible methods for assessing organization effectiveness to be used along with gross end results or economic measures. Organizational unit outcomes and economic measures may be difficult to obtain and frequently are contaminated by irrelevant factors such as economic conditions, windfall innovations, fortuitous competitive conditions, and political or governmental variations.

These measures of organization climate seem to be important correlates of organizational effectiveness. If managers were to

---

*See, for example, J. Price: *Organizational Effectiveness.* Homewood, Ill., Richard D. Irwin, 1963; C. Perrow: *Organizational Analysis: A Sociological View.* Belmont, Calif., Wadsworth Publishing Co., 1970; T. Mahoney and W. Wietzel: Managerial models of organization effectiveness. *Administrative Science Quarterly,* 14(No. 3):357–365, Sept., 1969.

†G. A. Forehand and B. Von Haller Gilmer: Environmental variation and studies of organizational behavior. *Psychological Bulletin,* 62:361–382, 1964.

institute changes so as to maximize such phenomena as clarity and acceptance of goals and improvements in planning adequacy, research suggests that organizational effectiveness would be favorably and significantly affected.

However, the correlates of organizational effectiveness are only a first approximation of the tasks that must be accomplished by top managers if the organization is to be successful. As stated before, additional study and discussion and research need to be conducted to determine clearly defined and highly specific tasks appropriate in various situations. On the following pages is a sample of items from a policy-formation questionnaire that has been tested in business and government.

Policy-Formation Practices Questionnaire

The statements listed on the following page describe some policy-formation practices. Rate each item, using the 1 to 5 scale of agreement-disagreement, on the degree to which the condition described in the item exists in the organization.

The 20 questions listed in the policy-formation questionnaire examine each of five previously identified dimensions from several perspectives. For example, the four questions 1, 6, 11 and 16 relate to the planning adequacy dimension. The questions have been arranged in mixed sequence for better reliability. However, they may be reshuffled into the dimensions or groupings indicated.* To obtain a composite picture of how those practices are rated, the data are extracted from the questionnaire and consolidated into a policy-formation practice summary form as follows:

Processing the data.

1. Transfer the scores (1 to 5) that are associated with each dimension.
2. Add the scores of all questions with each dimension and enter the total.
3. Divide the total by the number of questions in each dimension and enter the average score.

Finally, the average scores are transferred to a Policy Formation Profile Form where they are graphically displaced. These previous procedures, of course, may be handled with a computer program. It may be appropriate to develop such a policy-formation practices profile for each component and/or unit that is being studied. An alternative or supplementary approach would be to develop breakout tables for comparison of superior and subordinates responses and for comparison of unit and component responses. These comparisons could be made on an item by item

---

*The groupings are based on factor analysis. See F T. Paine and M. J. Gannon: Job attitudes of managers and supervisors. *Personnel Psychology,* Winter, 1973.

1. Important factors are frequently overlooked when plans are made. YES yes ? no NO
2. People get credit for good planning. YES yes ? no NO
3. People know pretty clearly what is expected of them. YES yes ? no NO
4. There is inconsistency or contradictions among policies and standards. YES yes ? no NO
5. People have freedom to use their abilities on the job. YES yes ? no NO
6. Important information is not considered when basic policies are made. YES yes ? no NO
7. Promotions are based on ability and talent. YES yes ? no NO
8. People know what they must do to make better plans. YES yes ? no NO
9. There is a conflict between objectives or directions that people or groups are expected to accomplish. YES yes ? no NO
10. People have enough authority to modify plans as they are implemented. YES yes ? no NO
11. Opportunities are missed because of poor planning. YES yes ? no NO
12. To succeed it is necessary to play "politics." YES yes ? no NO
13. The mission of _____ groups is clearly defined. YES yes ? no NO
14. Policies and strategies conflict with each other. YES yes ? no NO
15. People must get approval for decisions they should be able to make themselves. YES yes ? no NO
16. Policies and plans are made with great care. YES yes ? no NO
17. Getting ahead is a matter of luck and pull. YES yes ? no NO
18. Specific targets for improvement are made and understood. YES yes ? no NO
19. People give assignments or directives that conflict with each other. YES yes ? no NO
20. People can use their good ideas. YES yes ? no NO

basis or by grouping of items. The following abbreviated tables suggest one way in which the data may be organized and analyzed in preparation for discussions with managers or groups being assessed or in preparation for a report on the policy-formation process. After the examples of tables for grouping survey data, we turn to other programs for processing information from both the internal and external environment (e.g., market segments).

POLICY-FORMATION PRACTICES SUMMARY FORM

Planning Adequacy	Reward Orientation	Goal Consensus and Clarity	Conflict and Inconsistency in Policies	Skill Utilization Depth
Question Value	Question Value	Question Value	Question Value	Question Value
1 ___	2 ___	3 ___	4 ___	5 ___
6 ___	7 ___	8 ___	9 ___	10 ___
11 ___	12 ___	13 ___	14 ___	15 ___
16 ___	17 ___	18 ___	19 ___	20 ___
Total ___	Total ___	Total ___	Total ___	Total ___
Average ___	Average ___	Average ___	Average ___	Average ___

POLICY-FORMATION PRACTICES PROFILE FORM

Dimensions

Planning Adequacy	YES	yes	?	no	NO
Reward Orientation	YES	yes	?	no	NO
Goal Consensus and Clarity	YES	yes	?	no	NO
Conflict and Inconsistency in Policies	YES	yes	?	no	NO
Skill Utilization Depth	YES	yes	?	no	NO

TABLE OF RESPONSES TO QUESTIONNAIRE ITEMS

Unit _____

There are _____ managers and _____ staff in the unit.

Significant conditions in unit _____

Component _____

188 / ASSESSMENT AND ORGANIZATION DEVELOPMENT

TABLE OF RESPONSES TO QUESTIONNAIRE ITEMS
(Continued)

There are _____ managers and _____ staff in the unit.

Significant conditions in the component _____

_____

These are the percentage responses to the questionnaire administered in this unit. An asterisk designates that superiors and subordinates *in the unit* responded in a significantly different manner; a double asterisk indicates that supervisors and subordinates in the entire component had significantly different responses.*

*Significant differences in responses between superiors and subordinates can be ascertained by means of a statistical test (t-test). Where possible, efforts should be made to explore the reasons for differences within the unit.

		YES	yes	?	no	NO	No. of Responses
(Conflict)	There is conflict between objectives that people and groups are expected to accomplish						
	Unit	__%	__%	__%	__%	__%	( )
	Component	__%	__%	__%	__%	__%	( )
(PLN)	Important factors are often overlooked when plans are made	__%	__%	__%	__%	__%	( )
		__%	__%	__%	__%	__%	( )
(GC)	People know pretty clearly what is expected of them						
	Unit	__%	__%	__%	__%	__%	( )
	Component	__%	__%	__%	__%	__%	( )

Breaking Out Returns and Using the Results

Compare various groups.

Results from questionnaire, interview, observation and other sources are often useful when comparisons can be made between responses of participants in major components of the organization. By comparing attitudes or behavioral indications from major departments, divisions or satellite units, valuable leads may be discovered as to specific policy problems that are unique to one or more segments of the organization. For example, it may be useful to compare whether respondents in the unit answer in a manner significantly different from the respondents in the entire component. Feedback of such unit-component comparisons may be meaningful to the superior in charge of the unit in question.

In addition, a check could be made to see if there are any significant differences between those responding as superiors and those responding as subordinates. There is a tendency for persons to be clear about how much influence they have, would like to have and are encouraged to exercise when they are subordinates looking upward. It may be more difficult for them to fully accept the same operating guidelines when they look downward at their subordinates. Therefore, they may operate by a double standard. They may want to be involved and have influence with their superior but are unwilling to recognize and accept that their subordinates feel the same way in the organization. Breakouts of data comparing superiors' responses with subordinates', may be helpful in getting such double operating standards out in the open for discussion. Bringing a group together to examine and interpret such policy-formation practices data may lead to the development of some policy-formation practices to correct the situation.

The group may need *practice* and *training* before it can achieve the full potential in this process. Interestingly, as a questionnaire is used with the same group of respondents over time the results may become more reliable and even move backward in terms of favorability of results, even though the environment has not changed significantly or at all. The results may move backward for another reason, namely, because of higher expectations in the group as to effective policy-formation practices.

Because of such reasons, the actual levels of descriptions, as indicated by the responses on the scale, are of less interest than what the policy-formation group in question (and other such groups) are doing to bring about improvements. Used as a basis for group discussions, the questionnaire's main purpose is to serve as a catalyst to start the improvement process, rather than as a research or analytical instrument.

Use as a catalyst.

Using Market Segmentation Breakouts

Breakouts of questionnaire, interview, sales forecasts or other data from relevant parties who are not normally considered members of the organization (e.g., clients or customers) need to be as carefully considered as the data breakouts from those within the organization. For example, it may be useful to breakout groups who are similar in their reasons for needing or wanting or not needing or not wanting a particular type of service or product.

Identify choice criteria used by various groups.

The characteristics (i.e., age, sex, income, education, geographic location) of the various groups may give an indication that different strategies or policies could beneficially be adopted for various groups.

An important factor in determining the scope of an organizational strategy involves the decision by analysts as to the key market segments to be exploited. The definition of market segment often presents the organization with artificial constraints that are difficult to overcome. This constraint can be similar to the situation discussed earlier in which the business limited its potential solutions by its definition of objectives.

Determine where to concentrate effort.

The key question asked here is what business the organization is in.* This determines the markets or segments of markets on which the organization will concentrate its efforts. Various methods of determining which segments to attack have been suggested by many authors. Traditionally, market research breakouts have been employed to spot these segments. The key question for the policy analyst involves what the basic types of segments might be.

Geographic segments.

One form of market segmentation involves differentiating geographic tastes, preferences and requirements. The housing industry understands that different geographic regions require or can withstand varying product standards and that local government regulations provide constraints on the type of building materials, styles and sizes of products that can be offered to the consumer. Other differences involve the needs of the consumer. Housing in the South requires less insulation to the cold than similar housing in the North. A similar example would involve the producers of flavored soft drinks. In the outset of the marketing of these products, it was determined that certain ingredients, particularly caffeine, were more desired by consumers in some areas (the South) than in other areas. Firms engaged in these industries, and others affected by similar types of problems, have adapted their products to these geographic preferences or requirements.

Same product for different types of customer.

Another form of segmentation involves producing the same basic product for several different types of customers. This policy is appropriate when different customers are using a basic product in different ways. An example would include the widespread practice of producing a product for both private label and brand label marketing. Food processors supply the same product to supermarkets for sale under different labels. The product remains the same, but the package and, usually, the price differ. The same practice is followed by many other industries supplying products to the consumer—tires, petroleum and clothing.

---

*T. Leavitt: Marketing myopia. *Harvard Business Review,* July-August, 1960, pp. 45–56.

This type of segmentation allows the organization to uilize its production capacity more fully. Problems arise, however, in that the organization may become overly dependent on one segment to the detriment of the others. Many organizations have found, after entering the private label market, that they have become captive suppliers to one customer. They become dependent on one large customer to absorb their increased capacity. It is also possible that attempting to reach different markets may dilute the efforts of the firm in some one segment.

A third of segmentation finds an organization attempting to attack several different markets with variations of a similar product. The organization perceives that customers do not all want exactly the same product. The firm attempts to tailor its product line to satisfy as many different customers as possible. The auto industry exemplifies this product and customer policy. The major producers all offer an extensive line of different models through different outlets to appeal to the broad range of tastes and preferences of the consumer. Even with the proliferation of models and lines by the major producers, there is still unfilled demand being captured by foreign producers and small specialists such as the Lotus Europa.

Vary product for several markets.

This type of policy may become expensive. Unless large production runs can be utilized, inefficiencies can develop within the organization. In the auto industry there is the need for large scale duplication of marketing and distribution efforts. This type of segmentation requires large investments in all phases of the organization. It also forces the organization to diversify its efforts among several different products and markets. The chance arises that if the various market segments are not large enough, resources may be misallocated among the various products. The policy analysts, while aware of potential difficulties, may find that experimenting with different breakouts of information from informants, clients or customers may give some clues to design market segmentation policies.

What are some potential difficulties?

Experiment with different breakouts of information.

To reiterate, managers and other policy analysts frequently use multiple sources and multiple methods in gathering and processing information. The results may serve as a vehicle to begin discussion and analysis. For example, the information network, report, observation and interview are regarded as assessment and development tools for identifying indications of possible strategy problem areas or leads to be explored. The results may be used:

As an opener for management discussions and conferences. Discussion of, say, interview results with key participants may be aimed at joint diagnosis of the situation to provide a basis for evaluation.

As an indication of potential demands and opportunities in the external *and* internal environment where in-depth analysis appears to be warranted. Questionnaire results may be considered before a product or customer policy is developed. Interviews and forecasting, for example, can be structured to follow up on the leads generated from the informal information network.

In Chapter 8 we shall explore the use of results from information gathering and processing activity in an interlocking chain of conferences down the hierarchy.

SUMMARY

An organization may need some sort of assessment and development approach for a variety of reasons, such as to aid in: (1) adapting to environmental changes, (2) adjusting to a new domain of operations, (3) maintaining its current position, or (4) improving its "steady state."

A number of strategies, sources, and methods for proceeding with assessment and development are presented in this chapter and the next two chapters. We are stressing a broadly defined organization development approach to policy formation, including management science as well as behavioral science programs. The activities in this approach are viewed as both problem solving and developmental in nature.

In particular, the action-research program is introduced in this chapter. Action research, as the term is used in this book, is a generalized procedure, including three parts: (1) information gathering from the internal and external environment; (2) organization, analysis and feed-in of such information with relevant parties or groups in the organization; and (3) joint action planning based on the analysis and discussion. The generalized procedure may be based (using considerable judgment in selecting content) on the framework suggested thus far in the book, e.g., environmental segments, strategy-generating structure, organization objectives and outcomes and strategy development.

This chapter has emphasized that while there is some supporting evidence validating the effectiveness of an action-research program approach for improving some aspects of the policy-formation process, a cautious "I don't know for sure" approach to prescriptions must be maintained. With additional study of the wide variety of applications of action-research programs in both large and small organizations in many countries, in business, government agencies, hospitals, universities and school systems, better insight and understanding may be developed in the next few years.*

This chapter also has paid considerable attention to developing a network and improving methods for information gathering and processing, i.e., the informal information network, the S11 network, face-to-face contacts, tours, forecasts, publications, re-

---

*See, for example, the recent study of D. G. Bowers: OD techniques and their results in 23 organizations: The Michigan ICL study. *The Journal of Applied Behavioral Science* 9(No. 1):21–43, Jan./Feb., 1973.

ports, and the questionnaire. We have provided several examples and illustrations so that the reader will have some familiarity with a variety of ways of finding out about the "state of things" in the organization and expected conditions in the external environment. Careful judgment and expertise are needed in selecting and using the appropriate sources and methods.

Finally, we introduce some programs for the processing and use of results of our information-gathering activities. Special recognition to the breakouts of information about *market segmentation* as a part of organizational strategy formation is given.

Next we shall turn to some management science programs (statistical decision making, models, simulations) that may be useful in generating and analyzing information for the action-research program.

DISCUSSION QUESTIONS

1. Select an organization with which you are familiar. Discuss why this chosen organization may need some sort of systematic assessment and development activities on a more or less continuous basis. What type of information is needed?

2. What is meant by an organization development approach to strategy formulation? In your judgment, how would it differ from more traditional approaches to strategy formation?

3. One of the many programs in the strategy-generating structure is an action-research program. What does this program involve? How might this program be linked or coupled with other programs?

4. Give an example of how the action-research program might be used in an organization with which you are familiar. Discuss possible difficulties that might be encountered. How would you overcome such difficulties?

5. Compare and contrast the observer approach for data gathering with the interview approach.

6. Identify some of the correlates of organizational effectiveness discussed in the chapter. These variables are measures of organizational climate. What is meant by organizational climate?

7. Organizational unit outcomes and economic measures are frequently said to be contaminated. What does this mean? Why are they contaminated?

8. Discuss two types of interviewing procedures that may be used for data gathering about strategy formation. Under what conditions would you recommend each type?

9. Identify and discuss several guidelines for effective data gathering with survey instruments in an organization.

10. Discuss a top management information system. What are some of the most effective methods and some of the more important sources? What cautions should be observed in using the system?

11. How does the type of question asked affect the usefulness of the assessment interview?

12. Take an organization of your choice. Explain precisely how you would assess the effectiveness of the strategies of that organization. What would be some of the more significant questions you would ask? What sources of information would you use? What methods of data collection would you use?

13. Why is it useful to break out results from data collection by major components of the organization?

14. Discuss the use of results from data collection with survey instruments. Why is the feedback process so important?

15. Identify some of the most useful sources of information for top managers and analysts.

Suggested Additional References for Further Research

Alter, S. L.: How Effective Managers Use Information Systems. *Harvard Business Review,* 54(No. 6):97–104, 1976.

Athanassiades, J. C.: The distortion of upward communication in hierarchical organizations. *Academy of Management Journal* 16(No. 2):207–226, 1973.

Carlson, E. E.: An interview with "visible management" at United Airlines. *Harvard Business Review,* 53(No. 4):90–97, 1975.

Charnok, J.: Can Hospitals Be Managed by Objectives? *Journal of General Management* 2.(No. 2):36–47, 1975.

Gluck, F. W., Foster, R. N., and Forbis, J. L.: Cure for Strategic Malnutrition. *Harvard Business Review,* 54(No. 6):154–165, 1976.

Kerlinger, F. N.: *Foundations of Behavioral Research.* New York, Holt, Rinehart & Winston, Inc., 1964.

Locke, H.: Innovation by Design. *Long-Range Planning,* 9(No. 4):34–39, 1976.

Mandell, S. L.: The management information system is going to pieces. *California Management Review,* 17(No. 4):50–56, 1975.

Mintzberg, H., Raisinghami, D., and Theoret, A.: The Structure of "Unstructured" Decision Making. Professional papers of the Academy of Management, Division of Business Policy and Planning, Boston, 1973.

Newell, A., and Simon, H. A.: *Human Problem Solving.* Englewood Cliffs, N.J., Prentice-Hall Publishing Co., 1973.

Scott, M.: A data base for your company? *California Management Review,* 19(No. 1):68–78, 1976.

Webb, R. J.: Organizational Effectiveness in Voluntary Organizations: A Study of the Institutional Church. Unpublished dissertation, University of Maryland, 1973.

7

USE OF MANAGEMENT SCIENCE APPROACHES IN STRATEGY FORMATION
    Quantitative Problems in Policy
    Discounting and Present Value
    Personal Probability
    Establishing Priorities and Rates of Return
    Cost of Delay
    Tracing Decisions into the Future
    "What If" Questions and Models
    Simulations With Risk Analysis
    Forecasting Models and Methods
    Scenarios
    Combining Expert Opinion

REASONS FOR SUCCESS AND FAILURE OF MANAGEMENT SCIENCE PROGRAMS

COMPUTER-AIDED STRATEGY ANALYSIS
    Applications of Computers
    Creativity and the Computer
    Complex Systems
        Human Reaction to Complex Systems

SUMMARY

DISCUSSION QUESTIONS

APPENDIX 1. SOLUTION TO PROBLEM I

APPENDIX 2. SOLUTION TO PROBLEM II

MANAGEMENT SCIENCE AND COMPUTER PROGRAMS

Some information-gathering and processing aspects of an action-research program have been discussed as a way to measure how an organization goes about its policy-formation process and as a way to assess environmental forces and market segments. The action-research program has been discussed also as a way to obtain an indication of what should be done to improve organizational strategies and policies and to improve the process by which they are made. In addition to, or supplementing, the action-research program there is a broad range of programs available to aid the manager or analyst in playing his role. The range covers a spectrum from rather ill-defined qualitative programs (e.g., some scanning or intelligence activities, Chapter 6) to traditional procedures such as financial analysis (Appendix to Chapter 3) to rather sophisticated quantitative programs such as capital budgeting, statistical decision making and simulations. These programs, of course, vary in their degree of usefulness, depending on the type of organization and the type of policy problem. Furthermore, in some situations these programs may be viewed as part of an action-research program, e.g., when they include information processing or analysis that is fed into the action-research program itself. Or, the generalized procedures may be considered as a group of programs that are part of the overall strategy formation process used to design, implement and review integrated organizational strategies.

USE OF MANAGEMENT SCIENCE APPROACHES IN STRATEGY FORMATION

We have recognized that if feasible and effective organizational strategies are to be developed and utilized, evaluation programs must be built into the policy-formation process. An understanding of some of the evaluation programs available to the analyst or manager is, thus, a necessity. This chapter will illustrate and briefly discuss some of the rather sophisticated programs for determining if the organizational strategy fits the relevant environment. We shall consider (1) various management science or quantitative programs for dealing with environmental uncertainties, performing futures forecasting and evaluating alternative organizational strategies, and (2) computer programs for improving creativity in the strategy process.

Kinds of programs discussed.

After study of this chapter the reader should be able to see the relevance of these programs for the manager or analyst, understand where and when they can be used, and recognize some of the limitations and difficulties in applying them. Our objective does *not* include teaching how to actually utilize the management science programs. This is done in functional courses.

Objectives of this chapter.

However, enough information is given about certain aspects of capital budgeting and statistical decision making so that application may be made directly to specific cases and field investigations.

Although these programs can have great value, it must be remembered that there is no substitute for the informed intuition and judgment of top management and influentials. Management science programs are only to supplement, not to replace, the manager's judgment in strategy and policy formation.

Dealing with uncertainty and future consequences.

Part of the complexity of the problems facing the policy analyst lies in the fact that he must deal with *environmental uncertainties* and he must evaluate *future consequences.* In order to explain these problems and to illustrate some of the assumptions made and some of the generalized procedures that have been proposed to help the analyst, we shall use a simple example of a policy situation involving capital budgeting and statistical decision theory. We shall describe the situation, then ask some questions about it. Then we shall answer the questions and indicate some additional quantitative problems for practice. A policy analyst may want to try to answer the questions before proceeding to the discussion that is provided.

Quantitative Problems in Policy

One problem we shall discuss involves financial investment and a change in technology in a very small organization.*

---

*This problem was adapted from M. Richards and P. Greenlaw: *Management Decision Making.* Homewood, Ill., Richard D. Irwin, 1966.

MANAGEMENT SCIENCE AND COMPUTER PROGRAMS / 197

The decision required may be viewed as one of a cluster of decisions. The cluster might include decisions about the product, the market and the source of funds, as well as technology and financial investment. For this very small firm the decision may be viewed as a strategic decision. The problem is as follows:

In the past, all financial investment decisions made in the Larroc Corporation have been based on the "intuitive" hunches of its president, A. N. Renim. Recently the president, heeding the advice of his astrologer, hired a young financial analyst, Mr. M. Nonnag, who, since he has been with the organization, has spent considerable time extolling the virtues of present value analysis to Mr. Renim. In a recent conversation between the two on this subject, the president made the following comments: "Your present value model is theoretically unsound because it assumes that future returns realized from investments are known for certain, whereas, in real life, they're not. For example, I have a chance to buy for $5,000 a new machine with an economic life of three years that will (1) effect labor savings of $2,200 in the first year, $3,630 in the second, and $2,662 in the third if business is good, but will (2) effect savings of only $1,100 in the first year, $2,420 in the second, and $1,331 in the third if business is bad. Our cost of capital is approximately 10 per cent.

Mr. Nonnag asked, "What probabilities do you assign to business being "good" as opposed to being "bad"?

"About 50–50," responded Mr. Renim.

"Well, then," said the analyst, "solving your problem is not difficult at all."

1. What do you suppose Mr. Nonnag's conclusion was? Why? Show all calculations.
2. What would the analyst's conclusion have been had the president assigned a probability of: (1) 0.3 to "good" business conditions and 0.7 to "bad" business conditions? (2) 0.4 to "good" conditions, and 0.6 to "bad" conditions?
3. What are the weaknesses of such management science programs for policy formation?

Discounting and Present value

One way to handle the problem would be as follows:

The pattern of benefits (savings) occurs over a three-year period. We recognize that a dollar today is worth more than a dollar next year, because we have the option of investing the present dollar and obtaining a positive return during the time period in which we would have to wait for the other dollar. A way to take the time value of money into account is called discounting or present value calculating. The simple arithmetic of compound interest may be relied on in calculations for an approximate solution (approximate because an assumption is made that the benefits are received at the end of each year). If the interest rate is r between year 0 and year 1, then $1 can be converted to $1 + r dollars in year 1. In similar fashion a dollar return in year 1 can be exchanged for $1/(1 + r)$ dollars in year 0. Thus, the present value of $1 in year 1 is $1/(1 + r)$ or, more generally, the present value of $1 in year n is $1/(1 + r)^n$.

For the problem given we would come up with the present value for each of the years' savings and then add them together for a total present value associated with a decision to invest followed by good business conditions. Follow a similar procedure for bad business conditions. But what is the r? The interest rate (r) is the cost of using money, and our indicated cost of capital is 10 per cent. We proceed as follows:

If good business, PV=2,200/1.1 + 3,630/1.21 + 2,662/1.33 = $7,000
If poor business, PV=1,100/1.1 + 2,420/1.21 + 1,331/1.33 = $4,000.

What is a conditional value?

The $7,000 and the $4,000 are referred to as present values (PV). They may also be referred to as conditional values (CV), that is, benefits dependent or conditioned on the business climate. Two alternative business climates have been indicated as possible; only two, of course, is a simplification.*

Personal Probability

What is an expected value?

So far the likelihood of probability of occurrence of each alternative climate has not been taken into account. In using management science procedure from statistical decision theory, one may take the probability of various outcomes into account by explicitly using the personal judgment of the decision maker as to the likelihood of the various outcomes. The policy analyst should carefully audit the environment and estimate this likelihood. Then the value of the outcome (or present value of outcome) should be weighted by the probability of occurrence of the outcome. The result is called the *expected value* (EV). Thus, the expected value of a conditional benefit is equal to the perceived probability of occurrence times the conditional benefit. In the problem that we have:

If good business: $7,000 × 0.50 = 3,500
If poor business: $4,000 × 0.50 = 2,000

Make adjustments for time pattern of distribution and for uncertainty in case analysis.

The two expected values ($3,500 and $2,000) may be added together, based on the assumption in our procedure that there is a 100 per cent probability of good business *or* poor business: $3,500 + $2,000 = $5,500. $5,500 is the total expected value of the benefits. Thus, the benefits have been adjusted for the time pattern of distribution and for uncertainty. We have used discounting to present value and personal probability to make these adjustments.

Before we go further it should be mentioned that in simplifying the problem we have ignored depreciation and corporate income taxes. These might be taken into account by subtracting annual depreciation from gross benefits, obtaining taxable income

---

*The problem may be adapted to a government organization by determining the financial value of benefits of services to the client under various conditions. The calculation of benefits, of course, is difficult and inexact.

(if a profit is being made). The taxable income times the income tax rate would give the taxes, and subtracting the taxes from the gross benefits would give us the net savings. The main thrust of the discussion here, however, does not have to do with taxes and depreciation.

The reader may wish to proceed with the calculations with part (2) of the problem to check the effect of variations on probability estimates that might be used. In addition, there are some variations in calculation procedure, but these are outside the scope of this book. For a discussion of the possibilities there are numerous books on statistical decision theory.*

Thus, present value is one procedure to be used in making the choice. It says, in summary, that a project should be undertaken if the sum of future returns minus costs discounted back to the present is positive; that is, if $PV > 0$.

Present value decision rule.

Case Problem I

The following problem illustrates the application of present value techniques to a strategic decision-making process:

A staff planner has been presented with three alternative strategic moves to offer to top management. The three strategic moves appear to be feasible relative to the external environment. He is not sure that they are financially feasible, however.

They all have differing cash flows, so that comparison is not obvious. The planner would like to know if any of the moves would be profitable and which would provide the greatest return based on net present value (NPV) criteria. He has already determined that the cost of capital for the firm is 7 per cent. The cash flows for the three moves under the same probability are shown below.

Strategic Move	Initial Outlay	Year 1	Year 2	Year 3	Year 4
A	100,000	15,000	45,000	60,000	55,000
B	125,000	50,000	40,000	25,000	20,000
C	75,000	30,000	25,000	20,000	15,000

Net Returns

Which of the strategic moves are economically feasible? If the firm can make only one strategic move, which should it make and why?

Establishing Priorities and Rate of Return

Projects seldom occur in isolation. The choice is not just whether we accept or reject this specific project; what is needed

---

*For example, see R. Schlaifer: *Applied Statistical Decision Theory*. Boston, Division of Research, Graduate School of Business Administration, Harvard University, 1961; and S. Kassarf; *Normative Decision Making*. Englewood Cliffs, N.J., Prentice-Hall, Inc., 1977.

Why do we need priorities?

is a priority approach for ranking competing projects. The present value method may be converted to a priority approach; or another criterion, the rate of return, may be used. Some readers may be familiar with this alternative approach, which asserts that a project should be undertaken if the rate of return is greater than the cost of capital (r > cost of capital). The rate of return (r) is the rate that equates the present value of the future stream of benefits with the present value of the future stream of costs; that is, PV = 0.

Rate of return

This rate of return criterion will indicate the same choice as the present value criterion for accept-reject policy problems. Furthermore, as indicated, the rate of return provides a basis for establishing priorities among competing projects. The present value also provides such a basis, but these methods do not always indicate the same order of rank; that is, under certain time patterns of benefits and costs, the present value rank order will not be the same as the rate of return rank order. This occurs because of the differences in the assumptions about the rate at which the benefits will be reinvested. Simply stated, according to the statistical decision theory, a decision maker in selecting an approach should check to see which assumption comes closer to his situation.*

Cost of Delay

Another difficulty with the rank order approach may be that the cost of delaying certain alternatives may not be considered. Some strategic moves may be better suited to present needs; others can be delayed profitably if, for example, the interest rate is expected to come down. A simple example using present values and assuming a $1,000 yearly budgetary constraint (a very small organization) is shown below.

Strategic Move	Cost	Present Value Year 1	Year 2	Cost of Delay
A Divest product line x	$1,000	$2,100	$1,800	$300
B Phase out distributors	$1,000	$1,300	$1,100	$200
C Begin search for sites	$1,000	$1,700	$1,050	$650

Examine cost of delay.

If we select the strategic move on the basis of rank order for each year, we select move A in the first year and move B in the second year (A has already been selected). Examining the cost of

---

*For a more complete explanation of situations in which the two methods produce different results, see H. Bieman, Jr., and S. Schmidt: *The Capital Budgeting Decision*. New York, The Macmillan Company, 1966.

delay, however, would lead us to a different choice, that is, C in the first year and A in the second year. This illustrates for us that choices cannot be made in a vacuum. As we discussed in Chapter 5, a portfolio of strategies (and budgets) should be taken into account that ties together short- and long-range opportunities and resources. The effects of alternatives should be closely analyzed to determine what interactions will occur in the long run. Strategic moves that appear beneficial in the short run can often become constraining influences in the long run.

Portfolio approach.

Tracing Decisions into the Future

Decision trees are one application of statistical decision making that is particularly useful for tracing decisions into the future, especially for capital budgeting decisions. Decision trees help the analyst to structure his decisions under conditions of uncertainty. By indicating the many possible events and the decision-making requirements that will be encountered, and using estimates of probability that each event will occur, this procedure helps the manager to assess the probable payoff from his decision.

Decision tree procedure.

The following diagram traces a simple decision tree problem. The analyst can make one of two investment decisions. Decision A has a 50 per cent probability of returning a net profit of $7,000 and a 50 per cent probability of returning $3,000. Decision B has a 60 per cent probability of returning $10,000 and a 40 per cent probability of no profit. The initial diagram would be drawn as follows:

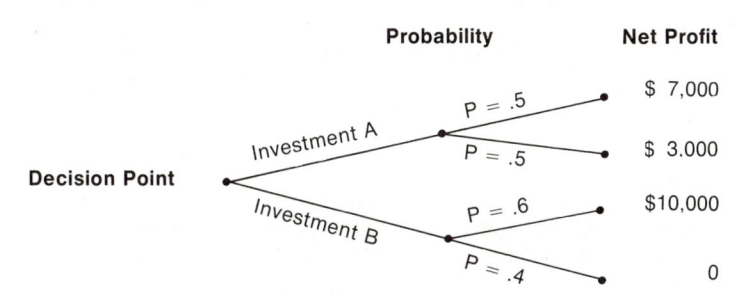

	Probability	Net Profit
Investment A	$P = .5$	$ 7,000
	$P = .5$	$ 3,000
Investment B	$P = .6$	$10,000
	$P = .4$	0

Decision Point

The solution would find the expected value for both investments, and a decision would theoretically be made based on the highest expected profit. (In this case, investment B would be chosen, since it has an EV = $6,000 versus an EV of $5,000 for investment A.)

A realistic view of the decision-making process, however, would consider how the various outcomes might affect the decision maker's future. The decision maker might decide to choose investment A regardless of the fact that investment B has a higher expected value. He might be led to this conclusion because there is a positive net profit from one, whereas there is a potential for no profit from the other. If, as we discussed in earlier chapters, individual rewards are based on not incurring negative results, then this would provide a "safer" decision.

Are managers finding statistical decision making useful? The situation is changing rapidly. However, a survey* of 40 United States companies indicates that 12, or 30 per cent, use general statistical decision-making procedures for planning for the following types of applications: to analyze factors in markets outside the U.S. to be considered in marketing lighting and home-entertainment products, to estimate costs, and to make general forceasts of economic conditions, deposits, earnings, and so on.

The survey also indicates that 15, or 38 per cent, use decision trees for planning for the following types of uses: to select research and development projects, to evaluate alternative new business opportunities, and to evaluate the outcome of strategic moves that are conditional, particularly in regard to product-planning decisions. Decision trees have become more commonly used by business managers, but they still have not achieved widespread acceptance. The main reason seems to be the difficulty in obtaining accurate information about the kinds of problems management faces and the computational complexity for all but the simplest problems. The following decision tree problem demonstrates the uses of this method in the strategy-formation process.

Case Problem II

A chief executive has requested his planning staff to analyze potential alternatives available to the firm. The alternatives involve expansion into new product lines related to their present efforts. They cannot afford to enter both areas at the same time, however. Both areas are relatively new, and information is not perfect. The expected returns under best and worst conditions are as shown below.

	Product A	Product B
Best results (0.4 prob.)	$7,000,000	$10,000,000
Worst results (0.6 prob.)	$6,000,000	$ 5,000,000

The planning staff has to decide if it is worthwhile to gather more information at a cost of $1 million. The estimated effectiveness of this research is not perfect, however. The staff estimates the probability of obtaining information favoring Product line A under the worst results is

---

*E. C. Miller: *Advanced Techniques for Strategic Planning*. AMA Research Study 104, New York, AMA, 1971. This excellent study has provided many examples and ideas, some of which are paraphrased in the following sections. See also B. W. Denning: *Corporate Planning: Selected Concepts*. New York, McGraw-Hill Book Co., 1972; M. K. Starr: Planning models. *Management Science, 13* (No. 4):115–141, 1966; H. Mintzberg: The science of strategy making. *Industrial Management Review, 8*:71–81, 1967.

0.7. Likewise, the probability of information that favors Product line B under the best conditions is 0.8.

Which product line should be chosen and why?

"What If" Questions and Models

In the adoption of any management tool the critical test is the test of usefulness. One great value is to enable management to ask "What if . . ." questions. The major contribution of models is their ability to ask questions and obtain answers that are an approximation of what might actually happen if a particular organizational strategy is followed.* This makes it possible for organizations to experiment with new strategies and policies before they select the one they will ultimately adopt. Models, therefore, are frequently designed to evaluate outcomes of organizational strategies, given various forecasts of future events.

Models.

A model is merely an artificial representation of a possible or actual occurrence. It is an abstraction used to represent conditions, relationships and processes. The model may be expressed in mathematical form. Although many managers tend to shy away from anything mathematical, they have, in fact, worked with a mathematical model of their business if they have worked with a budget. The budget is actually a quantitative forecast of future actions. Therefore, there should be nothing inherently threatening in the use of models.

Mathematical models vary in complexity from simple linear relationships used in break-even charts to highly complex linear programming techniques. The equation $y = k + av$ is an example of a simple model, where y equals total costs, k equals fixed costs, a equals variable costs per unit, and v equals volume in units. The equation is a symbolic representation of a real-world process.

Modeling has been aided by computers that process and store the tremendous quantities of data involved in modern business operations. The very act of constructing models, however, generates new insights into the nature of the factors that make it successful, or not.

Models can also be used to test the sensitivity of the end result sought, such as present worth or return on investment; to change certain input factors; and to test the impact of alternative courses of action. Some specific applications of models that have been reported include the following:

Sensitivity analysis.

(1) to evaluate the effect of alternative corporate strategies on profit; (2) to forecast cash flow; (3) to develop a corporate profit model; (4) to contribute to determination of research priorities and to estimate improvements in productivity from automation.

---

*See D. Schendel and G. R. Patton: *A Simultaneous Equation Model of Corporate Strategy*. Krannert School of Management, Purdue University Paper 582, December 1976.

The North American Rockwell Corporation, as an example, uses corporate models to assist it in acquisition planning.* They first use the model to uncover promising sectors of the economy in which it is anticipated that future growth will be above average for the economy as a whole. This is done with a model of the United States economy projected to 1980–1985. The company then carefully screens possible acquisitions. Once a promising possibility has been found, the company uses a computer-based financial model to determine what the effect of the acquisition would be on its overall financial resources.

Any kind of model is limited by the realism of the variables used to describe the actual occurrence. Too often models have been developed based on the perceptions of these occurrences by only one or a few individuals. The perception of the market, as an example, may differ substantially within different levels and functions within the organization. Some individuals may perceive many market factors, such as competitive reactions, pricing, and to some extent, even demand for the product, as external to the decision process of the firm. Others, however, may view these same factors as being key determinants of their actions.

If the model is to be an effective tool for answering "what if" questions, these differing perceptions must be coalesced into a consistent explanation of the effect of decision on outcomes. If they are not, using the previous example, the model would be invalid for at least one of the groups, at best. One group would be evaluating decisions with a model that did not express their views of the environment. Those policy analysts would be falling into the standard trap faced by anyone who uses models, computerized or not. That is the garbage in–garbage out syndrome; the results are only as effective as the inputs.

Caution: Garbage in, garbage out.

Simulations With Risk Analysis

Simulations involve the use of models to investigate what would result if we used different assumptions and forecasts about the organization and its environment. To the degree that the model is accurate, the simulation will show what would happen if certain circumstances occurred in the real world. In this sense, any model can be used to simulate. Analysts talk of using their models to ask "what if" questions; the operations involved in answering these questions define simulations.

Simulation has a long history. It is possible to trace the

---

*See Ansoff, H. I., et al.: Does Planning Pay? The Effects of Planning on Success of Acquisitions in American Firms. *Long Range Planning*, 3, December, 1970. This study of 93 firms provides some quantitative evidence supporting the effectiveness of long range planning (for acquisitions).

technique back to early war games. Although simulation is quite popular in other fields, it seems to have caught on as a useful business tool only recently.

Some examples of the use of simulation include: evaluating a new product, evaluating planning alternatives, assisting research and development planning and project selection, and studying possible divestments and consolidations. The Burroughs Corporation has a simulation model of the financial structure of the entire company. Xerox Corporation uses simulation to aid in marketing decisions. American Can developed a family of models to help to make the many different planning decisions it faces.

Risk analysis is a kind of simulation used to assess the relative attractiveness of alternative plans.

Consider use of risk analysis.

Alternative plans typically depend on many inputs that will occur in the future. Among these may be market size, selling prices, market growth rate, share of market, investment required, operating costs and useful life of facilities. Risk analysis allows an evaluation of the plans that take into consideration the uncertainties surrounding the inputs.

In applying risk analysis, the analyst would generate a probability distribution for values of *each* significant input (indicating the chances that the value would be achieved). Then sets of the inputs would be selected (at random) according to the chances they have of turning up in the future. The rate of return would be determined for each combination, and the process repeated until there is a clear portrayal of the investment (chances that the rate will be achieved).*

How to apply risk analysis?

Forecasting Models and Methods

A variety of management science models and methods may be useful to the manager in forecasting.† Econometric methods, for example, involve measurements of economic variables, frequently including correlation analysis. Using such analysis (and other techniques), the technocrat (an econometrician in this case) constructs equations that relate relevant variables to the factor being predicted and therefore develops predictive equations. Such equations have been used: (1) to forecast market sizes, (2) to forecast prices, (3) to forecast the relationship between volume of activity and costs, and (4) to relate profit to supply of raw materials.

These forecasts may be useful in the portfolio approach.

Econometric forecasting is a rapidly expanding field. Moreover, the models currently in use are no longer limited to short-range (six-

---

*For elaboration, see D. B. Hertz: *New Power for Management*. New York, McGraw-Hill Book Co., Inc., 1969.

†L. T. Sitmister and J. Turner: The development of systematic forecasting procedures in British industry. *Journal of Business Policy*, 3 (No. 2), 43-52, Winter, 1972-1973. See also discussion and references in Chapter 6.

to 18-months) forecasts of the economy as a whole. Long-range (up to five years) models are being built to forecast trends and changes for the entire economy, such as the Hickman-Coen model at Stanford. Short- and intermediate-term models for specific industries are also being developed.

Input-output models.

One econometric technique is the use of *input-output* models. Input/output analysis is a method for analyzing the interrelationships of a particular economy to uncover existing interdependencies. Through this method of analysis, the trend of development of the technical coefficients among the various economic sectors included in the input/output table can be combined to forecast the growth or decline of these sectors by some specified time in the future. Technical coefficients are ratios that show the proportion of each economic sector's output that is made up of input into that sector and all the other economic sectors under study. In broad terms, input/output analysis shows where all purchases by an industry come from and where all sales end up, as input either to other industries or to final-demand markets. This indicates the interdependencies that exist in the economy. It is only since the development of large computers that input/output analysis has become useful to the businessman. Even today it is not widely used. However, many feel it will be one of the essential planning tools of the near future as analysts become more sophisticated in their design and analysis of these techniques.

Detail forecasts by industry and market.

The main advantage of input/output analysis is that the interindustry forecasting provides detail by industry and by markets, which the aggregative econometric models do not.

Consider degree of supplier concentration and major changes in availability of raw materials.

The National Steel Corporation and the Celanese Corporation use input/output analyses developed specifically for their industries. By using forecasts of the technical coefficients that are projected for some specified time in the future, the input/output models contribute in both cases to the companies' long-term forecasts. Combustion Engineering, Inc., also uses input/output analysis for long-term economic forecasting.

Does model fit objectives of analyst?

When fully developed, these techniques could be of great assistance to the policy analyst in attempting to forecast future demand. A key factor, however, involves the determination of just how well the particular econometric model fits with the objectives of the analyst. The industry represented by the model must correspond specifically with that of the firm. The time span encompassed by the model must also correspond with the time span dealt with in the corporate strategy.

The policy analyst must realize that no econometric method is infallible; it is only as good as its component parts. All econometric models are based, in large part, on past experience. They cannot predict sudden changes in policy such as wage and price controls. The results of econometric models must be constantly analyzed and updated if they are to be used effectively in forming and evaluating organizational strategies.

Another rapidly growing field is *technological forecasting*. Technological forecasting has been defined as "the prediction, within a stated level of confidence, of the anticipated occurrence of a technological achievement, within a given time frame with a specified level of support."* Each forecast comprises five categories:

Technological forecasting.

1. *Background.* This section should identify the organizational objectives to which the fields of technology being forecast can contribute.
2. *Present Status.* The field of technology's current state-of-the-art should be quantitatively described.
3. *Forecasts.* Consists of a projection of the state-of-the-art as a function of time and cost with an indicated level of confidence.
4. *Product Implications.* This section should describe the effect on the corporation of the technological advances projected in the forecast.
5. *References and Associated Activities.* List the technical documents in the field that add credibility to the forecast.

Technological projections used to time resource allocation.

The methods used to forecast the future state-of-the-art are generally categorized as intuitive, growth analogy and trend correlation, with several techniques existing within each of these categories.

Technological forecasting has been utilized by public as well as private organizations. The U.S. Navy first prepared and published a technological forecast in 1968. This has aided them in determining what types of armaments might be possible in the future. This is particularly useful because of the long lead times involved in developing sophisticated weapons systems. Other public and private organizations have used technological forecasting for similar ends.

Scenarios

One step that may affect strategy making for large organizations is the development of scenarios, forecasts of possible future environments using various assumptions.

Alternative scenarios for an oil company, for example, might be developed with various assumptions about oil price increases, restraints on oil production, absorptive capacity problems, balance of payment problems, rate of inflation and economic recovery.

---

*Marvin J. Cetron and Donald N. Dick: Technological forecasting: Practical problems and pitfalls. *European Business* 21:13–24, April, 1969. See also J. R. Bright: *Technological Forecasting for Industry and Government*. Englewood Cliffs, N.J., Prentice-Hall, Inc., 1968; P. Thurston, Make TF Serve Corporate Planning, *Harvard Business Review*, Sept.-Oct. 1971.

Scenarios would endeavor to incorporate new input into strategy making: to cope with the possibility of many different futures; to provide scope for considering less likely possibilities, threats and opportunities; to provide greater scope for imagination and flair in perceiving major discontinuities. To be useful to the manager they would illuminate relevant uncertainties, broadly scan likely futures, be plausible and internally consistent, be dynamic and evolutionary, be comprehensive, yet simple and adaptable. Scenario building is difficult and time consuming, but if used by general managers, it may be helpful in dealing with new futures and latent opportunities.

Take the Changing Values scenarios developed by Shell Oil Co.* What effects might there be on industrial companies or on Shell if the scenario came to pass? The new emerging values in the Changing Values scenario are:

Smallness
Self-dependence
Concern with environment
Trade leisure for earnings
Resilience, stability
Large voluntary sector
Different criteria for success
Low GNP, low energy intensity

Contrast your answer to one that you would give in an alternative scenario, The Belle Epoch, came true. The necessary conditions for the Belle Epoch according to Shell are:
1. Strong political leaderships
2. Strong links into international trade system from national economies. Trade growth without distortions.
3. Government understanding of the wealth creation process, and adoption of policies that foster it.

Combining Expert Opinion

One problem with using scenarios or other management science programs is obtaining a consensus on the direction of growth for the firm. What apparently is required is a method of combining the opinions of key individuals within the organization for those purposes.

Consider using the Delphi method.

The Delphi method, as developed by the Rand Corporation,†

---

*G. Galer: Shell's Approach to Monitoring the Environment: An Application of Scenario Planning. Presented at *Analytical Approaches to Strategy,* INSEAD, Fontainebleau, France, Dec., 1976.

†N. C. Dalkey: *The Delphi Method: An Experimental Study of Group Opinion.* Rand Corp., 1969. Also see W. C. Wedley: Behavioral Implications at Delphi Strategy Formulation. *Analytical Approaches to Strategy,* INSEAD, Fontainebleau, France, Dec., 1976.

is a decision-making technique that is designed to gather consistent expert opinions from group members. The final decision, or analysis, should provide a consensual group point of view. Typically the problems attacked are ones in which uncertainty, through lack of complete information, is a key factor.

The technique requires three key ingredients: The first involves the precept that all responses by the expert members of the group should be anonymous. In this way undue emphasis is not placed on who originates the information, but on the content of the information itself. This is particularly important where the opinions originate from individuals within the organization. Without anonymity, formal or informal leaders would probably exert undue influence during the process.

What are three key ingredients?

The second factor involves the ability of the group members to refine their decisions and analyses through feedback of prior information. All members of the group are given an overall figure or piece of data (such as a median response) representing the responses of the group. They may then base their next decision on this overall information. This provides the experts with the ability to refine their assessments based upon more information than originally available. In this manner they can reassess their personal probabilities.

The third factor requires presentation of the results of each interaction in a statistical form that allows for breadth of opinion as well as noting what the consensus might be. The purpose is to allow for differences of opinion while also indicating the trend of the thinking of the group. This allows the experts to further adjust their projections based on their own analysis of future trends, consensus of other individuals and the spread of opinions. In this manner, diversity of thought is allowed in the decision-making process. The possibility of following diverse opinion is open to the respondents.

The purpose of the Delphi method is to combine these factors to aid the decision-making group in arriving at a consensus concerning the environment facing the firm. This process is designed to make arrival at the decision impartial and participative. Because of the results derived from this method, its application to risk analysis, personal probability and other forms of statistical decision making is enhanced. The Delphi method can help to overcome some of the previously noted problems of using management science programs.

Aid in arriving at consensus on environment.

This process is also particularly useful in arriving at a consistent projection of future trends. This is of assistance in determining if the various parts of the organizational strategy, both objectives for change and the action plan, are feasible relative to environmental trends. For an example of projections of future trends based on a Delphi approach using 70 experts at the Institute for the Future see Table 7–1.

If these projections are accurate how will they affect the organization?

TABLE 7-1 WHAT'S LIKELY TO HAPPEN BY 1985

Event	Per cent probability
Many chemical pesticides phased out	95
National health insurance enacted	90
Spending on environmental quality exceeds 6% of GNP	90
Insect hormones widely used as pesticides	80
Community review of factory locations	80
Substantial understanding of baldness and skin wrinkling	40
A modest (3%) value-added tax passed	40
Wide use of computers in elementary schools	25
Development of cold vaccines	20
Autos banned in central areas of at least seven cities	20
Breeder reactors banned for safety reasons	20

*Source: Institute for the Future, as presented in Business Week, 70 August 25, 1973.

REASONS FOR SUCCESS AND FAILURE OF MANAGEMENT SCIENCE PROGRAMS

Although schools of business have been teaching management science programs for some time, effective implementation of these programs has not occurred on any large scale. There are several reasons associated with this lack of success.

Understanding of strategy-formation process?

Quite often a key problem involves the inability of the management science expert to fully understand how the strategy process operates. This failure causes misunderstandings between the technocrats and managers who eventually have to use the programs.*

Conflict between the manager and the technocrat.

Both groups have their own languages as well as perceptions of what the programs should do. Until the technocrat and the manager can agree on the process itself and the applicability of management science programs to that process, effective use will be seriously impeded.

Furthermore, the role of the technocrat in the strategy process must be clearly defined. All too often, the technocrat is pressed into making decisions since he is the only one who can interpret output from what are perceived by other analysts as complex decision-making programs. When this occurs, antagonisms can develop between the two groups within the organization. Managers often view the technocrats as purposefully trying to usurp power within the organization on the basis of their technical expertise. This inhibits communications and exacerbates the problems noted previously.

---

*See W. K. Hall: Strategic planning models: Are top managers really finding them useful? *Journal of Business Policy,* 3:(No. 2):33–42, 1973; E. C. Miller: *Advanced Techniques for Strategic Planning.* op. cit. and C. J. Grayson: Management Science and Business Practice. *Harvard Business Review,* 51:41–48, July-August, 1973.

A complaint often voiced by the technocrat, however, is the lack of accurate data to use in the programs. Strategy formation, as we have noted, is not a precise science. Managers have learned to try to make decisions based on limited data. This "seat of the pants" type of decision making is usually abhored by the technocrat; he often feels frustrated by this inability to use management science programs in the ideal manner for which they were developed. This frustration may lead to a failure to adapt these programs to the data that are available.

Adequate data?

Also, the technocrat often complains that the traditional manager does not want to use new techniques. The technocrat feels that the manager's fears of unknown programs inhibits their application to business problems.

The manager replies that the main problem is that the technocrat is interested only in using a particular program. The manager feels that the technocrat is not interested in the problem posed by the strategy process. He is viewed as being interested primarily in experimenting with his program, often at the cost of an effective or efficient decision-making process.

All too often, when it is decided to use management science programs, sufficient preparation is not made within the organization. Top management sometimes decides for reasons of status, or simply because competition has implemented a particular program, that it is necessary for their organization to do likewise.

Preparation for use?

Management science programs, like any other type of innovative program, must have more than top management commitment. They must be understood by the managers who will eventually be required to use these programs. The organization can't simply hire a new group of managers who already understand the programs; it also can't wait for a new generation of managers who are trained in these programs to gradually replace current managers. What may be needed is a thorough training program for managers already within the organization.

At this point, however, most management science programs are used solely for evaluation purposes. An organizational strategy has to be devised by traditional methods before programs can be used to test its feasibility relative to constraints facing the organization. Too often the manager relies solely on imitation to develop the organizational strategy. This leads to an inability to properly analyze the organizational strategy through the use of management science programs. The organizational strategy has not been developed on a rigorous basis and, therefore, doesn't lend itself to quantification. The variables inherent in the strategy are not fully defined.

Fully defining and integrating the variables in the organizational strategy.

If management science programs are to be used effectively, the various phases of the strategy process must be defined and integrated. Strategy development and evaluation must be defined so that one can build on the other in a rational and well defined manner.

Many of the programs we have discussed may seem simplistic and commonplace to the student or teacher of Business Policy. It is becoming increasingly important, however, for most upper- and middle-level managers to utilize these programs to maintain their competitive posture.

In fact, the manager who utilizes these methods now finds himself with a comparative advantage in the marketplace. The position of the manager must take cognizance of the human factors and influences caused by use of sophisticated programs, however. Quite often the problems posed by implementation of new methods are increased through the introduction of computer-oriented approaches. Most management science programs are, after all, most efficiently used with computer facilities.

Applying programs to a creative process.

The key to these problems lies in applying formalized procedures to a creative process. Strategy formation must be viewed by managers as an uninhibited and nonthreatening procedure if it is to succeed.

COMPUTER-AIDED STRATEGY ANALYSIS

The use of management science, especially through computers, for all types of management functions has been proposed for some time. The first step in utilizing the computer, be it for simple mechanistic tasks or for more complex purposes, has been to attempt to understand the particular process. Our analysis of the strategy-formation process to this point has demonstrated several areas where the computer could potentially be of use.

There isn't total agreement as to the effectiveness of the computer over the full range of management decision making; however, the creative world of top management decision making resists quantification or model-building efforts in many areas.* This has been true because management decisions, particularly at the top, are seldom routine. The capacity of the computer to store knowledge and guidance procedures must be expanded if it is to be of greater use. More importantly, however, as mentioned, the strategy-formation process requires much better and more insightful understanding before use of the computer can be expanded in this area.†

We do understand the strategy formation process much better than it might appear. The process, as we have noted in earlier

---

*See Tom Alexander: Computers can't solve everything. *Fortune, 80*:126–129, October, 1969.

†See Martin L. Ernst: Stage three for computers: Management decision making. *Illinois Business Review, 27*:6–7, April, 1970.

chapters, can be divided into several phases or stages. All these stages share common characteristics. Probably the most important characteristic involves the need for creativity on the part of the individuals involved in the strategy formation. This creativity must be present not only in the formulation stage, where alternatives are generated, but also in the evaluation stage, where the organizational strategy is refined to its final form.

Divide strategy process into stages.

If we attempt to study the problem in parts, we might find our task a bit easier. For example, let's take creativity during a computer-aided formulation stage. Creativity, particularly in conjunction with the computer, requires confidence, knowledge, and effort on the part of the strategist; however, the key here is that the individual must be willing to follow some form of set procedure.* In line with this, however, the manager must have the knowledge necessary to be able to ask the types of questions most relevant to the problem at hand. Also, he must be willing to perform, at least to some extent, the function of combining, screening and recombining the data that are already available. Obviously this requires the potential for hard work and effort.

Must follow a set procedure.

Applications of Computers

Much of the application of the use of computers in management decisions has not really utilized the full potential of the computer. Most applications to date have used algorithmic types of programs. These are mainly of assistance in the evaluation phase of management decisions, as with the types of quantitative techniques discussed earlier in this chapter.

Middle management now is using the computer as a tool to generate and evaluate the data necessary to present top management with more alternatives from which to choose. The computer now allows top management to ask more "what if" types of questions of subordinates and expect rapid answers.

What applications to strategy process?

In addition, complex, interactive computer systems are now utilized in an effective manner over a whole range of managerial problems. This can be done, moreover, with individuals who have no strong background in the use of computers.

Creativity and the Computer

If it is true that many types of programs don't cause excessive fears, then it appears that the computer can be of significant assist-

---

*Roman R. Andrus: Creativity: A function for computers or executives? *Journal of Marketing,* 32:1–7, April, 1968.

ance in interrelating strategic decisions (e.g., the STRATANAL program discussed in Chapter 5).* First, the memory capacity of the computer can be of great assistance in the more mechanical phases of combining and, to some extent, screening data. Most of the previous references have shown how the computer is being used in this area now, and its use could be spread among higher levels of management, given the proper system and language. Of greater significance is the use of the computer as a guide during the creative phases of the strategy process.

There have been significant changes in computer technology which may overcome many of the utilization problems noted by their many detractors. Boulden and Buffa back this up strongly by stating:

> We feel that on-line, real-time decision systems are of great appeal to managers, partially because they do not require a basic structural change in a manager's role. He is not replaced by a supposedly optimizing mathematical model. On the contrary he remains the focus of the decision-making process, with a high premium placed on his judgment and intuitions.†

The main objection to this type of thinking is in use of the terms "nonrepetitive" or "nonprogrammable" problems. It may well be true that some problem, as a whole, may be nonprogrammable. But this does not necessarily mean that there are not individual subdivisions of the problem in which the computer can be of assistance in analysis. In particular, it appears that interactive computer programs might well be of assistance in providing the guidance required for a consistent and creative analysis of a strategic problem.

Complex Systems

The types of programs that would be useful along these lines would require an integrated, complex system. Systems must be designed with the ultimate goal in mind of the specific interaction desired; however, both the human and machine participants involved in the system must accept a common goal for the system if it is to be effective. Fortunately the human participant is adaptable to many environments and objectives. The question usually revolves about determining the proper incentives to encourage the man to adapt to a particular environment.

---

*For more information, see James B. Boulden and Elwood S. Buffa: Corporate models: On-line, real-time systems. *Harvard Business Review*, 47:65–83, July/August, 1970.

†James B. Boulden and Elwood S. Buffa: op. cit., p. 83.

Human Reaction to Complex Systems

As we have discussed earlier, one of the primary difficulties encountered involves the individual's fear that the program is actually performing the decision-making function itself. Ward Edwards states, "Since we want machines to help us solve problems, the more intelligent we are able to make it (the computer), the more unobtrusive it should be in providing this help."* Hopefully, by making the program as natural an aid as possible, adverse reactions to the use of a computer program as an aid can be held to a minimum or eliminated entirely.

This implies that the programming involved in the strategy process should be as flexible as possible. This presents a further problem. In actuality, the human is infinitely more programmable and easier to change than the computer. His flexibility and the ease and ability with which he can change increase the difficulties involved in attempting to produce a program that will maintain as little visibility as possible. The program, to do this effectively, should be able to adapt to each of the individuals using it as an aid.

To be able to adapt to the user requires a knowledge of the types of responses that one would expect a policy maker or strategist to produce for these types of decisions. It also requires a knowledge of the format of an efficient and acceptable strategy process. This follows the belief held by Edwards that man should be used to set up the basis for the decisions and hypotheses. The computer program should then be assigned the task of performing the heuristics necessary to achieve acceptable forms of solutions. The human policy maker can then decide, from a set of alternatives, which one he feels is the most appropriate for the structure and the environment that he is facing. Hopefully, the computer program would be able to assist him in this phase as well.

The key to the problem of computer-aided strategy making is to maintain the individual as the center of the strategy-making process. The storage and speed of the computer should be used to provide guidance to the strategist. The memory of the computer can be used to augment the memory of the strategist. In this manner, he can be totally concerned with questions of organizational strategy and leave to the computer the task of maintaining data as well as the more important task of attempting to ensure that the user does not make the same mistake more than once. Hopefully, the guidance function performed by the system would be able to accomplish this.

What is the key to the problem?

---

*Ward Edwards: Men and computers. *In* Psychological Principles in System Development, Robert N. Gagné, editor. New York, Holt, Rinehart and Winston, 1962, pp. 91–92.

SUMMARY

Although strategy formation may never be a science, there are aids to the process available from management science and the computer. The formation of objectives and actions for strategic and policy-making purposes relies primarily on the creative ability of the manager. This kind of creativity is usually learned as an art, rather than as a science. To enhance this creative ability, however, the manager requires a sound analysis of the relevant environment. Also, the effects of any projected moves by the organization on the environment and ensuing reactions must be known as much as possible if the manager is to be able to ensure the success of his projects. It is in this area, the evaluation process, that management science can provide useful programs that save the analyst time and aggravation.

In many situations, modeling of the organization and its environment can be of great use. Generalized procedures such as economic, technological, financial and market forecasts can be more easily tested if a realistic simulation of the relevant environment facing the organization can be formed.

The method by which these simulations and forecasts are built is crucial. Input-output analysis should be used cautiously to determine what critical factors affect the firm and, therefore, should be included in the model.

Simulations, models and forecasts are not infallible, however. They are only as good as the information used to form them. Most of these programs rely on a continuation of past trends for accurate results. Many situations in which trends are changing drastically or rapidly cause these programs to lose much of their validity. They do serve as a reasonable base from which to predict changes and the effects of those changes.

Of particular help in conjunction with modeling is the case of various types of risk and statistical analysis. Those programs allow the analyst to build confidence intervals about his projections. These types of programs allow the analyst to input the concept of the amount of risk acceptable to the individuals in the organization responsible for strategic moves.

Of equal assistance in analyzing the input and feasibility of strategic moves is knowledge of the financial condition of the organization. Various financial analysis techniques give the manager this type of knowledge. Widely used capital budgeting and cost analyses are not the only tools available, however. Some of the more mundane types of analyses such as ratio analysis are equally helpful in analyzing the condition of the firm.

It must be understood, however, that all these programs must be utilized within the context of an organization presided over by individuals. These individuals often fear the implementation of these programs by management. Methods must be found to make sophisticated analytical tools less threatening and, therefore, more acceptable to managers responsible for strategic moves.

The next chapter will discuss methods of gaining cooperation and assistance from members of the organization for strategic moves. Methods of structuring the activity of managers and staff for discussions based on available information and analyses will be highlighted.

DISCUSSION QUESTIONS

1. During what phase of the strategy process have management science programs found the highest degree of application to date? Why?
2. Which programs suffer greatest from a communication gap between technocrats and managers?
3. Is personal probability directly applicable to strategy formation for an organization? How can it be adapted for direct application?
4. What are some of the basic programs that are often used as building blocks for more complex management science programs? Are these basic programs fully understood yet?
5. What are some of the greatest problems faced in implementing management science programs in modern organizations?
6. How can the modern analyst help to gain acceptance for modern approaches within the organization?
7. What are the key factors inhibiting use of computers in the strategy process? Are they behavioral or physical?
8. Can creativity really be assisted through use of the computer, or is it hindered through computer interaction?
9. What is an input/output model and how can it be used in the strategy process?
10. Why is creativity so important for strategy makers?

Suggested Additional References for Further Research

Alexander, T.: Computers can't solve everything. *Fortune, 80*:126–129, 168, 171, 1969.
Andrus, R. R.: Creativity: A function for computers or executives? *Journal of Marketing, 32*:1–7, 1968.
Boulden, J. B., and Buff, E. S.: Corporate models: On-line, real-time systems. *Harvard Business Review, 47*:65–83, 1970.
Bowman, E. H.: Strategy and the weather. *Sloan Management Review, 17*:49–62, 1976.
Brady, R. H.: Computers in top-level decision making. *Harvard Business Review, 45*:67–76, 1967.
Burnett, G. J., and Nolan, R. L.: At last, roles for minicomputers. *Harvard Business Review, 3*(No. 3):148–156, 1975.

Ernst, M. L.: Stage three for computers: Management decision making. *Illinois Business Review,* 27:6–7, 1970.
Grayson, C. J.: Management science and business practice. *Harvard Business Review,* 51:41–48, 1973.
Grinyer, P. H., and Wooller, J.: Computer models for corporate planning. *Long-Range Planning,* 8(No. 1):14–25, 1975.
Grinyer, P. H., and Norburn, D.: Planning for existing markets: perceptions of executives and financial performance. *Journal of the Royal Statistical Society,* 136:70–97, 1975.
Hatten, K.: Quantitative research methods in strategy. Presented at Business Policy and Planning Research: The state of the Art Research Conference, Pittsburg, May, 1977.
Hatten, K. J., and Piccoli, M. L.: An evaluation of a technological forecasting method by computer-based simulation. Academy of Management Proceedings, Boston, Mass., 1973.
Hatten, K., Schendel, D. E., and Cooper, A. C.: A strategic model of the U.S. brewing industry, 1952-1971. Institute for Research in the Behavioral, Economic and Management Sciences, Purdue University Paper #580, November, 1976.
Holmberg, S. R.: Utility corporate planning. *Public Utility Fortnightly,* 90:July 6, 1972.
Jones, C. H.: At last: Real computer power for decision makers. *Harvard Business Review,* 47:75–89, 1970.
Kahalas, H.: An environmental decision model for dynamic planning. *Long-Range Planning,* 9(No. 1):81–88, 1976.
Klein, W. H., and Murphy, D. C.: *Policy: Concepts in Organizational Guidance.* Boston, Little Brown & Company, 1973.
Kriebel, C. H.: The strategic dimension of computer systems planning. *Long Range Planning,* 1:7-12, 1968.
Licklider, J. C. R.: Man-computer partnership. *International Science and Technology,* May, 1965, pp. 18–26.
McKinney, G. W.: *An Experimental Study of Strategy Formulation Systems.* Unpublished thesis, Stanford University Graduate School of Business, 1969.
Murdick, R., Eckhouse, R., Moor, R. C., and Zimmerer, T. W.: *Business Policy: A Framework for Analysis.* Columbus, Ohio, Grid, Inc., 1972.
Rue, L. W., and Fulmer, R. M.: Is Long-Range Planning Profitable? *The Academy of Management Proceedings,* Boston, Mass., 1973.
Swinth, R.: Organizational joint problem solving. *Management Science,* 8:(No. 2): October, 1971.

APPENDIX 1 TO CHAPTER 7

SOLUTION TO PROBLEM I

The following are the calculations needed for arriving at Net Present Value (NPV) decisions:

Year	NPV of $1 Received in Year...	Net Present Value of Returns Strategic Move A	Strategic Move B	Strategic Move C
1	.9346	$ 14,019	$ 46,730	$28,038
2	.8734	39,303	34,936	21,835
3	.8163	48,978	20,407.5	16,326
4	.7629	41,959.5	15,258	11,443.5
		$144,259.5	$117,331.5	$77,642.5
Initial outlay		−100,000	−125,000	−75,000
Net present value		$ 44,259.5	−$ 7,668.5	$ 2,642.5

If only one strategic move can be chosen, A should be the one. If resources are not that limited, A and C should both be followed, since they both offer positive net present values, i.e., they both offer returns greater than the cost of capital to the firm.

APPENDIX 2 TO CHAPTER 7

SOLUTION TO PROBLEM II

P = Probability
Worst = Worst outcome
Best = Best outcome
Res = Research
A = product A
B = product B
EV = Expected Value

$P[\text{Worst}] = .6 \quad P[\text{Best}] = .4$
$P[\text{Res A/Worst}] = .7$
$\therefore P[\text{Res B/Worst}] = .3$
$P[\text{Res B/Best}] = .8$
$\therefore P[\text{Res A/Best}] = .2$

$$P[\text{Worst/Res A}] = \frac{.7 \times .6}{(.7 \times .6) + (.2 \times .4)}$$

$$= .84$$

$\therefore P[\text{Best/Res A}] = 1 - .84 = .16$

$$P[\text{Worst/Res B}] = \frac{.3 \times .6}{(.3 \times .6) + (.8 \times .4)}$$

$$= .36$$

$\therefore P[\text{Best/Res B}] = 1 - .36 = .64$

Alt. 1 $\begin{cases} .6 \times 6 = 3.6 \\ + = 6.4 = \text{EV} \\ .4 \times 7 = 2.8 \end{cases}$

Alt. 2 $\begin{cases} .6 \times 5 = 3.0 \\ + = 7.0 = \text{EV} \\ .4 \times 10 = 4.0 \end{cases}$

Alt. 3a $\begin{cases} .84 \times 6 = 5.04 \\ + = 6.16 \times .5 = 3.08 \\ .16 \times 7 = 1.12 \end{cases}$

Alt. 3b $\begin{cases} .84 \times 5 = 4.20 \\ + = 5.80 \\ .16 \times 10 = 1.60 \end{cases}$

Alt. 3c $\begin{cases} .36 \times 6 = 2.16 \\ + = 6.64 \\ .64 \times 7 = 4.48 \end{cases}$

Alt. 3d $\begin{cases} .36 \times 5 = 1.80 \\ + = 8.20 \times .5 = 4.10 \\ .64 \times 10 = 6.40 \end{cases}$

Alt. 3a + Alt. 3d = 7.18
Alt. 3 − cost of information =
7.18 − 1 = 6.18

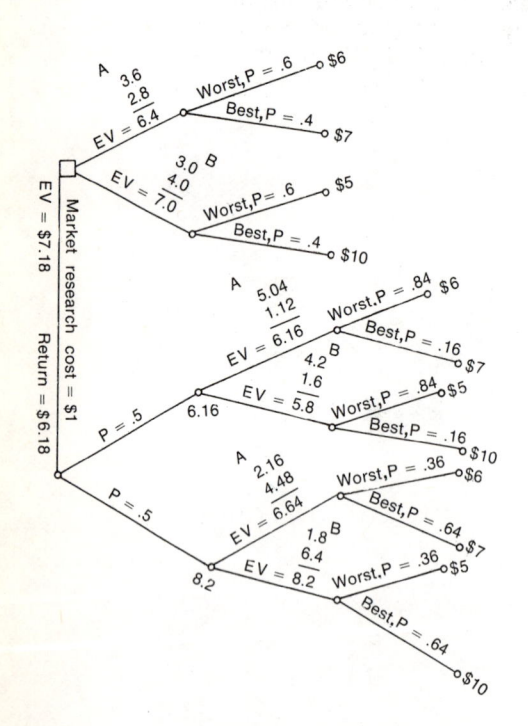

8

STRATEGIES FOR EFFECTIVE
CHANGE AND IMPLEMENTATION

INDIVIDUAL AND GROUP
PROBLEM SOLVING

OVERALL STRUCTURING OF THE
ACTIVITY: THE PLANNING
SYSTEM

TIMING OF THE ACTIVITY

SELECTING PROBLEM-SOLVING
SITUATIONS

TYPES OF STRUCTURED
ACTIVITIES — INDIVIDUAL
AND GROUP
    Strategy Formation Process
    Assessment of Leverage Points
    Managerial Activities and
    Capabilities

Stating and Analyzing
    Objectives
Priority Setting and
    Action Planning
Progress Review

EFFECTIVE GROUP SESSIONS

FEED-IN OF ACTION RESEARCH
AND MANAGEMENT SCIENCE DATA

QUESTIONS AND ANSWERS
REGARDING THE ACTION
COMPONENTS

SUMMARY

DISCUSSION QUESTIONS

APPENDIX 1. MANAGERIAL
ACTIVITIES AND CAPABILITIES

THE ACTION THRUST IN STRATEGY FORMATION: DEVELOPING INDIVIDUAL AND GROUP INVOLVEMENT

We have discussed previously several generalized procedures, including an overall strategy-formation program, an action-research program and various management science programs for data gathering and analysis. These programs (and others) may be coupled or linked together in a variety of ways. First, they may be arranged in pyramidal order with, say, the more general strategy-formation programs at the top and the more specialized management science programs lower down. The action-research program, as a general data gathering-feed-in-action-planning program, may construct and maintain control over lower level programs. The output from a management science program (e.g., a simulation) might serve as an input into the second process of the action-research program—the analysis and feed-in of data. In addition, the management science programs may be linked horizontally, with the output of one being the input of the other. For example, the forecasting program would provide input for a market survey at the Bike Lock organization that was discussed in the first chapter.

Used in appropriate combination for a given organization, these programs will generate useful input for those concerned with strategy making, implementation and evaluation. In a "one man show" organization, for example, the individual strategist could use such input to plan and to evaluate his actions. Most often, however, in larger organizations, and even in the case of the "one man show," more than one person will be involved in using such data input. Frequently, the manager will not be acting alone. He will need the support and assistance of others, not only to aid in the complex problem-solving process, but to assure that "the message gets through" to (and up from) various levels in the organization and to (and from) various divisions or groups.

Action components.

The manager may rely on the *action* components of the action-research program to gain such support and assistance. The action components include involving others in planning actions, coordinating actions, executing actions and evaluating actions. Data for such activity may be fed in from the other programs that have previously been mentioned.

This chapter will take up the matter of reliance on the action-research program for organization and strategy-improvement activities. The program should have two elements in proper balance —one that emphasizes change toward *integration* of the ongoing activities so that the organization can be efficient in its operations and one that facilitates *adaptation* to environmental opportunities and threats.* First, however, we shall present a general discussion of various strategies that may be used in implementing organizational change. Then we shall turn to the action component of the action-research program and discuss some structured activities or organization development interventions available to managers and to analysts or consultants, internal or external.† Though there are a large number of structured activities,‡ the main emphasis here will be on individual *and* group activities that are related directly to strategy reformulation and implementation.

Balance integration and adaptation

STRATEGIES FOR EFFECTIVE CHANGE AND IMPLEMENTATION

The organization development approach to strategy formation, as indicated, is basically a complex problem-solving process, with its activity focused more on the group or coalition than on the individual participants. As a process it deliberately attempts to set up effective group, intergroup and sometimes individual activities to:

Develop goals and plans of action.

---

*See P. Lorange and R. F. Vancil: *Strategic Planning Systems.* Englewood Cliffs, N. J., Prentice-Hall, Inc., 1977.

†Some student analysts may find only limited access to these activities but should have knowledge of the ideas put forth.

‡See W. L. French and C. H. Bell, Jr.: *Organization Development, Behavioral Science Interventions for Organization Improvement.* Englewood Cliffs, N.J., Prentice-Hall, Inc., 1978, P. A. Clark: *Action Research and Organizational Change.* New York, Harper & Row, 1973, and E. K. Warren: *Long-Range Planning: The Executive Viewpoint.* Englewood Cliffs, N.J., Prentice-Hall, Inc., 1966.

Gain understanding, acceptance and implementation of those plans throughout the organization.

Increase the capability of the organization for solving problems dealing with environmental changes in the future.

Group interaction does *not* mean that strategy decisions are turned over to subordinates as some might think; to follow this course of action might cause the organization's effectiveness to deteriorate. Group interaction does refer to the process that transforms an aggregate of individuals into a cohesively functioning team or group. In this context the word group means a face-to-face work or strategy-formation group that is characterized by its orientation to a series of objectives to achieve or problems to solve. Thus, the group of executives at Bike Lock, who form a committee are a work group, as are the top official and those subordinates who report directly to him.

Group interaction but strategy decisions not turned over to subordinates.

Another example of a work or strategy-formation group is a temporary or ad hoc team that is brought together for problem identification and solution. The team might be brought together by a manager or, alternatively, by an analyst or group of analysts interested in helping the organization. The team members might represent different divisions, functions or groups. Thus, we would have intergroup interaction.

These kinds of work group or conference activities have become the target for organization development practitioners and researchers. Many empirical studies have dealt with the attempts to improve organizational functioning, using to one extent or another the group structure and functioning. Greiner* has examined 13 such studies in an attempt to separate those organizations that have successfully dealt with implementing change and those that were not so successful. (In Chapter 6 you read several examples of these studies in various organizational situations.) These studies indicated that there were many strategies for introducing change and gaining implementation that could be placed along an Authority Distribution Continuum. Such a continuum is pictured below.

Authority distribution continuum.

Unilateral Authority Strategies	Shared Strategies	Delegated Strategies
By decree By replacement By technology-structure	By decision making By problem solving	By case study By T groups

---

*L. Greiner: Patterns of organizational change. *In* Dalton, G., Lawrence, P., and Greiner, L. (eds.): *Organizational Change and Development.* Homewood, Ill., Richard D. Irwin, Inc., 1970. See also P. Buchanan: Crucial issues in organizations development. *In* Watson, G. (ed.): *Change in School Systems.* Washington, D.C., National Education Association, 1967, pp. 51–67.

Success of entrepreneur in change.

Greiner's continuum starts with unilateral authority compliance but extends beyond the helper or shared approach to a delegated authority approach. Unilateral action can be accomplished in three ways: The most common strategy is called decree. It has its roots in centuries of military and government bureaucracies. It appears in the form of a policy statement, lecture, memorandum or verbal command. The entrepreneur may be quite successful in his decisive action approach to change. The second strategy in unilateral action is "by replacement." This rests on the idea that if a few key people cause a problem, their removal is the solution. The third form of unilateral action is "by technology structure." Currently this approach is under much study by behavioral scientists. Katz and Kahn,* for example, argue that changing the system (structure) is the most efficient way to introduce durable organization change. A basic assumption is that the way people behave can be importantly affected indirectly by changing the system or technology. Examples of this strategy include engineering the job to fit the man and adjusting formal authority in line with informal authority.† Later we shall discuss the issue of restructuring the organization for action.

Success of technostructural strategy.

Sharing the power is accomplished in two general ways, according to Greiner: First, by group decision making, in which the assumption is made that, given a problem, individuals develop more commitment to action when they have a voice in the choice of alternative solutions that affect them. Second, in group problem solving, in which both the definition and the solving of the problem are shared.

In delegated authority there is almost complete responsibility for defining and acting on problems. One form in which delegated authority appears is the case discussion. The teacher often does not impose analysis or solutions on the group. A second type of delegated authority is seen in sensitivity or T group sessions.‡ The purpose here is to increase the individual's self-awareness and sensitivity to group social processes. One assumption is that the method will unleash unconscious emotional energies, leading to self-analysis and therefore behavioral change.

Now that we have identified the authority yardstick, let us

---

*D. Katz and R. Kahn: *The Social Psychology of Organizations.* New York, John Wiley & Sons, Inc., 1966; see also, Bennis, W. G.: Theory and method in applying behavioral science to planned organization change. *Journal of Applied Behavioral Science,* 1:337–360, 1965.

†See F. Fiedler: *A Theory of Leadership Effectiveness.* New York, McGraw-Hill Book Co., Inc., 1967; and F. Herzberg: One more time: How do you motivate employees? *Harvard Business Review,* Jan.–Feb. 1968, p. 59.

‡For a discussion of the evidence see M. Dunnette and J. Campbell: Laboratory education: Impact on people and organizations. *In* Dalton, G., Lawrence, P., and Greiner, L. (eds.): *Organization Change and Development.* Homewood, Ill., Richard D. Irwin, Inc., 1970.

look at the results of the comparison of the organizations attempting significant change and adaptation. The organizations were compared on the conditions leading to change, the critical blocks and/or the facilitators encountered during implementation, and the more lasting results over a period of time. The comparisons were made on the basis of published reports. Perhaps unsuccessful attempts at change tend not to be published. Also, entrepreneurial change attempts were not examined.

Caution

Nevertheless, given the limitations of the data, the successful changes (those that accomplished stated organizational goals) generally appear to be those which:

1. Spread throughout the organization to include and affect many people.
2. Produce positive changes in line and staff attitudes.
3. Prompt people to behave more effectively in solving problems and in relating to others.

Successful changes sometimes use shared approach to collaborative problem solving.

Moreover, the relatively successful changes tended to use a shared approach to collaborative problem solving. The collaborative effort seemed to be more effective than organization change attempted unilaterally (e.g., by decree) or through delegation (e.g., T groups). The pattern of successful change can be viewed as a sort of filter, with external and/or internal forces causing pressure which then arouses management. That is the first step, be it planned or unplanned. The second step is an intervention and top management endorsement of an evaluation or re-evaluation. Third, there is a reorientation by management and a willingness to take a new look at "what things need to be different around here." Fourth, there is a specific shared diagnosis and recognition of problems. The less successful attempts at change seemed to avoid this step. If they took a unilateral approach, they tended already to "know" the problem. Those who took the delegated approach tended to abdicate responsibility by turning over authority to lower levels in such a nondirective way that subordinates questioned sincerity. The fifth step is sharing in the invention of solutions and becoming committed to them. The successful changes were characterized by widespread and intensive search for creative solutions. None of the less successful attempts at change reached this stage. Sixth, there is a process of experimentation and continued search. Some solutions were developed and tested and found creditable on a small scale before the scope of change was widened. Seventh, there is a period of reinforcement and acceptance. Early success experiences in experimentation bolster the confidence of the analysts and managers; they seem more willing to proceed with organization improvement.

Well outlined series of steps to change.

In short, then, according to this evidence successful patterns of change tend to follow a well outlined series of steps. These steps are characteristically seen as shared among the various levels in the organization. The bulwark of this sharing was cooperation and involvement. The extremes of unilateral authority and the delegated approach were avoided. There was heavy reliance on collaborative group problem solving.

INDIVIDUAL AND GROUP PROBLEM SOLVING

Individual problem-solving efforts and creativity.

We would caution that though group activity was relied upon, the importance of initiative and creativity in *individual* problem-solving efforts should not be downgraded or ignored. Individual brainstorming, for example, has consistently been shown to be superior to group brainstorming.* Time should be allotted for both individual and group problem-solving efforts. Some individuals are inhibited in group situations; furthermore, group participants sometimes tend to develop a similar perceptual set (people use the same framework in viewing the problem). Thus, creativity, which is a very important element in strategy making, may be reduced unless independent individual problem-solving activity takes place.

There is some evidence to suggest, however, that individual problem solving or creativity is improved if individual problem-solving activity follows a group problem-solving effort.† Some ideas may be picked up from the group activity that may be pursued and elaborated upon when one is alone. Recognition and support should be given to individual problem-solving activities. This holds true for the practicing manager, for the policy analyst, and for teams of students studying cases or conducting field projects.

Reasons for relying on the group.

There are, however, a number of reasons for relying on group activity for implementation and change in existing organizations. They are discussed by organization development specialists French and Bell‡ as follows: "First, much individual behavior is rooted in the socio-cultural norms and values of the work team. If the team, as a team, changes those norms and values, the effect on individual behavior is immediate and lasting. Second, the work team possesses the 'reality of configuration of relationships' that the individuals must in fact accommodate to and learn to utilize and cope with.... Effective (or ineffective) relationships with

---

*D. W. Taylor, P. C. Berry and C. H. Block: Does group participation when using brainstorming facilitate or inhibit creative thinking? *Administrative Science Quarterly*, 3:23–47, 1958; M. D. Dunnette, J. Campbell and K. Jaasted: The effects of group participation on brainstorming effectiveness for two industrial samples. *Journal of Applied Psychology*, 47:30–37, 1963; M. D. Dunnette: Are meetings any good for solving problems? *Personnel Administration*, 27:12–29, 1964; T. J. Bonchard, Jr., and M. Hare: Size, performance and potential in brainstorming groups, *Journal of Applied Psychology*, 54:51–55, 1970.
†M. D. Dunnette, J. Campbell and K. Jansted: op. cit., pp. 30–37.
‡W. French and C. Bell: *Organization Development, Behavioral Science Interventions for Organization Improvement.* op. cit., p. 61–62.

these people can have far-reaching effects on the individual's performance and behavior. Third, the work team is the source of most of individual's knowledge about organizational processes such as communications, decision making and goal setting. These processes are the processes that most influence the individual's behavior. Fourth, it is commonly believed that many of the individual's needs for social interaction, status, recognition and respect are satisfied by his work group, consisting of both peers and superior. Any process that improves the work team's processes or task performance will thus probably be related to central needs of the individual members."

It needs to be said, however, that though working through groups can be a powerful instrument in implementing organization change, poor handling of the process can have negative effects. Considerable expertise should be available if group intervention activities are being considered.

Caution.

OVERALL STRUCTURING OF THE ACTIVITY: THE PLANNING SYSTEM

Using organizational change evidence and assumptions, practitioners and academicians have devised structured activities or interventions to improve individual, group, intergroup and organization functioning. These interventions are sets of structured activities in which selected organization units (individuals or groups) engage in tasks that constitute *the action thrust* in strategy formation. In other words, the activities (including planning actions and evaluating actions) are the means for implementing change. Our discussion here will focus on the structuring of activities,* beginning with some situational design factors. Then we shall discuss several group *and* individual activities that seem to be helpful.

Action thrust.

Lorange and Vancil† distinguish between the task of structuring the activities for a larger, typically divisionalized and diversified organization versus a smaller organization, typically with less product/service diversity. They also discuss another contingency, namely whether the strategy process is relatively new or more mature and well established. Six structuring design issues are identified: the degree of explicitness in the communications of organizational objectives; the top-bottom/bottom-up flavor of the objective-setting process; the strategic (more detail) versus the

---

*See J. Shank, E. Niblock and U. Sandalls, Jr.: Balance 'Creativity' and 'Practicality' in Formal Planning. *Harvard Business Review,* January/February, 1973.

†For discussion see P. Lorange and R. F. Vancil: How to Design a Strategic Planning System. *Harvard Business Review,* Sept.–Oct. 1976.

	Situational Settings		
Systems Structuring Issues	"Small" Companies	"Large" Companies	
		New Planning Systems	Mature Planning System
1. Communication of Corporate Goals	Not Explicit	Not Explicit	Explicit
2. Goal-Setting Process	Top-Down	Bottom-Up	"Negotiated"
3. Corporate Environmental Scanning	Strategic	Statistical	Statistical
4. Subordinate Managers' Focus	Financial	Financial	Strategic
5. Role of the Corporate Planner	Analyst	Catalyst	Coordinator
6. Linkage of Planning and Budgeting	Tight	Loose	Tight

Figure 8-1 Structuring Issues for Strategic Planning Systems (Adapted from Lorange, P. and R. F. Vancil, op cit.)

statistical (less detail) approach of the top level environmental scanning effort; the strategic (identification and analysis of alternatives) versus financial (long-term detailed projections) nature of the subordinate planning focus; the role of the corporate planner (analyst for organization wide perspective, catalyst to line managers, or coordinator) and the degree of linkage between planning and budgeting. Each of these structuring issues should be solved differently, according to the contingency setting. Hypothesized solutions are summarized in Figure 8-1.

What type of environmental scanning in each division?

In a divisionalized company, for example, the general manager may be delegated authority to do detailed environmental analysis for his product line or service. This analysis would be used, together with whatever objectives, policies and other inputs he gets from headquarters, to make his long-range plans. A close linkage may be negotiated between overall corporate strategy and the subobjectives and substrategies developed by the division manager.

How close a link?

It may be advisable, as well, to have a close link between the first year of the long-range plans and the short-range operational budget summary. Such a link may help to keep long-range plans realistic. However, such a tight relationship may divert attention from long-range to short-range matters, such as this year's rate of return. As described earlier, this may present a serious problem if the manager involved sees his rewards based primarily on short-term results (e.g., he may avoid developmental expenditures). If the organization is serious about its long-range plans, care needs to be taken to see that those plans are reflected in the current operational budget making.

It should be stressed that these are hypotheses in Figure 8-1 which need testing. Other contingencies such as the degree of environmental uncertainty, the stage of life cycle or the requirements of the strategy itself may be important. The central idea is that there is no universal approach to structuring the activities in the strategy process. The organization's circumstances need to be taken into account, especially its major needs for environmental adaptation and for linking or integrating the ongoing activities.

In most organizations there will be a need for both adaptation and integration. A strategy process that is heavily based on long-term financial predictions but lacks the focus on environmental awareness may satisfy the integration requirements quite well but fall short on adaptation to discontinuities, threats, and opportunities. Conversely, a structuring of activities toward identification and analysis of strategic activities but which tends to neglect breakdowns in program development and coordination may contribute to adaptation but may be less effective for integration. Bringing proper balance to integration and adaptation may require a group effort.

Balance of adaptation and integration affected by situational design.

Some organizations have structured group activity into sessions that can generally be called *problem-solving conferences.* Such conferences fall into the process model category of assessing behavior, in that they aim at helping the participants perceive, diagnose and act upon events in their own environment. In other words, they aim at helping the problem-solving process.

Recently in an attempt to make "all cylinders function at the same time" and to avoid surprises, Sperry Rand set up a formal arrangement for quarterly, in-depth review meetings between the divisions and top management.* They report success with this approach, which was initiated for the first time by Chairman of the Board J. Paul Lyet. The approach includes a long-range planning system and a heavy emphasis on determining what the market needs before developing products. Lyet says about the meetings,

We are not controlling in a restrictive sense; we want to be sure the divisions are doing all the things necessary to grow and that they are not taking the short term view, generating profits now at the expense of the future. And we want to avoid surprises.

---

*The winning strategy at Sperry Rand. *Business Week,* February 24, 1973, pp. 50-58.

The new approach apparently has played some part in helping the company to avoid such surprises as "horrendous write-offs," which had previously been habitual in the company. Sperry Rand has experienced a solid turnaround after two straight declines in annual profits.

It is assumed, as mentioned before, that these collaborative meetings are more effective than organization change and implementation attempted unilaterally (e.g., compliance, or by decree) or through delegation (e.g., T groups). The lever that is used in attempting to change organizational behavior is the opportunity to obtain intrinsic rewards through influencing important activities in the organization. (Some might argue that this power distribution means a structural change.)

May use diagonal slice.

The group activity should be structured so that the relevant people are there. The relevant people are those most directly affected by the opportunity or the problem and those with necessary skills and knowledge. The consequences may involve intact work teams or ad hoc work groups. There may be a utilization of a joint team of managers and/or staff with internal or external analysts. Or the conference team, or a part of it, may represent a *diagonal** slice from top management down through the organization, including relevant functional or program areas. There may be separate action planning by teams at all levels.† Preplanning of the group composition is, of course, an important feature in structuring the activity.

Or a "bottom up" approach.

The group sessions should be structured to open lines of communication and, through the use of group dynamics, to establish personal and group commitment to improving strategy development and implementation. The aim is to identify major strategy issues and opportunities, to identify barriers to organization effectiveness, to establish a readiness to act, and to develop a plan of specific action for relevant parties.

Supplemental to these goals, the conference design should strive to emphasize that the re-evaluation activities are worthwhile and the outcome should have some important effects on the organization. Encouragement from top management through involvement, or at least endorsement, of the activities seems to be quite helpful. It does seem wise, though, to openly recognize the limits of manpower and money and to point out that there is no

---

*The diagonal slice may be used for the purpose of improving communication by avoiding the possible inhibiting effect of the direct superior-subordinate relationship.

†See Vancil, R. F.: The Accuracy of Long-Range Planning. *Harvard Business Review,* 48:98–101, September-October, 1970, and Formal Planning Systems, Cambridge, Mass., Harvard Business School, 1972. This research on the structuring of strategy formation indicates that long-range forecast accuracy seems to be greater when a "bottom up" approach is used than when a "top down" approach is used.

guarantee of acceptance of all or any results or outcomes. After all, the top official or officials will undoubtedly have veto power over important plans of action.

It is quite important that the conference goals be clear, as well as the way to reach the goals. Members of the organization are likely to be more highly motivated if they know what they are working toward and that what they are doing will contribute to goal attainment.

The team (teams) is (are) to provide major input to the group session or sessions and to be a major implementation link between various parts of the organization. It is hoped that organization members will establish a continuing series of activities for auditing the internal and external environment and improving their problem-solving ability. Policy analysts may provide support and assistance in helping the continuation of group interaction.

TIMING OF THE ACTIVITY

We have discussed the assessment process as well as the other phases of the policy-formation process in discrete terms. This is not to state, however, that these various phases are carried on in a discrete manner. The entire policy-formation process, including evaluation of alternatives, is followed on a continuous basis. Without continuous evaluation of alternatives and outcomes we would soon find ourselves with an outdated organizational strategy and direction for the organization. There are, however, three particular points in time during the policy-formation process when structured activities should be considered on a formalized basis: (1) the formation stage, (2) the postacceptance stage, and (3) the postcommitment stage. Structured activities during the formation stage may be extremely beneficial in that added information from external sources either within the organization or outside the organization will aid in developing the strategy. It is frequently easy to obtain criticism of the strategy at this stage. The individuals to be involved in implementing the strategy will often be wary of anything that might upset the status quo. These managers will often be eager to point up weaknesses in the proposed plan. This type of criticism can be extremely valuable for determining what additional information is needed for developing a feasible, acceptable strategy. The key here is not to allow criticism to harden into solid opposition to desired and required changes.

When should structured activities on a formalized basis be considered?

Structured activities during the postacceptance stage can often be most crucial. At this point, the strategy has been developed and accepted by the individuals affected by it. Quite often, great enthusiasm has been generated for this new direction. At this time, also, there is more information available to the analyst. Time has passed since the formation stage. The economy has

What information is available at each stage?

entered new stages, the organization has progressed (hopefully) and the market may have changed in the interim. Also, more importantly, valuable market research programs may have been progressing at the same time. This additional information should be utilized to present a more feasible, consistent overall strategy. The prime danger here is that pent-up enthusiasm generated so far may be stifled. A fine line has to be followed between the conservatism of assessment and the enthusiasm of conviction.

The third key stage for structured activities occurs after the plan has been implemented. In real terms, for example, the Edsel is on the showroom floors. The Ford Motor Company has already spent millions of dollars, and the auto buying public is staying away from Edsel dealers in droves.

It is at this stage that information is relatively easy to come by. Actual reports from the field are in and are easily analyzed. The decision must be made as to what the future course of action is to be. The organization must decide whether to continue with the original plan or to alter it to meet a changing environment or occurrences unforeseen during the formation of the original plan.

It was at this period, for instance, that Ford officials finally decided to cut losses on the Edsel and formulate new strategic moves for the future. Fortunately they were able to learn from their mistakes; they also were not frightened by the large losses incurred by this error. This was evident from their next attempts at finding and filling a new auto market. The Mustang and the Capri were developed and proved extremely successful.

Attention should be paid to this last point. Results achieved from implementation of a new strategic move should not overly influence the willingness of the organization to attempt further moves. Inhibitions caused by failure, or overenthusiasm caused by success, should play no part in future decisions, although these will be influenced by changes brought about in the resources available to the firm or changes in the external environment.

Structured activities, therefore, may be integrated into the formal policy-formation process on a periodic basis, and they should be given special consideration at certain points in time.

SELECTING PROBLEM-SOLVING SITUATIONS

The time it takes to reap the rewards that may result from the group sessions will depend to an extent on how often the opportunities are provided for the groups to interact. This means selecting situations wherein group problem-solving activity can be applied. (You will recall that the importance of individual problem-solving activity is fully recognized.)

Periodic staff or committee meetings are tailormade for beginning group problem solving because such meetings are frequently held quite regularly, and the participants are probably more or less comfortable at them. This presents an opportunity to begin by suggesting something like an examination of operating practices in order to improve acceptance and implementation of overall strategy. The group will need time to think about it and respond. Each member may be given a chance to contribute information and pose questions to other members. Some members may take an assignment to develop more detailed information about the various operating practices and to discuss the results at a subsequent meeting.

Regular group sessions or special purpose sessions.

In other words, no big deal has been made of the problem-solving conference approach. The group has been allowed to interact informally to a subject that presumably is of high interest to them. A goal is established (collection of data) that encourages communication and coordination among the participants. A reason for further discussion of the subject is established (interpretation of data.) This low key approach, using regular meetings as a basis for action research and group problem solving may be quite helpful. The discussion of the strategy-making process as well as the strategy output (goals and plans of action) is made a normal part of business.

However, to highlight the importance of *avoiding organizational stagnation*, it may be appropriate to put a special emphasis on the regular group sessions or even to set up special purpose sessions. Analysts with specialized expertise, say, in forecasting or in the problem-solving process may be brought in. *Orientation* and *"deciding what to do"* discussions with relevant parties seem to be especially appropriate before such sessions. To aid the subsequent communication of conference results, the relevant parties may include managers and staff not included in the actual conference sessions, along with conference participants. Several sessions may be necessary to provide enough information and experience pertinent to formulating "what to do."

Orientation and "deciding what to do."

The discussion time is used to clarify the purposes of the overall action-research program, including the conferences. Some time may be spent briefing participants and others about what alternative assessment and developmental methods (e.g., conferences, interviews, training sessions) could be used before the serious commitment was made to engage in the present effort. The participants may be allowed to decide the extent and the manner in which they feel the developmental programs should extend.

If staff experts or planners are to be included, time may be spent discussing an acceptable role for them.* Following the

---

*See W. Athreya: Guidelines for the Effectiveness of the Long-Range Planing Process, unpublished doctoral dissertation, Harvard Business School, June, 1967.

Role of corporate planners: analyst, catalyst or coordinator?

helper or shared approach to development, the planners would be there to aid the problem-solving process, not to unilaterally identify problems and give their solutions. The planners' role may include one or more of the following patterns of behavior: (1) to help the operating managers design and implement methods for obtaining information on the state of the environment and the organization; (2) to summarize all pertinent information collection; (3) to feed back information to individual managers and to the total conference groups; (4) to provide skill and expertise in designing meetings and in chairing such meetings or in sharing the chairmanship with operating managers; (5) to share in the analysis of information in the development of solutions; (6) to identify developmental methods for improved communication and problem solving; and (7) to act as part of the staff for the development program—preparing minutes, delivering background material, polishing language, streamlining presentations, as well as evaluating the views of operating managers.

An external expert may have been engaged to add professional skill, experience and objectivity to the role, whereas an internal planner may be relied on for his knowledge of the organization's environment or culture, his continuity of support and his availability for timely assistance.

Add outside experts?

Other subjects may be brought up during these initial sessions also. Based on past experience, it may be judged advisable to discuss with and inform the participants that the meetings:

1. Are a key part of a joint continuing assessment of policies and strategies.
2. Are an opportunity to influence important strategies and policies in the organization.
3. Have endorsement of top management (some top managers may be present; in fact, the conference may be chaired by a top manager).
4. Need openness and frankness. (State—and mean it—that there will be no penalty for expressing frank opinions.)
5. Are confidential* (including all working papers and discussion).
6. May include analysts who are there to help (not to report to certain people).
7. Will include tissues of special interest to the group.
8. Do not guarantee that all (or any) recommendations of the group will be accepted.
9. Should lead to certain outcomes (e.g., identification of priority issues, action steps for managers and staff, and a response from top managers where appropriate).

No one list of items to be covered in the initial sessions is appropriate for all situations; thus, judgment as to the unique

---

*Reasons for this include: (1) avoiding premature release of information that is not thoroughly analyzed, and (2) the need for openness. A judgment has been made about when and to what extent other members of the organization and parties external to the organization (e.g., competitors, columnists) are going to share in the information and results.

circumstances will need to be used in ascertaining what to include in and what to exclude from the discussions.

TYPES OF STRUCTURED ACTIVITIES—INDIVIDUAL AND GROUP

Subsequent to the early orientation and "deciding what to do" meetings, the problem-solving activity may turn to one or more of a number of structural activities. As we see it, some of the structured activities that may prove helpful to the practicing manager, the staff expert and perhaps to students doing field projects would include, but not be limited to, the following:

1. Strategy-formation process.
2. Assessment of leverage points.
3. Individual manager functioning.
4. Stating and analyzing objectives.
5. Priority setting and action planning.
6. Progress review.

Data collected from the previously discussed action-research program and the management science programs may prove useful as input to one or more of these structured activities.

Strategy-formation Process*

Focus is on early identification of the developmental needs of the groups engaged in the process of strategic choice. Various assessments may be made: perceptions of strategy issues, role perceptions, self-interests, strategy-formation practices, communication skills and patterns, authority and hierarchical problems, and intra- and intergroup conflict management procedures. Questionnaire and/or interview data may be collected from the group itself and from others. It may be analyzed as part of an individual research study of strategy making. The data may be summarized and fed back to the group for discussion and analysis. Plans of action may be developed. For example, skilled parties may be designated to help in the diagnosis, understanding and resolution of conflict of interest problems, e.g., between different teams or groups that must work together in the formation of strategy, such as a federal government agency and a county school board, labor representatives and management officials, line and staff, sales and engineering or separate organizations involved in a merger.

---

*For a discussion see F. T. Paine and C. R. Anderson, Strategic Management: An Intervention Approach. *Proceedings of National Academy of Management,* August 1977.

Assessment of Leverage Points

Stakeholders' leverage points vary with issues.

Focus here is on identification of those individuals within the organization or outside the organization (e.g., stakeholders) who have the authority (formal or informal), motivation and competence to influence the output of the strategy process as well as the understanding, acceptance and implementation of that strategy output. For strategy issues various assessments may be made: leverage points, types and amounts of political resources, reservoir of goodwill, trade-offs, phases through which the strategy issues proceed. It should be recalled that these assessments may vary with the type of strategy issue and with the phase that the issue is going through. The information gathered can be useful for independent study or for group discussion and analysis.

Organization learning also.

These first two interventions, moreover, carried out by qualified staff or managers, can serve not only to identify strategy problems, issues and individuals or groups of individuals that are judged important points at which to study the strategy process, but also to improve that process. That is, there may be some *organizational learning* while dealing with relevant organizational issues. The data gathering, for instance, may help people to learn not only about the strategy-formation process, but also about some new ways of producing data about the process. From this point we turn to additional structured activities that are potential building blocks for improvement of that process.

Managerial Activities and Capabilities

It is the contention of this book that a great deal of the effectiveness of strategic management is due to the actual managerial activities and capabilities used in dealing with issues and organizational constraints. Managerial thinking is directed toward changes to consider in such areas as follows:

    A. *Relationships*
        1. Identification of personal leadership style (internal and external). Use of group vs. one-on-one meetings, consideration of factors such as decision quality, information, time, type of task, acceptance, personalities of others, other motivations toward organizational goals, extent of conflict likely, development of others.
        2. Identification of internal and external relationships that must be built up for effective functioning.
    B. *Information Processing*
        1. Current use of information channels is identified, use of others for scanning activities, problems recognition procedures, opportunity and threat recognition.
        2. Emphasis placed on information dissemination, reliance on face to face contacts and communication; improving communication channels or setting up new ones is considered.
    C. *Decision Making*
        1. Current use of delegation of authority and decentralization.

Current problems of coordination due to independent decision making.
2. Analysis of organizational constraints and limits on strategic choice.
3. Time management techniques are explored, commitment of time to specific activities, in-depth analysis or superficial analysis activities.

At this point the manager or strategic unit is given feedback concerning the managerial activities suggested for effective functioning in this particular strategy situation. The feedback draws largely upon the normative propositions set forth in the relevant literature. Comparison and analysis rather than "the-one-best-way" are emphasized. See Appendix 1 to this chapter for a discussion of an experimental approach to self-study of managerial activities and capabilities.

See Appendix 1 to this chapter.

Stating and Analyzing Objectives

Key parties (e.g., manager-subordinate pairs, groups and analysts) in major segments of the organization engage in systematic, periodic performance reviews and target setting. An illustration of an approach for doing this has been presented in the chapter on the assessment guides. As indicated, a good bit of research suggests that such goal setting affects performance positively.*

Priority Setting and Action Planning

The focus is on formulating and reformulating action plans. The question may be raised as to what needs to be changed around here—policies, strategies, structure and so forth. Assessments may be made of such elements as the scope of support and resource deployment, what the scope should be, the basis of support for strategies, an inventory of organization resources and problems, changing environmental conditions, alternative opportunities and requirements for success, and possible combinations of alternatives for synergistic effects.

Use portfolio approach.

These priority-setting and action-planning sessions, of course, have many variations in their format and time schedule.† Special purpose sessions may be set up for (1) brainstorming on the effects of environmental or public policy changes, (2) devising an

---

*H. H. Meyer, E. Kay and J. R. P. French, Jr.: Split roles in performance appraisal. *Harvard Business Review*, Jan.–Feb., 1965, p. 129.

†See R. Beckhard: *Organization Development: Strategies and Models*. Reading, Mass., Addison-Wesley Publishing Company, 1969, and F. T. Paine: *Organization Effectiveness Conferences*. Washington, D.C., Civil Service Commission, 1970.

238 / THE ACTION THRUST IN STRATEGY FORMATION

Variations in format and time schedules.

"optimal" plan of organization to implement a corporate strategy, (3) devising standards and a plan for progress review, (4) translating functional plans into financial terms in the form of a pro forma profit and loss statement and perhaps a pro forma balance sheet, and (5) linking the top management objectives and action plans with the objectives and action plans forged at lower levels in the organization. Depending on the magnitude of the problem and the exigencies of the situation, there may be one- or two-day marathons or meetings spaced over a period of weeks, months or years.

Progress Review

This is to keep managers focusing on strategic variables and environmental changes and to maintain positive tension in the system.

1. Officials report and discuss progress, if any, on major

STANDARD PROGRESS REPORT (FOR THOSE WITH NO PROGRESS TO REPORT)

During the report period which encompasses the organizational phase, considerable progress has been made in certain necessary preliminary work directed toward the establishment of initial activities. Important background information has been carefully explored and the functional structure of component parts of the cognizant organization has been clarified.

The usual difficulty was encountered in the selection of optimum materials, available data, experimental methods, etc., but these problems are being attacked vigorously and we expect that the development phase will continue to proceed at a satisfactory rate.

In order to prevent unnecessary duplication of previous efforts in this same field, it was deemed expedient to establish a survey and to conduct a rather extensive analysis of comparable efforts in this direction, to explore various facilities in the immediate area of activity under consideration, and then to summarize these findings.

This Committee held its regular meeting and considered rather important policy matters pertaining to the over-all organization levels of the line and staff responsibilities that develop in regard to the personnel associated with the specific assignments resulting from these broad functional specifications. It is assumed that this rate of progress will continue to accelerate as these necessary broad functional phases continue further development.

Source: *Anonymous*

Figure 8-2.

strategies and issues in their SBA's or environmental segments.
2. Cycle begins again with a review of issues, priorities, barriers to improvement, and so forth.
3. Staff and officials keep probing for specific examples, actions taken from results of action, unresolved difficulties.

For situations in which there is no progress to report, we present (with tongue in cheek) Figure 8-2, Standard Progress Report (For Those with No Progress to Report).

We have indicated some focal points and activities that might be included in an intervention in the strategy-making process. These activities are available to the practicing manager or the staff planner. Some may be available to students doing field projects. In addition, students studying cases may find enough information in some cases so that partial analysis may be made. Both individual analysis and group discussion may be included.

The reader will note again that we are viewing the organization as going through a more or less continuous process of initiation, evaluation, choice, implementation and re-evaluation. The activities are not strictly limited to the action thrust of corporate strategy development; they include the diagnostic component of data collection about the external and internal environment.

EFFECTIVE GROUP SESSIONS

The structured activities that we are talking about include assembling an appropriate mixture of people "to work the problem." Certain assumptions are made. It is felt that if an aroused top management endorses a reorientation, others will develop an interest and readiness to act on strategy issues that are perceived as important. It is felt that open collaborative problem discussions on real organizational problems and opportunities will enhance involvement and commitment by group members. At the same time, it is assumed that the transfer to everyday work (implementation) is enhanced if the overall assessment and development design builds the expectation that strategy implementation activities will continue and expand, and if the design calls for periodic progress report conferences.

For some structured activities it is assumed that using small heterogeneous subgroup meetings would, on balance, help individuals to communicate and to use problem-solving skills as well as provide varied points of view for discussion. If successful experiences occur in the subgroups, a transfer of problem-solving efforts to groups in which the participants ordinarily work might also occur.

Many factors have a bearing on effectiveness.

Many factors have a bearing on whether the conference groups develop into effective operating teams — previous experience together and expectations, heterogeneity of group, type of problems, size of group, time pressure, amount of information available, personality and orientation of members, number of previous meetings, degree of consensus demanded, and so forth. The many factors have been discussed elsewhere;* we shall not discuss all of them here. We shall indicate that the conferences seem to depend to quite a degree on the skill and perceptiveness of those exercising leadership functions in the group.†

The role of chairman, for example, is a difficult one, requiring patience, a sensitivity to how much conflict is healthy, and the tough-mindedness to keep focus on the problem. Though there is *no one best way* to function as a conference leader, some ideas based on research and experience provide clues to the process of developing appropriate knowledge and skill to function more effectively in such a capacity. Norman Maier‡ provides such a set of ideas for planning and leadership in problem-solving conferences. These ideas are presented as a series of steps or phases which some conferences go through, as shown on page 242.

No one best way.

Some research and experience-based ideas.

These steps may occur in a series of sessions over several months or years or may be condensed into a much shorter period of time.

FEED-IN OF ACTION RESEARCH AND MANAGEMENT SCIENCE DATA

There may be data collection both before, during and after group sessions. There is a need to be flexible and to design and redesign the data collection and data feed-in process as the situation dictates. Some situations seem to call for an aggressive structured strategy, with much data input to the sessions prepared ahead of time. In other instances the conference members themselves will open the door, so to speak, and initiate the identification of problems and solutions. We should now illustrate different situations and conditions affecting data feed-in.

---

*B. E. Collins, and H. Guetzkow: *A Social Psychology of Group Processes for Decision Making.* New York, John Wiley & Sons, Inc., 1964. See also H. A. Shepard: Changing interpersonal and intergroup relationships in organizations. *In* March, J. G.: *Handbook of Organizations.* Chicago, Rand McNally & Company, 1965.

†R. F. Bales: In conference. *Harvard Business Review* 32:44–50, 1954.

‡N. R. F. Maier: *Problem-Solving Discussion and Conference Leadership Methods and Skills.* New York, McGraw-Hill Book Co., Inc., 1963; see also W. W. Burke and R. Beckhard (eds.): *Conference Planning.* Washington, National Education Association, 1970.

First, we shall give an example of a strategy in which the participants themselves generate information about their own problems, analyze the root causes, develop action plans and set a schedule for progress review. It is called the *confrontation meeting*.* In the confrontation meeting the top manager gives an initial challenge to a large segment of his management group. The challenge is a reorientation question, "What things need to be different around here—strategies, policies, structure?" The agenda is wide open. Out of such reorientation may come an interest and a readiness to act on problems seen as important. It is assumed again that open collaborative discussions on real organizational problems will enhance involvement.

Confrontation meeting.

There is some evidence to indicate that the strategy has worked successfully in business and government organizations. Conditions for its successful use are indicated by Beckhard:

There is a need for the management group to examine its own workings.
Very limited time is available for the activity.
Top management wishes to improve conditions quickly.
There is enough cohesion in the top team to ensure follow-up.
There is real commitment to resolving issues on the part of top management.
The organization is experiencing, or has recently experienced, some major changes.

Conditions for successful use.

As we have mentioned, it may be desirable to *feed in additional data* for the group to discuss during the sessions. The data may be fed in, allowing much leeway to the participants in interpreting the data and determining problems and solutions to the problems.

However, the relatively unstructured approach *may* fail if there are tight controls on delegation of authority, if there is perceived to be little or no articulated support from top management for openness in communications, if the purposes of the sessions are either not explained to or accepted by the conferees (i.e., if they feel they are participating in self-incrimination rather than in problem identification and solution), if there is little external or internal pressure for change, or if there is a need for more sophisticated data collection and analysis.

In these cases, more direction will be needed in order to develop the groups into effective operating teams. The direction may take the form of the session leader's initiating problem definitions and proposing solutions. Discussion, of course, is allowed. We call this generalized procedure the Situation Description Discussion Proposal Discussion (SDDPD) program. The program requires advance data collection and analysis, with prep-

A more structured approach—SDDPD program.

---

*R. Beckhard: The confrontation meeting. op. cit., p. 150. This article gives the steps to follow in such a meeting.

SOME STEPS IN CONFERENCE PLANNING AND LEADERSHIP

I. Provide orientation and explanation to relevant parties.
II. Provide for collection and sharing of appropriate data.
III. Discuss problems and issues with group.
   a. Check deviations from standards and goals.
   b. Ascertain factors impinging on mission accomplishment.
IV. Discuss problem priorities with group.
   a. Decide which problems to work on.
   b. Decide sequence of taking up problems.
V. Clarify problem(s) to be discussed.
   a. State in impersonal terms.
   b. Show how problem relates to their interests.
   c. State only one major objective (with limiting factors).
   d. State problem briefly and stop.
   e. Refrain from suggesting solutions yourself.
VI. Obtain possible solutions.
   a. Allow new idea evaluation.
   b. Be sure enough solutions are obtained; be patient; restate problem if necessary.
   c. Check understanding of ideas and solutions proposed.
   d. Write down solutions on chalk board or newsprint.
VII. Evaluate solutions.
   a. Get whole group involved. How?
      1. Ask by name how they feel about idea expressed.
      2. Create opportunities to indicate agreement or disagreement.
   b. Reward criticism.
   c. Bring hostility out into the open.
   d. Reduce list of solutions. How?
      1. Integrating solutions.
      2. Voting for best 3, and so forth.
   e. See if assumed cause is supported by the facts of the situation (get agreement on facts).
   f. See if solution addresses itself to assumed cause.
   g. List advantages and disadvantages of each solution on chalk board or newsprint.
   h. Eliminate solutions transferred from another situation unless situation is identical.
   i. Forecast effects of each solution.
   j. Use exploratory questions.
VIII. Choose solution.
   a. Choose one that most completely obtains the objective, one that does so most efficiently (least expenditure of time, money, energy).
   b. Choose one that is acceptable.
   c. Specify action to be taken.
      1. Duties of each member.
      2. Steps involved in implementation.
      3. Evaluation procedures to be used.
      4. Arrange for follow-up.
IX. Implement and test alternatives.
X. Provide for progress review sessions and further action.

aration of situation descriptions and solution proposals. The program allows sharing in the refinement of the situation and in the development and elaboration of relevant solutions.

The program has been used in various organizations (e.g., Babcock & Wilcox, Department of Treasury, Union Carbide, Department of Agriculture) and seems to increase involvement and commitment to action on the part of conference members.*

Specifically what is done is as follows:

An organization situation (e.g., opportunity or threat in environment) is described, checking with the group after each item in the description for agreement and discussion.

The situation description, which had been prepared ahead of time, is revised on newsprint as the group proceeds.

Similarly, the proposals are prepared ahead of time on newsprint and are revised as the group proceeds.

The proposals are presented and discussed, with the question, "Do we agree to do this?"

The most *valued* solutions or proposals are those that could be implemented by the conference group members themselves.

After each session a list of agreed-upon items is transcribed and distributed to each member of the conference as soon as possible.

The group is asked from time to time to stay with and bring up significant issues.

The conference leader keeps checking on the group process to see if what is being done is helpful. He checks on the accuracy of communication, protects minority points of view, keeps the discussion moving and summarizes from time to time.

This approach allows involvement as well as aggressive pursuit of problem areas in implementation of strategies or areas in which there may be opportunities for the organization to change practices or strategies.

An alternative way of feeding in data puts emphasis on debate and the examination of underlying assumptions, and the generation of new assumptions once old ones are exposed or demolished. It is called the *dialectical* program. Specifically what is done in this case is as follows:

Dialectical program.

An individual or subgroup develops a set of objectives and a plan of action.

Another individual or subgroup develops a similar set of objectives and a counterplan to attain the objectives.

The objectives and plans are presented and advocated to the total group.

The total group examines the underlying assumptions as they relate to environmental demands and support and the strategy-generating structure.

Opposing advocates interpret relevant information as supporting their views.

The total group is asked from time to time to judge the suitability of the various assumptions, objectives and action plans.

---

*See, for example, P. H. Chase: The creative management workshop. *Personnel Journal,* April, 1972, pp. 264–282.

244 / THE ACTION THRUST IN STRATEGY FORMATION

As with the SDDPD approach, the session leader keeps checking on the group process to see if what is being done is helpful.

Test your assumptions!

As reported by Mason,* in most cases in which this program has been tried, what seems to develop is either clear support for one alternative or a new composite approach that is superior to either of the original objectives or action plans. Moreover, the assumptions underlying the plans are made explicit and given a thorough examination, and new assumptions are generated. (See Fig. 8-3.) This approach lends itself to role playing.

The group activity may be preceded (or followed) by individual problem-solving activity. Thus, the advantages of both types of activity may be obtained.

An example of guidelines and a report and measurement plan.

To give more detail on some of the various activities in these sessions we shall give the guidelines and report and the measurement plan that resulted after orientation and discussion in a public organization.† The focal point in this particular illustration is *priority setting and action planning.* You will notice that there are multiple sources of data and multiple methods used, i.e., (1) self-generated data in the sessions, and (2) data fed in from outside sources (interviews, questionnaires, analysis of strategic moves and practices). You will notice as well that the design pays close attention to gaining understanding and acceptance of the measurement plan.

---

*R. O. Mason: A dialectical approach to strategic planning. *Management Science, 15*:403-414, 1969.

†The plan is a modification of the "confrontation meeting" approach used frequently in consulting by Professor Richard Beckhard of Harvard University, to whom we have previously referred.

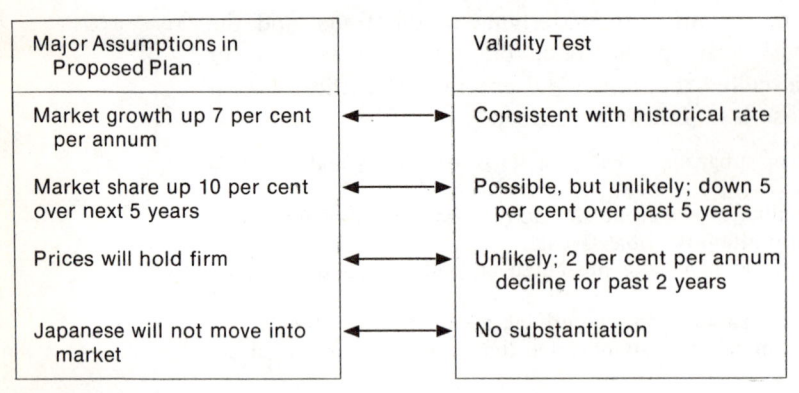

Major Assumptions in Proposed Plan	Validity Test
Market growth up 7 per cent per annum	Consistent with historical rate
Market share up 10 per cent over next 5 years	Possible, but unlikely; down 5 per cent over past 5 years
Prices will hold firm	Unlikely; 2 per cent per annum decline for past 2 years
Japanese will not move into market	No substantiation

Net Assessment
1. Plan is unrealistically optimistic.
2. Highly unlikely that market share can be increased without substantial price reduction.
3. Competitive threat from Japanese not adequately dealt with.

Figure 8-3 Testing key corporate strategy assumptions. Adapted from L. V. Gerstner, Jr.: Can strategic planning pay off? Business Horizons, 15 *(No. 6),* 13, December, 1972.

PHASE I

(One or two half-day sessions.) Separate meetings across organization lines to collect information.
   a. Separate top management group (perhaps exclude organization head).
   b. Subgroups of five to eight people composed of others that they do not work with on a regular basis (may use a diagonal slice).
   c. Assignment for each group. Example: "We think this is a very good organization. We think this organization is highly creative in developing policies and strategies and in managing its people. We want to experiment and try to make things even better. We all want to help. Considering the changing environment, your needs and those of the total organization, what things should be different around here—strategies, policies, ways of implementing policies, structure, and so forth?"
   d. Each subgroup should develop a list for approximately one hour, put the list on newsprint and be prepared to report these back to the total group.

PHASE II

(One or two half-day sessions.) Total group meeting.
   a. Each subgroup reports its discussion.
   b. Areas of agreement and disagreement are identified and discussed.
   c. Issues are assigned to categories by the group, for example, by type of issue and by area of their authority, ability and motivation to have an impact on the issue.
   d. Barriers to improvement are identified and discussed (if time permits).
   e. Indication is given by top manager that additional information about improving organization effectiveness is going to be collected in a variety of ways. Examples:
      (1) All participants will anonymously and independently fill out an organizational effectiveness form. (See Appendix 2 for an abbreviated version of this form.) They will rate identified issues on importance and on effectiveness and rate barriers to improvement.
      (2) Special questionnaires will be sent to a sample of all organization members.
      (3) Interviews and discussions will be held with a sample of managers and supervisors.
      (4) Strategic moves and practices will be reviewed by task forces.
      (5) Some additional conferences will be held.
      (6) Studies of the strategic environment may be made if appropriate.

PHASE III

(Two or three half-day sessions.)
a. Subgroups go through list of priority issues and select one which affects their group and which is susceptible to their own efforts. They determine action plans (dimensions and tasks) that their group will take on those issues and a time-table for beginning subsequent work.
b. Subgroups identify what other relevant parties, staff supervisors and lateral groups might do to assist them.
c. One assignment might be to design an "optimal" organization of work for their part of the organization; another might be to determine a tactical plan for communicating what happened at the conference to relevant parties.

PHASE IV

(One half-day session).
a. The groups reconvene and each subgroup reports out its list of priority issues and its plans for dealing with them. Then each group reports suggestions for other relevant parties. A cumulative list of specific suggestions is maintained.
b. Top management officials of the unit respond to the list, making some commitment on each major policy and issue.

REPORT AND MEASUREMENT PLAN

A record should be kept of important actions and statements in the conferences. The report(s) would include:
a. A brief statement of methodology used in identifying issues and courses of action.
b. An identification of policy issues discussed, including the perceived relative importance and the degree of agreement on the importance of the issue.
c. Perceptions of dimensions of the managerial job and the staff job as they relate to the policies and the issues identified.
d. Specific tasks for each type of position to improve organization effectiveness.
e. Minority comment on appropriateness of recommendations.
f. A timetable for their completion.
g. Tactical plan for communicating what happened at the conference to relevant persons not there.
h. Methods for estimating how much has been accomplished. It is highly important to gain *understanding* and *acceptance* of the measurement plan. A management performance accomplishment plan might be developed by the conference groups as follows:
(1) Identify independent dimensions of performance relating to issues identified. These could be individual group dimensions or inter-team dimensions, e.g., managers support and reinforce investment spending among subordinates.
(2) Provide descriptions of these dimensions.
(3) Develop descriptions or samples of high, moderate and low levels of performance on each dimension, e.g., the manager isolates strategic work for objective analysis and profiling of strategies.
(4) Transfer the dimension and examples to a second group knowledgeable about the issues for discussion and editing. Discard dimensions and examples for which there is a lack of consensus on definitions and on ratings.
(5) Participants and outside analysts independently and anonymously rate organization and management performance as it stands at time of conferences and then rate again after a period of time, e.g., six months, 12 months.
i. Appendix could include summaries of information distributed.
j. Progress review sessions should be scheduled within six months.

QUESTIONS AND ANSWERS REGARDING THE ACTION COMPONENTS

Numerous questions about structured activities and their effectiveness and efficiency may occur to the reader. We can only proceed *tentatively* at the time, but some appropriate guidance may be gained from experienced judgment. Some questions and answers arising out of experience with the interventions are presented below. (Also some additional relevant research findings are introduced.)

Do the approaches work?

Before-and-after studies, case studies, direct observation and anecdotal evidence (we have already referred to some of this evidence in Chapter 6) seem to indicate some outcomes associated with these types of structured activities which are judged as at least temporarily improving the strategy-making process. The approaches are being adopted by practicing managers (often with external advisors). Additional studies of the structured activities mentioned and variations of them are being conducted in a variety of business and government settings across the country. To fully understand the complexities and unique problems of application of these structured activities, however, requires systematic controlled research and constructive dialogue between specialists in the field. More data are needed, for example, on the cost benefit relationship, the limitations for size and type of organization, the effects of extended reliance on outside help and the limitations of group versus individual problem analysis.*

How many organization managers should be included?

The desirable number will depend on such factors as how the unit's work is divided, what participation would contribute a good enough spread of experiences and viewpoints to give a good picture of the organization or the organizational unit. For break-out groups, approximately five to eight members tend to provide for a good balance. Greater resources are available for problem solving, which may result in improved group performance. However, there may be decreased member satisfaction and increased difficulty in reaching a consensus or a joint decision.†

Who should be organization participants in the session?

For regular meetings the normal participants in the meetings may be included. For special sessions consideration should be given to:

Type of strategy issues to be discussed.
Representation from significant strategy units.
Interests, knowledge and skills of potential members.
Heterogeneity of membership.

While heterogeneity will tend to increase the difficulty of building interpersonal relations, it will also tend to increase the problem-solving potential of the group, since errors are reduced, more alternatives are generated and wider criticism is possible.‡

---

*See F. R. Wickert: Book review of Addison-Wesley Series on Organization Development. *Personnel Psychology*, 23(No. 3):411–415, Autumn, 1970; D. C. Barnland: A comparative study of individual majority and group judgment. *Journal of Abnormal and Social Psychology*, 58:55–60; R. Beckhard and D. Lake: Short and long range effects of a team development effort. *In* Hornstein, H. A., et al.: (eds.): *Social Intervention*. New York, The Free Press, 1971, pp. 421–439.

†E. J. Thomas and C. F. Fink: Models of group problem solving. *Journal of Abnormal and Social Psychology*, 63(No. 1):53–63, 1961. See also A. P. Hare: *Handbook of Small Group Research*. Chicago, The Free Press of Glencoe, 1962.

‡See B. E. Collins and H. Guetzkow: *A Social Psychology of Group Processes for Decision Making*. New York, John Wiley & Sons, Inc., 1964.

Should there be substitutes for group session participants?

The policy and strategy issues being dealt with are important to the success of the organization. The conference members need to be made aware of the importance and to be personally present at each session unless there is a dire emergency. Experience indicates an increased risk of ineffectiveness if substitutes for conference members are sent to the sessions. Even a few substitutes seem to hamper the continuity of thought and interaction among participants.

What about timing and spacing of the sessions?

We have already discussed timing of the structured activities. We should add that group effectiveness seems to depend on the openness between participants. Such openness is a function of, among other things previously cited, the number of meetings the group has. There should be enough meetings to permit openness to develop, but not so many nor held so often as to make the meetings too time-consuming or nonproductive. It is difficult to say how many sessions should be held or how often; probably not more than one or two sessions a week seems to be a good guide based on experience thus far.

It seems desirable to have one session held just before presentation of findings and possible solutions to the top manager. At this time the group members need to discuss the key issues and the best manner of presentation.

How to present the plan or report?

This question is relevant when the higher level officials are not members of the group. The question may be answered by the participants themselves. Since the staff analysts tend to be more neutral in the face of possible conflict, some managers may prefer to have the analysts make the presentation. In any event, it seems desirable after the presentation for the official to respond and to discuss the report with the total group from his standpoint to attempt to gain agreement on timing and priority. The official, as indicated, along with the highest board (e.g., directors, commissioners, and so forth) has probably reserved the right to final choice.

What of findings that members fail to confirm or agree on?

As suggested before, various conflict management procedures may be used. Effort in the session is sometimes made to bring differing objectives, values and perceptions out into the open where they can be dealt with constructively. In addition, a basic tactic is to find the goals upon which the participants can agree and thereby establish an effective interaction.

If some findings are not confirmed or agreed upon there may be a need for further study, or the findings may be reported, with notations made of disagreements or lack of confirmation. This is a decision that will test the judgment of the participants and the analysts.

SUMMARY

We have covered some of the considerations necessary for developing individual and group involvement and for selecting change strategies. We have indicated: (1) that individual problem-solving efforts are a very important part of the action thrust in strategy formation; (2) that group interaction does *not* mean that strategy decisions are turned over to the group; (3) that relatively successful development efforts tend to include a shared approach to information gathering and to collaborative problem solving following a well outlined series of steps; (4) that sometimes it may be quite effective to use an enterpreneurial change strategy and/or a technostructural change strategy; (5) that group activity may permit participants to obtain intrinsic rewards while perceiving, diagnosing and acting upon relevant strategy issues; (6) that many factors, including the skill and perceptiveness of those exercising leadership functions, have a bearing on whether the groups develop into effective operating teams; (7) that it is assumed that a transfer to everyday work would be enhanced if the development design built expectations of continuation and expansion of strategy formation and implementation beyond the meetings and if the design called for periodic progress report sessions; and (8) a situational design approach to the structuring of activities is necessary to develop an appropriate balance between adaptation and integration.

A situational design of the planning system.

The structured activities, as posed, may be used in regularly scheduled meetings, or special sessions may be set up. Using structured activities is a *highly flexible* approach that may be used in conjunction with training and development sessions or feed-in or with observational, interview, questionnaire, report and management science data. The information gathered may be useful for individual research and independent study of strategy formation as well as for group discussion and analysis. Expertise is needed and the problem-solving process may be designed and aided by internal and/or external analysts. It may have several focal points, including (1) strategy-formation process, (2) assessment of leverage points, (3) managerial activities and capabilities (see Appendix 1), (4) stating and analyzing objectives, (5) priority setting and action planning, and (6) progress review.

These action components of an action-research program may be relied on to gain support and assistance by involving others in planning actions, coordinating actions, executing actions and evaluating actions.

DISCUSSION QUESTIONS

1. Can groups be used effectively and efficiently to create strategies within the organization? Why? Within what constraints does this action occur?

2. Discuss how authority and leadership patterns affect the ability of the organization to react to strategy changes.

3. What criteria are satisfied by organizations that generally deal successfully with strategic changes?

4. How can the group problem-solving activity be designed to implement the "best" strategic changes within the organization?

5. What stages of the strategy-formation process require particular emphasis during evaluation? Discuss the problems and benefits associated with structured evaluation at each of these phases.

6. Discuss the critical steps involved in setting up problem-solving conferences. Which key individuals should be included in this process? What should their roles be?

7. What types of activities lend themselves to group action? What is the focus of the group during each of these activities?

Suggested Additional References for Further Research

Archbold, St.: Dimensions of participation. *Journal of General Management, 3* (No. 3):52–66, 1976.

Bell, D. J.: Manpower in corporate planning. *Long-Range Planning, 9* (No. 2):31–37, 1976.

Bennett, P. W.: Participation in planning. *Journal of General Management, 2* (No. 1):12–16, 1974.

Cammann, C., and Nadler, D. A.: Fit control systems to your managerial style. *Harvard Business Review, 54* (No. 1):65–72, 1976.

Cleivett, R. M., and Stasch, S. F.: Shifting role for the product manager. *Harvard Business Review, 53* (No. 1):65–72, 1975.

Dill, W. R.: Integrating planning and management development. *Long-Range Planning, 8* (No. 5):8–12, 1975.

Eppink, D. J., Keuning, D., and deJong, K.: Corporate planning in the Netherlands. *Long-Range Planning, 9* (No. 5):30–41, 1976.

Leavitt, H. J.: Beyond the analytic manager: Part II. *California Management Review, 17* (No. 4):11–21, 1975.

Leyshon, A. M.: Market planning and corporate planning. *Long-Range Planning, 9* (No. 1):29–37, 1976.

Lorange, P., and Vancil, R. F.: How to design a strategic planning system. *Harvard Business Review, 54* (No. 5):75–81, 1976.

Lorsch, J., and Lawrence, P.: *Managing Group and Intergroup Relations.* Homewood, Ill., Richard D. Irwin, Inc., 1972.

Lorsch, J., and Lawrence, P.: Organizing for product innovation. *Harvard Business Review, 43* (No. 1):96–104, 1965.

Mintzberg, H.: The manager's job: folklore and fact. *Harvard Business Review, 53* (No. 4):49–61, 1975.

Nurmi, R.: Developing a climate for planning. *Long-Range Planning, 9* (No. 3):48–53, 1976.

Richards, M. D.: An Exploratory Study of Strategic Failure. Academy of Management Proceedings, Boston, Mass., 1973.

Rothwell, R.: Factors for success in industrial innovation. *Journal of General Management, 2* (No. 2):57–65, 1975.

Schneier, C.: Behavioral modifications in management: A review and critique. *Academy of Management Journal, 17*:528–548, 1974.

Shagory, G. E.: Development of corporate planning staff. *Long-Range Planning, 8* (No. 1):26–30, 1975.

Taylor, R. N.: Psychological aspects of planning staff. *Long-Range Planning, 9* (No. 2):66–74, 1976.

Tilles, S.: *Making Strategy Explicit.* Boston, The Boston Consulting Group, 1967.

Tuason, R.: Corporate Life Cycle and the Evaluation of Corporate Strategy. Academy of Management Proceedings, Boston, Mass., 1973.

# APPENDIX 1 TO CHAPTER 8

MANAGERIAL ACTIVITIES AND CAPABILITIES*

The purpose of this appendix is to present an experimental approach (Analysis of Strategic Activities of Managers or ASAM),[†] for the strategy maker to begin an analysis of his own strategic activities and capabilities and to develop some understanding of changes he might consider. The analytical approach can be, and has been, readily utilized by general managers. Though no controlled evaluation research has been completed, ASAM participants see it as helpful especially if self-study is given considerable thought and attention. Candid answers are necessary. The approach suggests self-study as a beginning—one part of a total effort to seek means of dealing with key issues in his strategy formulation activities.

ASAM consists of several iterative steps based on intervention theory (Argyris, 1970). Some of the steps include discussion with other managers and/or a consultant. First, a review of some of the characteristics of managerial work on strategy formulation as they relate to his situation is developed. Second, to aid the self-study groups of guideline questions are used. The questions are significant ones based on a review of research on strategy making. Third, the manager develops an inventory of forces, strengths, problems and expectations. Typically, general managers show an interest in discussing and comparing their results with others, so small groups can gather to do this. The managers can help each other by sharing ideas and developing summaries of results.

The choices that the strategy maker has in his job are affected by environmental as well as organizational constraints (or uncertainties). A next step then is an analysis of how to reduce those constraints and/or how to operate effectively within them. Finally, in the ASAM approach the strategy maker is asked to review his choices and to make a commitment to on-the-job changes that appear to improve his effectiveness.

Characteristics of the Strategy Maker's Job

One of the arts of strategy formulation is the recognition and exploitation of key choices on the job itself. Many managers seem to fail to use the choices that their jobs offer because they fail to recognize their existence (Stewart, 1976). One way of aiding recognition is to review the conditions or characteristics under which others in similar positions tend to operate. The review enables the manager to:
 (i) Sort out the relevance of the characteristics to his own job;
 (ii) alert him to characteristics which may be hazardous in his situation; and
 (iii) begin seeing possibilities for improving his effectiveness.
Groups of two or more managers may be included at this stage.

The authority of research on the general managers job is relied on to give descriptive evidence; normative implica-

---

*See F. T. Paine: Analysis of Strategic Activity of Managers presented at Analytical Approaches to Strategy, INSEAD, Fontainebleau, France, Dec., 1976.

[†]All rights reserved. No part of this exercise may be used or reproduced in any manner without the written permission of the author, F. T. Paine.

tions may be developed as the discussion proceeds relying heavily on the participating general managers for input. There is a rapidly developing body of research and also reviews of that research to draw upon (see references). It is not the intention to review the research here. That has been done elsewhere as indicated. The manager, however, would be given the major findings plus some explanations and examples, and encouraged to provide feedback and comment.

For discussion purposes the major characteristics have been associated with three types of inter-related work activities — relationships, information processing and decision making. The discussion may draw attention to the fact that some of the characteristics have not received much attention in traditional management literature, or in management development training, e.g., selling, trading and bargaining without authority or the "art of imprecision." In addition, studies of how executives operate may be referred to indicating frequency and duration of meetings, their desk work (letters, reports, etc.), telephone calls, observation tours and their pattern of activities during the day.

Some of the characteristics of the strategy maker's job to discuss are:

I. *Relationships — Linking Between Organizational Unit and Wide Variety of Contacts*
   (i) Much time in meetings, unscheduled as well as scheduled.
   (ii) Dealing with conflicting demands.
   (iii) Active in seeking cooperation of people over whom he has no authority.
   (iv) Personally selling, trading and bargaining with people external to the organization unit.

II. *Information Processing — Receiving, Storing, Transmitting*
   (i) "Weak signals" about discontinuities.
   (ii) Some information of doubtful accuracy.
   (iii) Preference for live action, current and specific information, verbal media.
   (iv) Used informal information systems.
   (v) Some difficulty in sharing information with relevant parties.
   (vi) Discretion important, could give away information of value.

III. *Decision-Making — Initiate Changes, Allocate Resources, Handle Crisis Situations*
   (i) Psychological readiness to face unpleasant and unfamiliar events and ability to solve unfamiliar problems.
   (ii) Being receptive to "weak signals" and taking measures for flexibility (Internal and external) and readiness.
   (iii) Using the "art of imprecision" and "muddling with a purpose."
   (iv) Not fully in control of own affairs.
   (v) Some hazard of superficiality; activity characterized by unrelenting pace, brevity, variety and fragmentation.
   (vi) Some difficulty in delegation.
   (vii) Exposure — live with possibility of serious mistake.

Guideline Questions

After discussion of these characteristics, a further aid to the process of self-study is given in the form of guideline questions. The questions direct thinking toward choices already made and about changes to consider.

On an individual basis, the manager is expected to skim through the questions and then carefully reread, noting matters of special interest in his particular strategy work.

As a prelude to the individual work it is desirable to check on the need for clarification of any concepts brought up in the questionnaire or the discussion. For example, some time may be spent on discussion of:
   (i) Styles of leadership and problem solving (Vroom and Yetton, 1974).
   (ii) Modes of strategy making — entrepreneurs, planners, adapters (Mintzberg, 1973).
   (iii) Measures for flexibility (internal and external) and readiness (Ansoff, 1975).

A sample of questions follows:
Relationships
   (i) Do I emphasize the interpersonal

influence style that fits the situation—Tell, Sell, Consult A, Consult B, Join? One-on-one vs. group meetings? Do I sufficiently consider the factors—decision quality, information, time, type of task, acceptance, personalities of others, other motivations toward organizational goals, extent of conflict likely, development of others?
 (ii) Are there certain kinds of external relationships (external to my organizational unit) that I need to build up? Can I improve my effectiveness in exercising a positive influence in those relationships?

Information Processing
 (i) Do I need to make better use of my contacts to get information? Can other people do more scanning for me? How can I become more aware of and have earlier recognition of problems, opportunities and threats for my organizational unit?
 (ii) Should I put more emphasis on disseminating and storing information in my organization? Do I tend to rely excessively on face-to-face communication, thereby putting all but a few of my subordinates at an informational disadvantage? How can I get more information to others so that they can make better decisions?

Decision Making
 (i) Do I need to delegate more authority so my subordinates can go ahead with their proposals? Do I have coordination problems because subordinates now, in fact, make too many of their decisions independently?
 (ii) Is there a need for more system to my allocation of time. Am I frequently just reacting to the pressures of the moment? Do I need to commit more scheduled time to do the specific things I want to do? Do I need to be more reflective and probe more deeply into certain issues.
 (iii) Do I need to make the objectives and strategy for my organizational unit more explicit in order to better guide the decisions of others? Or do I need more flexibility to change these "plans" at will?
 (iv) Should I place more emphasis on dealing with changes that are needed? On managing disturbances and conflicts that might develop? Has sufficient analysis and anticipation been given to these changes and disturbances?

Inventory of Forces, Strengths, Problems and Expectations

The general manager has read through and noted a number of guideline questions for self-study. Using the guidelines as a base, he is asked to think over what he actually does and what he can do (e.g. in scheduled meetings, desk work, unscheduled meetings, telephone calls, observational tours). He is asked to be as objective as possible in answering the following questions:
 (i) What kinds of specific on-the-job actions do you take that contribute most to your managerial work?
 (ii) What kinds of specific on-the-job actions seem to be needed to improve your work as a manager?
 (iii) What changes would you like to make in the allocation of your managerial time? More time doing what? Less time doing what?
 (iv) Expectations—To what extent and how do you expect to be able to actually implement the suggested changes in your managerial work? Any difficulties? How to overcome?

These questions are answered individually by the executive. Self-study is at best difficult. The answers can be shared with relevant others (managers, staff, consultants), others can play the role of devil's advocate and challenge whether the answers are realistic and feasible. The degree of impact, the importance and the effectiveness of various changes can be considered. Group summaries of the most important changes can be developed. Individuals, of course, must make the judgment of what is most relevant and important for their own strategy formulation situation.

Dealing with Constraints

Some managers going through the exercise have asked themselves: "What constraints are hindering the effectiveness of my work?" and "What can I, should I, do in dealing with them?" Constraints may be related to several factors: the scope of the job, suppliers, customers and environmental uncertainties among others. Let's face it, sometimes there is little that one can do. For example, the nature of the market may be an environmental constraint, which is virtually unchangeable (at least temporarily), or there might be government imposed wage and price controls. Thus, one must operate within the constraints.

There are, however, a number of actions that can be discussed in ASAM which may help to reduce constraints. An aggressive, bold entrepreneurial approach may, in a sense, enlarge the managers job and shape the environment. Of course, a psychological commitment (Mintzberg, 1976) to a strategy may build up eventually restricting the choice (the psychological commitment of top strategy makers at Volkswagen may be an example). An adaptive approach, on the other hand, where the manager is groping around in a confusing environment (but taking flexibility measures) may avoid the explicit commitment to a strategy, thus preserving the choices of activity in his own job.

More specifically, however, utilization may be made of bargaining power and political tactics to enhance one's position and reduce constraints. The process of bargaining is difficult and requires special understanding and skills. But the process goes on and tactics to use have been described in the literature. (For example, some "advice" on tactics is given in Chapter 2 of this book.)

Political tactics are, of course, commonly used by some organization members for their own private gain as well as reducing constraints. Some of the tactics are in contrast to the proposals of some behavioral scientists and practitioners for open communication, participation and a democratic atmosphere. A rationale needs to be developed for the non-hypocritical use of power or political tactics. However, these tactics are presented in ASAM because there are lessons in them for the individual manager. The implications of their use, however, need to be considered. "What if" scenarios have been used, and provoke a lively discussion.

Conclusions

To conclude, the general manager needs to think analytically about different ways in which his job can be done as well as various ways to deal with constraints and uncertainties. Too often choices are not seen. Too often the manager operating in his live action verbal world has fallen into a pattern of activities that need reconsideration. While the manager himself knows the intricacies of his situation better than anyone, to tell him to be introspective about changes in his job is not enough. Some program is needed to bring in the research, the experiences of others, and the testing of ideas with feedback. ASAM attempts to do that.

It should be emphasized that there are no simple solutions to the complex problem of strategy formulation. A number of other analytical approaches to strategy can perhaps provide some help; but if the strategy maker is to improve his own work, ASAM can perhaps help him ask the right questions. He must provide his own answers.

References to Appendix 1

Allison, G. T.: *Essence of Decision: Explaining the Cuban Missle Crisis.* Boston, Little, Brown & Company, 1971.

Anderson, C., and Paine, F. T.: Managerial perceptions and strategic behavior. *Academy of Management Journal, 18*:811–823, 1975.

Ansoff, H. I.: Managing strategic surprise by response to weak signals. *California Management Review,* 18(No. 2):21–33, 1975.
Argyris, C.: *Intervention Theory and Method.* Reading, Mass., Addison-Wesley, 1970.
Campbell, J. P., Dunnette, M. D., Lawler, E. E., III, and Weick, K. E., Jr.: *Managerial Behavior, Performance and Effectiveness.* New York, McGraw Hill, 1970.
Hofer, C. W.: Towards a contingency theory of strategic behavior. *Academy of Management Journal,* 18:775–810, 1975.
Mintzberg, H.: Strategy making in three modes. *California Management Review,* 16(No. 2):44–53, 1973.
Mintzberg, H.: A new look at the chief executive's job. *Organizational Dynamics,* 5:49–61, Winter, 1973.
Mintzberg, H.: Strategy Formulation as an Evolutionary Process. Presented at Conference: Strategy Formulation—Different Perspectives, Aix-en-Provence, May, 1976.
Mumford, E., and Pettigrew, A.: *Implementing Strategic Decisions.* London, Longman, 1975.
Paine, F. T., and Anderson, C. R.: Contingencies affecting strategy formulation and effectiveness. *Journal of Management Studies,* 14:147–158, May, 1977.
Stewart, R.: *Contrasts in Management.* London, McGraw Hill, 1976.
Vroom, V. H., and Yetton, P.: Decision making and the leadership process. *Journal of Contemporary Business,* 7:47–64, Autumn 1974.
Wrapp, H. E.: Good Managers Don't Make Policy Decisions. *Harvard Business Review,* 45(No. 5):95–104, Sept.-Oct., 1967.

9

TRENDS IN STRATEGY AND STRUCTURE

BALANCING THE ENVIRONMENT—STRATEGY—CAPABILITY

INTEGRATED CONTINGENCY MODEL

STRATEGIC MOVES IN EACH QUADRANT

RELATED INFLUENCES ON CAPABILITY
  Differentiating by Organizational Level
  Keeping the Organizational Strategy in Mind

OVERALL SUMMARY
  Practical Problems for You to Solve
  Questions to Answer
  Policy Makers

DISCUSSION QUESTIONS

APPENDIX 1. SOME ACTION STEPS IN CASE ANALYSIS

ENVIRONMENT—STRATEGY—CAPABILITY

What you should learn.

See appendix for case analysis suggestions.

Up to this point we have concentrated on a model of strategy and policy formation, guides for assessment, and methods for assessing and developing strategies and policies and the policy-formation process. A variety of ideas and methods have been presented. Their use as given or in revised form, alone or in combination, rests with the judgment and skill of the manager, analyst or student. Of course, there will be some "muddling through" owing to various uncertainties and pressures. We are assuming, however, that the planning and structuring of activities would be helpful.

In the preceding chapter we discussed some structured activities that might help the organization both to initiate and to implement organizational strategies. In this chapter we shall discuss some general trends in strategy and structure (for large corporations where there is significant evidence), some considerations in balancing the environment-strategy-capability of the organization and a contingency model that provides a framework for analysis. We shall also provide an overall summary of the book. Finally, in the appendix to this chapter we shall summarize some action steps along with several categories of questions that, when answered, should be a help in starting a planned approach.

TRENDS IN STRATEGY AND STRUCTURE

We have discussed earlier that strategy may be linked to aspects of the structure in a coherent organization design. A historian, A. D. Chandler,* has pointed out that as firms grow larger over time

---

*A. D. Chandler: *Strategy and Structure.* Cambridge, MIT Press, 1962.

TABLE 9-1 RELATIONSHIP BETWEEN STRATEGY AND STRUCTURE*

Stage	Product-Market Scope (Degree of Diversification)	Number of Companies	Structure Functional	Structure Divisional
I.	Single product	30	30	0
II.	Dominant product	70	25	45
III.	Related products	300	15	285
IV.	Unrelated products	100	0	100
		500	70 (14%)	430 (86%)

*Adapted from B. R. Scott: *Stages in Corporate Development, Part II.* Harvard Business School, 4-371-295 BP 999, 1971.

and diversify into new businesses or integrate their operations they have to decentralize because the business has become so complex that top management does not have the technical knowledge or because it just takes too long to send the problems up to the top for a decision.

In addition, the hypothesized relationship between strategy and structure has received strong support from an analysis of firms in the Fortune 500 (1967) by Wrigley* (see Table 9-1). The analysis, as reported by B. R. Scott, indicates that among the largest industrial corporations in the United States all the single product firms were found to be functionally organized, all the highly diversified and 85 per cent of the related product diversified group to have a divisional organization.

Furthermore, previous analysis of organizations in the United States indicated a trend over the last several decades toward the growth of markets involving increased volume in a product or service line associated with more specialized manpower and equipment. The development of an integration strategy and a centralized, functional structure to exploit the opportunities occurred frequently.

Integration and a functional structure

However, a more predominant recent trend, which also stems from the growth of markets, includes the development of new products and services to serve them, the increased impact of product-or-service oriented research and development activities within the organization, and the development of a strategy and a structure to exploit the market, namely, diversification and divisionalization. Growth via diversification has become the most common corporate strategy in Western Europe as well.‡

Diversification and divisionalization.

---

*As reported by B. R. Scott: *Stages in Corporate Development, Part II.* Harvard Business School, 4-371-295 BP 999, 1971.

†See, for example, J. K. Galbraith: *The New Industrial State.* Boston, Houghton Mifflin Company, 1967.

‡They're sniping at Galbraith again. *New York Times,* March 11, 1973, p. 16.

Success of "diversifiers."

The evidence (of Scott) also indicates that diversified companies (e.g., E. I. Dupont, Eastman Kodak, General Electric, General Foods. Olin Textron) have performed better in growth by sales, earnings and earnings per share (especially if they had related products) than nondiversified companies (e.g., U.S. Steel, Scott Paper, Texaco). There are some exceptions, of course, such as the high-performance, vertically integrated* and dominant-product enterprises like IBM, Polaroid and Xerox.

These exceptions have occurred where the organization was able to gain a leadership position in a single, rapid-growth industry and to retain that position. The "diversifiers" were able to achieve a redistribution of sales and assets toward more favorable growth and profit prospects by using a multi-industry strategy and a divisional form of management.

While the trend toward diversification and divisionalization for large corporations is clear, the transition is quite difficult for an organization (e.g., Jones & Laughlin, Goodrich, and Armour) "caught" with large investments in vertically integrated operations in an industry with a low to moderate growth rate. For these companies it takes very substantial investments in new areas in order to achieve significant diversification. Many of the companies do not have a high price/earnings ratio and are not in a strong position from which to diversify by acquisition. Yet "to diversify into attractive areas with rapid growth prospects they almost surely face the prospect of buying companies with high price earnings ratios. The result is a dilution of earnings per share, and possibly further downward pressure on the price of their stock. To pay cash, on the other hand, places a burden on the treasury in industries where recourse of outside capital is typically a continuing need. In addition, cash transactions may require a premium price in order to offset tax advantages for the seller."† Financially speaking, therefore, some dominant product companies (with low or moderate growth) are somewhat boxed into a situation where a significant redistribution of sales and assets is a slow process.

Neverthless, many firms (dominant product and otherwise) seem to be going through this process and likewise toward the use of a divisional form of management. Continuing research is needed to describe more fully the trend toward increasing product market diversification and divisionalization.‡

---

*Vertical integration may include growth by adding units closer to the final end-use market (forward integration) or to its original raw material sources (backward integration).

†B. R. Scott: *Stages in Corporate Development, Part II.* op. cit., p. 6.

‡See also R. Rumelt: *Strategy, Structure and Economic Performance in Large American Corporations.* Cambridge, Harvard University Press, 1974.

BALANCING THE ENVIRONMENT–STRATEGY–CAPABILITY

While recognizing the limits of our current knowledge, it has been demonstrated that policy analysts need to give careful consideration to the organizational strategy *and* the managerial capability.*

Refer back to the policy formation model in Chapter 2.

The managerial capability of the organization may be broadly conceived as the ability to carry out the strategy. The capability, as we have said, would include a variety of components such as processes, power, attitudes, skills and knowledge, which would provide the appropriate degree of internal flexibility, as well as roles and programs (structure).

Moreover, earlier in discussing aspects of our policy-formation model, we have noted the accelerating pace of change in the economic, technological, social, political, competitive and social responsibility forces. Organizations significantly affected by this kind of turbulent environment would need an organizational strategy that allows more rapid modification of itself now than in the past. And with each shift in strategy, the appropriateness of the existing elements in the overall capability for each organization will need to be re-examined for balance.

There are several important considerations for the analyst. Determinations need to be made on the specialization by level and/or function plus coordination of specialized jobs in order to focus activity on organizational objectives. What is the most effective way to divide the work — functional group, product division or geographic division? Will it be helpful to group closely the units that are now required to integrate their activities? What skills are appropriate for coordinating specialized jobs and for managing conflict situations? Will a wide or narrow span of control be most useful? What management information-gathering processes will generate relevant and timely data? Are managers playing leadership roles that are appropriately matched to the situation? Are the measurement and motivational programs designed to encourage role orientations that are appropriate to the unit task? The action research program previously discussed will help to answer those questions on overall capability.

Your previous learning should help in judging some significant considerations.

Recent advances in understanding the environment-strategy-capability relationships have centered around the role of the general manager as a mediator between the internal characteristics of the organization and the important attributes from the external environment.† In general, managers (or policy makers) perceiving a

---

*H. Igor Ansoff: Strategic Posture Analysis. Presented at Analytical Approaches to Strategy, INSEAD, Fountainbleau, France, Dec., 1976.

†J. Child: Organization structure, environment, and performance — the role of strategic choice. *Sociology*, 6:1–22, 1972.

highly uncertain environment are likely to use different decision patterns in strategy formation than those managers perceiving a high degree of certainty in the environment.* For example, an adaptive mode including incremental, remedial decisions arrived at in part through bargaining among members of a power coalition may occur where environmental uncertainty is perceived; a planning mode including systematic, integrated decisions may be possible and occur where conditions of certainty are perceived.†

Similarly, the perception of a need for change in some strategy or internal capability of the organization may lead to different

---

*J. Galbraith, *Organizations Design,* Reading, Mass.: Addison-Wesley, 1977, p. 55.

†See Allison, G. T.: *Essence of Decision: Explaining the Cuban Missile Crisis,* Boston: Little, Brown & Company, 1971; H. Mintzberg: Strategy Making in Three Modes, *California Management Review,* 16(2), 44–53, 1973; and H. Mintzberg: Policy as a Field of Management Theory, *Academy of Management Review,* Vol. 2 (No. 1):88–103, 1977.

TABLE 9-2 PROFILE OF LEVELS OF UNCERTAINTY IN AN ENVIRONMENTAL SEGMENT

	Low			Medium		High	
State of Knowledge about T/O (See Chapter 4)							
Intensity	1	2	3	4	5	6	7
Importance	1	2	3	4	5	6	7
Price Competition							
Intensity	1	2	3	4	5	6	7
Importance	1	2	3	4	5	6	7
Promotion and Distribution Competition							
Intensity	1	2	3	4	5	6	7
Importance	1	2	3	4	5	6	7
Technological Changes	Slow			Medium		Fast	
Intensity	1	2	3	4	5	6	7
Importance	1	2	3	4	5	6	7
Technological Diversity	Low			Medium		High	
Intensity	1	2	3	4	5	6	7
Importance	1	2	3	4	5	6	7
Societal Pressures							
Intensity	1	2	3	4	5	6	7
Importance	1	2	3	4	5	6	7
Customer Pressures							
Intensity	1	2	3	4	5	6	7
Importance	1	2	3	4	5	6	7
Product Life Cycle	Long			Medium		Short	
Intensity	1	2	3	4	5	6	7
Importance	1	2	3	4	5	6	7
Stage of Product Life Cycle	Maturity	Early Growth		Late Growth		Emergence/ Decline	Shift in Stage
Intensity	1	2	3	4	5	6	7
Importance	1	2	3	4	5	6	7

decision patterns. For example, managers in a new, rapidly growing firm who perceive a situation in need of change may follow a mode or pattern of action different from those managers who perceive more of a commitment to the status quo. Bold, risky, entrepreneurial strategy making may occur in the former; a more conservative course of action may occur in the latter.

Uncertainty in the firm's environmental segments can be profiled for a number of attributes such as lack of knowledge of threats and opportunities, price competition, promotion and distribution competition, technological change, technological diversity, societal

TABLE 9-3 PROFILE OF LEVELS OF NEED FOR CHANGE

	Low			Medium			High
Processes							
Intensity	1	2	3	4	5	6	7
Importance	1	2	3	4	5	6	7
Skills							
Intensity	1	2	3	4	5	6	7
Importance	1	2	3	4	5	6	7
Knowledge							
Intensity	1	2	3	4	5	6	7
Importance	1	2	3	4	5	6	7
Attitudes							
Intensity	1	2	3	4	5	6	7
Importance	1	2	3	4	5	6	7
Power							
Intensity	1	2	3	4	5	6	7
Importance	1	2	3	4	5	6	7
Roles							
Intensity	1	2	3	4	5	6	7
Importance	1	2	3	4	5	6	7
Programs							
Intensity	1	2	3	4	5	6	7
Importance	1	2	3	4	5	6	7
Reallocation Strategies							
Intensity	1	2	3	4	5	6	7
Importance	1	2	3	4	5	6	7
Flexibility Strategy							
Intensity	1	2	3	4	5	6	7
Importance	1	2	3	4	5	6	7
Business Strategies							
Intensity	1	2	3	4	5	6	7
Importance	1	2	3	4	5	6	7
Environmental or Conflict Strategies							
Intensity	1	2	3	4	5	6	7
Importance	1	2	3	4	5	6	7
Resource Strategies							
Intensity	1	2	3	4	5	6	7
Importance	1	2	3	4	5	6	7
Evaluation Strategies							
Intensity	1	2	3	4	5	6	7
Importance	1	2	3	4	5	6	7
Change Strategies							
Intensity	1	2	3	4	5	6	7
Importance	1	2	3	4	5	6	7

pressures, customer pressures, a short product life cycle, changes in the life cycle, sociocultural change, and unpredictable shifts in government policies.

The profile in Table 9-2 highlights the extent (intensity) of the uncertainty as well as its relative importance for each attribute. Careful analysis and judgment of the situation relative to other organizations, units, or environmental segments is necessary to develop the profile.

Caution!

The attributes in the profile can be combined into a composite measure of environmental uncertainty because increases in uncertainty in any of the attributes increases the amount of information that must be processed by the organization. Therefore, variations in broad strategy and capability are hypothesized to be variations in the actions of the organization to process information about events that could not be anticipated in advance. For example, adjusting a strategy towards more integration improves the organization's capability to process information relating to uncertainties among its suppliers and/or distributors.

The magnitude of the gap between the firm's current position (in terms of economic performance) and its desired position should be measured. When this is done the firm could plot where it should be and where it is in order to determine the need for change in its environmental segments, strategy process, strategy content, and capabilities (see Table 9-3). Why is this so?

INTEGRATED CONTINGENCY MODEL*

Starting with the observation that the broad strategy should reflect the degree of environmental uncertainty, it is postulated that the broad strategy will differ based on the extent of gap between the present position and the goals of the organization. Using these two factors—environmental uncertainty and gap—a matrix of appropriate contingency strategies and capabilities may be developed (see Fig. 9-1). Hypotheses for the four corner cells are indicated. However, certain assumptions are made and limitations exist.

Assumptions

The following assumptions have been made in the design of the integrated contingency model:

1. The model is applicable to situations in which a single individual formulates strategy or a single individual dominates a

---

*Some of the material in this section has been adapted from C. R. Anderson and F. T. Paine: Managerial Perceptions and Strategic Behavior. *Academy of Management Journal,* 18(No. 4):811-824, 1975; and F. T. Paine and C. R. Anderson: Contingencies Affecting Strategy Formulation and Effectiveness. *Journal of Management Studies,* 14 (No. 2) 147-158, 1977.

ENVIRONMENT—STRATEGY—CAPABILITY / 263

Figure 9-1 An integrated contingency model.

Gap Between Present Position and Goals

	Low	High
Certain	**Cell 1** 1. Fixed and well defined 2. Optimization; maintenance; efficiency 3. Adaptive planning; maintain competence, stability, defend the domain, known technology 4. Closed/stable/mechanistic 5. Commitment to existing power structure; less active search for environmental information; defender	**Cell 2** 1. Need for identification and readjustment 2. Optimization; improve economies of operation; planned change 3. Planning search for market share; integration, improve distinctive competence, new technology 4. Closed/stable/mechanistic 5. Systematic; moderate search for environmental information; "integrative" planner
Uncertain	**Cell 3** 1. Continually adjusted to feedback 2. Satisfying; maintain flexibility; portfolio balance 3. Adaptive entrepreneurial, penetration, diversification into related products and markets; flexibility 4. Open/adaptive/organic; product divisions, matrix 5. Seek familiar change; active information gathering; adaptor	**Cell 4** 1. Varied and flexible 2. Satisfying; survival; develop creative problem solving 3. Entrepreneurial; divestiture; merger; diversification; major reallocation among SBA's; novel technology 4. Personal control; venture management 5. Search for external information; risk taking; "sharp departure" entrepreneur; create change

(Left axis: Perceived Environmental Uncertainty)

KEY:
1. Mission or Domain
2. Objectives
3. Strategy Process and Broad Strategies
4. Organization Form and Style
5. Role Performance of Policy Maker

coalition of strategy formulators. It is also applicable where there is a nondominated coalition, but moderator variables such as the risk propensity of the group and conflicting perceptions (decision making by compromise) add complexity to the problem of making predictions about strategic behavior.

2. The environment (especially environmental uncertainty) is a relatively constant factor in the formulation process that cannot be substantially influenced by the decision maker. This assumption does not preclude the organization from taking action to influence

the environment as a result of selected strategies. It is assumed that during the formulation process, environmental factors comprise a series of conditions over which the decision maker has no control.

3. It is assumed that there is a set of strategy-related behavior types that are relevant for each of the four model quadrants. Literature review provides support for this assumption. The model discussion expands this data base.

4. Every environment contains a certain degree of uncertainty or uncontrollable elements. However, the degree of environmental uncertainty is extremely variable and depends on both absolute characteristics and, more importantly, managerial perceptions. Similarly, organizations only rarely face conditions when there is no need for internal change. Need for change is assumed to be a function of absolute characteristics and, more importantly, managerial perceptions.

5. The important assumption is made that strategy formation must be consistent, for behavioral (implementation) reasons, with perceptual rather than with absolute characteristics of the environment. The contention of this model is that maximum effort toward implementation of strategy will be achieved only when strategy is consistent with perceptions of the environment and internal capabilities.

6. It is also assumed, following the arguments of Cyert, March, and Simon, that individuals will be motivated to reduce uncertainty if uncertainty is perceived. Behavior therefore is predictable in several quadrants. Similarly, predictable behavior is expected to occur with regard to the "Perceived Need for Change" dimension, since individuals are motivated to reduce "gaps" between existing and desired states.*

Applications of the Model

Hypotheses about these strategy-capability relationships have not been proved through substantial empirical research dealing with managerial perceptions. Only tentative patterns of perceptual relationships can be identified from earlier research efforts. Therefore, the following discussion of the model quadrants imputes managerial perceptions to their "most likely" situations.

The discussion can be viewed as suggesting several areas of research need in the perceptual/strategy framework. This initial step of identifying tentative patterns can be of major importance in understanding strategic behavior. The model can be applied to the

---

*MacCrimmon, K. R. "Managerial Decision-Making," in J. W. McGuire (Ed.), *Contemporary Management: Issues and Viewpoints* Englewood Cliffs, N.J.: Prentice-Hall, 1974.

study of policy making in organizations in various stages of development. For example, the significant differences in characteristics between the small, young growth-oriented organization and the stable, mature organization could be better understood by the use of some of the quadrants in the model. Those institutions that are trying to become established are characterized by an active flexible search for environment-related information about appropriate changes to reduce the gap and to reduce the perceived uncertainty. A larger, more mature organization has built up commitments to existing power centers, processes, and traditions; it may carry out its environment boundary relationships in a more routine, standardized way reflecting a combination of the adaptive and planning models.

Capability variations

Systematic variations are expected in the information search behavior of policy makers operating in environments characterized by varying levels of uncertainty or scarcity of strategy related information. Those policy makers who perceive high uncertainty are expected to use all information sources more frequently, to rely more on external information sources, to allocate more time to information gathering activities, and to make more use of informal sources than are those policy makers who perceive low uncertainty.*

STRATEGIC MOVES IN EACH QUADRANT

While there is (depending on the stage of development, share of market and forecasted market growth rate) an opportunity to exercise a great deal of discretion in each quadrant, each seems to be associated with a set of broad strategic moves (or outputs) for the organization or division, based on the appropriate perceptions. A sample of suggested, or hypothesized, moves will be discussed here. In addition, however, the detailed strategies would be formulated by processes and structures consistent with the above factors. The model predicts that firms, or divisions, operating in Quadrant I have an adaptive planning orientation, have a less active search for environment related information and are stability motivated.

The model predicts that firms operating in Quadrant II have a planning orientation, resort to a moderately active search for environment related information and have a high motivation to change.

---

*J. S. Blandin, W. B. Brown, and J. L. Koch: Uncertainty and Information Gathering Behavior: An Empirical Investigation. Paper presented at the National Academy of Management Meeting, 1974.

Model Quadrant III is described as implying a more active search for environment related information, an adaptive entrepreneurial orientation and stability (internal) motivation. Familiar change is sought.

Firms operating in Quadrant IV would engage in more active search for environment-related information, have an entrepreneurial orientation, and be characterized by internal change motivation. It is not proposed that every organization or division will fit exactly into one of the quadrants described. It is proposed, however, that the perceived uncertainty – perceived gap condition provides one basis for describing possible outcomes from the organization-environment interaction.

Quadrant I. In Quadrant I the mission or domain would tend to be fixed and well defined; the objectives would be operational and would emphasize optimizing, efficient performance and maintenance. Broad strategies would tend to stress defending the domain with stability but with allocations for maintaining distinctive competence.* Some expansion may take place in "sure bet" areas. There might be some attempts to reduce whatever uncertainty is perceived by integration to protect supplies and/or markets. Resources would be allocated to maintain an efficient technological process and to maintain market share. The organization form and style would incline toward being closed/stable/mechanistic.

The Quadrant I type is found in many lines of endeavor – the retirement division of Civil Service, a paper mill, an established beer distributor. The Volkswagenwerk situation from 1949 – 1965 (after it integrated, before it diversified) also illustrates Quadrant I, as does the Ford Motor Company during the 1930s. In both cases, the need to change was not perceived soon enough.

Quadrant II. In Quadrant II the current mission or domain of the organization or division might need some identification and readjustment. However, the objectives are likely to be planned change in internal capabilities to improve economies of operation. The broad strategies and policies tend to include integration for synergistic effects, improving distinctive competence in technological process, funding search for market share, market segmentation, and concentration on a few product types for economy. The organization form and style is likely to be closed/stable/mechanistic.

Nordhoff, when he integrated the Volkswagenwerk in 1948, exemplifies improving strength. And in the mature field of

---

*C. C. Snow and R. E. Miles: Managerial Perceptions and Organizational Adjustment Processes. Unpublished paper; see 13, p. 256. See also R. Miles, C. Snow, et al.: *Organizational Strategy Structure and Process.* In press, 1978.

aerosol packaging, Barr-Stolfort planned several allocations to improve its technology and to concentrate on a limited number of product types for economy. Both of these firms appear to illustrate Quadrant II.**

In Quadrant III the domain of the organization is somewhat more varied than in Quadrants I and II and is continually adjusted to feedback. The objectives include maintaining sufficient flexibility and a balanced portfolio. The broad strategies and policies include market penetration with allocations to continue active search for advance environment related information,† and some diversification into related products and markets (if the firm is mature). Product differentiation and market segmentation may be relied on to reduce uncertainty. Also, imitation may be used sometimes to serve the same purpose. The organization form and style is likely to be open/adaptive/organic. Divisionalization may occur.‡ A matrix structure may be introduced.

Quadrant III.

Quadrant III is illustrated by Kodak and Dupont, with their diversification into related products and by American car manufacturers with their divisionalization and imitation of European small cars and luxury cars.

In Quadrant IV, with perceived uncertainty and a high gap, the mission is varied and flexible. The objectives would be to develop (or acquire) creative problem solving with satisfying models and to survive. Some rather bold strategies and policies appear to be associated with this quadrant. Taking action to reduce the gap and reduce uncertainty may require some tough divestiture decisions. Acquisition and/or merger may bring strength, or disaster. The organization may act like an enthusiastic prospector searching for new ventures or a new domain. Diversification into related or even unrelated products is another way of coping with the environment. On the other hand, a conservative organization may follow a more modest course of product imitation rather than allocating resources to an R & D search.§ The organization seems to need a more personal control with perhaps matrix, project or new venture components. An entrepreneurial role for the policy maker

Quadrant IV.

**See *Aerosol Techniques, Inc.* (ICH 13G155). Barr-Stolfort is discussed in Chapter 5.

†S. Terreberry: The Evaluation of Organizational Environments. *Administrative Science Quarterly.* 12:590–613, 1968.

‡B. R. Scott: *Stages in Corporate Development, Part II.* Harvard Business School. 4 371 295 BP999, 1971.

§S. Schoeffler, R. Buzzell, and D. Heany: Input of Strategic Planning on Profit Performance. *Harvard Business Review, 52* (No. 2): 137–145, 1974.

may be followed in which he dominates the coalition and takes action to reduce uncertainty; a sharp departure from the status quo is made. Or sometimes an adaptor role for the policy maker(s) may be used where there is a divided coalition of influencer forces. Changes may be slower and perhaps even too late in some cases with the adaptor role.

The Quadrant IV situation can be seen in many organizations—the young organization trying to get established, the mature organization in crisis, organizations suddenly faced with a changed environment. Bike Lock, Franklin National Bank, Penn Central, and Head Ski are examples. In fact, many organizations find themselves in Quadrant IV today.

RELATED INFLUENCES ON CAPABILITY

Consider nature of participants, stage of development and complexity.

Although analysis of the environment-strategy-capability balance in terms of perceived environmental uncertainty and perceived need for change seems helpful, the dynamic set of relationships in the organizational situation should not be underestimated. Other influences are at work. Richard Hall,* after reviewing extensive empirical research on organization strucutre and process concludes that environmental-technological factors, together with the related consideration of the nature of participants and the stage of development and complexity, are important determinants of the capability requirements of an organization at any particular time. We shall give a few examples of such influences in strategy and capability situations.

There are many case studies that have explored the ways in which firms have tried to adapt to changing environments. We often see the problem encountered by the entrepreneur when he realizes that his organization has outgrown his ability to control it. He views the company as his pet and is unwilling to give up control of all aspects of the policy-formation process. In many instances, he struck upon a new product or an improved method of producing or supplying a particular product or service. Howard Head, inventor of the metal ski and founder of Head Ski Company, is an example of this type of individual.

The type of organization usually developed by these individuals is highly centralized, but loosely structured. The innovator, or

---

*R. Hall: *Organizations Structure and Process.* Englewood Cliffs, N. J., Prentice-Hall, Inc. 1972. See also J. P. Gibbs and H. L. Browning: The division of labor, technology, and the organization of production in twelve countries. *American Sociological Review, 31*(No. 1):81–92, February, 1966.

entrepreneur, frequently makes all significant decisions himself. There is rarely a formal organizational structure. The individual will define his task in relation to the environment, "plan" his activities over the long and short run and then carry them out to achieve his objectives.

As the organization grows and becomes more complex, formal structure and processes are usually imposed. The entrepreneur will usually try to maintain control as long as he can. Frequently some crisis, such as sustained losses, forces him to relinquish that control. The organization is then often turned over to managers who play a professional role and implement formal controls within a centralized structure. The organization may be strong enough so that a centralized structure is still the most effective method of operating the firm. Most organizations stay at this level of operations. Sometimes the family of the founder will maintain control of the organization and continue as its managers even after a formal structure has been imposed. Often, however, as mentioned, professional managers are brought in and perpetuated within the formal organization.

The organization, by committing its resources with strategic decisions, may gradually lock itself into specific strategies, certain roles and programs, and demanding coalitions. The managers may become adaptors as they go through the policy-making process, reacting in a difficult environment that imposes many problems and crises. Other organizations as they mature tend to commit more and more of their resources to the development of controlled, orderly change through planning.

Consider changes needed in the roles of policy makers.

The policy makers in these organizations (or segments of an organization) are of the belief that formal analysis can provide prediction of the environment sufficient to influence it. They may be faced with rather stable environmental-technological demands.

Both the "planning" and the "adaptor" organizations may, at some point, need to regenerate themselves through a new period of entrepreneurship. In addition, a built-in provision for self-criticism, for challenging present strategies, for revising objectives and actions may be needed as a deliberate way of preventing stagnation. The provision may allow periodic consolidation of power in the hands of a strong newcomer to override entrenched factions. Thus, in this fashion the organization (or segment of an organization) may be "turned around."

Differentiating by Organizational Level

Occasionally the products or services supplied by the organization will develop increasing environmental support and will provide for a high rate of sustained growth. The managerial team is presented with a critical decision concerning organizational capability. The continued growth often leads to more levels of management being introduced into the organization. The organization may, as mentioned earlier, be differentiated into three levels; strategic, coordinative and operating.*

The complexities of a multilevel organization often increase coordination and communication problems. At this stage, top management has to consider decentralizing some of the operating and coordinative decisions. Strategic decisions may be made centrally. If the organization becomes geographically dispersed, coordinative and operating decisions may be made by regional managers with policy guidance being given centrally. In a diversified, divisionalized organization all operating decisions may be made locally, with broad organizational strategies and interdivisional coordination developed centrally. More detailed coordinative management may be carried on within divisions.

How to differentiate?

In this chapter we have looked at several influences on characteristics of an organization. Differentiating by role expectations and competencies (say, of entrepreneurs or professionals), by stage of development and complexity, and by various levels, as well as by the environmental situation, compounds the difficulties in identifying patterns of relationships and/or configurations among organizational characteristics.

Organizational forms co-exist.

We have also tended to emphasize the capabilities for the whole organization or SBU. For example, we have assumed that there is one set of environmental demands for processing information and that one design predominates. For some single function organizations this holds true. However, many organizations or SBU's do not fall into a single type of design. Firms often have more than one type of structural arrangement operating at the same time. An example would be a hospital. The medical staff is highly decentralized. Each physician expects to play a professional role, having the responsibility and authority to make his own decisions involving patient care. The administrative staff, however, is often centralized and reports to a single individual, the hospital administrator. The administrator sets policies for his subordinates. The two organizational forms coexist and are able to implement their combined, overall mission of providing medical care.

---

*T. A. Petit: A behavioral theory of management. *Academy of Management Journal*, Dec. 1967, pp. 341–50; and T. Parsons: *Structure and Process in Modern Societies*. Chicago, The Free Press of Glencoe, 1960.

There are other examples of this type of coexistence of different organizational forms. The matrix organization, where products or project-oriented groups are superimposed on a functional organization, is probably the best known. Defense-related industries often use this type of design to achieve collaboration, teamwork and integration among participants where needed. The defense-related industries are committed to supplying a constant array of new products. The firms within these industries, moreover, have environmental support to continue to produce older products. They, therefore, have adopted the matrix organizational form to achieve their strategic objectives.

Keeping the Organizational Strategy in Mind

Basically, changes in the direction and strategy of the organization have direct effects on the organization's capability requirements. Balance in the strategy-capability design seems important whether the organization is simple or complex, large or small, private or nonprofit. The policy analyst has the difficult task of considering a whole mosaic of factors in planning a capability. While considering arranging the many parts of the organization, he may refer back to key elements in the success of the organizational strategy and then ask whether the capability design gives proper emphasis to those elements. In thinking through the refinements of a design he would not want to lose sight of the results expected or the specifically defined objective, goal or statement of future accomplishment that contributes to the organization's overall socioeconomic purpose.

Consider key elements in organizational strategy.

For example, "new knowledge" may be a key element in an organizational strategy to attain the objectives of growth and survival. The designed relationship between research and development and marketing and production depends upon the prime focus of the new knowledge. If new technological innovations develop rapidly, closer grouping of activities for integration between research and development and production than between research and development and marketing should be considered. On the other hand, if the technology for making new products is widespread and the new knowledge consists primarily of rapidly changing market information, the research and development department probably would be integrated to a greater extent with marketing than with production.

New knowledge.

Another key element in an overall strategy may be financial

Financial synergy.

synergy or the ability of organizational combinations to obtain external funds and to be able to allocate capital to various divisions. Some firms with unrelated products do *not* attempt to achieve operational and coordinative integration among various divisions. However, they do attempt to achieve financial synergy with centralized allocation of financial support to the most promising divisions. This approach to strategy and capability has important advantages for the firm with unrelated products: it makes it much easier to divest existing divisions and to acquire new organizational units. Substantial integration at the operating and coordinative levels would make such changes more difficult.

Use contingency approach.

The foregoing discussion suggests that the type of organization capability is contingent upon a number of factors. The policy analyst is required to make an effective matching of the overall strategy with the environmental-technological situation as well as a number of related considerations, including the stage of development and complexity of the organization and individual role expectations and competencies.

OVERALL SUMMARY

This book is concerned with what the analyst (student, manager or assessor) can do in a business or non-profit institution to study and to improve the process of dealing with policy and strategy issues. Policy or strategy formation is seen as a complex problem-solving process by which the organization makes choices relating to the internal and the external environments. The policy activities have wide ramifications, have a long-time perspective, use critical resources and include a social process as well as an intellectual process.

Conceptual framework.

The book was written for use as a conceptual framework for information gathering on policy and for organizing and analyzing such information. It has been our experience in a variety of situations that use of the book with additional practice materials for information processing seems to be helpful in several ways, such as (1) conceptualizing the policy-formation process; (2) developing comprehension, skill and knowledge for diagnosing and dealing with specific strategy situations; (3) analyzing the organization's environment and its policy-generating structure; (4) developing administrative and communication skills in presenting and developing solutions to policy problems; (5) integrating or tying together concepts, principles and skills learned separately in more specialized courses; and (6) being cautious in accepting the many prescriptions that exist in the literature on policy.

Practical Problems for You to Solve

In this book we have asked you to assume you were being hired to design and implement an approach for solving policy problems in a business or public body. You would be asking questions about what needs to be done, what resources are available, what characteristics of the environment would be worth knowing, and so forth. To elaborate, suppose that it was an organization whose rate of growth had leveled off in the last few years that had hired you to increase that rate of growth. You might first want to know if the organization merely wanted to increase the growth or whether it was also important to change the image of the organization for the stockholders or the general public. Does the organization want to be seen as an aggressive, innovative yet stable organization in addition to increasing the growth rate? It would be important to know the time period within which you had to work. Changes that are meant to occur quickly would probably be more expensive and difficult to produce. As a policy advisor, hired to develop significant changes, the questions you might want answered before you proposed and implemented your approach would be numerous.

Questions to Answer

In this book we have developed sets of questions concerning the policy or strategy situation. One set has to do with preliminary information on how significant choices in policy "should be" made and how significant choices are made. Another set has to do with further conceptualization of policy formation, including various strategies for "negotiating" with the environment to form organizational objectives, resource allocations, and so forth. A third set that you would surely want to consider deals with ways of learning about policy through case study, field and library projects, field research, dynamic computer games, simulations, observation, informal contacts, publications and so forth.*

---

*See D. E. Schendel and K. J. Hatten: Business Policy or Strategic Management: A Broader View for an Emerging Discipline. Paper presented at Academy of Management National Meetings, Division of Business Policy, August, 1972.

Multiple guides, sources and methods.

The remaining sets of questions that you might want to ask would deal with (1) guides that could be used for assessing the current situation and the changing environment and for developing strategies; (2) assessment and development methods from behavioral science and from management science; (3) processes by which there is an action thrust in organizational strategy formation for involving others in planning actions, coordinating actions, executing actions and evaluating actions; and (4) factors related to the environment-strategy-capability balance of the organization as it develops in the environment. These are the main questions for which this book has tried to provide some answers.

Policy Makers

We have seen policy or strategy makers as "negotiating" to find solutions to policy issues that will (1) satisfy environmental demands or requirements, (2) win external and internal support (coalitions are formed), and (3) partially satisfy self-interests. "Negotiating" has been described as sometimes like muddling through, with an impossibility of determining in advance exactly what the solution should be. Thus, policy makers are sensitive to feedback from the environment. They analyze their present situation and forecast what environmental demands and support will be. Then, with their self-interests as basic premises, they make choices that may emerge into patterns of decisions or strategies that influence future decisions.

Various modes of strategy-making.

Some policy makers seem to dominate and seek bold opportunities to reach established goals (the entrepreneur); some are more adaptors or reactors in a nondominated coalition (the adaptor); some seem to rely more heavily on an analytical, highly integrated, one-point-at-a-time approach to formulating strategy (the planner); some mix the modes of strategy making (e.g., adaptive entrepreneur or adaptive planner).

We have suggested in this book that the analyst can go about the process of strategy formation more effectively by using the conceptual framework previously discussed and by using technology, some of which is associated with applied behavioral science and some with management science.

Action research.

It appears that *action research*, a behavioral science program sometimes associated with organization development, holds promise for helping to initiate successful change in the strategy-formation process. Although the literature includes an inventory of self-reports, anecdotes and some before-and-after studies, there appears, so far, to be very little data to provide a firm base for prescription.

Our approach has been a cautious one, suggesting that keen judgment is needed in making choices of variables to emphasize and methods of assessment and development to use. As mentioned, there will be some muddling through owing to various uncertainties and pressures.

Keen judgment needed.

In summary, however, the process of action research applied to strategy formation can be described in the following way:

First, it involves the generation and explanation of pertinent information regarding the organization's environment, structure and functioning, and organizational strategy. It includes the use of various *management science* programs. In other words, outputs from management science programs feed into the action-research program.

Second, it involves an evaluation of that information and a diagnosis of the current position and what the position might be.

And, *finally,* it involves adjusting the portfolios, gaining defensible segments and balancing the environment-strategy-capability.

The program provides for continuing assessment of the opportunities, threats, problems and progress reviews in an attempt to avoid organizational stagnation and deterioration.

Continuing assessment.

DISCUSSION QUESTIONS

1. Discuss the structure (i.e., roles and programs) of an organization with which you are familiar (e.g., a university or a restaurant).

2. How does this organization adapt to changing environments?

3. Discuss the relationships between product line, diversification and organizational structure. What has been the traditional line of development of structure and internal factors?

4. Discuss the benefits and problems of decentralization versus centralization, particularly as the structure relates to strategy formation.

5. How can strategy-capability be blended to perform effectively under varying environmental conditions?

Suggested Additional References for Further Research

Baker, C. R.: Behavioral aspects of corporate planning. *Long-Range Planning,* 9 (No. 4):72–75, 1976.

Baker, F. (ed.): *Organizational Systems: General Systems Approaches to Complex Organizations.* Homewood, Illinois, Richard D. Irwin, Inc., 1973.

Carroll, S. J., Paine, F. T., and Miner, J. B.: *The Management Process: Cases and Readings.* 2nd Edition. New York, Macmillan Company, 1977.

Chandler, A. O.: *Strategy and Structure.* Cambridge, Mass., MIT Press, 1962.

Filley, A. C., and House, A. J.: *Managerial Process and Organizational Behavior.* Glenview, Ill., Scott Foresman & Company, 1976.

Friedman, Y., and Seger, E.: Horizons for strategic planning. *Long-Range Planning,* 9 (No. 5):84–89, 1976.

Guth, W.: Toward a Social System Theory of Strategic Planning Proceedings of the Midwest Meetings of the Academy of Management, April, 1973.

Hedley, R. A.: Organization structure and managerial control: A case study of organizational change. *Journal of General Management,* 2(No. 4):55–69, 1975.

Hutchinson, J. G.: *Management Strategy and Tactics.* New York, Holt, Rinehart and Winston, Inc., 1971.

Katz, D., and Kahn, R. L.: *The Social Psychology of Organizations.* New York, John Wiley & Son, Inc., 1966.

Kraushar, P. M.: Organization for corporate development. *Long-Range Planning,* 9 (No. 3):43–47, 1976.

Likert, R.: *The Human Organization: Its Management and Value.* New York, McGraw-Hill Book Co., Inc., 1967.

Litschert, R. H.: Some characteristics of organization for long-range planning. *Academy of Management Journal* 10:247–256, 1967.

Miner, J. B.: *The Management Process: Theory, Research, and Practice.* New York, MacMillan Company, 1973.

Parsons, T., and Shils, E. A. (eds.): *Toward a General Theory of Action.* Cambridge, Mass., Harvard University Press, 1951.

Pugh, D. S., et al.: Dimensions of organization structure. *Administrative Science Quarterly,* June, 1968, pp. 65–105.

Starbuck, W. H.: Organizational growth and development. *In* March, J. G. (ed.): *The Handbook of Organizations.* Chicago, Rand McNally & Company, 1965, pp. 467–633.

Thompson, J. D.: *Organizations in Action.* New York, McGraw-Hill Book Co., 1967.

Thompson, P. H. and Dalton, G. W.: Are R&D organizations obsolete? *Harvard Business Review.* 54 (No. 6):105–116, 1976.

APPENDIX 1 TO CHAPTER 9

SOME ACTION STEPS

Our conceptual framework focuses attention on information and theory about complex problem solving, that is, problems that affect the long-term development of the organization. In order to develop skill in handling these problems, it is important that the reader actually process complex problems; that is, more information gathering and processing activity seems to lead to greater skills in the strategy formation process.

The manager and the staff analyst have opportunities for on-the-job experience in information processing activity. He or she may assess the relevance of theory in practice or, in other words, link the theory with practice. In colleges, universities and development programs, however, the participants may need other ways to link theory and practice and develop skill in information-processing activities. Other ways include dynamic computer models (e.g., STRATANAL), field projects, role plays, debates and some form of the case study method. Of these, clearly the case study method is most often used at present for policy courses in colleges, universities and in development programs.

In Chapter 2 a descriptive model of strategy formation is presented along with some environmental strategies. In Chapters 3 to 5 are presented some Assessment Guides for Strategy Development including the important diagnostic process. In this chapter we have presented a contingency model for balancing the environment-strategy-capability. Here we provide a rather extensive set of *action steps* devised for case analysis in policy at Ohio State University along with the Framework for Long Range Planning. You may wish to adapt or modify the approaches for your information processing in the study of cases and incidents.

EXAMPLE OF POLICY MATERIAL USED AT OHIO STATE UNIVERSITY

I. Case Preparation for all Cases

a. Read each case a minimum of three times
   general idea
   detail
   notes
b. Analyze the organization and determine major strengths and weaknesses
   trends
   developments
c. Prepare a statement of the major and minor problems facing the organization (outline form)
d. Determine the feasible alternatives available to the organization and analyze the pros and cons of adopting each alternative
e. Arrive at a recommended course of action for the organization

II. Oral Presentation

Each team is scheduled for two oral presentations during the quarter. These presentations should be between *20* and *30* minutes in length and should be organized to clearly indicate the major and minor problems, the alternatives, and the recommended course of action. Visual aids may be employed but must be of such size as to be visible to the entire class. The use of an overhead projector and screen should be scheduled, in writing, with your professor at least two days before needed. The only other ground rule for oral presentation is that *all team members must be involved in the oral discussion.* Teams are encouraged to use imagination and resourcefulness in researching, preparing, and presenting their scheduled oral case discussions.

III. Discussion of Oral Presentation

At the end of the three oral presentations, some members of the class will be selected to analyze and evaluate the initial presentation. The discussions will be designed to point out *strengths and weaknesses of the presentations and to indicate major areas of difference in their analysis and recommendation.*

IV. General Class Discussion

Following the critiques of the oral presentations, there will be some time devoted to general class discussion of the case. Students and the instructor may direct questions or suggestions to individual teams, team members, or the entire class.

V. Suggestions for Analyzing a Case

a. Read through the case quickly to determine its general nature. Then reread and begin to sort out facts. During subsequent readings it will probably be desirable to outline and rearrange the material in the case, or to prepare tabulations and charts that permit the more ready comparisons of available data.
b. After you have mastered the facts and other information in the case, isolate the major problems to be solved.
c. Then determine the major topics around which the analysis is to be undertaken. Some major points

for analysis commonly encountered in problem analysis are:
(1) The market and its influence on problem and decision
   (a) present
   (b) potential
   (c) size and/or characteristics of
   (d) buying habits and motives of
(2) The product and its influence on problem and decision
   (a) characteristics of
   (b) classification of
(3) Channels of distribution and/or outlets and influence on problem and decision
(4) Reaction of middlemen, customers, or others (if not included in (1) above) and influence on problem and decision
(5) Reaction of salesmen and/or other company personnel and influence on problem and decision
(6) Competition—types of; reaction of; probable future action of, and influence on problem and decision.
(7) Effectiveness of retaliation (of competition, middlemen, personnel, others) and effect on problem and decision
(8) Importance of good will and effect on problem and decision
(9) Position of the company in the industry and effect of this on problem and decision (if not included in (6) above)
(10) Financial position of the company and effect on problem and decision
(11) Importance of price; elasticity of demand, and effect on problem and decision
(12) Effect on other product lines and/or affiliated companies
(13) Organizational and managerial effectiveness
(14) Capabilities and limitations of personnel
   (a) work force
   (b) management
   (c) sales
(15) Congruency between personal and corporate objectives
(16) Appropriateness and effectiveness of control policies and procedures
(17) Technical capabilities of plant and equipment
(18) Seriousness of the problem: degree of urgency; time and funds available before action must be taken, and the effect or influence of these factors on decision
(19) Legal implications and their influence on problem and decision
(20) Economic conditions within and without the industry, and effect on problem and decision
(21) Effect on volume, costs, and profit, and the influence of these factors on problem and decision
   (a) Immediate
   (b) Short run
   (c) Long run
(22) Probable profit commensurate with risk involved?

d. The foregoing list is *not* intended to be all-inclusive or necessarily in order or importance. Not all points will require consideration in each case, and some cases will involve areas of analysis not listed above.

c. Proceed with the analysis of the major points or areas.
(1) For the purposes of this course, the analysis is the most important part of the report. *The reasoning* used to develop the recommended course of action *carries more weight than the actual decision.*
(2) The analysis consists of studying the problem from many different aspects and attempting to foretell the probable effect upon, or reaction of, the many factors which influence the success or failure of a certain course of action.
   (a) As the analysis proceeds, alternative courses of action or possible solutions to the problem will come to mind. These must be examined also and their feasibility appraised in

much the same way as is the original problem. In fact, as the analysis progresses, it may be discovered that the problem as originally stated requires modification, or that the whole approach to the case needs to be changed.
- (b) To be complete, the analysis must take into consideration not only the strong points of each argument presented, but the weaknesses of each as well. The analysis of one set of factors will indicate one course of action. The analysis of others may indicate a different solution. It is important to recognize the alternative solutions.
- (c) Occasionally some assumptions must be made. These should be logical and set forth clearly. Do not make unnecessary assumptions or assumptions which are contrary to facts already given in the case.
- (d) In many instances, more data may be desirable. Use should then be made of the secondary sources available in the library or elsewhere.

(3) Based on the analysis, arrive at one or more possible decisions as to the proper course of action to be taken in order to solve the problem facing the firm. If, as is customary, more than one solution appears reasonable, choose the one which, all factors considered, seems to contain the greatest strength and the fewest disadvantages. Be sure that your arguments are based upon the facts in the case, upon logical and clear-cut reasonings, and upon such assumptions as are made.

VI. Form for Comprehensive Case Analysis

When writing a case, the following form should be used:

Major Divisions of the Comprehensive Outline Analysis

Your outline should be divided into five major parts. Each part should be designated by a Roman numeral and labeled as follows:

I *Statement of the Problem* — What is (are) the central issue(s) in the case?

II *Solution or Decision* — State your final conclusion or decision. Your conclusion should be stated in sentence form.

III *Analysis* — This section is the heart of the report. It involves the selections of the factors or pertinent areas which must be considered in order to solve the problem — and the analysis of these factors. It involves the marshalling of evidence and the evaluation of the significance of this evidence. And it involves the determination of the relative importance of the various factors.

A. Analytical Presentation.
1. Make your report consist of analysis rather than mere restatement of the facts.
2. Show specifically how a particular factor affects the problem.
3. Do not present just the arguments that support your decision. The purpose of the analysis is to find the best decision possible; hence, all phases of the problem must brought out, regardless of the decision they suggest. In some instances, you may well incorporate into the analysis sound suggestions or alternatives to the decision.

IV *Conclusions* — This section should represent a summary of the conclusions reached concerning each of the major elements in the case. It should not be a listing of all the arguments presented in the analysis.

V A detailed statement of a plan for implementing your recommendations including the steps to be taken, their timing, and the resources required to implement each step.

VII. Mechanics of the Outline Analysis Report

Written cases will be graded on substance of arguments, form, and organization of material. Effective display and correct handling of mechanical details will add prestige and conviction to your reports. The following instructions will help you set up your reports in an attractive, readable manner:

1. Four copies of your report should be typewritten on standard $8\frac{1}{2} \times 11$ unruled white paper of good quality and should not exceed 5 pages in length, exclusive of appendices. (If typing is impossible, legible penmanship may be substituted.)
2. Do not use a separate page as a title page, but begin with statement of the problem immediately under the title of the case.
3. Identification of the report:
   a. In the upper left-hand corner of the first page, place the following information:
      Policy—
      Date report is due
      Your assigned number
   b. The name of the case should be centered on the first page approximately two inches from the top of the page.
4. Never crowd the bottom of the page. Always allow a margin of approximately seven to nine spaces.
5. Double space throughout.
6. Use only one side of each sheet of paper.
7. Make sure that you've used proper spelling, grammar, and sentence construction. Carefully reread and check the copy for these points and for typographical errors. You are expected to be capable of effective writing, correct spelling, and proper usage of words, grammar, and punctuation. Failure to maintain high standards in these respects will detract from the general merit of your report. Carelessly prepared papers will be returned for rewriting.
8. Clip or staple the sheets in the upper left-corner *only.* Do not fold the report when handing it in.

The following procedure is to be observed in presenting your written reports:

The reports should be turned in at the beginning of the class period. Late work will not be accepted. If you cannot attend class on the day a report is due, discuss this fact in advance and arrange to submit the report on time.

VIII. Framework for Long Range Planning

1. What are the Fundamental Objectives of the Company in Terms of:
   A. Profitability
   B. Market position
   C. Ownership
      1) Family
      2) One or more "outsiders"
   D. What the company wants to become
      1) Specialist in one line
      2) Diversified producer of related types of products
      3) Diversified into unrelated lines
      4) Size
2. What are the Major Strengths and Weaknesses of the Company?
   A. Present market position
      1) Market share
      2) Reputation
         a. overall
         b. in different market segments
   B. Product line
      1) Quality
      2) Extent of line
      3) Relationship to market demand patterns
   C. Nature of the market
      1) Rate of growth of market for

general type of products produced
2) Rate of growth for specific products or types of products
3) Prospects for future growth
4) Nature and extent of competition
   a. Strategies being followed by competing firms
   b. Strengths and weaknesses of actual and potential competitors
D. Financial capability
   1) Availability of internal funds
   2) Borrowing capacity
   3) Earnings potential
   4) Ability to attract outside capital
E. Production capability
   1) Costs compared to those of competitors
   2) Production potential
      a. quality levels
      b. flexibility of product mix
      c. availability of production capacity
   3) Facility location
      a. ability to expand
      b. access to markets
F. Marketing capability
   1) Advertising and sales promotion
   2) Sales force
      a. Technical skills
      b. Size
      c. Number of "personal" customers
G. Management capabilities
   1) Depth
      a. Will loss of any one individual affect company's ability to compete?
      b. Are capable people available?
         1. To replace present members of management if necessary
         2. For meeting needs caused by growth of business
   2) Managerial ability of present management team
      a. ability to handle present job
      b. ability to handle future responsibilities in light of growth prospects for firm

H. Personnel
   1) Availability of capable technical people
   2) Labor relations
   3) Skill level of labor force
   4) Size of labor force
3. Identify Overall Strategies Available to Organization
   A. Purpose of strategy—formulate overall plan of action enabling company to attain its goals.
4. Identify Requirements for Implementing Alternative Strategies
   A. Required resources for each strategy
      1) Production capability
         a. facilities
         b. capacity
      2) Additions or deletions to present product line
      3) Marketing capabilities
         a. Necessary marketing strategies
      4) Management
         a. Skills
         b. Numbers
      5) Technical Personnel
      6) Labor
         a. Numbers
         b. Skills
      7) Money
   B. Timing of strategy execution
      1) Time when each type of resource required
      2) Amount of resource required at that time
   C. Probable results of strategy
      1) Type of results expected
      2) Time at which or over which results are expected
      3) Size of results expected
5. Bases for Evaluation of Alternative Strategies
   A. Internal consistency
      1) Are the policies and goals outlined in formulating the strategy consistent with one another and with company objectives?
   B. Consistency with the environment
      1) Does the strategy make sense in light of present market and competitive conditions?
      2) Does it make sense in light of expected changes in the environment, for example,

changes in the demand pattern for various types of products?
C. Consistency of resource requirements and resource availability
   1) Must balance goals against the availability of needed resources
   2) Do requirements leave margin of error with respect to needs?
      a. To meet unexpected business downturns
      b. To cover requirements in case strategy does not yield expected results
         1. May be more successful than anticipated
         2. May be less successful than anticipated
D. Does the strategy have an acceptable degree of risk?
   1) How much risk is management willing to take?
   2) How much risk does the strategy involve?
      3) Aspects of risk
         a. Amount of resources whose value or continued existence is not assured
            1. Skills
            2. Specialized facilities
         b. Time period of commitment
            1. Length of time required to recover capital commitment
            2. Saleability of usefulness elsewhere in company of committed resources if strategy is abandoned
            3. Rapidity with which environment changes
      4) Proportion of company's resources committed to a particular strategy
6. If a particular strategy meets all of these tests then it is an appropriate one to follow.

AUTHOR INDEX

Ackerman, R. W., 51, 109
Addleman, R., 139
Aguilar, F. J., 167
Aiken, M., 34
Aldag, R. J., 34, 105
Alexander, T., 212, 217
Allison, G. T., 18, 30, 82, 254
Alter, S. L., 194
Amory, C., 96
Anderson, C. R., 16, 35, 80, 124, 235, 254, 255, 262
Andrews, K. R., 12, 52
Andrus, R. R., 213, 217
Ansoff, H. I., 12, 35, 37, 60, 64, 80, 94, 118, 167, 171, 204, 255, 259
Archbold, S., 250
Argyris, C., 121
Arthreya, W., 233
Athanassiades, J. C., 194
Ayres, C. V., 180

Baier, K., 180
Baker, F., 275
Baker, C. R., 275
Bales, R. F., 240
Banks, L., 29
Barber, R. J., 55
Barkdale, G. T., 55
Barnes, J., 68, 114, 123
Barnes, L., 164
Barnhill, J. A., 12
Barnland, D. C., 247
Bass, B. M., 46
Bauer, R. A., 16, 33, 39, 55, 107, 172, 175
Beckhard, R., 164, 165, 237, 240, 241, 247
Bell, C. H., Jr., 165, 222, 226
Bell, D. J., 250
Bennett, P. W., 250
Bennis, W. G., 161, 224
Berry, P. C., 226
Bieman, H., Jr., 200
Blake, R., 161, 164
Blandin, J. S., 265
Block, C. H., 226
Bloom, P., 139

Blumberg, A., 46
Boehm, G. A. W., 109
Bonchard, T. J., Jr., 226
Bonge, J. W., 62
Boulden, J. B., 213, 214, 217
Bower, J. L., 16, 52
Bowers, D. G., 192
Bowman, E. H., 109, 217
Brady, R. H., 217
Brandt, S. C., 23, 30
Brearly, A., 55
Bridges, F. J., 12
Bright, J. R., 207
Broom, H. N., 12
Brown, W. B., 265
Browning, H. L., 269
Brunner, G. A., 183
Buchanan, P., 223
Buffa, E. S., 213, 214, 217
Burke, W. W., 240
Burnes, T., 34, 139
Burnett, G. J., 217
Buskirk, R. H., 12
Butcher, B., 109
Buzzell, R. D., 268

Camillus, J. C., 29
Cammann, C., 250
Campbell, J. P., 121, 122, 224, 226, 255
Cannon, J. T., 12, 55, 78
Carlson, E. E., 194
Carroll, S. J., 75, 276
Carter, E. E., 14, 45
Cetron, M. J., 207
Chambers, J. C., 180
Chandler, A. D., 10, 256
Chandler, A. O., 276
Chapman, P. E., 109
Charnok, J., 194
Chase, P. H., 164, 243
Chesser, R. J., 139
Chevalier, M., 139
Child, J., 259
Christensen, C. R., 12
Clark, P. A., 222
Clarke, D. G., 139

285

AUTHOR INDEX

Cleary, M. J., 109
Cleivett, R. M., 250
Cohn, J., 52
Cole, E. N., 39
Collings, R., 172
Collins, B. E., 240, 247
Connell, C. F., 173
Cooper, A. C., 139, 218
Corey, R. E., 139
Costello, T. W., 158
Crockett, W. J., 158
Cummings, L. K., 132
Cyert, R. M., 14, 81

Dahl, R. A., 41
Dalkey, N. C., 208
Dalton, G., 46, 162, 164, 165, 223, 224, 276
Davis, K., 55
DeClerk, R. P., 37
DeJong, K., 250
Demuzzio, E., 139
Denning, B. W., 202
Dexter, L., 39
Dick, D. N., 207
Dill, W. R., 29, 250
Drucker, P. R., 70, 76, 153
Dunnette, M. D., 121, 122, 174, 224, 226, 255
Dyer, W., 158

Easton, D., 36
Eckhouse, R., 218
Eddy, W., 158
Edwards, W., 215
Emery, J. C., 29
England, G. W., 18, 29
Eppink, D. J., 250
Ernst, M. L., 212, 218
Eyring, H. G., 29

Farmer, R., 55
Fenn, D. H., Jr., 107
Fiedler, F., 224
Filley, A. C., 43, 276
Fink, C. F., 247
Finn, R. H., 139
Ford, H., II, 62
Forehand, G. A., 184
Foster, G., 165
Foster, R. N., 56
Fouraker, L. E., 18

French, J. R. P., Jr., 237
French, W. L., 161, 165, 222, 226
Friedman, M., 52, 109
Friedman, Y., 276
Fruhan, W., 127
Fulmer, R. M., 218

Gagne, R. N., 215
Galbraith, J., 260
Galbraith, J. K., 55, 257
Galer, G., 208
Gannon, M. J., 185
Gardner, J., 162
Gergen, K. J., 16, 55, 172, 175
Germane, G. E., 29, 110
Gerstner, L. V., Jr., 100, 120, 244
Gibbs, J. P., 269
Gilmer, B. V. H., 184
Gilmore, F. F., 12, 111, 139
Gluck, F. W., 55, 194
Glueck, W., 12, 29
Goldembiewski, R. J., 46, 158
Goldner, F. H., 40
Gordon, R. L., 173
Gossett, W. T., 109
Granovetter, M., 168, 172
Grayson, C. J., 210, 218
Green, M. J., 31
Greenlaw, P., 196
Greiner, L., 46, 162, 164, 165, 223, 224
Grinyer, P. H., 22, 218
Gross, N. C., 38
Guetzkow, H., 240, 247
Guth, W. D., 12, 16, 18, 276

Hage, J., 34
Haire, M., 109
Hall, R., 34, 269
Hall, W. K., 137, 210
Hare, A. P., 247
Hare, M., 226
Harrison, F. L., 56
Harsangi, J. C., 41
Hatten, K. J., 139, 218, 274
Hayes, R. L., 37
Heany, D., 268
Hedley, R. A., 276
Heenan, D. A., 139
Hershey, R., 109
Hertz, D. B., 205
Herzberg, F., 224
Hicks, E. J., 139
Hickson, D. J., 40
Higgins, R. B., 29
Hill, W., 72
Hille, S. J., 183
Hinnings, C. R., 40
Hodgetts, R. M., 56
Hofer, C. W., 117, 129, 131, 139, 255
Hogue, W. D., 55
Holden, P., 29, 110
Holmberg, S. R., 218
Hornstein, H. A., 164, 247
House, A. J., 276
House, R. H., 43
Howell, R., 139
Huberman, J., 139
Hussey, D. E., 109
Hutchinson, J. G., 276

AUTHOR INDEX / 287

Jackson, D. W., Jr., 105
Jansted, K., 122, 226
Jones, C. H., 218

Kabus, I., 109
Kahalas, H., 218
Kahn, R. L., 68, 121, 173, 224, 276
Karger, D. W., 55
Kassarf, S., 199
Kast, F. E., 16, 34
Katz, D., 68, 121, 224, 276
Katz, R. L., 12
Kay, E., 237
Keegan, W., 172
Keeney, R. L., 139
Kerlinger, F. N., 174, 194
Kerr, S., 74
Keuning, D., 250
Khandwalla, P., 16, 35
King, P., 139
Kirschner, W., 174
Kitching, J., 139
Klein, W. H., 110, 218
Kline, C. H., 69
Koch, J. L., 265
Kotler, P., 139
Kraushar, P. M., 276
Kriebel, C. H., 218
Kristol, I., 55
Kudla, R. J., 29

Lake, D. G., 164, 247
Lanford, H. W., 109
Lawler, E. E., Jr., 255
Lawrence, P. R., 34, 44, 46, 56, 162, 164, 165, 223, 224, 250
Learned, E. P., 12
Leavitt, H. J., 29, 250
Leavitt, T., 139, 190
Lee, C. A., 40
Lenz, R. C., Jr., 109
Leontiades, J. C., 64, 71
Levitt, T., 109, 139
Leyshon, A. M., 250
Licklider, J. C. R., 218
Likert, R., 182, 276
Lindblom, C. E., 42, 56
Lirtzman, S., 43
Litschert, R. H., 276
Locke, E., 72
Locke, H. B., 194
Logan, J. P., 12, 29, 126
Lorange, P., 29, 73, 222, 227, 228, 250
Lorsch, J. W., 34, 44, 56, 250
Luthans, F., 56

MacCrimmon, K. R., 264
Mace, M. L., 139
MacMillan, I. C., 56
MacMillan, J. C., 139

Maddocks, R., 158
Mahoney, T. A., 184
Maier, N. R. F., 22, 240
Malik, Z. A., 55
Mandell, S. L., 194
Mann, R., 110
March, J. G., 14, 39, 81, 240
Marley-Clarke, B. W. G., 56
Marrow, A. J., 158
Mason, R. O., 244
Mason, W. S., 38
McColough, C. P., 55
McCormick, A. D., 165
McEachern, A. W., 38
McGinnis, M., 140
McGuire, J. W., 264
McKinney, C. W., III, 218
McNichols, T. J., 12, 29
Meyer, H. H., 237
Migliore, H. B., 109
Miles, R. E., 266
Miller, E. C., 202, 210
Miller, J. G., 109
Miner, J. B., 276
Mintzberg, H., 16, 29, 37, 62, 73, 79, 80, 81, 111, 167, 194, 224, 250, 255, 260, 265
Moffett, J. W., 158
Moore, R. C., 218
Morris, G. K., 109
Mouton, J., 161, 164
Mullick, S. K., 180
Mumford, E., 255
Murdick, R., 218
Murphy, D. C., 110, 218
Murray, E. A., 37

Nader, R., 56
Nadler, D. A., 250
Nagashima, Y., 109
Nash, A. N., 183
Naumes, W., 136
Naylor, T. H., 139
Newell, A., 194
Newland, C. A., 79
Newman, W. H., 10, 12, 29, 126, 135
Nibloc, E., 227
Nolan, R. L., 217
Norburn, D., 218
Nurmi, R., 250
Nutt, A. B., 109

O'Connell, J., 12
Olm, K. W., 12

Paine, F. T., 16, 35, 37, 46, 80, 124, 183, 185, 235, 237, 251, 254, 255, 262, 276
Parsons, T., 37–38, 270, 276
Patchem, M., 30
Patel, P., 113

AUTHOR INDEX

Patton, G. R., 203
Pederson, C. A., 29, 110
Pennings, J. M., 40
Perrow, C., 72, 184
Petit, T. A., 14, 80, 270
Pettigrew, A., 255
Piccoli, M. L., 218
Pool, I., 39
Price, J., 184
Pugh, D. S., 276
Punt, T., 56

Raia, A. P., 74
Raisinghani, D., 81, 194
Rescher, N., 180
Richards, M. D., 196, 250
Riker, W. H., 56
Rizzo, J. R., 43
Rondinelli, D. A., 56
Rosenzweig, J. E., 16, 34
Rothwell, R., 250
Rue, L. W., 218
Rumelt, R., 258

Sandalls, U., Jr., 227
Sandbrook, R., 109
Saunders, C., 63
Schein, E., 45, 158, 182
Schendel, D. E., 203, 217, 274
Schlaifer, R., 199
Schmidt, S., 200
Schneck, R. E., 40
Schneier, C. E., 250
Schoeffler, 268
Scott, B. R., 257, 258, 268
Scott, G. M., 194
Selznick, P., 18
Sethi, S. P., 31, 56
Shagory, G. E., 250
Shank, J., 227
Shepard, H. A., 240
Sherif, M., 44
Shils, E. A., 37–38, 276
Simon, H. A., 39, 56, 194
Sitmister, L. T., 205
Smith, D. D., 180
Snow, C. C., 266
Solem, A. R., 122
Sprague, L. G., 109
Stagner, R., 139
Stalker, G. M., 34, 139
Starbuck, W. H., 276
Starr, M. K., 202
Stasch, S. F., 250
Steiner, G. A., 31
Steinhoff, D., 164

Stevenson, H., 139
Stewart, R., 80, 255
Storey, R., 34
Sumner, C. E., Jr., 12, 135
Swinth, R., 218

Tagiuri, R., 18
Taylor, B., 29, 48, 56, 109, 116
Taylor, D. W., 226
Taylor, R. N., 250
Terleckyj, N. B., 180
Terreberry, S., 268
Terry, P. T., 29
Theoret, A., 81, 194
Thomas, E. J., 247
Thompson, J. D., 34, 37, 276
Thompson, P. H., 276
Thurston, P., 207
Tilles, S., 250
Tock, D., 139
Tosi, H., 34, 75
Tuason, R., 250
Turner, J., 205

Ulmer, S. S., 36
Underwood, W., 158

Vancil, R. F., 29, 73, 222, 227, 228, 230, 250
Vroom, V. H., 255

Warren, E. K., 135, 222
Watson, G., 223
Webb, R. J., 178, 194
Wedley, W. C., 208
Weick, K. E., Jr., 255
Weitzel, W., 184
Wheelwright, S. C., 139
White, B. F., 165
Wickert, F. R., 247
Wildavsky, A., 47
Woodward, H. N., 139
Woodward, J., 34
Wooller, J., 218
Wrapp, E. H., 42, 43, 73, 255

Yetton, P., 255

Zald, M. N., 40
Zand, D., 83
Zarecor, W. D., 139

SUBJECT INDEX

Abt Associates, Inc., 107
Action plan. See *Plan of Action*.
Action-research. See *Organization, development of*.
Action, thrust, 4, 221–255. See also *Organization, development of*.
 defined, 227
Agriculture, Department of, 243
American Can, Inc., 205
American Motors Corp., 11–13, 100, 128
Assessment, 4, 57–92
 and development methods, 156–194
 guides to, 57–92
  main types of analysts using, 58
 objectives of, 58
Authority distribution continuum, 223

Babcock & Wilcox, Inc., 164, 243
Baldwin Locomotive Works, 93
Bargaining, 45–46, 260
Bike Lock Company case, 23–28, 64–65, 127–128
Boston Consulting Group, 68, 114

Celanese Corp., 206
Choice process, 11–16. See also *Decision-making and problem solving*.
 collective, 18
 individual, 18
 policy formation and, 11–21
 theories relevant to, 16
Climate, organizational, 184–185
Coalition, 14, 32, 40
 bargaining and negotiating to maintain, 15, 260
Computer, decision making and, 212–215
 programs from, creativity and, 213–215
 reformulating organizational strategy, 135–137
Conditional value, 198

Conflict, 16, 38, 42–46
 management, 42–46, 78–79
 over unshared goals, 15, 44–45
Contingency approach, 34–35, 117–120, 259–269
Cost, effect of accumulated experience on, 115–118
Creativity, 226–227
 related to computer programs, 213–215

Decision-making, 30–33, 212–214, 253. See also *Problem-solving*.
 assumptions of classical model violated, 30, 31
 computer-aided, 212–214
 theory of, descriptive, 17–19
  elite, 18
  group, 18
  normative, 17
 typical model of, 30–31
Decision tree. See *Program(s)*.
Delphi technique. See *Program(s)*.
Diagnosis, 60–62
 cautions in, 62
 defined, 60
 identifying causes in, 62
 pinpointing problems in, 61–62
Dialectical approach. See *Program(s)*.
Digital Equipment Corp., 11

Eastman Kodak, Inc., 7, 101, 258
Entrepreneur. See *Policy makers*.
Environment, 33–36
 analysis of threats and opportunities from, 94–108
 assessing basis and location of support from, 65–69
 competitive factors in, 100–102
 demands from, 33–35
 economic considerations in, 95–96
 interdependence of factors in, 36
 level of uncertainty and need for change in, 260–262
 monitoring of, 93–108

289

290 / SUBJECT INDEX

Environment (*Continued*)
 negotiating with, 42–46
 observation of, 178–179
 political inputs of, 98–99
 related to strategy capability, 259–262
 segmenting of, 64–66
 social influences on, 104–108
 social responsibility of, 51–53
 stable, 36
 support from, 36
 technological advances and, 96–97
 technological demands of, 269–270
Evaluation, 158–161, 238–239
 approaches to, 158–161
 of objectives and outcomes, 73–74
 timing of, 231–232
 using quantitative evidence in, 196–217
Expected value, 198
Experience curve theory, 115–116

Forecasting, 60–61, 179–180, 205–210
 economic, 179–205
 input-output models for, 205
 social, 179
 scenarios, 207
 technological, 179, 206

General Electric Corp., 70, 258
General Foods, Inc., 258
General manager, 16, 37
 role of, 79–82
General Motors, Inc., 39, 63, 70
Goals. See *Objective(s)*.

Head Ski, Inc., 168, 269
HMH Publishing Co. (Playboy), 11

IBM, 11, 70
Implementation. See *Strategy(ies), implementation of*.
Information, gathering of, 165–192
 processing program for, 81–82
 questionnaire in, 181–189
  organizational effectiveness related to control of, 184
  processing results of, 188–189
  restrictions on, 68
 sources of, deviant individual as, 168
  main, for policy analyst, 167
  marginal individual as, 168
  transitional individual as, 168
Informational network, 170–178
Interviews, 172–178
 choosing approach for, 172, 203–206
 focused, 174–176, 200

Interviews (*Continued*)
 guides to, 174
 pitfalls in, 174
 structured, 173, 176–178

Kaiser Industries, 128

Leadership, 259
 of policy conferences, 239–248
Lear Jet, Inc., 168
Lotus Europa, 191
LTV, Inc., 168

Management science. See *Program(s)*.
Managerial capability, 259–268
 relationship of, to environmental strategy, 259
Market growth, 113–120
Marketing concepts, review of, 140–144
Means-end chain, 5–11
 need for, 10–11
Mission(s), 5, 65, 107
 defined, 5
 identifying, 65
Models, of policy formation, 30–55
Motivation, and self-interest, 39–40, 77–78
Multinational competition, 101–102

National Affiliation of Concerned Business Students, 52
National Distillers, 67
National Steel Corp., 206

Objectives, 31, 42, 71–76, 110–120
 assessment of outcomes and, 71–76
 defined, 6
 derivation of, 6, 71
 in strategy formation, 10
 relation of, to means-end chain, 7
 trading off of, 119–120
Observation in action-research program, 178–179
Office of Management and budget, 67
Olin Textron, 258
Organization, climate of, 184–185
 development of, 161–163
  action-research in, 163–193
  defined, 163
  processes involved in, 163
  use of results of, 240–241
Organizational processes theory, 14–16

SUBJECT INDEX / 291

Plan, of action, 11–16, 163, 222, 237, 245–247
  detailing provisions of, to link overall strategy with operations, 134–135
Playboy Enterprises, 11–12
Polaroid Corp., 100
Policy(ies), 7, 45, 71, 76, 112
  defined, 5, 7
  descriptive model of, 33–35
  distribution, 76, 112
  financial, 70, 75–76, 112, 117, 196–197
  formation of, 30–35, 259
    and choice process, 11–21
    use of probabilities in, 195–210
  investment, 117–125, 195–210
  personnel, 71, 112
  pricing, 112, 130–131
  product, 76, 112, 117–125, 185–192
    differentiation of, 129, 189–192
  promotion, 112, 130–131
  review and evaluation, 112, 238–240, 246–247
Policy makers, 31, 37–39, 110–111, 274–275
  as adaptors, 37, 274
  as entrepreneur, 37, 274
  as planners, 37, 274
Political resources, 40–42, 77
  defined, 40
  tactics in using, 40–42
Portfolio approach, 111–120, 201, 205, 237
Present value, of business, calculation of, 197–198
  decision rule in, 199
  defined, 197
Problem solving, 161, 226–227. See also *Decision making and diagnosis*.
  brainstorming, 226
  group, 226
  individual, 17–18
  policy, effective group sessions in, 240–242
    selecting situations for, 232–235
    testing assumptions in, 244
    types of structured activities for, 235–238
Product maturation cycle, 114–120
Program(s), 8, 37–38, 76, 81–83
  action-research, 163–165
  capital budgeting, 195
  computer, creativity and, 212–214
  decision tree, 201–202
  defined, 8
  delphi method, 208–210
  dialectical program, 244
  financial analysis, 84–92
  information processing, 81–83
  management science, 195–217
    reasons for success and failure of, 210–212

Program(s) (*Continued*)
  pert, 134
  sensitivity analysis, 203
  standard operating procedure, 82
  STRATANAL, 135–136

Rand Corp., 208
Rate of return, as basis for priority, 200
Reward(s), as influence on behavior, 77–78
Role, 8–9, 37–39, 43, 76–83
  conflict, 37–39
  consensus, 38
  defined, 8–9
  general, 80
  of management, at various levels and stages, 80, 268–270
  of technocrat, 89, 230, 234
  resolution of conflict in, 43

Scope. See *Mission(s)*.
Scott Paper, Inc., 258
Sears, Roebuck Corp., 70
Segmenting, 120–133. See also *Strategic business areas*.
  of organization's environment, 64–65, 72
Self-interest(s), 39–40
  motivation and, 39–40, 77–78
  influences on behavior, 77–78
  need to determine, 77
Shell Oil Company, 208
Simulation(s), 204–205. See also *Program(s)*.
  risk analysis, 204–205
Slimey Oil Co. (role play), 49–51
Small businesses, 145–155
  assessment guides for, 145–152
  help for, 153–155
Social responsibility, 51–53, 102–108
Southern Pacific Railroad Co., 6
Sperry Rand, Inc., 229–230
Stakeholders, 35–37, 77
Strategic business areas (SBA's), 64–68, 94–108
  effect of environment on, 94
  objectives and targets for, 72
Strategic business units, 5–6
Strategic stakeholder areas (SSA's), 77
Strategy(ies),
  defined, 4–7
  diversification, 114–119, 256–257
  divestiture, 112, 117–119
  expansion, 112
  integration, 112
  niche, or segmentation, 11, 112, 120–126, 189–192
  portfolio approach to, 111–120, 201, 205, 237
  push-pull model of, 111

Strategy(ies) (*Continued*)
  penetration, 112
Structure, organizational, 9, 37–42, 256–258
  assessment of strategy generating, 76–83
  defined, 9
  divisionalization of, 258
  functional, 257
  matrix, 271
  roles and programs as, 9, 37
Synergy, 126, 272
  defined, 126
  financial, 272
  negative, 127
  product, 126
  technological, 126

Technology, forecasting changes in, 96–97, 207
Treasury, Department of, 243

Union Carbide, 243
U. S. Navy, 207
U. S. Steel, Inc., 258

Vulnerability problem, 66

Western Union, 67

Xerox Corp., 205